THE COLOSSAL BOOK OF CRAFTS

FOR KIDS & THEIR FAMILIES

THE COLOSSAL BOOK OF CRAFTS FOR KIDS & THEIR FAMILIES

by Phyllis Fiarotta with Noel Fiarotta

Two Volumes in One

Originally Published as:

Sticks & Stones & Ice Cream Cones
and
Snips & Snails & Walnut Whales

BLACK DOG
& LEVENTHAL
PUBLISHERS
NEW YORK

This edition published by arrangement with Workman Publishing Company, Inc.

Published by   Black Dog & Leventhal Publishers, Inc.
                    151 West 19th Street
                    New York, NY 10011

Distributed by   Workman Publishing Company
                    708 Broadway
                    New York, NY 10003

Printed and bound in the United States of America.

j i h g f e d c b a

ISBN: 1-884822-57-6

Library of Congress Cataloging-in-Publication Data

Fiarotta, Phyllis.
    The colossal book of craft for kids and their families / by Phyllis Fiarotta
    with Noel Fiarotta.
        p.   cm.
    Reprint. Two volumes in one originally published as:
    Sticks & stones & ice cream cones, 1973 and Snips & snails & walnut whales, 1975.
    Summary: provides directions for a variety of craft projects using items from
    around the house and from nature.
    ISBN 1-884822-57-6
    1. Handicraft--Juvenile literature. 2. Nature craft--Juvenile literature.
    [1. Handicraft. 2. Nature craft.] I. Fiarotta, Noel.
    II. Fiarotta, Phyllis. Sticks & stones & ice cream cones. 1973.
    III. Fiarotta, Phyllis. Snips & snails & walnut whales. 1975. IV. Title.
TT160.F5   1997
745.5--dc21   97-24530
                                                       CIP
                                                        AC

TABLE OF CONTENTS

Sticks & Stones & Ice-Cream Cones

Snips & Snails & Walnut Whales

Sticks & Stones & Ice Cream Cones

Foreword to parents

The return to craftwork is on. How-to-make-it items are displayed everywhere you look, and men and women alike discover the pleasure of making quality products themselves. Children especially love craftwork, and should at last be given the chance to create and use handmade games, toys, and things of beauty. *Sticks & Stones & Ice Cream Cones* provides the opportunity. It is the first book of its kind to offer youngsters a full range of craft projects on their own level; to help them explore completely all craft techniques.

This book belongs to the younger generation. It is written for children to understand. All specific measurements (inches and feet) are omitted, leaving the total creative process to the young craft designer. For easier construction, many of the projects are illustrated in exact project-sized patterns. No guesswork is needed.

Some crafts will appeal to your children, others will not. Don't force them, just for creativity's sake, to make something they won't use. Let them choose the objects they would like to construct. They will automatically select the things most appropriate to their age group. Your children know themselves very well and what it is that they most enjoy making.

The adult plays an important part in the construction process. Read through this book before you hand it over to your children. Look at all of the craft items and see how the instructions are written. **You will notice the symbol ** in front of a direction. This means that potentially dangerous household equipment is called for, or that the execution of the step so marked may be too difficult for a child.** It is advisable for you to supervise this activity. Keep in mind your children's physical abilities and limitations. If you feel they cannot perform a particular task, you will have to do it for them. Allow youngsters to feel, however, that they are the ones creating the objects, even though it is you who have just bored a hole in a piece of wood or cut a piece of string.

Every craft item in this book has three parts: the drawing, the instructions, and a list of craft materials. Children should be encouraged to read through the instructions several times before they begin, and to study the drawings carefully. You will provide them with the necessary craft supplies. Almost all materials can be bought in a stationery or art supply store, or at the stationery counter of department stores. Other needed items will be found in your kitchen or in the family tool box. One of the greatest pluses of the craft boom is that it recycles paper and metal products. Coffee cans, oatmeal boxes, and shirt cardboard are just a few of the many items that can be reused. Save all throwaways for future craft use.

It is now time to present this book to its rightful owners, your children. There are hours of fun and creativity—of toy, craft and game making—between its covers. And if, by chance, you find yourself the recipient of one of the beautiful, handmade craft objects, consider yourself lucky indeed. Your reward is a gift from the heart—your child's special sense of accomplishment.

Just for you

This is *your* craft book. It contains many interesting things for you to make all by yourself. Crafts like macrame and candle making; all kinds of toys and games; even a complete puppet show for you to design, produce and perform. There are toys to make from other lands, things which fly, things to grow. Holiday decorations, party favors—beautiful gifts for special people . . .

Look through the book and see all the great things you can do. Decide which item you would like to make first. It is very important that you read all directions—not just once, but several times before you begin. If there is something you don't understand, have someone explain it to you. It is important to study the drawings well, too. You will be better able to understand the directions if you see how a craft is put together. Your mom and dad will buy and help you find all the materials you'll need for the projects you choose. If you have difficulty cutting, threading, sewing or *anything*, ask for a helping hand. Once you learn the way to handle tools and materials, the construction of the items will be easier.

Now choose the items that you would like to have or make the most. Take your time with the projects and do the best job you can. If something does not turn out to be as perfect as you would like it, don't worry. Your individuality will add a personal touch to every craft you make. Besides, there's always more to try, again and again. Think of this book as a chocolate layer cake: one slice is never enough.

All about the things you need

PAPER

• **White drawing paper** is important in craft projects as well as for drawing. Drawing paper is heavy, smooth paper that comes in pads or packages.

• **Colored construction paper** is heavy paper that comes in many wonderful colors. The sheets are sold in packages, and many paper sizes are available. Try to pick the correct size for the craft you will be making. Save all large scraps in a box or bag. You never know when you might need a little bit of color.

• **Tracing paper** is very important for many of your craft projects. It is very light, transparent paper. When it is placed on a drawing, you can see the drawing through it. Tracing paper comes in pads.

• **Typewriter paper** is a white paper that is lighter than white drawing paper but heavier than tracing paper. You can see a drawing under it. It comes in packaged sheets.

• **Cardboard** is very heavy paper. You can find it backing shirts which come from the laundry or in packages of new clothes. Other boxes found around the house—like shoe and hat boxes—are made of it. Cardboard may also be bought in art supply stores. Save all pieces of cardboard you find in your home.

GLUES AND PASTES

• **Liquid white glue** comes in plastic bottles with pointed caps. This glue makes a strong bond when it dries and is used, therefore, for hard-to-glue crafts.

• **Liquid brown glue,** or mucilage, comes in a bottle with a rubber cap that is used for spreading. It is a light adhesive.

• **Paper paste** is a white, thick adhesive. It comes usually in a jar, and has a plastic spreader. Paper paste is best for sticking paper to paper.

• **Wallpaper paste** is a powder paste that you mix with water. Although it is used in putting up wallpaper, we will use it for making some of the crafts.

COLORINGS

• **Poster paints** are paints that can be removed from your hands with water. They come in many colors and are sold in jars.

• **Watercolor paints** are little tablets of hard color that must be daubed with a wet brush to use. The paints come in a tin which has at least six colors in it.

• **Crayons** are colored wax sticks that are used for drawing.

• **Colored felt-tipped markers** are tubes or "pencils" of enclosed watercolor with a felt coloring tip. You draw with markers as you would with crayons.

• **Indelible felt-tipped markers** are special markers that use unremovable or unwashable "inks" for coloring. Use indelible felt markers only for the crafts that ask for them specifically.

BRUSHES

• **A watercolor brush** is a small brush that is used for fine drawing, like painting pictures of faces.

• **Paintbrushes** are larger. They are used to paint large surface areas, like the sides of a box.

FABRIC

• **Felt** is a strong, heavy fabric that comes in many colors. It is sold in small squares. It can be glued to a surface with liquid white glue.

• **Scrap fabric** is odds and ends of cloth that your mom saves from her sewing projects. You can also cut up old clothes for scrap fabric.

How to trace patterns from this book

HOW TO TRACE PATTERNS FROM THIS BOOK

There are many projects in this book you make with your imagination. All it takes is some scissors and paper and—puff—you have a beautiful craft. There are other things for which you will need a little more than just your imagination. For these crafts you will need to make a pattern.

The patterns in this book are drawn with a heavier line than the other illustrations. Instructions about patterns will always be given along with the directions on making the craft.

TO TRACE A PATTERN

1. Place a sheet of tracing paper over the page that has the pattern you wish to trace, Fig. a.
2. Follow the outline of the pattern with a soft pencil on the tracing paper. Do not press hard or you will see pencil marks on the page.
3. After you have traced the pattern on tracing paper, cut it out with your scissors, Fig. b.

(Never cut any pattern out of your book.)
4. Put the new cutout pattern on the paper you wish to use, Fig. c.
5. With a pencil, trace around the edge of the cutout pattern, Fig. c.
6. Remove the cutout pattern and cut out the new drawing from the paper. Now you are ready to continue with your project, Figs. d and e.

TO TRACE A PATTERN WITH A PENCIL RUBBING

Another way of tracing from this book is with a pencil rubbing. With this method, you do not have to cut out the pattern from the tracing paper.

1. Place a sheet of tracing paper over the page that has the pattern you wish to trace.
2. Follow the outline of the pattern with a soft pencil, Fig. a.
3. After you have traced the pattern from the book, turn the tracing paper over, and rub along the back of the tracing outline with the

side of the pencil lead. Make sure the back-and-forth scribbling covers all of the pattern outline, Fig. f.

4. Place the tracing over the paper you wish to use, scribbled side down, Fig. g.

5. Draw over the lines of the original tracing with a pencil. Press hard on the line as you draw. The rubbing will act like carbon paper.

6. Lift up the tracing paper.

7. The lead that you scribbled on the back of the tracing paper will have come off on the paper where you drew with your pencil, Fig. h.

8. Cut out the drawing from the paper and continue with your project.

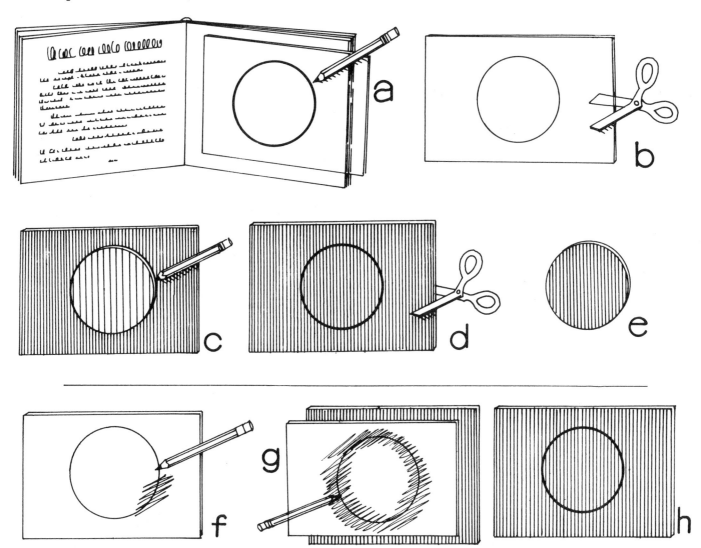

Flying through the air with the greatest of ease

For a second or two, the man on the flying trapeze soars gracefully through the air. He flies over his audience without wings of feather or tail of steel, caught—just in time—in the mighty hands of his partner. After one good swing he rockets upward again, returning in triumph to his lofty perch. Once his feet are safely on the platform, the audience applauds his marvelous flying stunts.

Have you ever tried to fly? No doubt you had a few problems. Only birds, bats, bees, butterflies, and other flying insects can move freely through the air. Of course, there are machines that fly—things like jets, gliders, helicopters, and rockets. With these, man has managed to get closer and closer to the sun, moon, and stars. Wouldn't it be great if you could do that anytime you wanted?

In this chapter you almost can. You can bring the sky and some of its wonders right into your very own bedroom. The toys included here will let you take an imaginary trip to the moon, make your very own star, decorate your ceiling with all kinds of flying creatures. You may not really be the man on the flying trapeze, but you can feel something like the way he feels, just by creating the objects which follow.

Spinning Star Wheels

"Twinkle, twinkle little star, how I wonder what you are . . ." These are very familiar words to you. Have you ever looked at a cloudless evening sky and seen the stars twinkling? They don't, really. Because stars are so far away, their light has to travel millions and millions of miles before you can see it. The light shines through space dust and other objects surrounding the earth, and this is what makes them seem to twinkle.

Maybe stars spin. Since you cannot take a rocket ship into space to find out for yourself, you'll have to use your imagination. Bring a piece of the sky into your hands. Create a special star. This one will catch the wind and whirl in dizzy circles, like a crazy earth spinning around the sun. If the air is still, hold the wheel in your hand and twirl yourself in circles. You will enjoy seeing your star go round and round.

Things You Need

1 square piece of colored construction paper
scissors
1 nail with a large head
1 new pencil
stick-on gold stars
1 bead

Let's Begin

1. Start with a square piece of construction paper; you choose the color. Be sure all sides are of equal size.
2. Draw a line from corner to corner. This forms an X on the paper, Fig. a.
3. Cut along these lines up to O, as shown in Fig. a. Do not cut all the way to the center.
4. Number the corners as shown: 1, 2, 3, 4.
5. Bring corner 1 to the center, Fig. b.
6. Bring corner 2 over corner 1, Fig. c.
7. Bring corner 3 over corner 2.
8. Bring corner 4 over corner 3.
9. Ask Dad or Mom for a long nail with a large head. Push the nail through the four points and all the way through the center of the star wheel.
**10. Hammer the nail through the eraser of a new pencil.
11. Glue a bead over the point of the nail that came through the other side of the eraser.
12. Stick gold stars onto the wheel.
13. Hold star to the wind or whirl around.

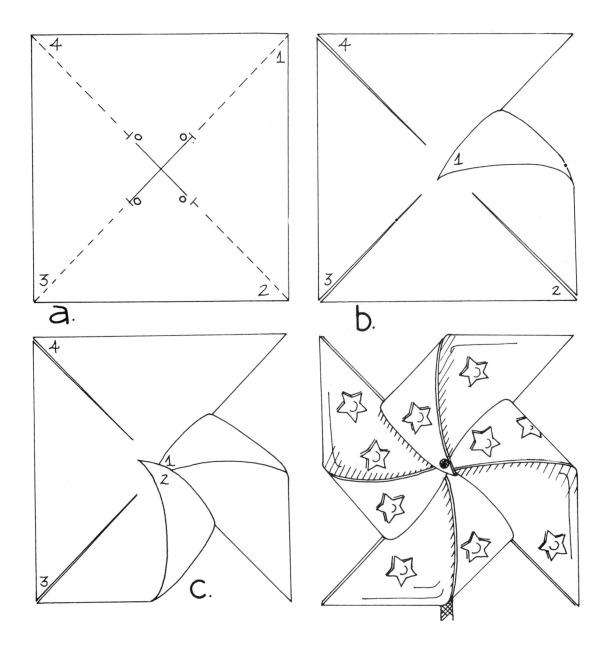

a.

b.

c.

Gliding Paper Airplanes

A glider rides the rising air currents without the roar of a turning propeller. The only sound that can be heard is the wind blowing over the wings of the plane. You've probably never been in a gliding airplane, but you can build your very own. All it takes is a piece of paper, a paper clip, and a little energy you supply to make this aircraft fly.

If you really enjoy "piloting" your first paper airplane, make dozens of them. You might be the captain of your own air force, or the owner of a flying school. You and your friends can have hours of fun racing planes, seeing how high they can fly, competing to design the best-looking models.

Things You Need

1 sheet of typewriter paper

1 paper clip
crayons or colored felt-tipped markers

Let's Begin

1. Fold a sheet of paper in half along the long side, Fig. a.
2. Keep the folded side on the bottom. Corner X (Fig. a.) is folded over to lie on the folded side, Fig. b.
3. Do the same with the other corner.
4. Corner Z (Fig. c.) is then folded over to lie flat on the folded bottom. This will cover Corner X, Fig. a.
5. Do the same with the other corner.
6. You now have two wing flaps, Fig. e. Fold these on each side of the plane in such a way that Y is lower than the bottom folded side, Fig. f.
7. Slip a paper clip near the front point.
8. Draw designs with crayons or markers.

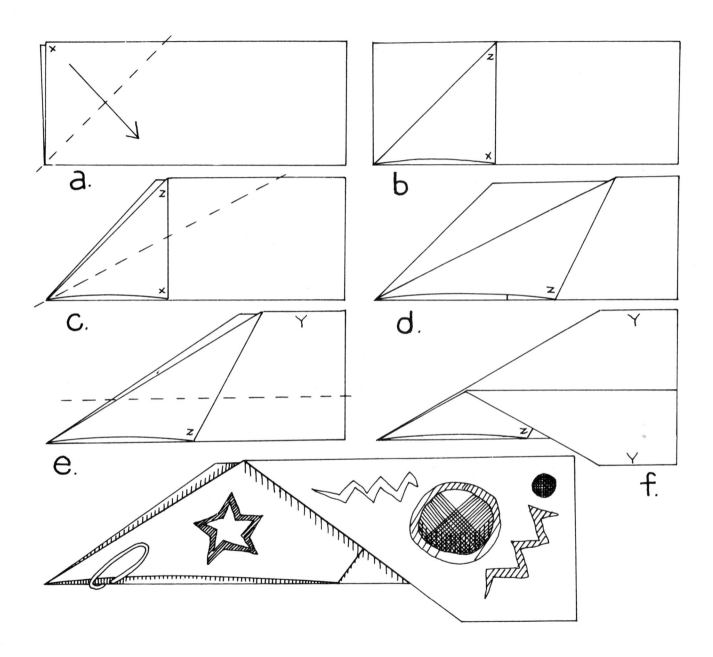

a.

b.

c.

d.

e.

f.

Noisy Sun Rattlers

"Happy New Year!" "No more school!" "Happy birthday!"

There are many times when you are very happy. So what do you do? Celebrate. And what is a celebration without a lot of noise? You don't want to be too noisy, but you do want everyone to know how you feel. Why not do it with these out-of-space sun rattlers? The noise from your sun rattlers will shake up a merry beat.

Things You Need

2 deep paper plates
1 handful of dried beans
liquid white glue
crayons or colored felt-tipped markers

Let's Begin

1. Ask Mom or Dad for two paper plates with a raised rim.
2. Draw a happy sun face on the bottom or underside of each plate. Use crayons or colored felt-tipped markers.
3. Place a handful of dried beans inside one plate, Fig. a.
4. Put white glue on the rim of the plate containing the dried beans.
5. Place the empty plate over the plate that has the white glue around the rim.
6. Let the glued plates dry overnight. From the side, the rattler will look like Fig. b.
7. Hold in your hands and shake for fun noises.

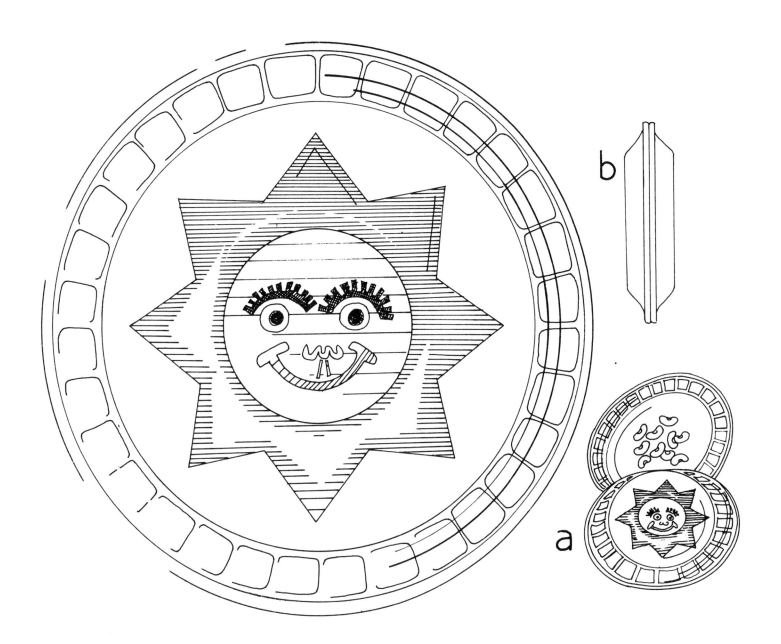

Lacy Snowflakes

It has been said that no two snowflakes look the same. Can this really be true? Since nobody can see all of the snowflakes during a snowstorm, there might just be twins. When it snows, what fun it is to catch snowflakes softly on your glove or coat. You could look at them for hours. Each one is so beautiful and appears unlike any other—maybe it *is* true that no two snowflakes look alike.

Whether you live where there is too much snow or where snow never comes, you'll want a blizzard in your bedroom. Make as many Lacy Snowflakes as it'll take, and hang them from your ceiling, place them around your mirror, or just save them for holiday decoration. These are very special snowflakes. No matter how warm your room is, they'll never melt.

Things You Need

4 drinking straws
1 large paper doily
liquid white glue
stapler
tape
string

Let's Begin

1. Take two straws and cross them, Fig. a. Now tape them together where they meet.
2. Do the same with the other two straws.
3. Place the two crosses on top of each other, Fig. b.
4. Staple the two crosses together in the center. (You may tape them together if you'd rather.)
5. Cut out the round shapes from a paper doily.
6. Glue a round doily shape to the end of a straw, Fig. c.
7. Cover each straw end with a round doily shape.
8. When you are finished put a piece of string through one of the holes of the doily rounds and hang.

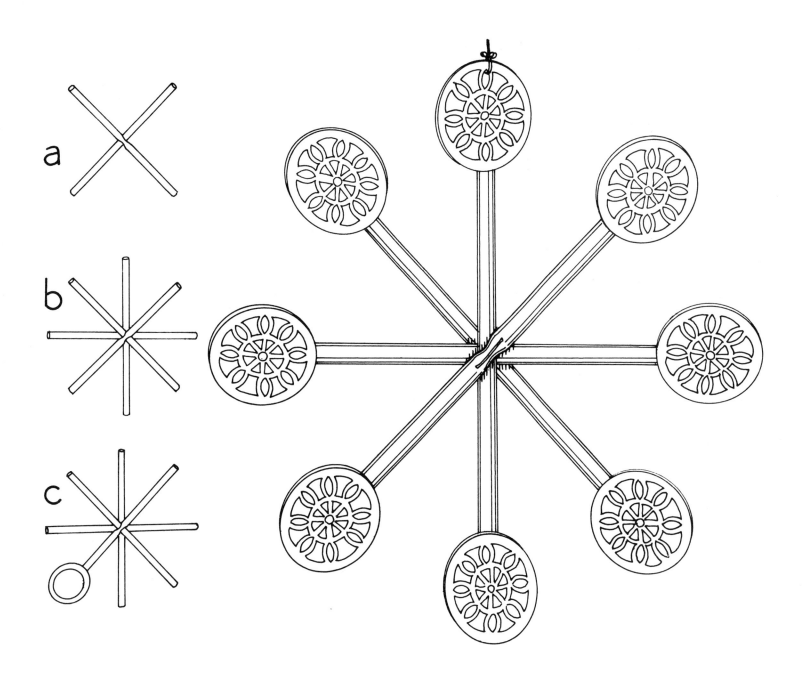

a

b

c

Cardboard Butterfly Printer

Everyone likes to watch a butterfly dance gracefully about the flowers and trees. As it flutters around, it looks as if the sky has a flower flying in it. Butterflies are very pretty because they are so colorful, but don't forget what it takes for them to get that way. They are caterpillars when they are first born. A caterpillar lives in large trees, eats plenty of green leaves, then spins a silky cocoon. It sleeps all winter in that cocoon and, come spring, finally emerges—a beautiful butterfly.

You don't have to wait until spring to see a butterfly. You don't even have to find a caterpillar. With a piece of cardboard and a pair of scissors you can make a butterfly printer. Hundreds of colorful butterflies can be yours—all you have to do is print them on paper, walls, book covers, or anywhere you want a little beauty for your own.

Things You Need

1 sheet of tracing paper
liquid white glue
watercolor brush
drawing paper
scissors
1 piece of cardboard
poster paint
pencil
crayons
colored felt-tipped markers

Let's Begin

1. Trace the butterflies from the book onto the tracing paper.
2. Cut out the tracings, and using them as patterns, trace shapes onto cardboard.
3. Cut out the cardboard butterflies and glue each to other pieces of cardboard with liquid white glue. The backing cardboard pieces should be larger than the butterfly shapes, Fig. a. Let the glued butterflies dry.
4. Paint a thin layer of poster paint over a butterfly shape only. Don't let the paint dry.
5. Print a butterfly immediately by turning the cardboard upside down and pressing the printer onto a piece of paper.
6. Lift the printer off the piece of paper.
7. Let the paint dry.
8. Add butterfly designs to print with crayons, felt-tipped markers, or poster paints.

a

Soaring Rocket Ship

How would you like to be an astronaut? You may be too young to fly a real rocket ship, but why not build your own? Just think, you can have a blast-off right in your own home. Travel your house, making each room a different star or planet. You're in control. Land on a meteor (that looks suspiciously like an armchair) or hop about the moon craters. When your exciting trip is over, lay your rocket safely in your room and think about tomorrow's fantastic journey. What about visiting your neighbor's galaxy next door?

Things You Need

1 cardboard tube from paper towels
poster paints
1 sheet of tracing paper
colored construction paper
scissors
tape
liquid white glue
paint brush
pencil

Let's Begin

1. You will need a cardboard tube, the kind found inside a roll of paper towels, for the body or fuselage of the rocket.
2. Get the tube and paint it a good rocket color with poster paints.
3. Trace Shapes a, b, and c from the book onto tracing paper.
4. Cut out the tracings and, using them as patterns, trace shapes onto construction paper. Make one tracing of Shape a, four of Shape b, and two of Shape c. Use different colored construction paper for each kind of shape.
5. Cut all shapes out of construction paper.
6. The nosecone is Shape a. To form it, keep point x (see book) on top as you roll paper so that corner Y meets Z. Tape the nosecone together, Fig. a.
7. The tail of the rocket is made from the four Shape b's. Fold each shape along the dotted line as shown in Fig. b.
8. The blasting flames of the rocket are made from the two Shape c's. Cut slits along the bottom of each shape, see dotted lines in Fig. c.
9. Attach all of the rocket parts to the fuselage with liquid white glue as follows:
10. Glue the nosecone over the top of the tube.
11. Glue the four tails on the bottom of the tube. Be sure they are equally spaced.
12. Glue the two flames inside the bottom of the tube.
13. Add a paper door and round windows.

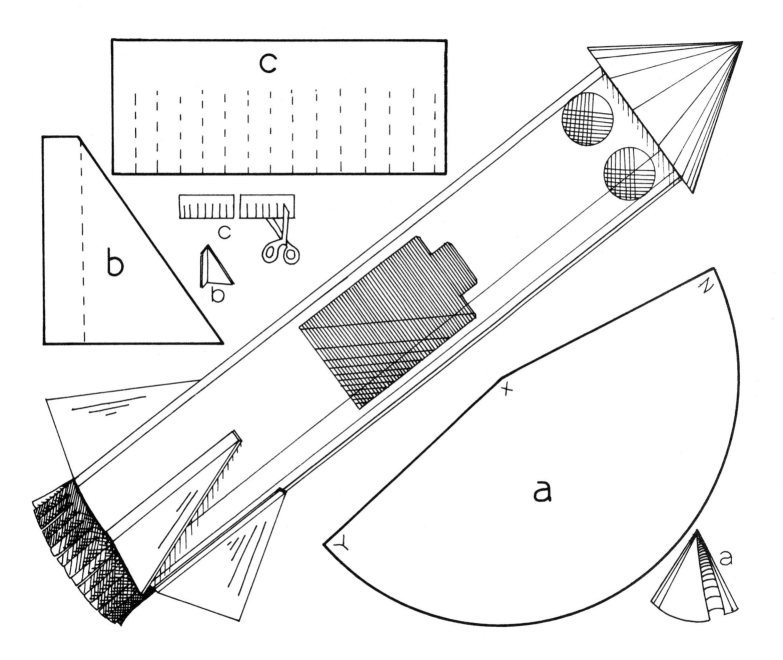

Twirling Copters

A toy helicopter won't fly. You have to move it along the ground. A Twirling Copter will go high into the sky. It is very simple to make and what fun you will have when you throw it into the air. The exciting part is watching it spin to the ground. The two blades look like they are playing a game of tag with each other. When the Twirling Copter lands, it is time for you to toss it into the sky again.

Things You Need

1 strip of paper
1 paper clip

Let's Begin

1. Cut out a long, narrow strip of paper, or trace the strip from the book.
2. Fold the strip in half, Fig. a.
3. Fold one top end of the folded strip down so that it points to the right, Fig. b.
4. Turn the paper over, Fig. c.
5. Fold the other top end of the folded strip of paper just as you did before, Fig. d.
6. Place a paper clip over the bottom folded part of the copter, Fig. d.
7. Throw it high into the air.

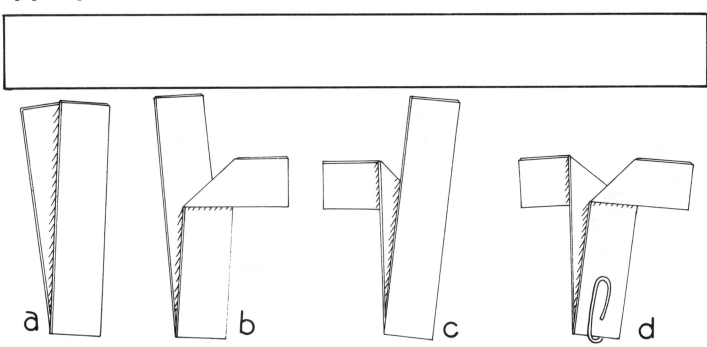

a   b   c   d

Whirling Birds

"A bird in the hand is worth two in the bush." Have you ever heard these words? What they mean is to be happy with what you have for the meantime. Now you'll have a "bird in the hand" for your very own. It won't fly away because it is attached to a stick. With your help, this feathered friend will do all kinds of tricks for you.

Things You Need

1 Twirling Copter (see page 36)
1 sheet of tracing paper
1 piece of cardboard
colored construction paper
liquid white glue or paper paste
1 new pencil
paper punch or sharp pencil
poster paints
1 straight pin
crayons or colored felt-tipped markers
length of yarn
1 cork

Let's Begin

1. Trace the bird, Shape a, from the book onto tracing paper.
2. Cut out the tracing and, using it as a pattern, trace the shape onto a piece of cardboard.
3. Cut out the cardboard bird.
4. Make a hole near the bird's beak with a paper punch or the point of a sharp pencil.
5. Paint the bird with poster paint.
6. Trace the bird's wing, Shape b, from the book onto tracing paper.
7. Cut out the tracing and, using it as a pattern, trace two wing shapes onto construction paper. Cut these out.
8. Put liquid white glue or paper paste on the rounded part of the wing.
9. Glue a wing onto each side of the bird.
10. Use crayons, colored felt-tipped markers, or paint to draw feathers on the wings and body.
**11. Have Mom or Dad cut a slit on the wide end of a cork from a bottle, Fig. c.
12. The tail is a Twirling Copter. It is attached to the bottom of the cork.
**13. To attach the tail, push a straight pin through the inside of the tail and into the cork. Don't push the pin in all the way, Fig. c.
14. Push the tail end of the bird into the slit in the cork.
15. Tie and knot a length of yarn through the hole on the bird's beak. Tie the other end of the yarn to a pencil.
16. Whirl the bird over your head.

33

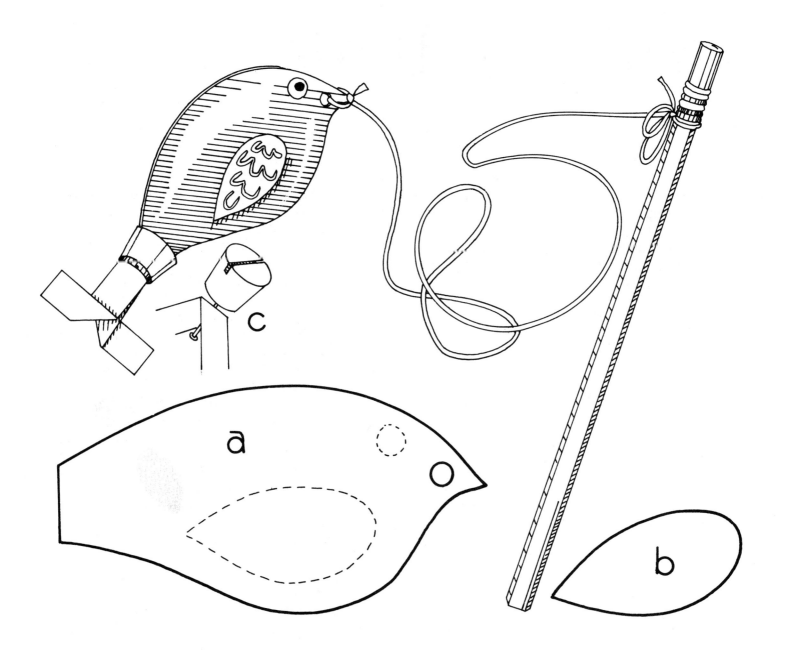

"The owl and the pussycat went to sea"

It was a long journey for the two weary travelers. The owl and the pussycat had set sail in search of a wedding ring. Since airplanes, cars, buses, and trains had not yet been invented, they traveled by boat. Riding on top of the blue ocean, the little craft with its crew of two finally reached land. When the ring was found—bought from a piggy for a shilling—the animals could at last be married and dance "by the light of the moon."

Have you every traveled the ocean in a boat, or merely looked at it? Standing by the shore, the sea is like a blue carpet being pulled by the beach. It is actually a gigantic home for millions of sea creatures. They have lived there longer than any other animals have lived on earth anywhere. In fact, the first land animal was probably some kind of fish that was ready to jump out of the ocean and check out the shore. He liked it so much that he dove back and told all his friends about the new dry world. After hundreds of millions of years, that fish's descendants evolved into all different types of land creatures. People today think that all creatures on earth came originally from the sea. Do you like that idea?

The next time you go to a beach, think about all this. Look down into the water and you will see some of the animals that make the ocean their home. Many of them, as you know, leave their shells behind on shore. Gather a bagful, and then see what beautiful "sea things" you can make in this chapter.

"Going Fishing" Game

"You should have seen the one that got away!"

Many fishermen say these words after a day of fishing. If this is true, there must be many big fish in the lakes, streams, and oceans. Big fish *are* hard to catch. They seem to be a little more careful than the smaller ones.

Big or small, it's hard to land a fish at home. But you can make a "Going Fishing" Game to play whenever you like with your friends. With it, there should be no reason why you can't catch your limit of fish—you might even be the best fisherman in your home!

Things You Need

1 sheet of tracing paper
cardboard
pencil
poster paints
watercolor brush
plastic shower-curtain hook
scissors
length of yarn
1 new pencil
1 gift box (shirt size)

Let's Begin

1. Trace the fish shape from the book onto tracing paper.
2. Cut out the tracing and, using it as a pattern, trace six fish shapes onto a piece of cardboard. Cut out the cardboard fish.
**3. Cut out or punch the large hole in the top of each fish.
4. Paint and decorate each fish.
5. Turn the gift box upside down.
6. Paint the box with green poster paint.
**7. Cut two rows of slits. Each row should have three slits equally spaced, see illustration.
8. Put one fish into each slit.
9. Tie a plastic shower-curtain hook on one end of a length of yarn.
10. Tie and knot the other end of the string around the top of a new pencil.
11. Try to fish by catching the plastic hook in the top hole of the fish. Pull the fish out of the box.

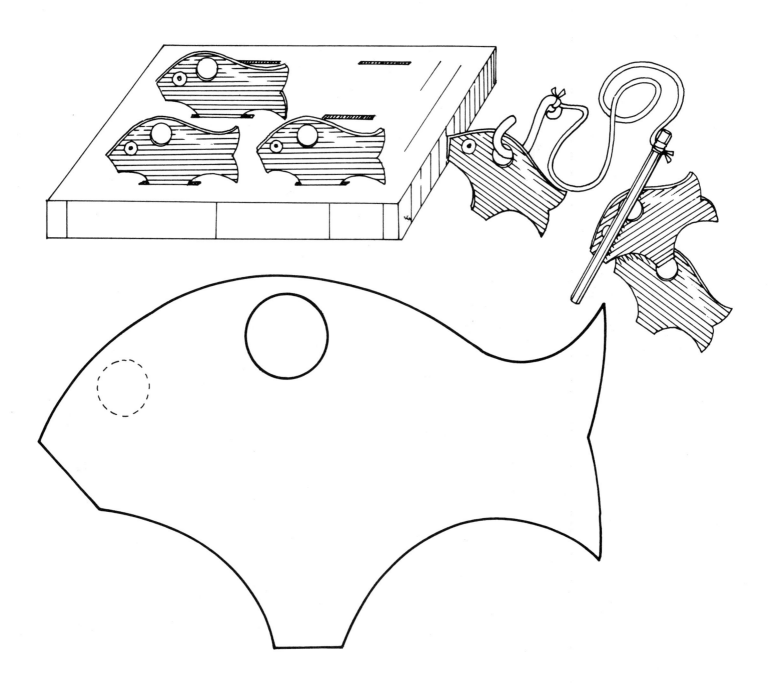

Tinkling Shell Wind Chime

If you are lucky enough to live near the ocean, you know how much fun it is to collect seashells. Hold the larger ones to your ear. You should hear a sound like the ocean's roaring waves.

There are many things you can make with seashells. For this craft idea you'll need at least eight pretty specimens. They should all be fairly small, but they needn't all look alike! The Tinkling Shell Wind Chime will make a lovely sound when the wind blows through it.

Things You Need

8 seashells (available, away from the beach, at craft supply stores)
1 plastic coffee-can lid
knitting yarn
liquid white glue
sharp pencil or paper punch

Let's Begin

1. Glue each shell to the end of a short piece of yarn. Use liquid white glue.
2. Dry overnight.
3. Punch eight holes equally spaced on the top of a plastic coffee-can lid. Use a sharp pencil or a paper punch.
4. Hold the lid with the rim facing up. Push the eight pieces of yarn through the eight holes of the underside of the lid.
5. Tie the end of each piece of yarn in a large knot. Make the knot bigger than the hole so the yarn will not slip through.
6. Punch two more holes on opposite edges of the lid.
7. Push one end of a large piece of yarn from the top of the lid through one hole. It should come out on the underside of the chime.
8. Tie a large knot.
9. Push the other end of the yarn through the other hole and knot it.
10. Hang the chime on the branch of a tree or in your window.

Seashell Candy Dish

What type of candy do you like? Candy bars, rock candy, candy canes, lollipops, jelly beans —there are an endless variety of delicious sweet treats. How about making a special dish for the candy you can't quite get to now, but will definitely eat later?

The next time you go to a beach or go shopping, look for a large clam shell. With a little paint you can turn it into a beautiful candy dish. Be careful! When Mommy sees it she will want to have it for her own. Then you might find yourself making two candy dishes instead of one.

Things You Need

1 large clam shell
poster paints
white kitchen cleanser
watercolor brush
3 beads or 3 small seashells
liquid white glue
clear nail polish

Let's Begin

1. Add some of Mom's white kitchen cleanser to your poster paints so they will stick to the inside of the shell.
2. Paint the entire inside of the shell a light blue for the sky. Let dry.
3. Paint green water, Fig. a.
4. When dry, paint in the boat's hull or bottom and the center mast, Fig. b.
5. Paint in the sails and a triangle-shaped flag, Fig. c.
6. Paint in a fluffy cloud and a bright sun, Fig. d.
7. With liquid white glue, stick three beads or three small seashells to the bottom of the shell, spacing them the same distance from one another, Fig. e. Dry overnight. The beads make a stand so the candy dish will not wobble when placed on a table.
8. To protect the painted scene in the shell, brush clear nail polish—the kind that Mom uses on her nails—all over it.
9. Let the shell dry, and your candy dish is ready to use.

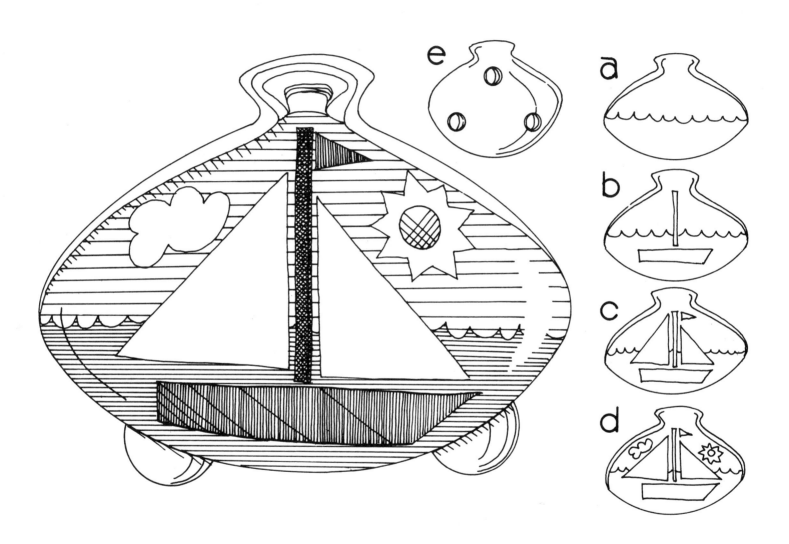

Braided Yarn Octopus

Imagine being an octopus and having eight arms! With all the chores you could get done at one time, you would be the most popular member of your family (with Mom and Dad at least). Well, what about an octopus for a friend? Not a real one, of course. It would have to live in a fish tank. The octopus you will make can go almost anywhere you go. *Except* in the water. Strange, isn't it?

Things You Need

1 package (skein) of colored yarn
1 sheet of cardboard
1 rubber ball
ribbon
scissors
liquid white glue
colored scraps of felt

Let's Begin

1. Wrap the entire package (skein) of colored yarn around a very long rectangular piece of cardboard, Fig. a. You can find cardboard of the right size behind the shirts Dad gets back from the laundry.
2. Clip a small piece of yarn off the free end of the wrapped yarn, and slip it under all the strands on one end of the cardboard.
3. Draw all the strands together on this end by tying a tight knot with the piece of yarn, Fig. a.
4. With the scissors, cut through all of the yarn at the other end of the cardboard, Fig. a.
5. Place the yarn, with the knotted part on top, over the rubber ball, Fig. b.
6. Push the yarn strands together so that the entire ball is covered.
7. Tie the yarn under the ball tightly with a piece of extra yarn, Fig. c.
8. Divide all the yarn under the head into eight equal parts.
9. Tie the eight sections very loosely to keep the yarn separated, Figs. c and d.
10. Take one section and divide it into three equal parts, Fig. e.
11. To braid the parts, study Figs. f and g. Number 1 strand-group goes over Number 2 (the strands on the left go over the middle strands). Then Number 3 strand-group goes over Number 1 (the strands on the right over the middle strands).
12. Repeat the operation, Number 2 strand-group going over Number 3 and so on, until you have just a little bit of yarn left on the bottom.
13. Tie the bottom of the braid with a piece of yarn or thin ribbon.
14. Braid the seven other arms of the octopus.
15. Tie a big bow under the octopus' head.
16. Glue on felt eyes and mouth with liquid white glue.

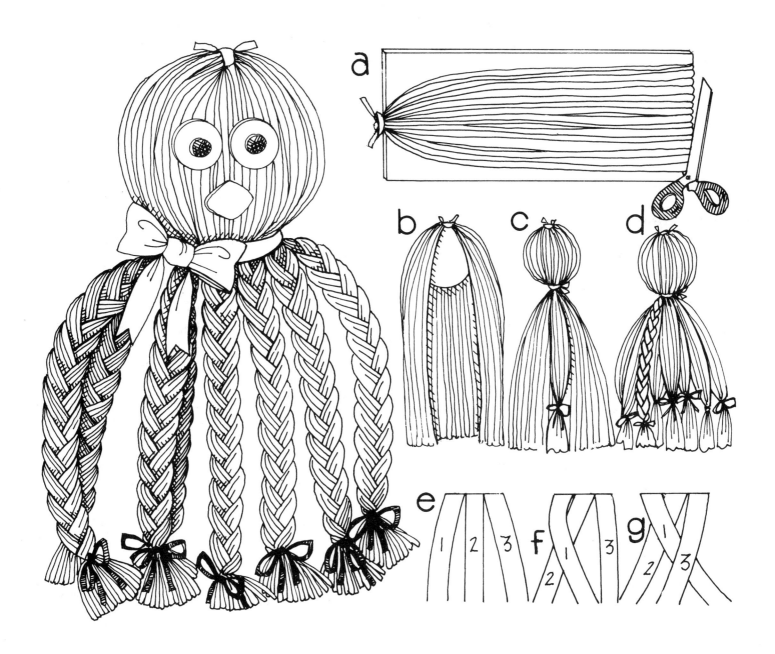

a

b

c

d

e
1 2 3

f
1 3
2

g
1
2 3

Sandcasted Footprint

Dinosaurs lived on the earth many years ago—some, maybe, in your back yard. When they were thirsty, they would go to a lake or stream for a drink. After they finished, they would go away, leaving their footprints in the mud. The mud turned very hard, and today, millions of years later, we can still see where the dinosaurs walked.

You can do the same thing the mighty dinosaur did long ago. For this project you will get your foot a little wet and sandy. No, you don't have to go down to the river for a drink before you start. It can be done in your bedroom and takes only a few minutes. Little enough time when you remember how many millions of years it took the dinosaur's footprints to make their own lasting impression.

Things You Need

shoe box
beach sand
coffee can
mixing spoon
aluminum foil
water
plaster of paris
your foot

Let's Begin

1. Press a sheet of aluminum foil into a shoe box, molding it to fit and cover the inside completely.
2. Fill the shoe box a little more than half full with sand.
3. Sprinkle the sand with water. Use a watering can or dip your fingers in a dish of water and sprinkle. Do not overwater. The sand should be just wet enough to hold together.
4. Place your bare foot in the sand and step down to form a footprint. Remove your foot.
5. Mix plaster of paris in an old coffee can.
6. Add water to the powder slowly while stirring. The plaster should have the consistency of a thin cream.
7. Pour the liquid plaster of paris into the footprint. Don't let it overflow the footprint impression.
8. Let the plaster dry for a week.
9. After a week, take out the hardened footprint. Brush away any loose sand.
10. Use it as a paper weight, for scaring people, or any way you want.

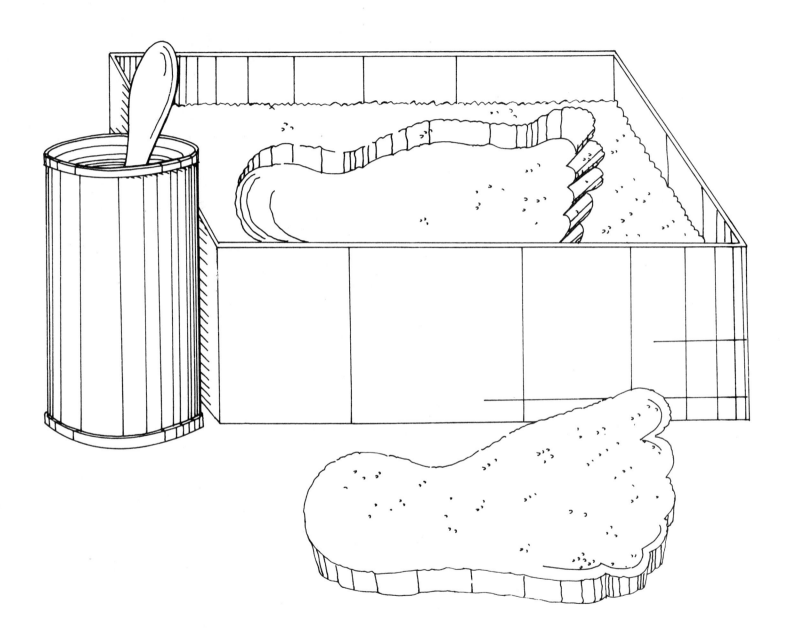

Huck Finn's Log Raft

Huckleberry Finn floated down the Mississippi. What sights he must have seen! Picture yourself on a river, passing farms, homes, and forests. When you are tired of being on the water, you set sail for the shore. The land is your home and the ground is your bed. You go to sleep by the comforting sound of a crackling fire . . .

Since you can't build a raft large enough for you to climb aboard, make a smaller one. Next time you are in the forest, or anywhere near trees, gather some twigs. With them, you can make a raft that will sail just as smoothly as Huck's did many years ago. Although your Mississippi may be a bathtub, you will still be captain of all you survey.

Things You Need

11 twigs of equal thickness
liquid white glue
1 sheet of white paper
colored crayons or colored felt-tipped markers
wax paper

Let's Begin

**1. Break or cut the twigs a little longer than the logs shown in the illustration.

2. Place six of the twigs on a sheet of wax paper. Glue the twigs together with the liquid white glue to form the raft, Fig. a.

**3. Break or cut two twigs to fit the width of the six glued twigs, Fig. b.

4. Glue these two twigs near the ends of the raft, Fig. b.

5. Let the raft dry overnight. When dry turn upside down.

**6. Cut a twig to form the mast and glue it, standing up, to the center of the raft.

**7. Cut the last two twigs to fit the width of the raft.

8. Glue the remaining two twigs to both sides of the mast, Fig. c.

9. Dry overnight.

10. Cut the sail from white paper. With crayon or marker, draw the letters H and F (*H*uckleberry *F*inn) on it, or use your own initials.

11. Push the paper sail through the standing twig, Fig. d. You are now ready to sail.

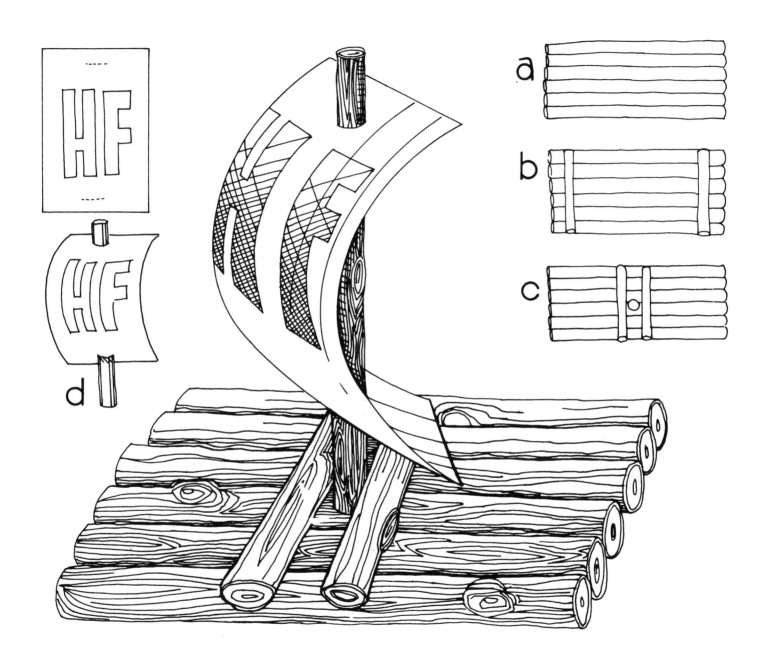

a

b

c

d

Slowpoke Stone Turtle

It was indeed the turtle who won the race. The hare thought he was the best, but the turtle kept a steady pace and came in first. Turtles don't move very quickly on the ground, but they can swim fast in the water. They carry their house on their backs. On land, it's a heavy load.

The Slowpoke Stone Turtle is as slow as the best of them. He won't move along the ground very well or in the water, but he will look very pretty on a table or in Mom's room. Before you start making the turtle, find his house. Look for a large, smooth stone in the woods, at the beach, or in the garden. When you find the best stone, you are ready to begin.

Things You Need

1 large, smooth stone
poster paints
watercolor brush
6 wood ice-cream spoons
liquid white glue

Let's Begin

1. Paint the large, smooth stone with green poster paint.
2. When dry, paint a light green shell design on the top of the stone.
3. Paint circles or shell markings on top of the shell design.
4. Turn the stone upside down when dry.
5. Paint the spoons green.
6. Make the turtle's head and tail by gluing the handle of one spoon onto the "bowl" of another, Fig. a. Glue both spoons to the stone as shown.
7. Make the front legs by gluing the handles of two spoons to the handle of the spoon that forms the head, Fig. b.
8. Make the back legs by gluing the handles of the last two spoons to the "bowl" of the spoon that forms the tail, Fig. c.
9. Dry overnight.
10. Add two eyes to the head of the turtle with white paint.

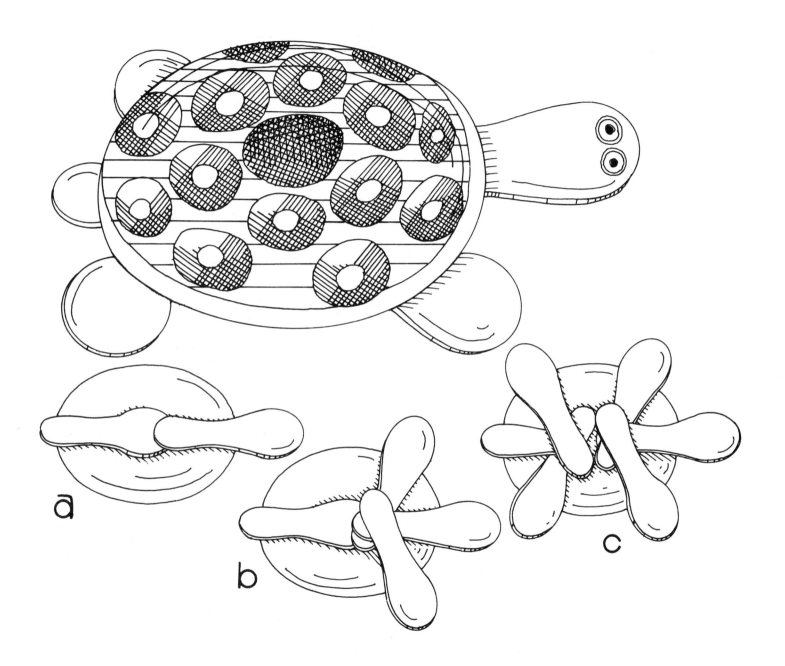

a

b

c

Crazy Stones

When you are at the beach, by a stream, or in the woods, look for small, smooth stones. Gather a whole bunch of them. With them, you can make many happy, funny, or nutty things. Give the Crazy Stones as gifts, trade them with your friends, or—why not keep them all for yourself?

Things You Need

small, smooth stones
poster paints
watercolor brush
colored construction paper
crayons or colored felt-tipped markers
liquid white glue

Let's Begin

The following are examples of Crazy Stones you can make. Follow them, or invent your own designs. In all cases, you will be drawing or painting on a stone.

- Draw a flower and glue a green paper leaf next to it, Fig. a.
- Draw a funny face and glue bits of yarn to the top for hair, Fig. b.
- Write your name, or the name of someone special, Fig. c.
- Draw symbols: stars, circles, lines, etc., Fig. d.
- Make a lovenote to Mom with a heart. Write "I Love You" in the heart, Fig. e.
- Draw a lion face. Glue a scalloped circle cut from orange paper to the back of the stone, Fig. f.
- Paint a clown face and glue a colored construction paper triangle on top of it for a hat, Fig. g.
- Draw a happy face, Fig. h.

Flowers, trees, and other growing things

In the words of a song written long before you were born, ". . . the best things in life are free." Just what does that mean?

Go outside and look around. If you're not a city kid, chances are you'll see some sky, a tree or two, the wavy grass. These are the things you couldn't buy for all the money in the world. People put prices on things as if that told you what they were worth. A tree makes you feel somehow more real. There's no money you can get that will buy that feeling.

You may not be able to enjoy nature whenever you want, but you can bring a bit of its beauty indoors. Or you can let it inspire you to imitate it in "made" things—almost as good. Some of the projects in this section call for actual materials from nature; some require things found in a store. All the projects should give you some sense of the great outdoor world—you'll even be able to sow your own grass seed and watch it grow.

Wax Leaf Collage

Look out of your window and you will see one of nature's most beautiful creations, the leaf. Leaves come in all sizes and shapes. How pretty they look on the trees! It's as if the trees are wearing fluttery green cloaks.

You can bring part of a tree into your bedroom. (No, you won't be hoisting the stump of a giant oak through the window.) You are going to make a beautiful leaf collage. This craft will make a lovely present for someone special, and looks really great when the light shines through it.

Things You Need

leaves of different shapes and sizes
2 sheets of waxed paper
crayons
butter knife or crayon sharpener
glitter
a clothes iron (ask Mom)

Let's Begin

1. Place the leaves on a sheet of waxed paper.
2. Remove the protective paper covering from the crayons.
3. Scrape crayon shavings over the leaves, or sharpen crayons, allowing shavings to fall on them.
4. Sprinkle glitter over the leaves and crayon shavings.
5. Cover this collage of leaves, glitter, and crayon shavings with a second sheet of waxed paper.
6. Ask Mom where you can iron your leaf collage.
**7. Iron over the waxed paper using a medium hot iron.
8. Let all the wax melt into the leaves. Your collage is now permanent. Hold it up to the window and see how beautiful it looks.

Eggshell Garden

Whoever thought that eggshells could be used as flower pots? You can't really grow flowers or trees in them, but you *can* grow grass. (Your Mom will be more than happy to supply you with the empty eggshells you need—she has been throwing them away for years.) It will be very exciting to see the grass grow higher and higher. When it's time to cut it, don't use a lawnmower. Scissors will do the trick.

Things You Need

1 broken eggshell

1 small piece of sponge
grass seed (available at garden supply stores)
water

Let's Begin

1. Place the piece of sponge into the eggshell, Fig. a. Wet the sponge.
2. Sprinkle grass seed on top of the sponge, Fig. b.
3. Sprinkle a little water on the sponge every day, Fig. c.
4. The grass should start growing in a week, Fig. d.

a

b

c

d

Oak-Leaf Seed Painting

For thousands of years people have been writing and drawing. Prehistoric man made paintings of animals on the walls of his cave. Some American Indians wrote on rocks. Today we write and draw on paper mostly. And what do we use to do it? Pens, pencils, crayons, chalk, and paintbrushes.

Now you are going to "draw" with seeds. The seeds you'll need are found in fruits like watermelon, cantaloupe, or honeydew melon. Save as many as you can, and let them dry thoroughly. (You can see that this craft has some good eating as well as good "making" involved in it.) You will also need some of Mom's spice seeds—things like poppy or fennel seeds. With this grain palette you are ready to take a giant step forward in the drawing history that caveman began.

Things You Need

dried watermelon, cantaloupe, and honeydew melon seeds
seeds from Mom's spice rack, like poppy, fennel, caraway or mustard seed
liquid white or brown glue
1 small cup
1 sheet of typewriter paper
paper paste
pencil
scissors
1 sheet of tracing paper
watercolor brush

Let's Begin

1. Trace the oak design from the book onto a sheet of typewriter paper.
2. Paste the paper with its tracing onto a sheet of cardboard with paper paste.
3. Pour liquid white or brown glue into a small paper cup.
4. Use a watercolor brush to brush glue into one area of the design, for example, an oak leaf.
5. Arrange the large seeds (watermelon or cantaloupe seeds) along the outline of the glued area first, then work them inward until the whole space is filled.
6. To work with the smaller seeds (poppy or fennel seeds), merely sprinkle seeds onto the glued area and blow away any that do not stick. Proceed to glue and fill all areas in the way that pleases you most.

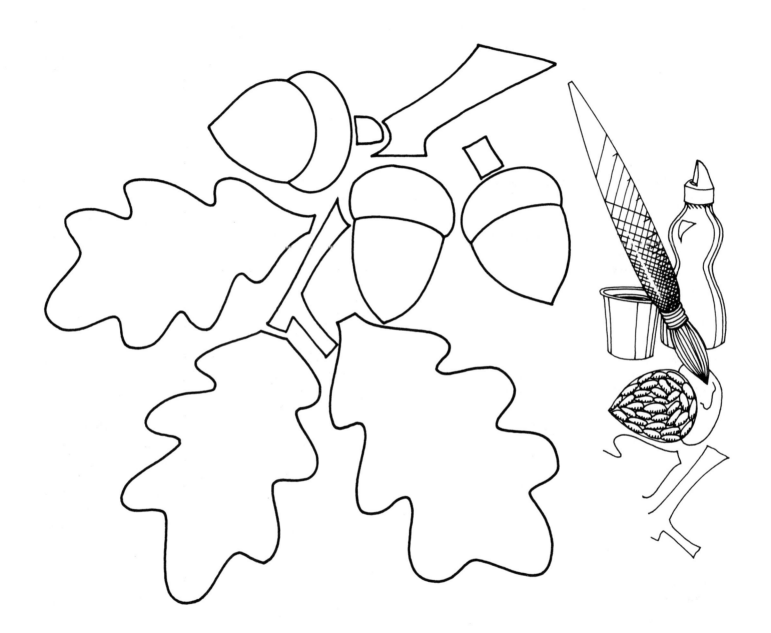

Vegetable String Painting

In Mexico they make paintings of string. They use different colored yarns, and make wonderful designs with it. You can do the same type of craftwork. It's a lot of fun seeing how string can be turned into very pretty vegetables. All you have to do is follow the directions. They will look good enough to eat.

Things You Need

1 sheet of tracing paper
pencil
scissors
paper paste
liquid white glue
paper cup
watercolor brush
scraps of colored knitting yarn
1 sheet of colored construction paper

Let's Begin

1. Trace the four vegetables from the book onto a sheet of tracing paper. The carrot is Shape a; the ear of corn, Shape b; the beet, Shape c; the pea pod, Shape d.
2. Cut the vegetables from the tracing paper and paste one or all of them onto a sheet of colored construction paper.
3. Pour some glue into a paper cup. Brush glue into the carrot, Shape a.
4. Put the string into the wet glue along the outline of the design.
5. Start outlining the carrot and work your way in.
6. Keep working the yarn in until you have filled the entire shape. Don't forget to work yarn in the carrot top "coil." Use a contrasting color of yarn for this part.
8. Proceed in a similar fashion with the other vegetables. Remember to differentiate by color the kernels of corn (the squares inside the corn) and the peas inside the pod.

Papier-Mâché a Super Strawberry

What's your favorite fruit? If it's strawberries, then you're in luck. Even if you don't like this sweet fruit, you'll want to have one of these super berries. You won't find this one in your garden or even in a jar of strawberry jelly. If you did, it would probably take you two weeks just to eat it. This strawberry will be the center of attraction in your bedroom.

Things You Need

1 round balloon
string
newspaper
wallpaper or flour paste
poster paints
large watercolor brush
green construction paper
scissors

Let's Begin

1. Blow up a round balloon and tie the end.
2. Rip up newspaper into small strips.
3. Make a paste from the wallpaper paste or from cooking flour and water. In either case, add water slowly to the dry substance while you stir. You want the paste to be the consistency of soft mashed potatoes. Don't add too much water.
4. Dip the strips of newspaper into the paste.
5. Place a pasted strip on the balloon, Fig. a.
6. Keep pasting strips of newspaper over the balloon until it is covered.
7. Repeat the operation with a second layer of newspaper strips, Fig. b.
8. And with a third.
9. Remove the extra paste from the paper on the balloon with your fingers.
10. Let the balloon dry for one to two days.
11. When dry, paint the balloon with white poster paint. Let dry.
12. Paint the balloon **again**, this time with red poster paint. Let dry.
13. Paint in brown seeds.
14. Cut the strawberry leaf from green construction paper. Cut the paper in the shape of a circle.
15. Cut wedges out along the circle's perimeter, Fig. c.
16. Poke a hole in the center of the leaf.
17. Push the balloon's rubber "stem" through the hole. Your Super Strawberry is complete.

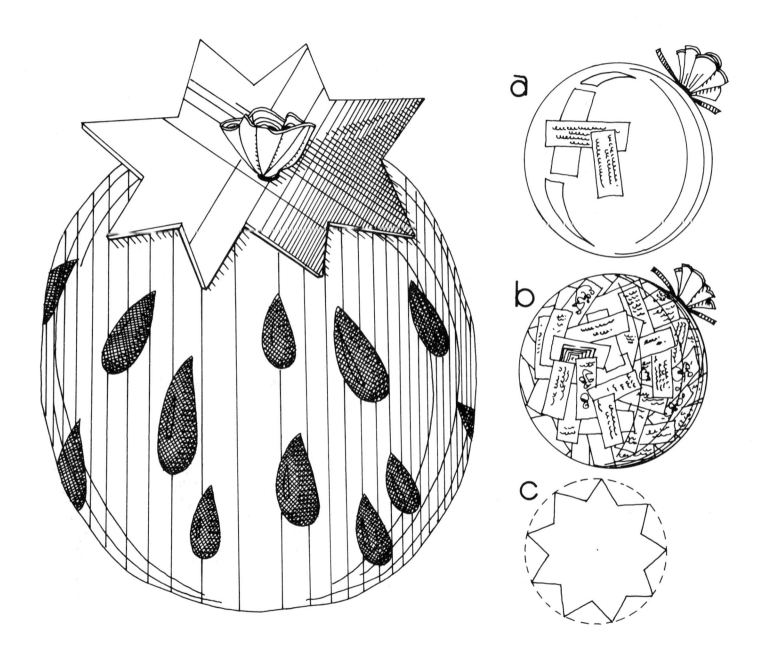

Embroider a Special Flower

If you like to paint with string you will really like to learn how to embroider. Embroidering is a lot of fun once you've mastered a few basic stitches. You can't wait until your stitching is finished. This is a long project, so you might as well get started right now.

Things You Need

1 sheet of tracing paper
pencil
scissors
yellow, brown, and green embroidery thread
1 needle with a wide eye
1 piece of scrap fabric
embroidery hoop
safety pins

Let's Begin

Preliminaries

1. Ask Mom to help you find an embroidery hoop at the five-and-dime store.
2. Cut a piece of fabric larger than the hoop.
3. If the fabric is thin enough to see through, trace the flower from the book onto the fabric before you put it on the hoop. Fit it onto the hoop.
4. If you cannot see through the fabric, first trace the flower onto a sheet of tracing paper.
5. Put the fabric onto the hoop. Trim the tracing of the flower to the size of the fabric showing in the hoop.
6. Use safety pins to pin the tracing paper with design onto the fabric.
7. Embroider the design right through the tracing paper.
8. When all the design has been embroidered, pull away all of the tracing paper.
9. Remove your embroidery from the hoop.

Stitching the Fabric

Once the design is on the fabric, and the fabric on the hoop, you will start to embroider. Proceed with the following stitches:

The Outline Stitch

A. Fig. a shows the outline stitch in action. Use it to embroider the petals. To do the stitch, first thread the needle with yellow thread, and knot the end.**
B. Push the needle through the fabric from under the hoop. Make the needle come out on the outline of the petal.
C. Push the needle back through the fabric along the same line, making a small stitch.
D. Push the needle up through the fabric

(continued on page 65)

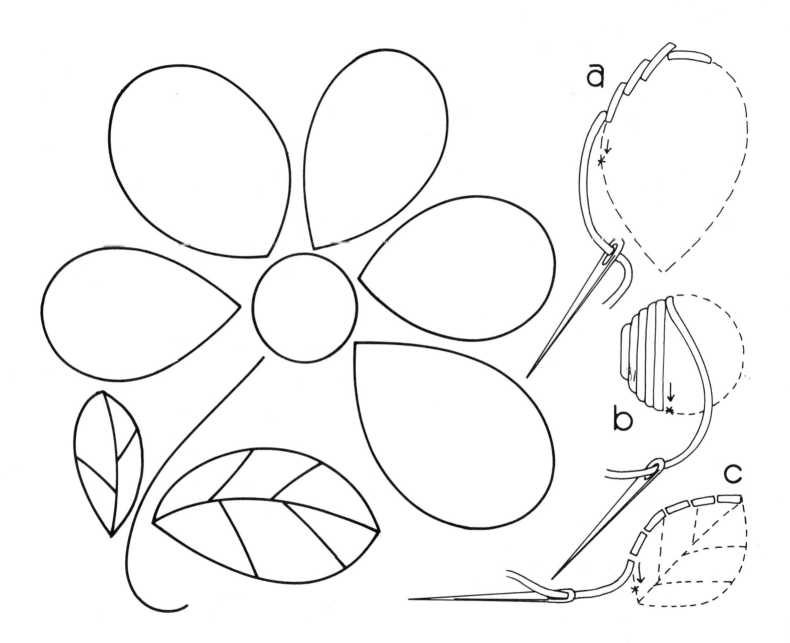

a

b

c

again. Make it come out to the left of the bottom of the stitch you just made.

E. Push the needle back through the hoop, following the line. You will have just made another stitch.

F. Do the rest of the stitches in the same way. Cover the entire outline of the petal with stitches.

G. After the last stitch, sew the thread under one stitch on the underside several times.

H. Cut the extra thread.

The Satin Stitch

A. Fig. b shows the satin stitch in action. Use it to make the bud. To do the stitch, first thread the needle with brown thread, and knot the end.**

B. Push the needle through the fabric from under the hoop. Make the needle come out on the bottom left of the circle's outline.

C. Push the needle back through the fabric on the line at the top of the circle, making a stitch across the circle.

D. Push the needle up through the fabric again. Make it come out on the top line of the circle to the immediate right of the stitch you just made.

E. Push the needle back through the fabric on the bottom line of the circle, making a stitch back across the circle. You have just

made two stitches. They should be close to each other.

F. In this manner, fill in the entire bud with stitches.

G. After the last stitch, sew the thread under one stitch on the underside several times.

H. Cut the extra thread.

The Running Stitch

A. Fig. c shows the running stitch in action. Use it to make the leaves and stem. To do the stitch, first thread the needle with green thread, and knot the end.**

B. Push the needle through the fabric from under the hoop. Make the needle come out on the outline of a leaf or the stem.

C. Push the needle back through the fabric on the same line, making a small stitch.

D. Push the needle up through the fabric again. Make it come out on the line, with a little space between it and the preceding stitch.

E. Push the needle back through the fabric on the line, making a small stitch as before.

F. Cover all outlines of the leaves and stem with this stitch.

G. After the last stitch, sew the thread under one stitch on the underside several times.

H. Cut the extra thread.

Link a Daisy Chain

You'll look as fresh as a daisy with a daisy chain around your neck. But that's not all you can do with this craft. If you make the chain long enough, it can border your mirror. You can even string chains all around your bedroom. Daisy chains are so bright and cheerful, no matter where you put them it will seem like a sunny spring day.

Things You Need

1 sheet of tracing paper
pencil
scissors
white, yellow, and green construction paper
paper paste

Let's Begin

1. Trace the flower, Shape a, from the book onto a sheet of tracing paper.
2. Cut out the tracing and, using it as a pattern, trace the flower onto white construction paper as many times as you will want flowers.
3. Trace the bud, Shape b, from the book onto tracing paper.
4. Cut out the tracing and, using it as a pattern, trace the bud onto yellow construction paper multiple times.
5. Trace the leaf, Shape c, onto tracing paper.
6. Cut out the tracing and, using it as a pattern, trace the leaf onto green construction paper multiple times.
7. Cut out all the flowers, buds, and leaves, from the construction paper.
8. Cut along the dotted lines on the flowers, (Fig. a) to form the petals.
9. Paste the buds to the center of the flowers.
10. Paste a flower to a flower at the ends.
11. Glue the flowers into a circle large enough to fit over your head or as large as you want to make the chain.
12. Glue the leaves onto the underside of some of the flowers.

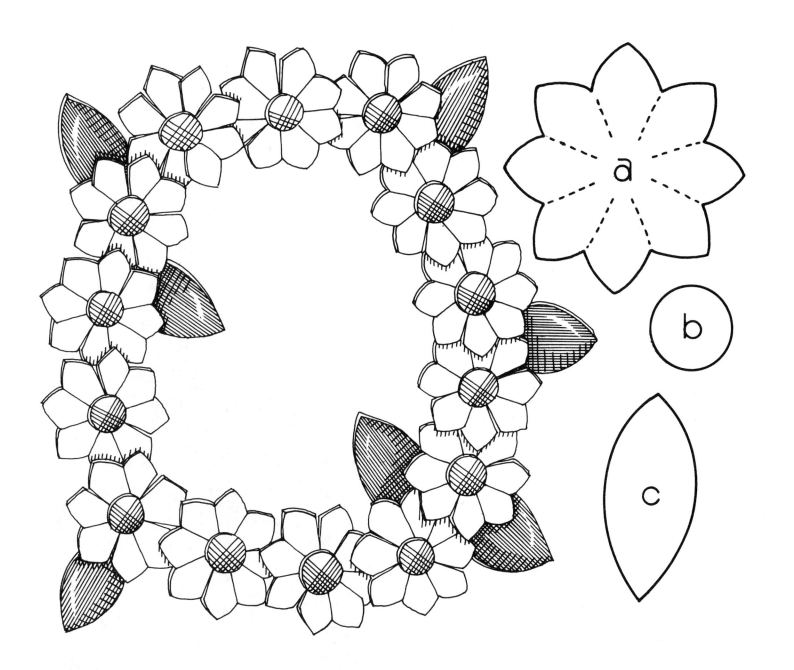

A Bouquet of Dried Flowers

Nothing can be as beautiful as a fresh flower "growing" in a vase. But fresh flowers are not always available. Why not try a bouquet of dried flowers?

Pick some of your favorite flowers when they are in bloom. (If they are in your garden, better ask Mom or Dad if it's okay.) Gather as many as you like. Then dry them following the directions below. The flowers will add a touch of beauty to wherever you put them.

Things You Need

summer or autumn flowers
string
scissors
1 wire coat hanger

Let's Begin

1. Remove most of the leaves of the flowers you have gathered, but leave the stems on.
2. Tie the flowers together at the stems with a string. Be sure the knot is tight.
3. Tie the string to a wire coat hanger.
4. Hang the flowers in a dark, dry place like a closet or an attic for about two weeks. Some flowers will dry better than others.
5. Untie the dry flowers and put in a vase.

Animals are friendly friends

"A man's best friend is his dog." You may wonder why this is true. It's simple. Dogs are very friendly animals. They love their owners and their owners love them. You have lived with your Mom and Dad for many years. During this time you have grown to love them. They give you food, comfort, and a place called home. It's a matter of love. A person who owns a dog gives him the same things. He takes care of the dog, and the dog gives him companionship in return.

Do you have a pet? Many people enjoy having an animal around the house. It's like having an extra brother or sister to play with. (Sometimes it's better.) Turtles, fish, birds, cats, even alligators and raccoons make wonderful pets. How nice it is to have an animal friend to fondle, love and talk to. Most animals like to hear the sound of your voice, even though they don't know what you are talking about. If you talk softly to them, they will be friendly to you.

What if you don't have a pet? If you like animals, you can have a roomful of friendly friends anyway. No, these aren't live creatures, but they look so good it's like having a zoo right in your bedroom. Just read the following sections and make a collection of animals all for yourself.

Silly Salt-Box Animals

If you walk into the woods you'll never see a raccoon, a deer, and a rabbit together. Animals like to live with their own kind. You can change this by making a collection of salt-box animals. With them, all kinds of animals will spend many happy hours sitting together on top of your dresser. You will enjoy playing games with them.

Things You Need

3 salt, oatmeal, or kitchen-cleanser containers
colored construction paper
pencil
scissors
tape
paper paste

Let's Begin

1. Cut a piece of white or colored construction paper as tall as your container.
2. Wrap this piece of paper around the container, Fig. a.
3. Tape the paper in place, Fig. b.
4. Outline the top of the container on the same colored paper with a pencil, Fig. c.
5. Cut out this circle.
6. Paste the circle on top of the container, Fig. d.
7. Cut out animal faces like the ones in the book.
8. The raccoon has black pointed ears, a brown nose, and a red mouth.
9. The monkey has a brown face, white eyes, a black nose, and a red mouth. To make the ears, cut a construction-paper circle in half.
10. The rabbit has long white ears with smaller pink ears inside them. Make a pink nose, red mouth, pink cheeks, and a purple bow tie from construction paper.
11. Put the faces on the containers with paper paste.

a b c d

The Grapefruitiest Animal

Do you like grapefruit? It doesn't taste as sweet as other kinds of fruit. Grapefruit is good to eat when you are sick in bed with a cold.

Did you ever think that you could be best friends with one of these sour yellow fruits? Well, you can. All you need is a well-shaped grapefruit, some paper, and a few other things. It will be the most interesting pet you've ever seen.

Things You Need

1 sheet of tracing paper
pencil
scissors
colored construction paper
1 grapefruit
toothpicks

Let's Begin

1. Trace all of the shapes from the book onto a sheet of tracing paper: the eyes, Shape a; the noses, Shape b; the mouths, Shape c; half a mustache, Shape d; the eyebrows, Shape e; the cheeks, Shape f; and the ears, Shape g.
2. Cut out all shapes from the tracing paper.
3. Using the tracings as patterns, trace all shapes onto colored construction paper.
4. Cut out the colored face shapes with a scissors.
5. Pin a silly animal face onto the grapefruit with toothpicks. Mix up the face shapes. Keep your grapefruit animal in the refrigerator when you are not playing with it.

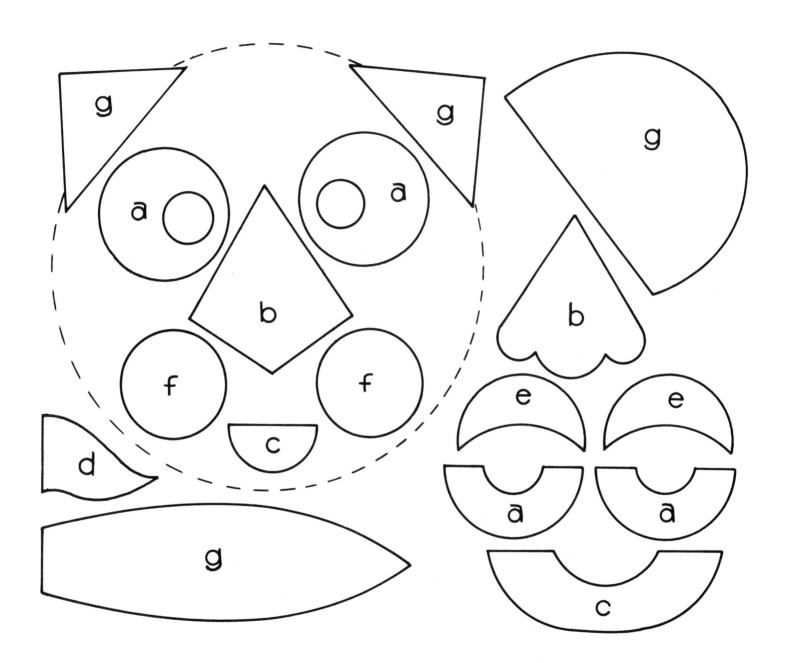

Rocking Horse

You don't see too many horses nowadays. People in the country see horses, and use them on their farms. If you don't have your own horse, now is the time to make one. With some paper and glue you can make a horse that rocks back and forth. Put it on the floor and imagine you are riding across the wide open fields.

Things You Need

1 sheet of tracing paper
pencil
scissors
colored construction paper
white glue or paper paste

Let's Begin

1. Trace the horse from the book onto a sheet of tracing paper.
2. Cut out the tracing and the shape inside the tracing which separates the horse from his rocker.
3. Using the tracing as a pattern, trace the horse shapes onto colored paper twice.
4. Cut out the construction-paper horses and cut along the lines on the neck.
5. The two shapes will be joined together with paper boxes. To make a box, first cut out a strip of paper about as long as the horse is from nose to tail. It should be as wide as the dotted box on the horse (see book).
6. Cut out two strips and fold them into five parts, Fig. a.
7. Fold each into a four-sided box.
8. Glue each box closed.
9. Face both horse shapes in the same direction. Glue the two boxes between both horses at the places indicated by the dotted boxes (see book and Fig. b).

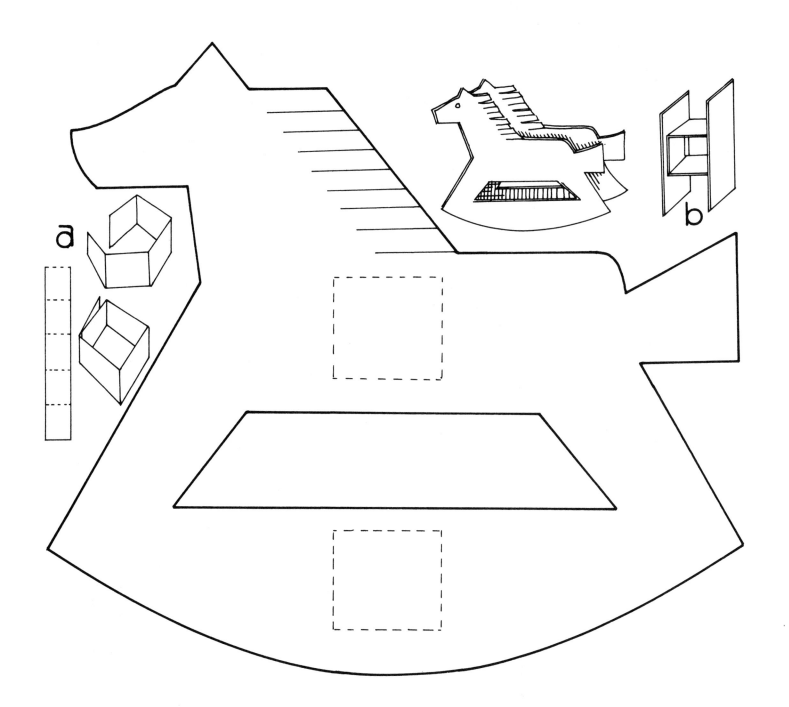

a

b

Plastic Piggy Penny Saver

"Oink! Oink! Oink!" says the little pig. What he really means is: Save your pennies for a rainy day. The more pennies the piggy eats, the more fun you will have when he is full. When that happens—and the rain is falling—your pennies may be good for an exciting picture show.

Things You Need

1 gallon plastic bleach bottle
indelible felt-tipped markers
pink paper
1 pipe cleaner
1 sheet of tracing paper
pencil
scissors
4 thread spools made of wood
white liquid glue

Let's Begin

1. Wash the gallon plastic bleach bottle.
2. Place the bottle in front of you with the handle on top. Draw flower designs on it with the indelible felt-tipped markers.
3. Draw on an eye and a smiling mouth.
4. Trace the pig's ear, Shape a, from the book onto a sheet of tracing paper.
5. Cut out the tracing and, using it as a pattern, trace the ear shape *twice* onto pink paper.
6. Cut out the ears, and glue one to each side of the handle.
7. Punch a small hole in the middle of the bottom of the bottle using a sharp pencil.
8. Push a pipe cleaner into the hole. Use a dab of glue to hold the tail in place.
**9. Cut a slit on top of the bottle. Make sure it is big enough to let pennies drop in.
10. The legs of the piggy bank are made from the sewing spools. Glue the spools to the bottom or underside of the piggy bank with white liquid glue, Fig. b.
11. Let the glue dry overnight.
12. Unscrew the bottle cap—the pig's snout —when you want to borrow some pennies from the bank.

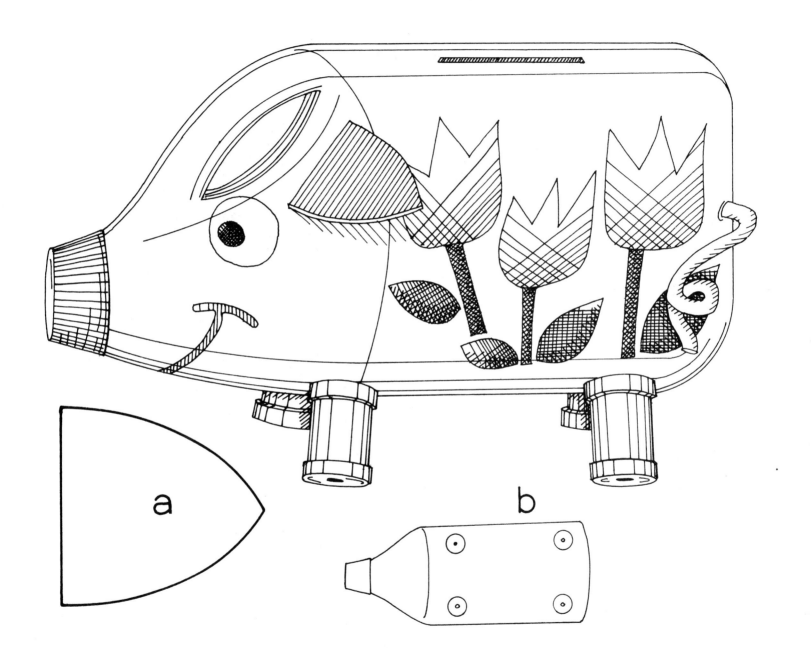

a

b

Bean-Bag Fun

Bean bags are fun to play with. The ones you are going to make are very special. They look like two of your favorite circus animals, the lion and the horse. Use these animal bean bags to play catch with your friends. They've probably never held a lion or a horse in their hands.

Things You Need

colored felt
drawing paper
pencil
needle
scissors
thread
dried beans

Let's Begin

Cut three felt squares for the horse Bean Bag; two for the Lion Bean Bag. All squares should be the same size.

The Horse Bean Bag

1. To make a horse-head pattern, first cut a piece of drawing paper to the same size as the felt squares.
2. Draw a diagonal line (a line from corner to corner) on the paper, Line P, Fig. a.
3. Draw a line across the width of the pa-per right in the middle, Line Z, Fig. a.
4. Draw another line across the width of the paper, this time halfway between Line Z and the top of the paper: Line O, Fig. a.
5. Draw a line from the top to the bottom of the paper, right in the middle: Line Y, Fig. a.
6. Fig. b shows how to draw the horse-head shape:
   draw a line from O to Y;
   draw a line from Z to X;
   draw a line from X to P.
   These lines are shown by the heavy lines in Fig. b.
**7. Pin the horse drawing onto one square of the felt.
8. Cut through the paper and the felt following the outline of the horse-head drawing, Fig. c.
9. Make the ear from a triangle of felt, and the mane from small felt rectangles. Use scrap felt for ears and mane.
10. To assemble the bean bag, first lay another of the felt squares on the table.
11. Put the ear on top of the felt square a little over the top edge, Fig. d.
12. Place the rectangles on top of the felt square, a little over the edge of the right-hand side, as shown, Fig. d.

(continued on page 80)

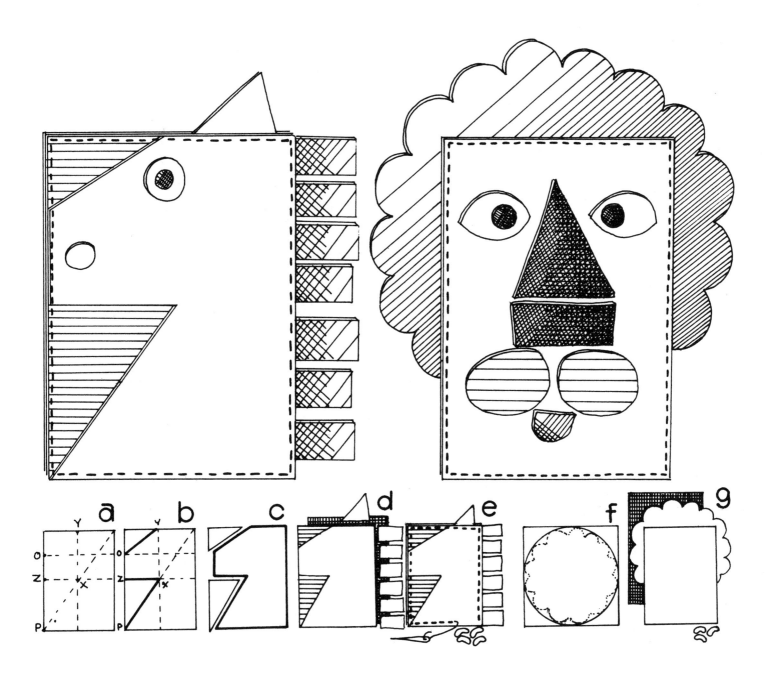

a   b   c   d   e   f   g

13. Lay the last square of felt on top of the other square, sandwiching the ear and mane between them.
14. Place the felt horse head shape on top of the bean bag, Fig. d.
**15. Pin everything in place.
**16. Thread a needle, and sew around the sides of the bag (see dotted line, Fig. e).
17. Leave a little part of the bag unsewn on the bottom, Fig. e.
18. Fill the bag halfway full with dried beans.
19. Sew the unsewn part of the bag closed. Go over the last stitch many times, then cut the thread.
20. Glue on round felt eyes and nose made from felt scrap.

The Lion Bean Bag

1. Cut a circle out of drawing paper which is larger than the size of the felt squares.
2. Scallop or cut out small circles along the edge of the large circle, Fig. f.
**3. Pin the scalloped circle onto felt and, following the outline, cut out felt replica. This will be the lion's mane.
4. Place the first felt square for the bean bag on the table.
5. Put the scalloped felt circle on top of the felt square. It should stick out above the top, Fig. g.
6. Place the second felt square on top of the scalloped circle, aligning it to the first square.
7. Sew the bean bag in the same manner as the horse, Fig. g, leaving open a little part of the bag, filling bag with beans, etc.
8. Cut lion's face shapes (see book) from felt and glue to top felt square of the bean bag. Use liquid white glue.

Join a Dancing Bear

One of the best loved acts in the circus is the dancing bears. These lumbering animals move about the ring with surprising grace. It looks as if their arms are hardly attached to them and are going to fall off any minute.

Now is your chance to have your own dancing bear. It comes apart and snaps together in seconds. You can carry your dancing friend in your pocket and amaze people with him wherever you go.

Things You Need

1 sheet of tracing paper
pencil
scissors
brown construction paper
5 large clothing snaps
colored scrap paper

Let's Begin

1. Trace onto tracing paper the bear's head, Shape a; the leg, Shape b; and the arm, Shape c.
2. Cut out the tracings from the paper. Using them as patterns, trace one head, two legs, and two arms onto brown construction paper.
3. Cut out all of the bear parts from the brown construction paper.
4. Make the body of the bear from a circle cut out of the same brown paper. Trace around a small dish to get the circle.
5. Cut out the circle.
6. Ask Mom for five large snaps.
7. Punch one side of the snap through the circle on the bottom of the head (see book).
8. Punch a tiny hole through the body near the edge of the circle.
9. Push the other half of the snap into this hole and, turning circle over, snap the head onto the body.
10. Punch two more holes through the body, one on either side of the head (see book). Punch holes in arms and snap to body.
11. Attach legs on the bottom of the circle, the same way as you did the arms.
12. Paste a paper nose, eyes, and mouth on the bear's face.

a

b

c

Circus Animal Car

The news is out: The circus is coming to town.

It's a very exciting time. The ringmaster, clowns, elephants, and cages of wild animals parade down Main Street. They are marching to the big top where you can see the Greatest Show on Earth.

It's a good thing the lions and tigers are in sturdy cages. You wouldn't want them to escape and scare everyone. You'd better make some animal cages for yourself. Why? Because later on you will make some wild animals, and they are going to need to be put behind bars!

Things You Need

small soap-powder boxes
cardboard
pencil
scissors
tracing paper
poster paints
paintbrush
brass paper fasteners
cellophane tape
colored construction paper

Let's Begin

**1. With scissors, cut open the top of a soap-powder box, leaving one short side uncut, Fig. a.

**2. Cut rectangles out of the box on one side, Fig. a. You can cut out as many rectangles as you want. Try to keep all the cutout shapes the same size and in a straight line.

3. Paint and decorate the box with poster paints. If the paint doesn't stick to the box, add some kitchen cleanser to the paint.

4. Make the four wheels from circles cut out of cardboard. Use a glass to trace the circles.

5. Paint the wheels a bright color.

6. Punch a hole through the center of each wheel with a sharp pencil point.

7. Punch four holes in your box where the wheels will be fastened. Locate the holes near the bottom and away from the ends of the box, Fig. a.

8. Push a paper fastener through the holes in the wheels and through the holes in the box. Fasten all four wheels to the box by spreading out the two prongs of the fastener.

9. Trace the handle shape from the book onto tracing paper.

10. Cut out the tracing and, using it as a pattern, trace the handle onto construction paper.

11. Cut out the handle and glue it to the side of the box.

12. Tape the flap closed when an animal comes to stay, Fig. b.

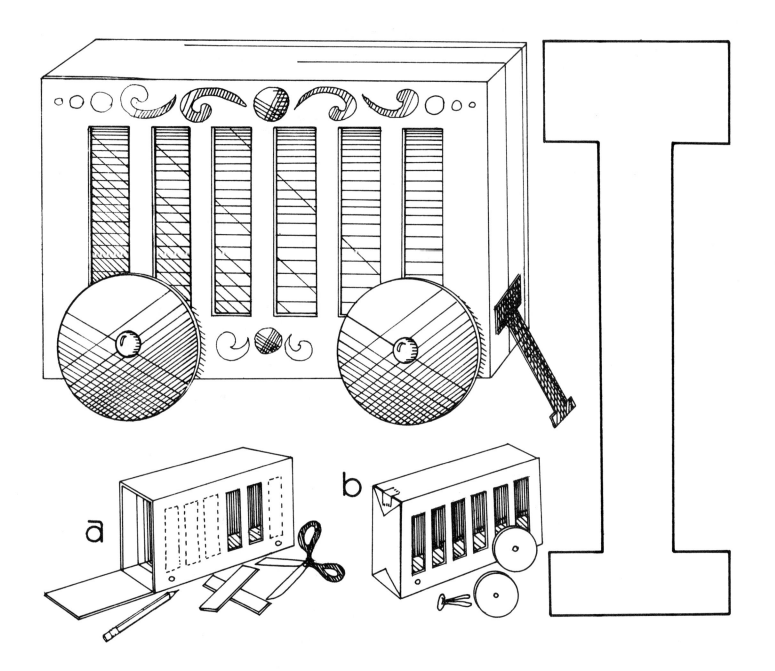

a

b

Friendly Circus Animals

These animals came all the way from Africa to be with you. That's where they live. The elephant and the giraffe like to eat the leaves in the trees. As you may imagine, the giraffe has it all over the elephant in treetop leaf-eating. The hippo couldn't care less about the two, preferring instead to staying in the cool river water. In the evening he goes for a nice grassy dinner on the shore.

Your three African animals should each have his own cage to live in (see preceding project). You might have to cut a hole in the top of one of the cages so that the giraffe can stretch his neck. The elephant and the hippo will fit very nicely in their new homes. With this new collection of animals, your room will be a circus of fun for you.

Things You Need

tracing paper

colored construction paper
cardboard
crayons or colored felt-tipped markers
tape

Let's Begin

1. Trace each animal shape onto tracing paper.
2. Cut out each tracing.
3. Using tracings as patterns, trace the animals onto colored construction paper.
4. Cut out the animals from the colored construction paper.
5. Add fun designs to each animal with colored felt-tipped markers or crayons.
6. Place an animal in each circus wagon.
7. Use a little tape to keep the animals standing.

Sugar and spice and everything nice

What kind of little girl are you? Are you made of sugar and spice—of pinks and pastels, frills, bows, and jump ropes? Or of sterner stuff, like softballs and cowboys and tree-climbing? It's not ungirl-like to do big, active things—where would Alice have been if she hadn't told the Queen of Hearts' courtiers that they were nothing but a pack of cards?

Of course, the important thing is to be yourself and to enjoy as much as you can of every day. The projects in this section should help you to do just that. Whatever kind of girl you are, you probably like dolls, and this chapter should add a few beauties to your collection. Included here also are several items you can actually use, like the Little Moppet Hand Mirror, plus a découpage project that's really fun. Of course, if you see nothing in this section which especially interests you, why not skip to the next one for boys? There's no law around which says you can't build a robot or make a spooky totem pole . . .

Little Moppet Hand Mirror

You can turn your hand mirror into a very pretty little girl. Her name is Little Moppet. She's a young girl who likes being with you when you want to look pretty. When she is not with you, she deserves a place among your favorite play friends. From now on, there will be two pretty little girls in your room: you and Little Moppet.

Things You Need

plastic hand mirror
pink paper
crayons or colored felt-tipped markers
paper paste
scrap knitting yarn
1 piece of cardboard
scissors
liquid white glue
ribbon

Let's Begin

1. Make Little Moppet's hair by wrapping yarn around a small square of cardboard, Fig. a. About twelve "wraps" should do it.
2. Slip a short piece of yarn under the wrapped yarn on the cardboard and push to the end of the square.
3. Using the piece of yarn, tie all the yarn together in a tight knot.
4. Cut open the yarn coil at the bottom of the cardboard, Fig. b.
5. Make two more hair pieces as you did the above.
6. Cut a circle out of pink paper to fit the back part of the mirror, Fig. c.
7. Draw a face on the circle with crayons or colored felt-tipped markers.
8. Paste the circle to the back of the mirror, Fig. c.
9. Glue a hair piece to each side of the mirror, Fig. d.
10. Glue the last piece of hair to the top of the mirror, Fig. e.
11. Dry overnight.
12. Tie a bow with the ribbon onto the handle.

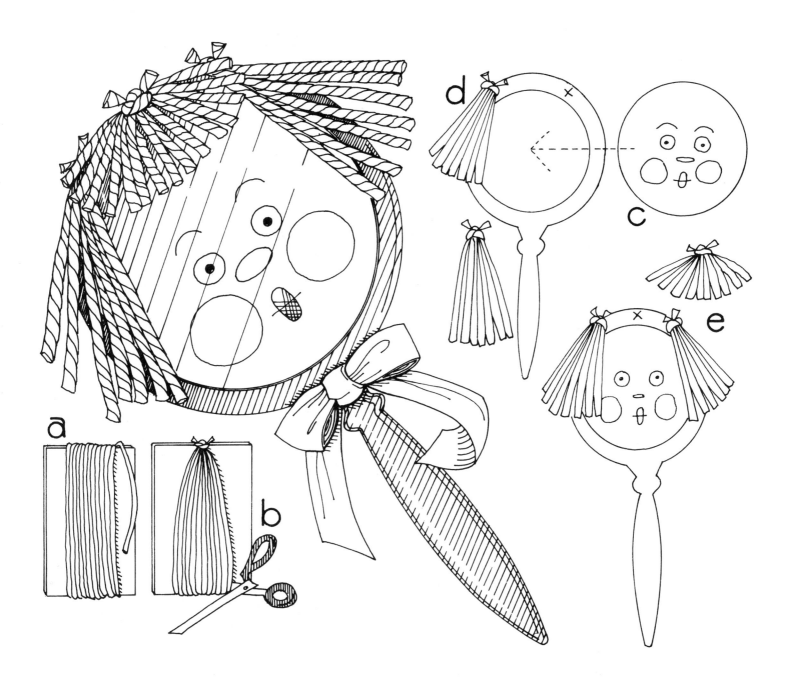

a

b

c

d

e

Tie a Yarn Doll

A marionette is a doll that has strings attached to it. A Yarn Doll has no strings but, as you might imagine, a lot of woolly yarn. The yarn forms the arms, legs, body, and head. You make the doll move without strings. In fact, she is at her best when given the chance to let her arms and legs dangle freely.

Things You Need

one 4-oz. package (skein) of yarn
small rubber ball
scissors
1 piece of cardboard
two small buttons

Let's Begin

1. Wrap the entire package of yarn around a long rectangle of cardboard.
2. Slip a short piece of yarn under the wrapped yarn on the cardboard and push to the end of the rectangle.
3. Using the piece of yarn, tie all the yarn together in a tight knot. Cut the yarn open at the bottom of the cardboard.
4. Place the knotted yarn over a small rubber ball. Keep the knot on top of the ball, Fig. a.
5. Arrange the yarn around the ball.
6. Tie the yarn under the ball in a tight knot with another piece of yarn, Fig. b.
7. Divide the hanging yarn in half.
8. Divide one of the halves in half again, Fig. c.
9. Tie these sections halfway down with small pieces of yarn.
10. Trim off the yarn from a little below the knots, Fig. d. You have just made the arms.
11. Tie the remaining yarn halfway down with another piece of yarn. Make a tight knot.
12. Divide the hanging yarn into two parts, Fig. e.
13. Tie each section near the bottom in a tight knot, Fig. f. These are the legs.
14. Glue on button eyes.

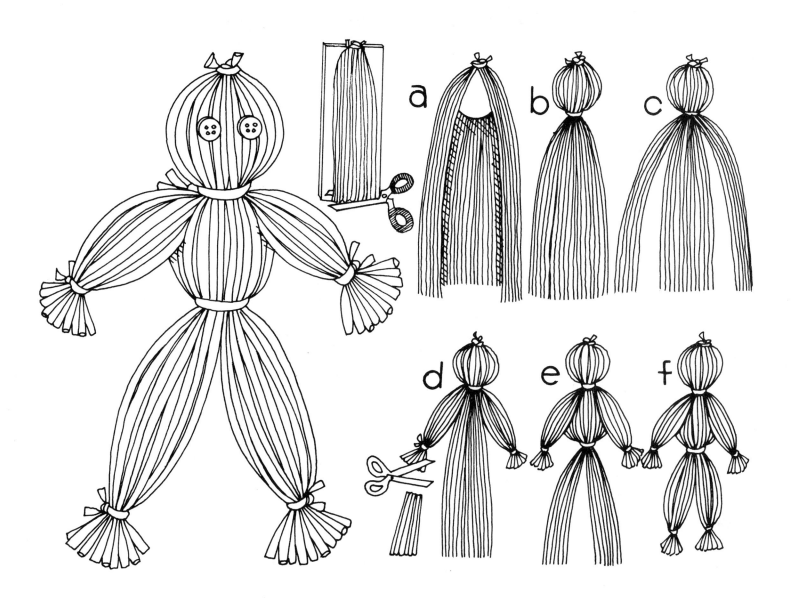

a b c

d e f

Hoop-Skirt Dottie

You may never own a hoop skirt, but why not make a doll that wears one? Your Hoop-Skirt Dottie doll stands very tall on her pretty round skirt. With her arms folded and her skirt in place, she will add a charming touch to your room. Be careful! A handsome young prince might take her away when you are asleep.

Things You Need

1 sheet of tracing paper
pencil
scissors
white drawing paper
crayons or colored felt-tipped markers
cellophane tape

Let's Begin

1. Trace the doll from the book onto a sheet of tracing paper.
2. Cut out the tracing.
3. Use the cutout to trace the doll shape onto white drawing paper.
4. Draw on hair, face, and dress designs with crayons or colored felt-tipped markers.
5. Cut the doll out from the paper.
6. Cut slits on the hands along the dotted lines (see book).
7. Cut slits on the tabs of the skirt along the dotted lines (see book).
8. Curl the skirt back. Fit one tab into the other tab, Fig. a.
9. Put a piece of tape on the tabs to hold them in place.
10. Curl the arms forward. Fit one slit into the other slit, Fig. b.

Découpage a Jewelry Box

Do you know what découpage is? It is a way of decorating an object with pictures, photographs, and designs. (The designs are protected from dust and dirt under many layers of varnish.) You can découpage almost any smooth surface, like a wastepaper basket or a piece of wood. You can make many wonderful gifts for the people you love the most.

Your first découpage project will be something special for your room. You are going to make a very pretty jewelry box. Put your jewelry and any personal things you might have in this precious box, or give it as a special present to someone who'd like it.

Things You Need

1 cigar or gift box
poster paints
paintbrush
large paper doilies
scissors
liquid white glue
paper cup

Let's Begin

1. Paint the box any color you want with poster paints, Fig. a.
2. Let the box dry.
3. Cut a large doily into large and small designs, Fig. b.
4. Brush liquid white glue over the entire cover of the box, Fig. c. If your bottle of glue is too small to allow a paint brush to fit in, pour the glue into a paper cup.
5. Place the cut doilies on the glued surface. Use as many doily shapes as you wish, Fig. d.
6. Glue doily shapes to the sides.
7. Let the glue dry.
8. When dry, paint the entire box with liquid white glue.
9. Let the glue dry.
10. Brush at least four layers of glue on the box.
11. Let each layer of glue dry before you brush on the next layer. On your next project, instead of doilies try using magazine cutouts, small drawings, or scraps of torn paper.

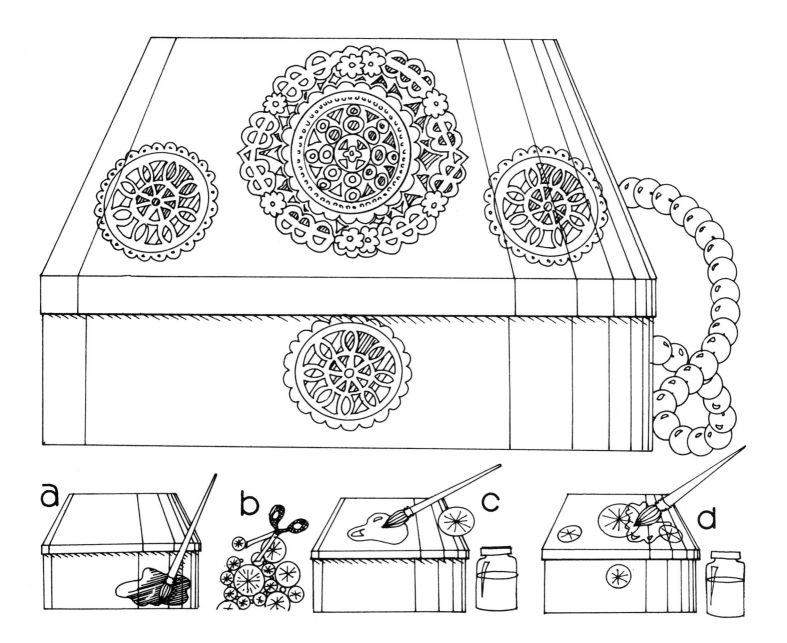

a

b

c

d

Shoe-Box Kitchen

Are you too young to cook? You probably are, but that doesn't mean you can't help Mom around the kitchen. There are many jobs you can do that will help her prepare a meal. It's a lot of fun using a stove and going to the refrigerator, but these are not toys you can play with. So why not make your own kitchen? You can have your very own stove and refrigerator and invite your friends over for a lesson in cooking. When you are old enough to have learned more about cooking, Mom will let you prepare supper for the family.

Things You Need

2 shoe boxes
cardboard
scissors
colored paper
white poster paint
paintbrush
crayons or colored felt-tipped markers

Let's Begin

THE REFRIGERATOR
1. Stand a shoe box on its end with the opening facing you.
2. Cut shelves from the cardboard the same size as the inside of the box.
3. Add a tab to both sides of each shelf before you cut out the shelves, Fig. a.
**4. Cut a slit into both sides of the box for each shelf (see book).
5. Push out the sides of the box to fit in the shelf, Fig. a.
6. Fit the tabs of the shelves into the slits in the sides of the box.
7. Paint the box white.
8. Add door handles with crayons or colored felt-tipped markers to the front cover.
9. Cut pictures of food from magazines or make different shapes using colored paper and store in your refrigerator.

THE STOVE
1. Lay the second box down with the opening facing up.
**2. Cut out a door on the side facing you. Follow the dotted line, Fig. b.
3. Paint the box white.
4. Cover the box and add knobs and top burners with crayons or colored felt-tipped markers.

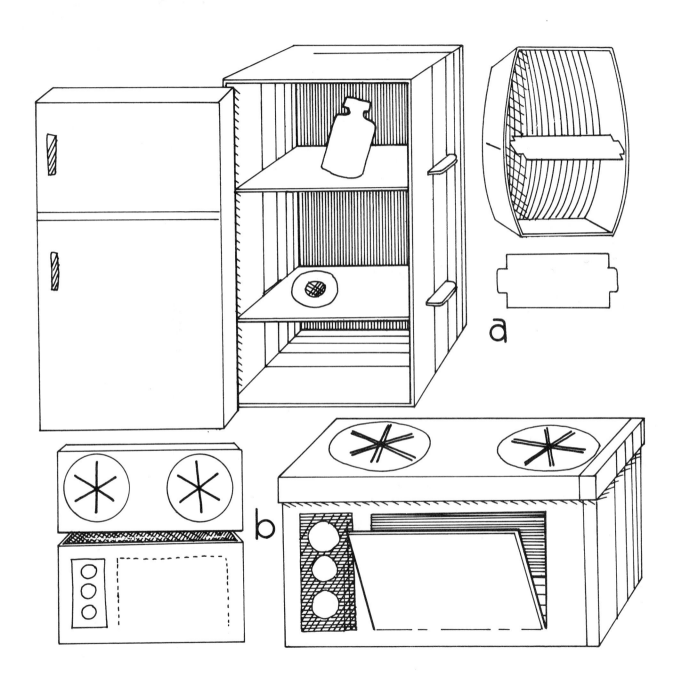

a

b

Build a Dollhouse

If you don't have a dollhouse of your own, make one. It's not as difficult as it looks. You won't need a hammer or nails, or glass for the windows. With four shoe boxes and a few sheets of colored construction paper, your small dolls can have a lovely two-story home. There'll be a kitchen, a living room, a bathroom, and a bedroom. All you need now is a family that wants to move in.

Things You Need

4 shoe boxes
colored construction paper
white liquid glue
crayons or colored felt-tipped markers

Let's Begin

1. Glue the four shoe boxes together with the open sides facing you (see book).
2. Fold in half two sheets of red construction paper as wide as the box front.
3. Place the folded sheets of construction paper on the table with the fold on top. These will make the roof.
4. Draw shingles and windows on both sides of the folded paper roofs with crayons or markers.
5. Glue (or tape) one sheet of folded paper to each of the top boxes.
6. Cut out tree shapes from colored construction paper, and glue one to each side of the house.

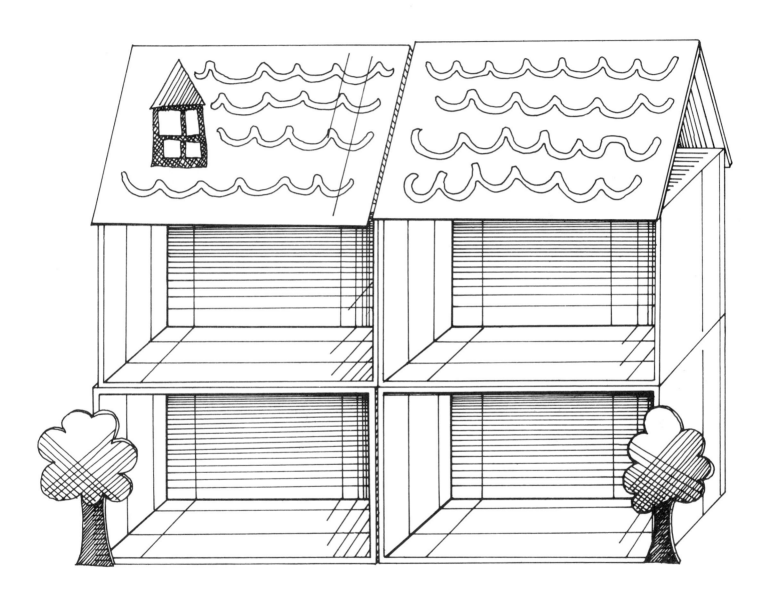

Folded Furniture

Now that you've got a dollhouse, it's time to make the furniture for it. Each piece of furniture is simple to make. All it takes is one strip of paper for each. You must fold the strips as shown in the drawings. Study the pictures. It is very important that you fold the paper correctly.

Things You Need

tracing paper
scissors
pencil
colored construction paper
paper paste
crayons or colored felt-tipped markers

Let's Begin

GENERAL INSTRUCTIONS

1. Each piece of furniture has its own letter pattern, its own illustration and corresponding figure. Figures show how to fold paper strips. Trace the furniture patterns from the book onto a sheet of tracing paper and cut out the tracings. (See specific instructions which follow.)
2. Using tracings as patterns, trace each pattern onto a different colored sheet of construction paper.

3. Cut out the patterns from the colored construction paper.
4. Following the figures (heavily outlined drawings), fold the strips. Paste strips closed along tabs.
5. Each strip requires four folds making five sections. The fifth section is shorter than the rest. This is the tab that will be pasted to close the strip.
6. Draw designs on finished furniture with crayons or colored felt-tipped markers.

WORKING THE PATTERNS

1. Notice that Patterns a, g, f-1, and f-2 are individually drawn, while b, c, d, and e are shown as part of a larger pattern block. To trace b, c, d, and e, use arrows as guides to a given pattern's width. Dotted lines indicate where a pattern should be cut from the larger block (Pattern e comprises the entire block). Fold all patterns along heavy horizontal lines.

   Pattern a is the chair. Fold as shown in Fig. a, furniture illustrations.

2. Pattern b is the clock. Fold as shown in Fig. b, furniture illustrations.
3. Pattern c is the television. Fold as shown in

(continued on page 103)

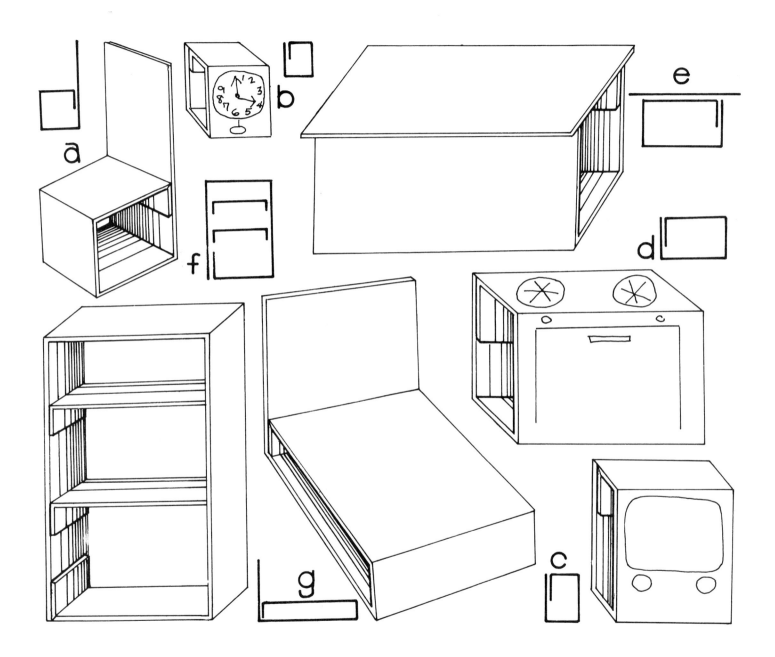

a

b

e

d

f

c

g

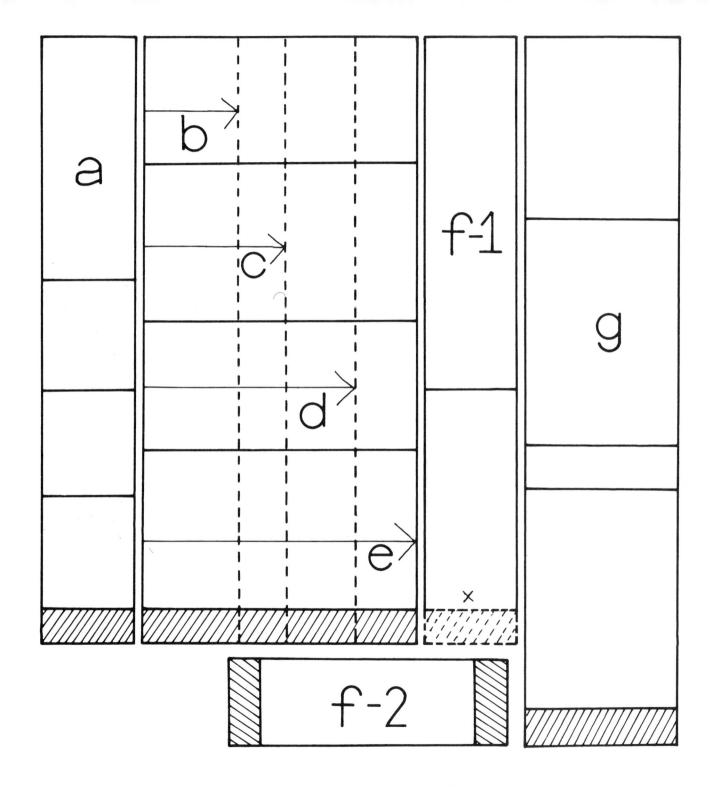

Fig. c, furniture illustrations.

4. Pattern d is the stove. Fold as shown in Fig. d, furniture illustrations.

5. Pattern e is the table base. Fold as shown in Fig. e, furniture illustrations. Make the table top from a small square of construction paper. Paste top to base.

6. Pattern f-1 is one-half the entire cabinet. Trace the pattern twice, end-to-end. That is, the larger rectangular segment of the first tracing should butt the shorter of the second (paste over tab at Point x). Fold as shown in Fig. f, furniture illustrations (one tab remains for closing the whole strip).

7. Pattern f-2 is the shelf. Make two shelves, and fit within cabinet, paste along bent tabs.

8. Pattern g is the bed. Fold as shown in Fig. g, furniture illustrations.

Snips, snails, and puppy dog tails

What is a little boy? A volcano of energy, a zoo keeper of wild animals, a Hall of Fame baseball player. Or maybe a movie director, a musician, the greatest chef in the world. What happened to the snips, snails, and puppy-dog tails? Any boy with a puppy-dog tail would probably find himself in a circus sideshow.

Boys are anything they want to be. They can catch fish or make furniture for the house. They like action—but they like to see and make beautiful things too. How do you feel, as a boy, when you hold a little kitten? Just as much yourself as when you swing that bat at a speeding fast ball or throw that fantastic pass. It's good to win, but it's also good to sit down and relax and start to work with your hands.

This chapter should provide an ample opportunity to do just that. There's a bug cage to make, a telescope, and even a milk-container village. You will have many hours of fun creating toys from objects that are usually thrown away. More to the point, you will have fun creating. Isn't that part of what being a boy is about?

Paper-Cup Army

You have to prepare your soldiers for a very important battle. You are the captain, and not one man must be lost. During the fighting you will be moving your soldiers around the battlefield so that you will win your make-believe war. When the big battle is over, you can put your soldiers away for another day of fun.

Your paper-cup army can be as large as you want it to be. Two different armies can be made by changing the color of the paper that is wrapped around the cups. Have a blue army fight a green army. If you win enough battles, you just might be a general before you know it.

Things You Need

8-oz. drinking cups (as many as you want)
colored construction paper
paper paste
tape
scissors
crayons or colored felt-tipped markers

Let's Begin

1. Wrap a piece of blue construction paper around a paper cup, Fig. a.
2. Tape the paper together around the cup.
3. With the scissors, trim all the extra paper that may go above and below the cup.
4. Make the face from a strip of pink, brown, or yellow paper. Cut it the size of the face in the book. Make it long enough to go around the top of the cup.
5. Wrap the face around the cup close to the top, Fig. b.
6. With crayons or colored felt-tipped markers, draw a face and a black hat brim on the strip (see book).
7. Paste a yellow paper feather onto the top of the cup.
8. Glue a red paper X to the front of the cup.
9. Cut out a triangle from the bottom of the cup to form the legs, Fig. c.

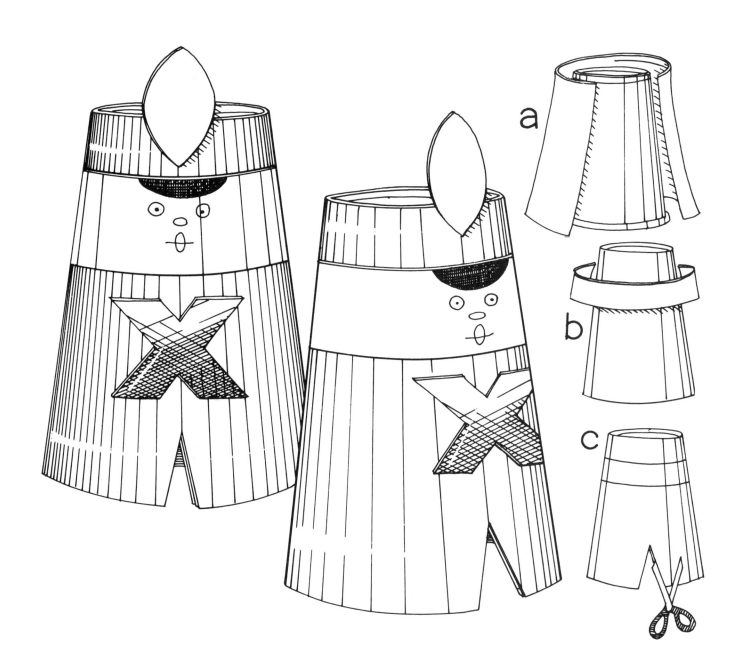

a

b

c

Oatmeal-Box Bug Cage

Now you can have a small insect zoo in your very own room. If you like catching insects, then you will want to make one or more bug cages. The cages are easy to construct and will hold many bugs or beetles. Add a little grass or a few leaves to the bottom of the cages, and don't keep any bug population too long! You wouldn't want to stay too long in a cage yourself. Remember to ask Mom if you can keep the bugs in your room. She may not like them as much as you.

Things You Need

1 oatmeal box
piece of screening, preferably plastic
pencil
scissors
yarn or cord
crayons or colored felt-tipped markers
poster paints

Let's Begin

1. Paint an empty oatmeal box a light color with poster paints.
2. Let the box dry.
3. Draw flower shapes on the box with a pencil.
4. Poke a hole in the center of each flower with a pencil, Fig. a.
**5. Put one blade of a pair of scissors into each hole, and cut out the flowers from the oatmeal box, Fig. b.
**6. Cut a piece of screening. Plastic is best. It should be as tall as the box and long enough to fit around the inside.
7. Roll the screening, and fit it into the box, Fig. c.
8. Poke a hole on both sides of the box near the top. Use a pencil.
9. Thread a long piece of cord or yarn through both holes.
10. Tie both ends together, Fig. d.
11. Pull the cord so you can put the cover on the box.
12. Draw leaves, a sun, or clouds on the box with crayons or colored felt-tipped markers. Don't forget to keep the lid on the box when bugs are inside.

a

b

c

d

Coffee-Can Totem Pole

The Indians made totem poles to honor the gods they worshiped. To make them, they had first to find a very tall, very straight tree. The bark would be removed, and faces of animals and evil spirits carved into the wood. When it was finished, the totem pole was placed in the ground. It stood very tall. There were many totem poles in a village.

How would you like to have a totem pole? You don't really have to be an Indian to have one. Your totem pole will not be *very* big, but it is large enough for you to invite your fellow braves to your house. You can have a powwow by your totem pole every week.

Things You Need

coffee cans with lids
colored construction paper
tape
scissors
paper paste

Let's Begin

1. Wrap a piece of colored construction paper around each can, Fig. a.
2. Tape the paper together around the cans, Fig. b.
3. Trim away any extra paper that may go above and below the cans.
4. Cut out three feather shapes from colored construction paper. Paste them to the top of one of the cans, Fig. c.
5. Paste a long strip of paper to the back of that can. Glue feather shapes to this strip, Fig. d.
6. Cut out funny paper eyes, noses, mouths, and crazy war-paint shapes.
7. Using these, paste a face to each can.
8. Make the totem pole by putting one can on top of the other.
9. The more cans you make, the taller your totem pole will be.

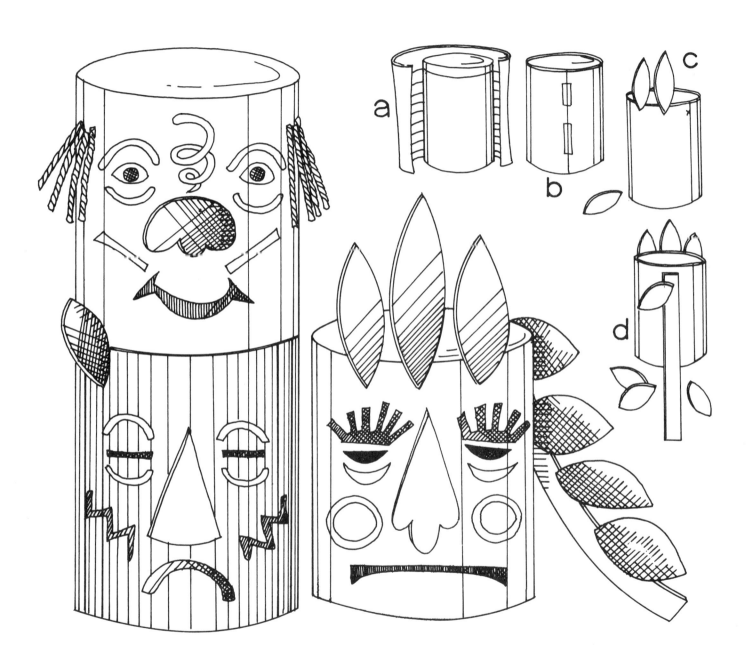

a

b

c

d

Paper-Plate Warrior Shield

If you were a Knight of the Round Table you would need two important things. The first would be your sword. It would have to be razor sharp. You would have to know how to use it to defend yourself. You would also need a shield. A shield would protect you from your enemy's strong sword flashing.

Today, swords and shields are no longer used. Most of them are in museums or hanging on a wall. You may not have a warrior's shield on your wall, but you can easily make one. This shield is not the one used by the knights of long ago, but somewhat like the kind the brave warriors of Africa still treasure.

Things You Need

1 large paper plate
colored construction paper
paper paste
tape or stapler
1 sheet of tracing paper
pencil
scissors

Let's Begin

1. Cut out design shapes from colored construction paper like the ones you see in the illustration.
2. Paste these shapes to the underside or bottom of a paper plate.
3. Make the handle for the shield from a paper strip cut a little longer than the size of the plate. Tape or staple it to the other side of the plate, Fig. a.
4. Trace the feather, Shape b, from the book onto a sheet of tracing paper.
5. Cut out the feather from the tracing paper.
6. Use the feather cutout to trace three feathers onto different-colored construction paper.
7. Cut out these feathers and paste to the bottom front of the shield.
8. Play with your shield by holding the handle on your arm or hang the shield on your wall as a decoration.

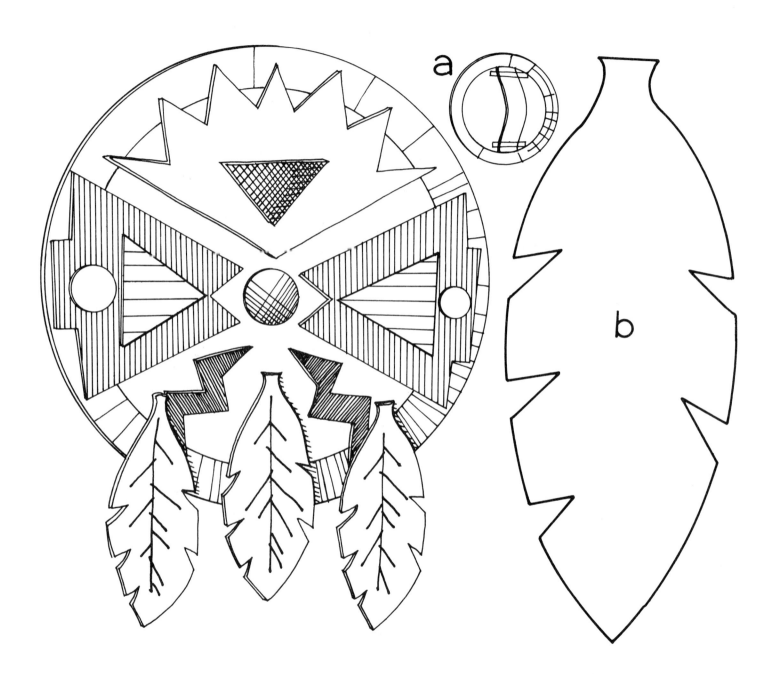

a

b

Milk-Carton Village

Some of the towns out West are small enough for one man to own. There are several houses, a grocery store, and maybe even a candy store. How would you like to own your own village? It's very possible. This is a very healthy town —the buildings are made from milk cartons. If you like to drink milk, then who knows? Your little village might develop into a large city.

Things You Need

milk cartons
colored construction paper
scissors
tape
paper paste
crayons or colored felt-tipped markers

Let's Begin

1. Cut a sheet of colored construction paper as tall as the carton is straight-sided.
2. Wrap the paper around the carton, Fig. a.
3. Tape the paper together around the carton, Fig. b.
4. Cut out window, door, flower box, and flower shapes from colored construction paper.
5. Paste the house decorations onto the carton.
6. Cut the roof from a piece of red or orange construction paper. It should be long enough to overhang the carton slightly when folded in half.
7. Make the stairs from a piece of construction paper by folding it back and forth, Fig. c. Paste stairs under the door.
8. Make the chimney from a construction-paper rectangle with a point at the bottom, Fig. b. Draw a brick design on it.
9. Cut a small slit on one side of the folded roof. It should be smaller than the point on the chimney.
10. Draw a roof design on both sides of the folded roof. Use crayons or colored felt-tipped markers.
11. Push the pointed end of the chimney shape into the slit in the roof.
12. Glue or tape the finished roof and chimney to the top of the carton, Fig. b.
13. Use cream or Half and Half containers for smaller houses. Decorate them the same way you did the big house.
14. Make a village for your trains or racing cars.

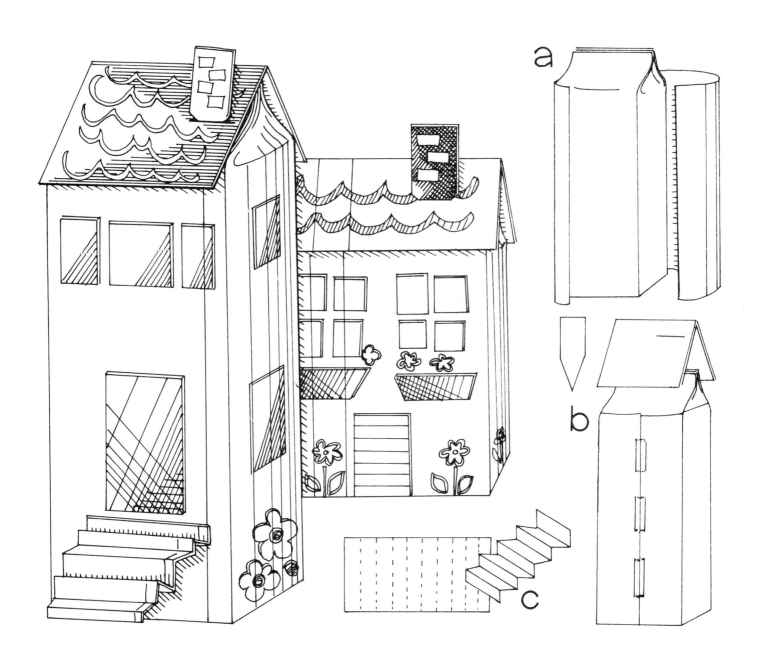

a

b

c

Soap-Box Wagon

You may not have a real red wagon but you can make a small one. Next time Mom finishes using a box of laundry detergent, ask her for it. With it, a fun pull wagon can be yours. It is not big enough for you to sit in it, but you can cart your toys in it.

Things You Need

1 large soap-powder box
tape
scissors
4 brass paper fasteners
cord or yarn
pencil
poster paints
paintbrush

Let's Begin

1. Tape the open end of the soap box closed, Fig. a.

**2. Cut away the front side of the box, Fig. a.

3. Use a pencil to punch two holes into each end on the long side of the box for the wheels, Fig. b.

4. Punch two holes close to each other on one of the short sides of the box for the pull cord, Fig. b.

5. Paint the box with red poster paint.

6. Use a large glass to draw four wheels on heavy cardboard. Cut out wheels.

7. Punch a hole through the center of each wheel with a sharp pencil.

8. Push a paper fastener through the wheels and through the holes punched in the long sides of the box, Fig. c.

9. Open the fastener prongs inside the box to keep the wheels on.

10. Tie a long length of yarn or cord through the two holes on the short side of the box.

11. Tie the cord in a knot.

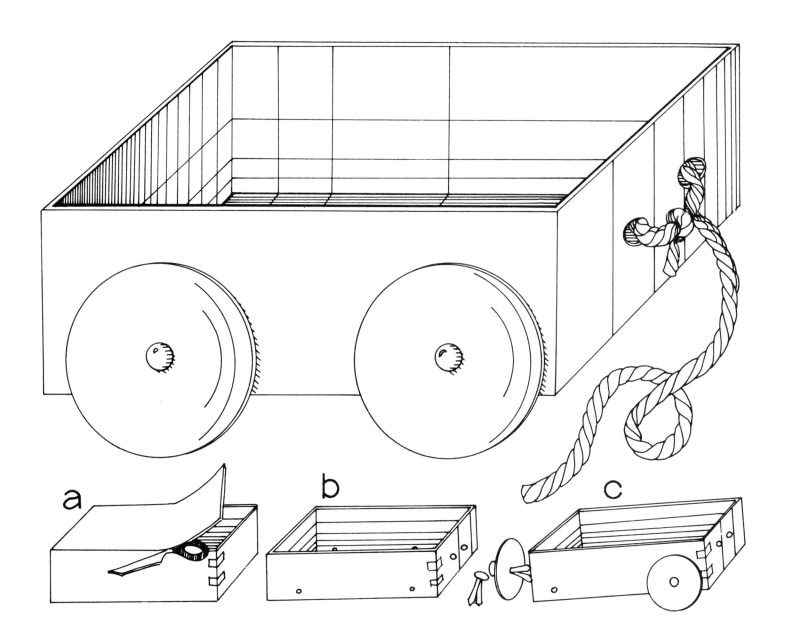

a

b

c

Odds-and-Ends Robot

Is it a creature from outer space or did a mad scientist make it?

Robots are machines that do the same things that people do. They walk and talk, though they are made of metal. *Your* robot will be made from things that are usually thrown away. Look around the house for the "junk" needed to build him. The odds and ends you use all together suddenly combine to make a wonderful mechanical man.

Things You Need

oatmeal box
tuna-fish can
2 cardboard tubes from inside rolls of paper
   towels
waxed-paper box
straw
2 beads
pencil
liquid white glue
poster paints
crayons or colored felt-tipped markers
watercolor brush

Let's Begin

  **1. Remove the lid from a tuna-fish can.

  2. Glue the can to the top of an oatmeal box, open side down, Fig. a.

**3. Cut one of the cardboard tubes in three equal parts.

  4. Punch a hole with a sharp pencil completely through the center of one of the tube sections. You can use a paper punch.

  5. Glue this tube to the top of the tuna fish can, Fig. b.

  6. Push a straw through both holes of the tube, Fig. c.

  7. Glue a bead to both ends of the straw, Fig. d.

  8. Glue the other two sections of the cut tube to the oatmeal box, close to the top, Fig. e.

**9. Cut off one end of an empty waxed-paper box.

  10. Glue the waxed-paper-box section to the front of the oatmeal box, Fig. f.

  11. Cut the other cardboard tube into two equal parts.

  12. Glue both parts of the tube to the bottom of the oatmeal box, Fig. g.

  13. Paint the robot with grey poster paint.

  14. Paint red circles on the tuna-fish can, and blue circles on the front box.

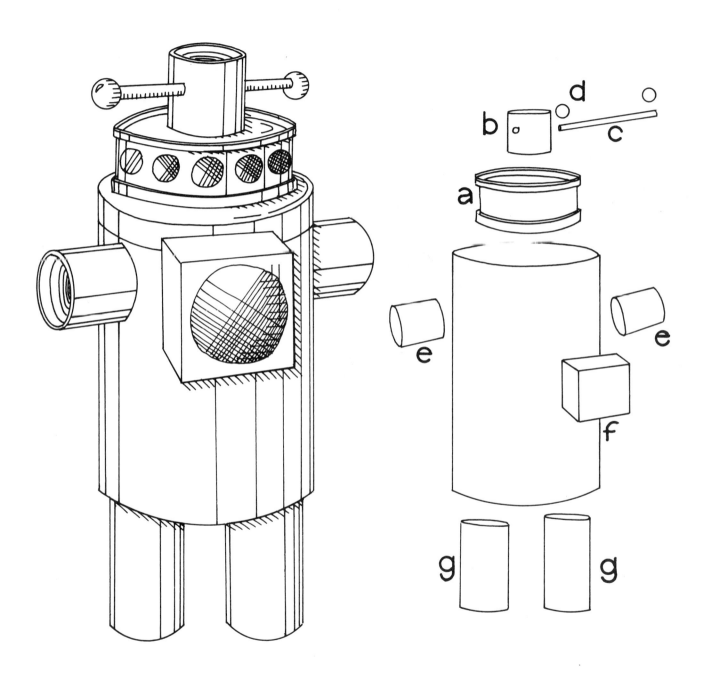

Sewing-Spool Telescope

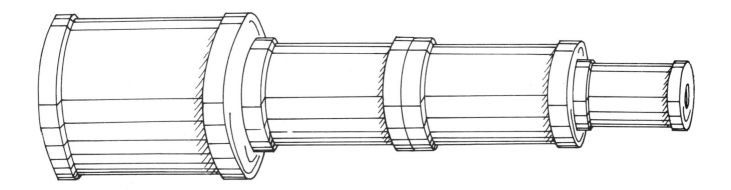

You have been sailing on the ocean for many days. There is blue all around you. Blue sky and blue ocean. Finally, the sailor in the crow's nest shouts the words you have wanted to hear. "Land, ahoy!" What is the first thing you are going to reach for? That's right. You take your telescope in your hand and place it to your weary eye. It's true. There is land ahead of you at last . . .

It's fun to imagine you are the captain of a sailing ship or maybe an evil pirate. With your sewing-spool telescope you can sail the high seas and always spot the land which lies just across the horizon.

Things You Need
sewing-thread spools of different sizes
1 drinking straw
liquid white glue
poster paints
watercolor brush

Let's Begin
1. Place the straw into the hole of a large sewing spool.
2. Put the spool on a piece of paper with the straw standing up.
3. Add a little liquid white glue to the top of this first spool.
4. Stack two or three medium-sized spools onto the straw, gluing them together with liquid white glue.
5. Glue a small spool on the straw last.
6. Remove the straw. Be careful not to move the spools. (If you keep the straw in the spools, trim when dry.)
7. Dry overnight.
8. Paint the telescope with poster paint.

My room is a special place

Your home is a place where everyone in your family stays dry when it rains, eats food when he is hungry, and sleeps safely when he is tired. It is a comfortable place with a friendly kitchen and a cozy living room. Best of all, there is a room for you. It may not be as big as you'd like it to be, but it is your own special place.

Look around your room. Your Mom and Dad and you have made it a friendly place. There must be a picture or two of your favorite real or make-believe people. Toys are probably neatly placed all around (or are they?). There might even be an airplane hanging from the ceiling, or a pretty marionette dancing on the wall. Are you happy with the way your room is decorated? Although your imagination can turn it into a castle keep or an Old West city, maybe it could use some real-life embellishment.

Now is the time to decorate that bare ceiling or those colorless out-of-the-way places. In this chapter you will make things for many of the important parts of your room. There's a mobile for that ceiling, a carton to keep your toys in, even a braided fabric rug. How about a stained-glass window shade? Since only one room of your home is really yours, make it a place that you really love and don't want to leave unless you have to.

Collage a Special Container

There must be hundreds of paper objects around your home—from your old report cards to postage stamps. Any object made of paper can be used in this collage project. If you remember, a collage is lots of paper things pasted together to make a picture or to decorate an object. Pick out your favorite pictures, greeting cards, or any paper scraps. Then find tin cans, boxes, or even a waste-paper basket—you can collage almost anything. With a little glue, you can then turn these objects into lovely things for your room. You might even want to make a present for someone special in your family.

Things You Need

greeting cards, stamps, pieces of fabric, magazine cutouts, invitations, food labels, etc.
colored construction paper
paper paste
liquid white glue
crayons or colored felt-tipped markers
waste-paper basket
coffee can with plastic lid
large box
small paintbrush
paper cup

Let's Begin

1. Paste the special things you have collected onto a waste-paper basket, coffee can, or a large box. Paste each piece close together so that no part of the basket, can, or box shows. Cover the entire container with pictures.
2. If you want to make a special can or box, write the name of what is to be put in it on a piece of colored construction paper.
3. Glue the name on the container.
4. Pour liquid white glue into a paper cup.
5. Brush glue over all of the pictures.
6. Let the glue dry overnight.
7. The next day, brush another coating of glue over the pictures.
8. Let the second coating dry completely.
9. Glue and dry at least two more times.
10. When making the box, you might cover the entire box or just the lid.

Pillow-Case Pajama Bag

Before you start your evening fun, you usually want to get comfortable. You can't wait to take off the clothes you've been in all day. What could be more cozy than your pajamas. Now let's see! Where did you put them? They are probably in a dresser drawer. Or hanging in your closet. Maybe Mom put them on your bed. Since they are so special and personal, why not make a home just for them—somewhere you'll know they'll always be? With the Pillow-Case Pajama Bag, you will never have a problem finding them. Your pajamas will be behind your door waiting for you every night.

Things You Need

plain pillow case
small curtain rod
scissors
indelible felt-tipped markers

Let's Begin

**1. Cut six evenly spaced slits on one top edge of a pillow case, Fig. a.
2. Draw the design on the other side of the case with indelible felt-tipped markers (see book).
3. Draw the Letter A with a red apple next to it.
4. Draw the Letter B with a yellow banana next to it.
5. Draw the Letter C with an orange carrot next to it.
6. Draw green leaves on the apple and the carrot.
7. Push both ends of a curtain rod, from opposite sides, in and out of the slits, Fig. b.
**8. Fit the rods together to the size of the pillow case.
**9. Attach the pajama bag to the back of your closet door.

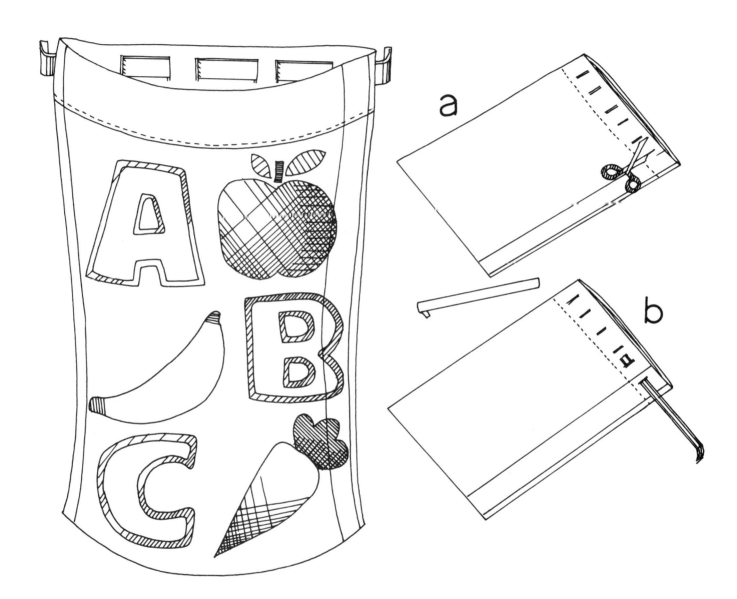

a

b

Drinking-Straw Mobile

The ancient sailors used stars to guide them across the ocean. It is difficult to see stars, much less be a navigator, in your bedroom. What about a star mobile, then? With it, a galaxy of stars will orbit inside your room. They will lead you to whatever shores you wish to dream . . .

Things You Need

4 drinking straws
1 sheet of tracing paper
pencil
scissors
colored construction paper
needle and thread
1 small two-hole button

Let's Begin

1. Trace the bottom star (with the circle on it) from the book onto a sheet of tracing paper.
2. Cut out the star.
3. Use the cutout star to trace nine stars onto yellow or blue construction paper.
4. Cut out the nine stars.
**5. Thread a needle, knot the thread, and sew through one point of a star. Now sew the star to one end of one of the straws, Fig. b, leaving enough thread between star and straw to allow star to dangle. Knot thread around straw. Repeat this operation for eight of the stars. Every straw should have two stars dangling from it, one at each end.
6. Place the four straws on top of each other. Form an evenly spaced star by crossing the straws at their centers, Fig. a.
7. Crush the straws with your finger at the place they meet.
8. Thread a needle with a long length of thread.
9. Sew down through the centers of the straws.
10. Pass the needle through one hole of the button placed underneath the juncture of the straws.
11. Sew up through the other hole of the button and back through the center of the straws.
12. Knot the thread.
13. Sew the last star through the center of the mobile.
14. Hang the mobile from the ceiling with tape.

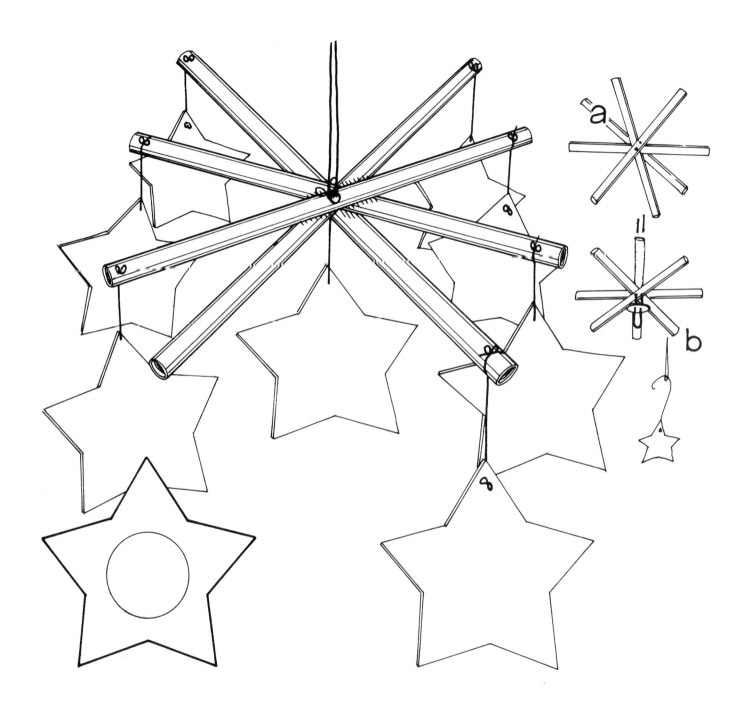

a

b

Stacked Carton Toy Box

Your toys are very special. When you are finished playing with them, why not put them in a safe place? Build a toy box; in fact, build an apartment house of toy boxes. Stack one toy box on top of another. Mom will be very happy. She likes to see your toys put neatly away.

Things You Need

3 same-sized sturdy cardboard cartons with
   lids intact
large sheets of colored construction paper
tape
paper paste
scissors

Let's Begin

1. For small boxes, tape colored construction paper to the box. The paper should be cut to the same size as the sides of the box, Fig. a. For large boxes, paint the box a bright color with poster paint or paint you can borrow from your dad. Paper or paint each box a different color.

2. Make the triangular covers for the corners of the box from small yellow squares of construction paper cut from corner to corner, Fig. b.
3. Paste a triangle to each corner of each box, Fig. c.
4. Cut the letters that spell TOY and BOX from square pieces of colored construction paper. Use the letter drawings in the book as a guide.
5. Cut two of each letter except the letter O. Cut four O's.
6. Stack the boxes and paste on the letters T O Y, one letter to one side of each of the boxes. The boxes should be arranged so that T is on the top box, O is on the middle box, and Y is on the bottom box.
7. On the next sides of the boxes, paste the letters B O X, top to bottom.
8. On the next sides of the boxes, paste the letters T O Y, top to bottom, as before.
9. On the last sides, paste the letters B O X.
10. Fill the boxes with toys. Try scrambling and unscrambling the letters by stacking the boxes in different combinations.

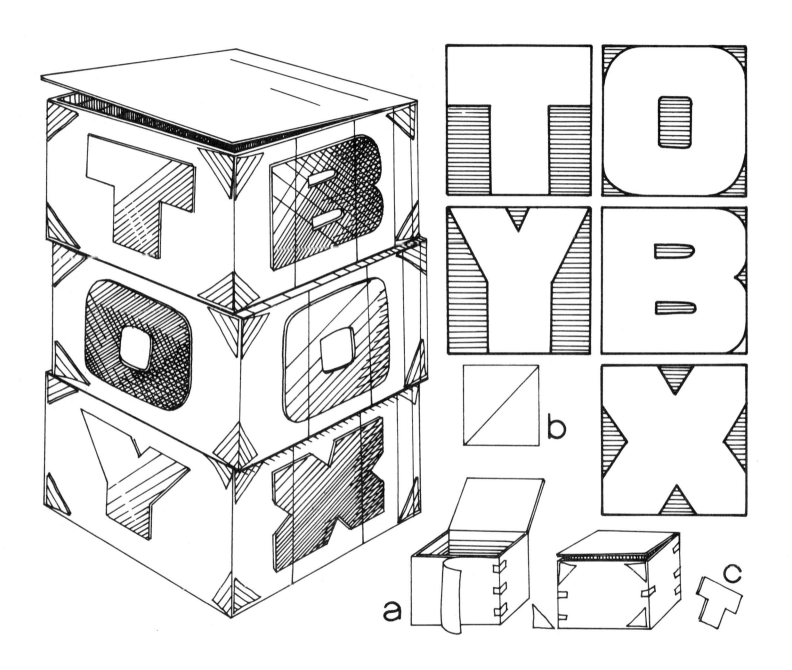

b

a

c

A Braided Fabric Rug

Little girls like to braid their hair. It makes them look so very cute. Hair isn't the only thing you can braid. A warm and cozy rug starts as the longest braid you have ever seen. This rug will be pretty because it has many colors. All of your old favorite worn-out clothes can become a braided-rug foot warmer for chilly mornings.

Things You Need

strips of colored fabric
needle with a large eye
heavy thread
scissors

Let's Begin

**1. Cut strips of fabric from old clothes or from new fabric that is bought in the store.
2. Cut each strip no wider than the two lines between which the arrows are pointing (see guide in book). Make each strip as long as you want.
3. Tie three strips together in a knot, Fig. a.
4. To braid strips, start by folding strip Number 1 over strip Number 2, the middle strip, Fig. b. After you have done this you will notice that strip Number 1 is now in the middle.
5. Fold strip Number 3 over the new middle strip, Number 1, Fig. c. After you have done this you will notice that strip Number 3 is now in the middle.
6. Now, strip Number 2 goes over the new middle strip, Number 3, Fig. d. What you are doing is always putting the right strip over the middle strip and then the left strip over the middle strip.
7. When the strips start to get short, sew a new strip onto each with a needle and thread, Fig. e.
8. Start making the rug by rolling the braid around the knot you made when you tied the strips together, Fig. f.
9. Sew the braid to itself in a circle as you roll the braid around the center knot. Sew and braid as you go, adding new strips to the three main strips as you need them, Fig. g.
10. When the rug is the size you want, tie the ends of the three strips into a knot.
11. Tuck the knot and a little bit of the braid into the underside of the rug.
12. Sew the knot to the underside of the rug.

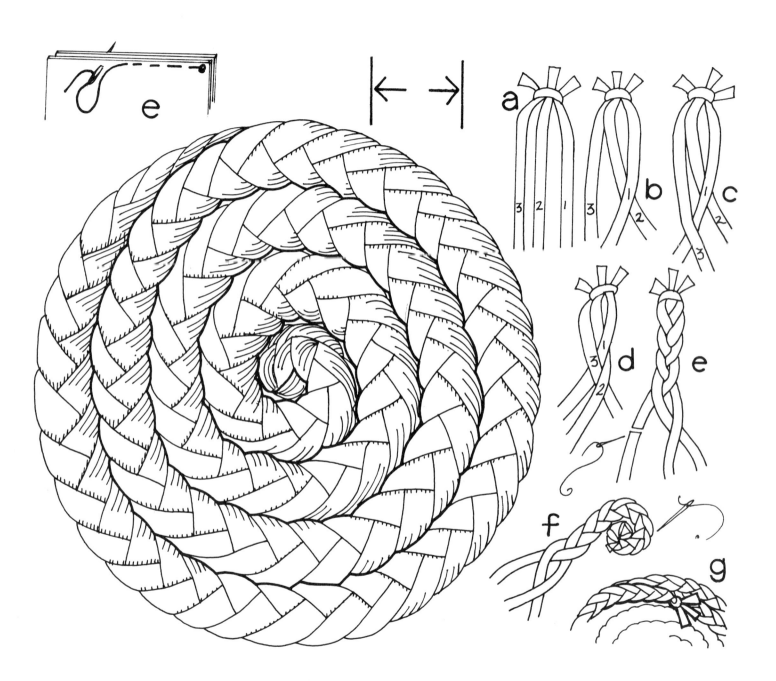

Stenciled Curtains

The curtains on your bedroom windows make your room a cheerful place. If you want to brighten your room even more than it is now, why not stencil designs on the window curtains? You can buy stencils in the store, or you can make them yourself, as we will do here. The circle and diamond shapes will brighten up old or new curtains. After you've practiced a little, why not make up your own stencil shapes and patterns?

Things You Need

plain window curtains
piece of cardboard
pencil
scissors
indelible felt-tipped markers
tracing paper

Let's Begin

**1. Remove your curtains and wash them.
2. Trace the diamond and circle designs from the book onto a sheet of tracing paper.
3. Rub a pencil on the back of the tracing paper, covering the lines from below.
4. Place the tracing on a piece of cardboard with the drawing facing up.
5. Retrace the lines of the circle and the diamond, pressing hard on the paper, Fig. a. The designs will appear on the cardboard when you lift up the tracing paper.
6. Poke a hole in the center of the cardboard diamond and circle, Fig. b.
**7. Put your scissors into the hole and begin to cut out each shape along the pencil lines on the cardboard, Fig. c.
8. Place the cardboard stencils near the bottom of your curtain and close to one side. You can arrange the stencil so that the circle is over or under the diamond.
9. Ink in all the fabric that shows through the cutout diamond and circle with an indelible felt-tipped marker, Fig. d.
10. Make as many designs as you can fit across the bottom of the curtain.
**11. Hang the curtains on your window.

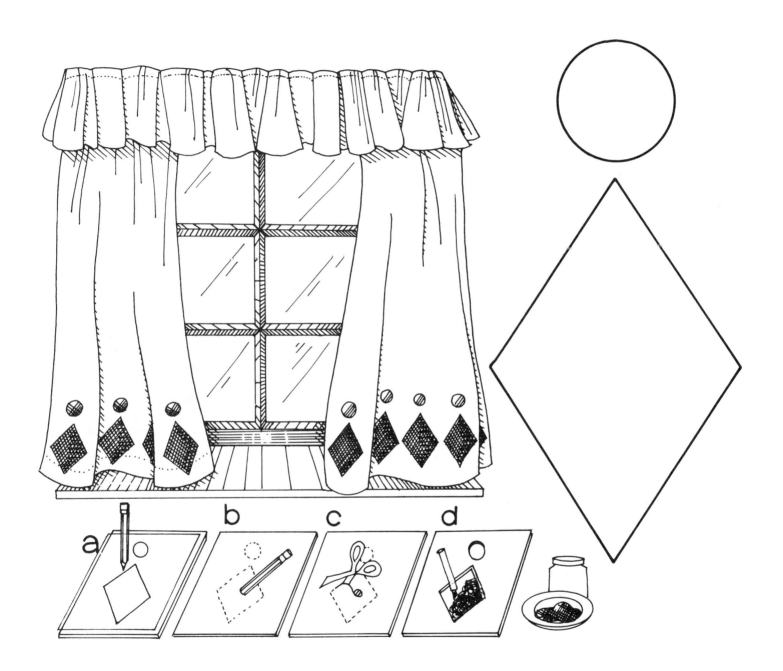

a   b   c   d

Stained-Glass Window Shades

Does the morning sun, peeping around your window shade, awake you? Maybe it would help if the shade was prettier. What you can do is stencil designs on it. The stenciled fish design will make it seem like you are waking up under the ocean or in a small submarine. The light of the morning sun will paint a beautiful picture as it tries to come through your window shade. You won't mind so much getting up in the morning.

Things You Need

1 white paper shade
1 sheet of tracing paper
pencil
scissors
indelible felt-tipped markers

Let's Begin

1. Trace the fish design from the book onto a sheet of tracing paper and, following the directions for the preceding craft, cut out a stencil from cardboard.
**2. When you have made your stencil, take down the shade from your window.
3. Unroll the shade and lay it flat on the floor.
4. Using the stencil, ink in the fish and tail design on the cardboard with the indelible felt-tipped markers.
5. Draw eyes and tail designs onto shade with different-colored indelible felt-tipped markers.
6. Draw green seaweed and blue bubbles.
**7. Hang the shade on your window, and see how the fish glisten.

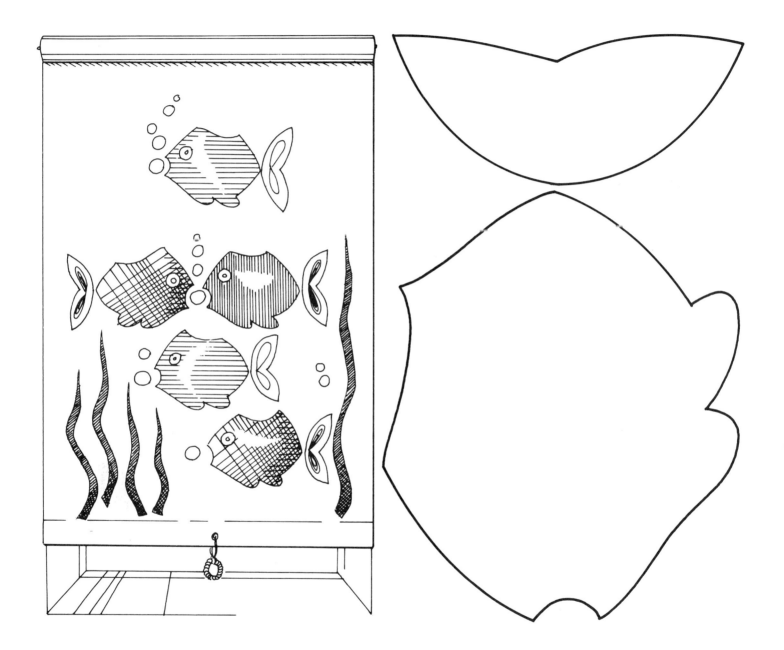

Mirror Decals

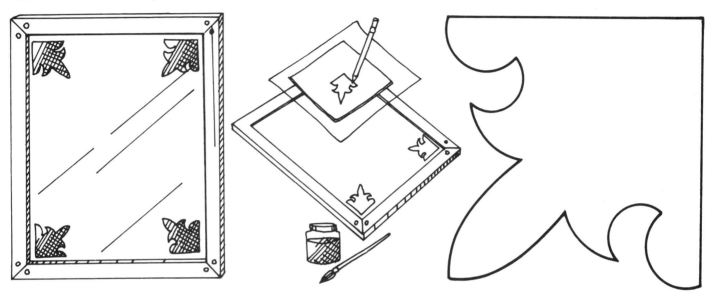

"Mirror, mirror, on the wall . . ." Are you the fairest one of all? Of course you are. Look in the mirror and see yourself. You look fine, but what about the mirror? What your room needs is a special decaled mirror. Every time you look in it, your face will be surrounded by pretty decal designs. With some waxed paper and paint, your decal mirror will be the best-looking of them all.

Things You Need

1 mirror in a frame
1 sheet of tracing paper
pencil
piece of waxed paper
poster paints   paper cup
kitchen cleanser   watercolor brush

Let's Begin

1. Trace the design from the book onto a sheet of tracing paper.
2. Put a sheet of waxed paper over one corner of the mirror.
3. Place the tracing paper over the waxed paper. The corner of the design should be fitted into the corner of the mirror.
4. Draw over your pencil lines with a pencil.
5. When you lift up both pieces of paper you will see the design drawn in wax on the mirror.
6. Repeat the procedure for all four corners.
7. Mix your colored paint with a little bit of kitchen cleanser in a paper cup.
8. Paint in each design.

What shall I wear?

Your clothes are the closest things to you. They keep you warm when it's cool, cool when it's warm, and make you look the way you want to look every minute of the day. You are rather lucky. When your clothes wear out, your Mom goes shopping at the clothing store. Just imagine if you were a person living in a cave many millions of years ago. You would have to hunt for your clothing. Cloth was not yet invented and primitive man used animal skins to make his wardrobe. This was good for the cave man. Besides getting a new suit he also ate a delicious supper.

It wasn't easy making clothing, even if you had a deer or bear hide. The skin had to be treated so that it was soft enough to wear. The Eskimos in Alaska used and still use seal-skin hides to make boots, gloves, and heavy coats. If you lived in Alaska, you would need heavy fur clothing to protect you from the cold weather. In other primitive parts of the world, making clothing is one of the chores people have to do in order to stay alive.

It's a little easier for you today—still, there are a few items of clothing you probably don't have but have always wanted. Headbands, string belts, love beads, and many more. With your hands, a snip of the scissors, and a needle and thread, you can be on your way to a world of fun fashions. You thought you were good-looking? Wait until you finish making all of the items of clothing on the following pages. You are going to be the best-dressed person on your street. Your friends might even ask you to make something for them.

Tie-Dye Tee Shirt

Everyone is wearing wild tee shirts. These crazy shirts have all kinds of designs and different sayings on them. Don't be seen without one. Make your own tie-dye tee shirt. All it takes is string and some dyes. You can design many beautiful patterns and have a sunburst of exciting colors. Your tee shirt will be extra special because there won't be anyone in your neighborhood with one like yours. The great thing about tie-dyeing is that no two designs look the same. Once you get started, you'll want all of your clothes to be colored that way.

Things You Need

1 light-colored tee shirt
boxed dyes of various colors
elastic bands or string
small bowl.

Let's Begin

1. Gather a section of the tee shirt and tie it with an elastic band or with strong string. Make a very tight knot, Fig. a.
2. Tie a second knot halfway down from the first, Fig. b. Repeat this procedure, gathering and knotting material in various places all over the shirt.
3. In some gathers, but not all, tie a third knot halfway down from the second knot, Fig. c.
4. Pour yellow or another light color of boxed dye into a small bowl. Mix with a small amount of water.
5. Dip the entire shirt into the dye. Ring out.
6. Pour light green, or another medium shade of boxed dye into a small bowl. Mix with a small amount of water.
7. Dip all of the gathers into the dye, this time only as far as the middle knot, Fig. d.
8. Add blue, or another dark color of boxed dye to a small bowl. Mix with a small amount of water.
9. Where gathers make three knots, dip into dye, dyeing the last section only.
10. Let the tee shirt dry without removing any of the knots.
11. When dry, remove the elastic bands or tied string.

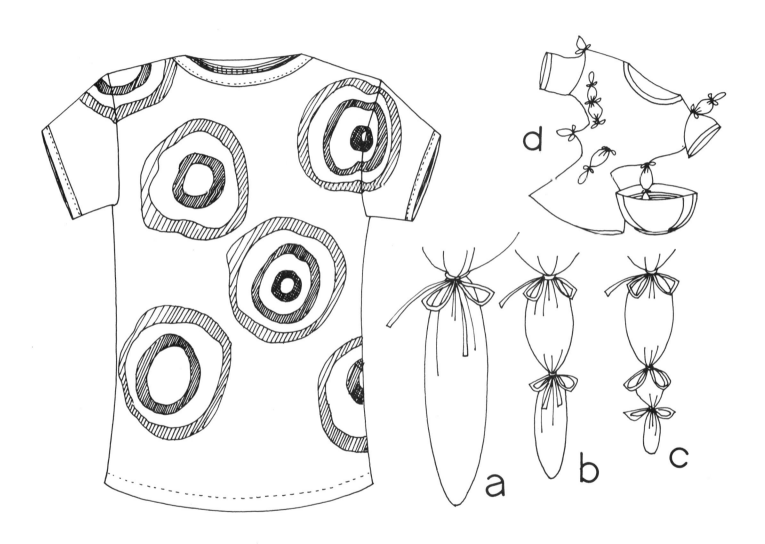

a

b

c

d

Crayon-Batik a Scarf

Did you ever wonder how designs are put on fabric? Most designs are printed just the way a newspaper is printed. Long before printing machines were invented, though, clothing had designs and patterns. One of the ways this was done was by batiking the fabric. When you batik a piece of fabric you start with a light, solid-colored piece of material. With wax and dyes, the batiking process adds colorful designs to the fabric. You will not be using wax and dyes the way people did hundreds of years ago. Crayons will do just as well. Your batik scarf will look absolutely lovely on your head.

Things You Need

white silk scarf
crayons
boxed dyes of various colors
bowl
clothing iron
paper toweling

Let's Begin

1. Place the corners of the scarf on the heart, diamond, and circle design on the bottom right of the scarf illustration in the book. Trace onto the scarf with a pencil.
2. Color in all the hearts on the scarf with a heavy coating of red crayon, Fig. a.
3. Place each corner between two sheets of paper toweling.
**4. Use a medium-hot clothes iron to iron each heart so that all of the wax melts into the silk, Fig. b.
5. Mix a light-color dye into a small bowl with water.
6. Dip the entire scarf into the dye, Fig. c.
7. Let the scarf dry completely.
8. When the scarf is dry, color in all the diamond shapes on the scarf with a heavy coating of green crayon, Fig. d.
**9. Iron the diamonds the same way you ironed the hearts.
10. Dip the scarf into a medium-dark dye solution.
11. Let the scarf dry completely.
12. When the scarf has dried, color in all the circles on the scarf with a heavy coating of blue crayon, Fig. e.
**13. Iron the circles the same way you ironed the hearts and diamonds.
**14. Iron the whole scarf before you wear it.

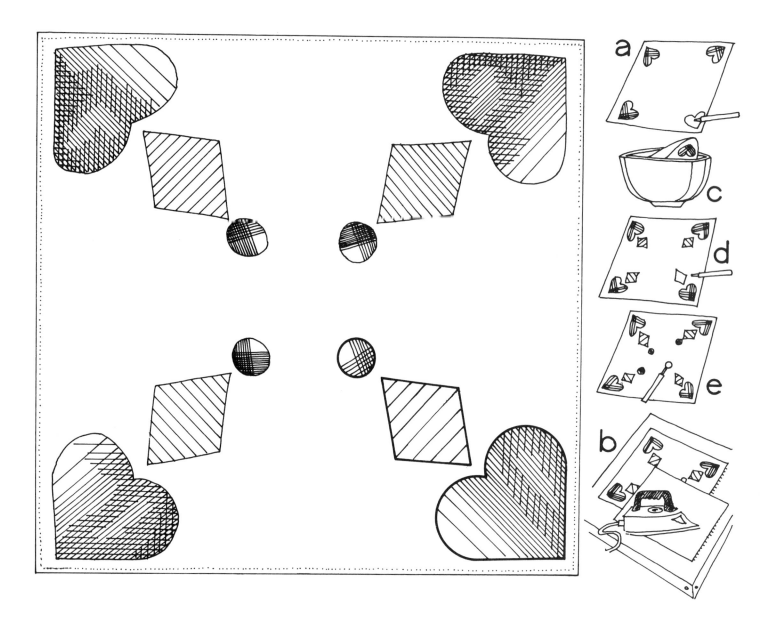

Macramé a Belt

If you like to dress in the latest funky fashions, then you will need a macramé belt. Most belts are made from leather. The belt you are going to make is made of yarn or heavy cord tied into interesting knots. The knots were invented by sailors during their long voyages across the sea, and the process is called macramé. You need only two things for this project: a piece of yarn or cord and a lot of patience.

Things You Need

yarn or heavy cord

Let's Begin

GENERAL INSTRUCTIONS

1. You will work with four strands of cord. To more easily depict the knots, each group of two strands is shown in the drawings as one.
2. The single-headed arrow will always indicate the right two strands. When tied, they will always return to the right side.
3. The double-headed arrow will always indicate the left two strands. When tied, they will always return to the left side.

TO MACRAMÉ

1. Fold two very long lengths of yarn or cord in half, Fig. a.
2. Tie both lengths of cord at the loop tops, Fig. b.
3. Start by bringing the right cords (single-headed arrow) over the left cords (double-headed arrow), Fig. c.
4. Form a loop on the right side, Fig. c.
5. Bring the single-headed arrow cords behind the double-headed arrow cords, and then through the loop on the right, Figs. d and e.
6. Next bring the left or double-headed arrow cords over the right or single-headed arrow cords, Fig. f.
7. Form a loop on the left side.
8. Bring the double-headed arrow cords behind the single-headed arrow cords, and then through the loop on the left side, Figs. g and h.
9. Continue to tie these knots going from the right and then to the left.
10. When you are near the end, make a knot in the belt.
11. Tie a different color of yarn or cord to both ends of the belt. Use these to fasten the belt around your waist.

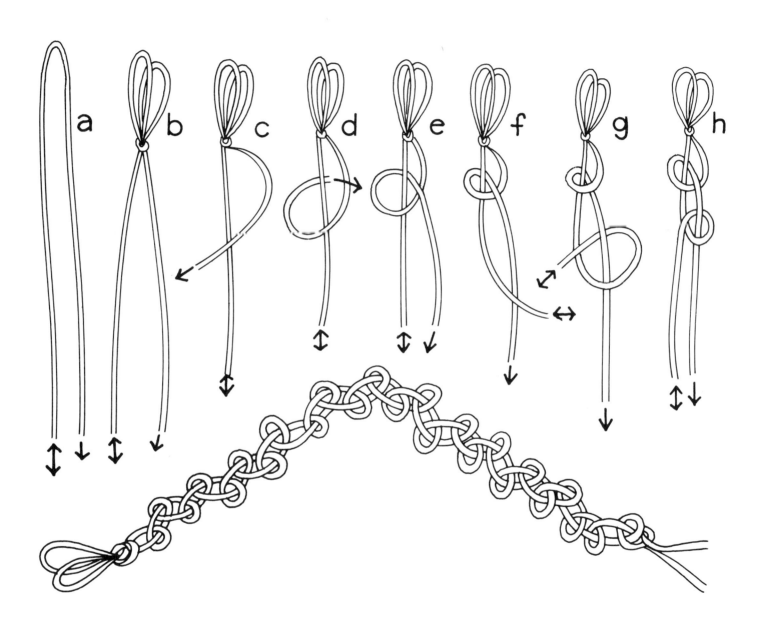

a   b   c   d   e   f   g   h

Ball-Fringe Apron

Do you like to help Mom in the kitchen? If you do, then you probably wear an apron. Aprons are important because they keep your clothes from getting soiled and messy. If your Mom lets you do some of the cooking, why not make yourself an apron? After you make the first one for yourself, surprise Mom and give her one.

Things You Need

washable fabric
ribbon
ball fringe
needle and thread
scissors

Let's Begin

1. Choose a piece of fabric that is wide enough to fit completely around your waist. You can make it as long as you want.
2. Fold a little of the side edges of the fabric over and sew down with a simple running stitch. **To do the running stitch,** first thread the needle and knot the thread. Sew over and under through the fabric, making stitches a little distant from each other. (Figs. a and b.)
3. Sew a running stitch along the top side of the fabric, and a little bit down from the top edge, Fig. b.
4. Pull the thread until the fabric begins to gather.
5. Gather the fabric enough to fit across the front of your waist, Fig. c.
6. Knot the thread several times before you cut away the excess.
7. Turn the apron around.
8. Cut a piece of ribbon long enough to fit around your waist two times, Fig. d.
9. Sew the center of the ribbon over the stitches that formed the gathers, Fig. e.
10. Sew several "tacking down" stitches on the end before you cut off the thread.
11. Turn the apron around and sew a bottom hem, folding the fabric over onto the back side of the apron, Fig. f.
12. Sew a length of ball fringe across the bottom edge of the front of the apron.

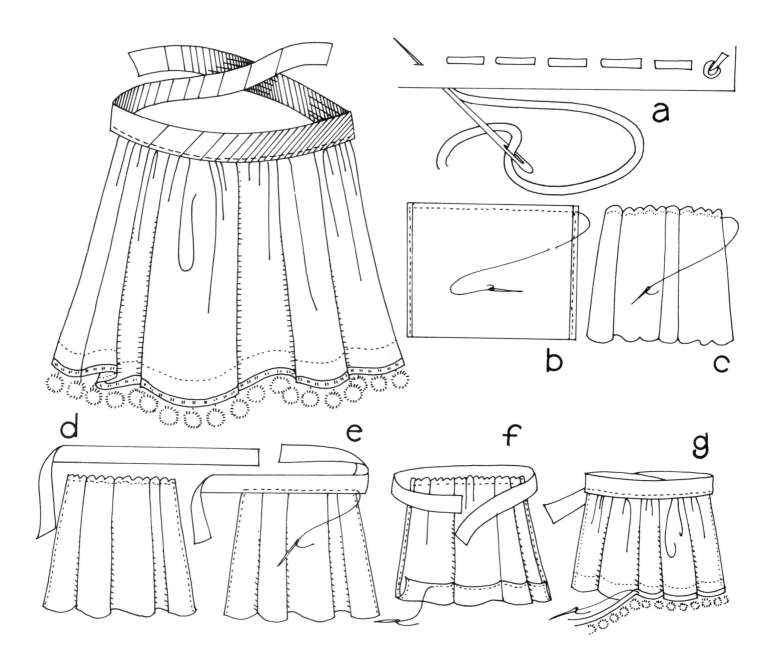

a

b

c

d

e

f

g

String a Necklace

Necklaces are beautiful because of the wonderful things they string together. Seashells, wooden beads, and pearls are some of the popular necklace items. Most of the beads and shapes for these decorative necklaces are in your home, and are very easy to make.

Things You Need

colored construction paper
tracing paper
tube macaroni
drinking straws
string
yarn
pencil
paper paste
scissors

Let's Begin

PAPER BEADS
1. Trace the triangle, Shape a, from the book onto a sheet of tracing paper.
2. Cut out the tracing and, using it as a pattern, trace the triangle onto colored construction paper as many times as you want beads for your necklace.
3. Cut out the triangles.
4. Cover one side of each triangle with paste.
5. Starting at the wide side of the triangle, roll it around a straw with the pasted side on the inside.
6. Press all of the edges down.
7. Roll all of the triangles on the straw, or on others if you need them.
8. When the beads have dried, cut off the straw at the edges of each bead, string the beads, and knot the ends of the string together, Fig. a.

MACARONI BEADS
1. String different sizes of tube macaroni, Fig. b, on yarn or string. Knot ends of string together.
2. Color macaroni with colored felt-tipped markers.

STRAW BEADS
1. Cut drinking straws on an angle with a pair of scissors, Fig. c.
2. String the straws on yarn or string. Knot the ends of string together. Color straws with colored felt-tipped markers.

PAPER SHAPE CHARMS
1. Cut different kinds of shapes from colored construction paper, like the ones shown in the illustration (Fig. d).
2. Poke a hole in the center of each shape. Use a sharp pencil.
3. String the charms on colored yarn. Tie string ends together and wear.

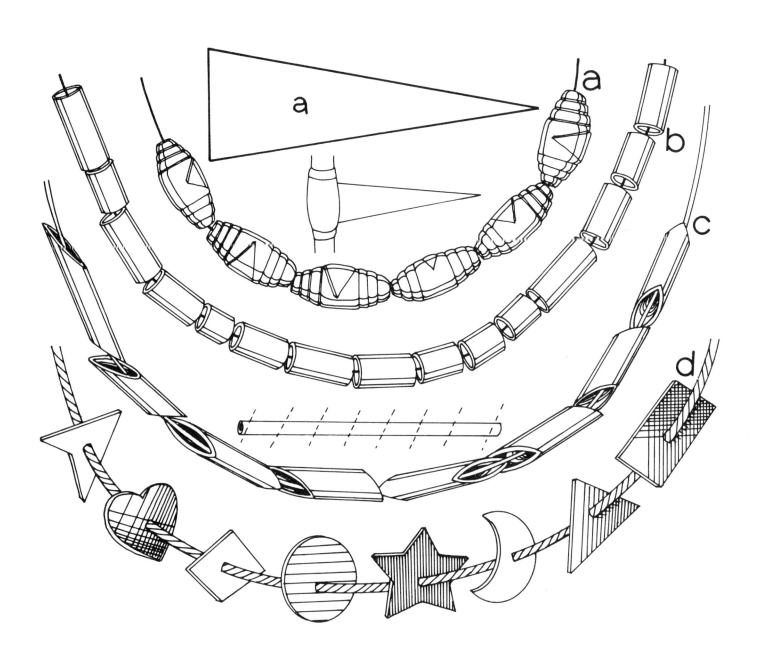

a

a

b

c

d

Headbands

When you think of headbands, the Indians probably come to mind first. There were very few Indians who didn't wear them. The long, straight, black braided hair of the Indian men and women was tucked neatly behind them. Today, many young people are beautifying *their* foreheads with headbands. It adds a little color to the top part of a person's body. The headband you are going to make will look just like the ones worn by the Indians. After you make your first one, you will probably start designing your own.

Things You Need

colored construction paper or colored felt
liquid white glue or brown glue
1 sheet of tracing paper
pencil or colored felt-tipped markers
scissors
paper punch
two lengths of yarn or cord

Let's Begin

1. Trace either headband and its designs from the book onto a sheet of tracing paper.
2. Cut out the headband shape from the tracing paper.
3. Trace this shape onto colored construction paper with a pencil. If you are using felt, use colored felt-tipped markers.
4. Cut out the headband shape from the paper or felt.
5. Cut out the designs from the headband tracing.
6. Use these cutouts to trace the shapes on paper or felt, depending upon what your headband is made of.
7. Cut out the colored shapes, and glue them to the headband, Fig. a. Follow the illustration for the correct positioning of the designs.
8. Make two holes on both sides of the headband with a paper punch or a sharp pencil, Fig. b.
9. Put a piece of yarn through both holes on each side of the headband. Tie the yarn to itself on each side, Fig. c.
10. Tie the yarn ends together to fasten the band around your head.

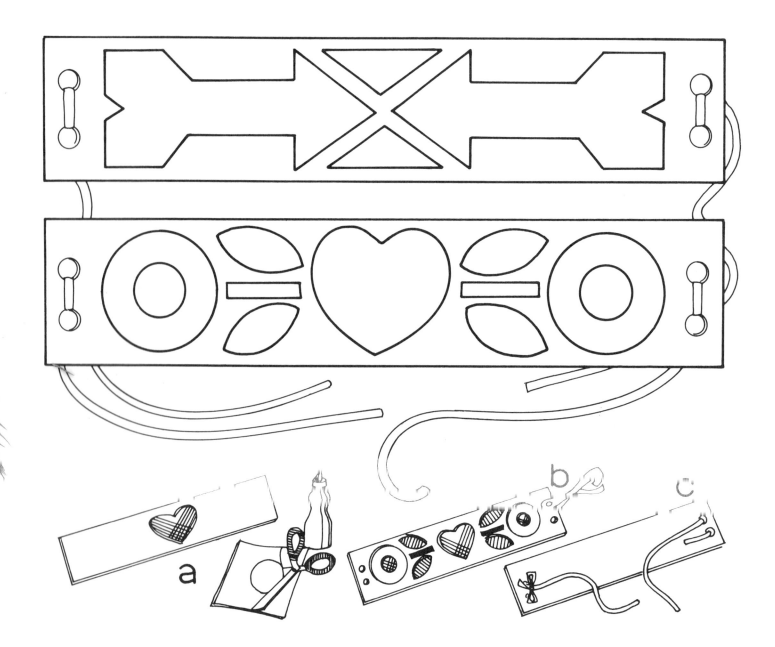

a

b

c

Hair Bows

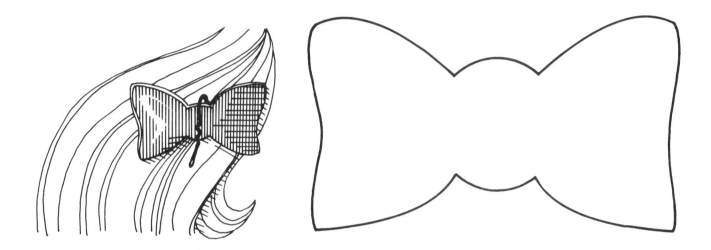

Are you the type of little girl who likes to put things in her hair when she wants to look pretty? Headbands, barrettes, and clips are good for holding your hair in place. What if you want just a little decoration in your hair? Do it with these pretty hair bows. Make a collection of all sizes and shapes.

Things You Need

1 sheet of tracing paper
pencil
scissors
colored construction paper or felt
bobby pin

Let's Begin

1. Trace the bow from the book onto a sheet of tracing paper.
2. Cut out the tracing and, using it as a pattern, trace the bow on a sheet of colored construction paper or scrap felt.
3. Cut out the paper or felt bow.
4. Attach it to your hair with a bobby pin.

Special crafts for special gifts

You have many friends. Your two best friends are your Mom and Dad. They have loved and cared for you long before you can remember. The other members of your family come next. Your younger sister or older brother are perhaps among the best friends you will ever have. Then, of course, there's your pet. Even though he can't talk, he still likes being with you. He is a good and loyal friend.

When you leave your home, there is always a friend to greet you. Walking to school together, sitting in the same class, or playing outside—your pal is fun to be with. Do you like your teachers? Although they don't play with you they are frequently friends. Aunts, uncles, Grandmother, and Grandfather are other friends. How many times have they given you presents when they came to visit the family?

If you ever want to say "I love you" to one of your friends, there are several ways to do it. The best way is to say it, simply, and give the person a big hug or kiss. The second way is to give a beautiful gift. Gifts can be bought in the stores, but the best ones you can give are the ones you make all by yourself. Everyone loves a homemade gift. In this chapter there are many pretty gifts to make. Look at a calendar and see if someone special in your family is going to have a birthday soon. Maybe Mother's Day or Father's Day is coming. You don't really have to wait for a special day, though. A handmade present from you will be accepted anytime.

Appliquéd Wall Organizer

To appliqué means to sew one piece of fabric on top of another larger piece. If you have some empty wall space, why not make this pretty appliquéd wall organizer? Bobby pins, hair clips, bows—almost any small object can then find a home on your wall.

Things You Need

colored felt
curtain rod
embroidery thread
needle with a wide eye
tracing paper
safety pins
cotton stuffing or soft tissues
liquid white glue

Let's Begin

PRELIMINARIES
1. There are lettered shapes and lettered figures. Trace all of the letter shapes from the book onto tracing paper. Include all inner dotted-line designs where they appear. Trace two extra circles, Shape a or h. These will be used to make the snail and the lollipop.
2. Cut four pockets from the felt. Use the heavily outlined form in the illustration as a guide to the correct size.
3. Cut a large backing piece out of the felt. It should be big enough for the four pockets to fit comfortably on it, leaving a good margin of felt at the top (see illustration).
4. Sew a hem on top of the backing using a running stitch (to do this stitch see Ball-Fringe Apron, page 143). The hem should be large enough to allow a curtain rod to fit through it, Fig. a.

To Make the Pockets

THE FLOWER
1. Cut out Shape a from your tracing paper.
2. Pin the tracing on a piece of felt, and using it as a pattern, cut out the circle. Do not remove the tracing from the felt.
3. Hold a thin layer of cotton stuffing or two sheets of facial tissue behind the circle.
4. Trim the cotton or tissue a little smaller than the circle.
5. Pin the circle in the center of one of the felt pockets, keeping the cotton stuffing sandwiched in the middle.
**6. Thread a needle with embroidery thread.
7. Sew the circle with its tracing to the

(continued on page 153)

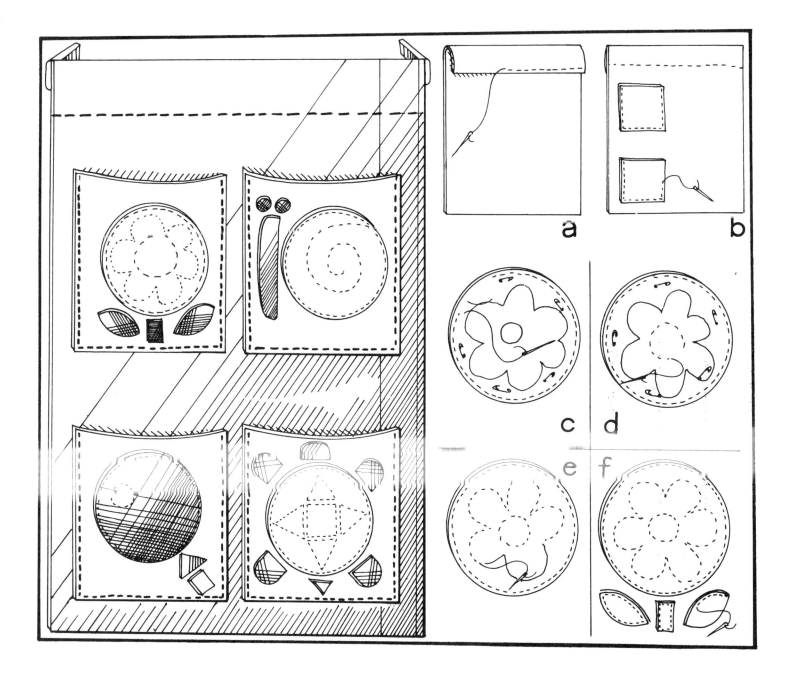

a

b

c

d

e

f

pocket around the outline of the circle, Fig. c. Use a running stitch.

8. Sew around the outline of the center circle design, Fig. d.
9. Sew around the petal outline, Fig. e.
10. Pull away the tissue. Cut out Shape c and Shape b from the tracing paper, and use them to cut out the shapes from the felt.
11. Sew the felt stem (Shape b) and leaf (Shape c) beneath the flower, Fig. f. Your flower is now complete.

THE SNAIL

1. Cut out one of the extra circles you drew on tracing paper.
2. Draw a spiral line on the tracing starting from the outer edge and curling into the middle.
3. The snail's body is Shape d and his antenna is Shape e. Following the procedure outlined for the flower, appliqué shapes to a pocket. Sew along inner swirl outline. See large illustration for a guide to the placement of body and antenna shapes.

THE LOLLIPOP

1. Cut out the other extra circle you drew from the tracing paper.
2. Draw a small inner circle on the tracing.
3. The lollipop stick is composed of Shapes f and g. Appliqué shapes to a felt pocket as above. See illustration for shape placement.

THE TURTLE

1. The turtle's shell is Shape h. His head and arms are Shape j, and his tail is Shape i. Follow procedures outlined above for appliquéing turtle shapes to the last felt pocket. Don't forget to sew along inner design of Shape h.

To Finish the Project

**1. Pin all pockets to the felt backing, Fig. b.
2. Sew pockets to backing using the running stitch. Sew along bottom and sides of pockets only, of course.

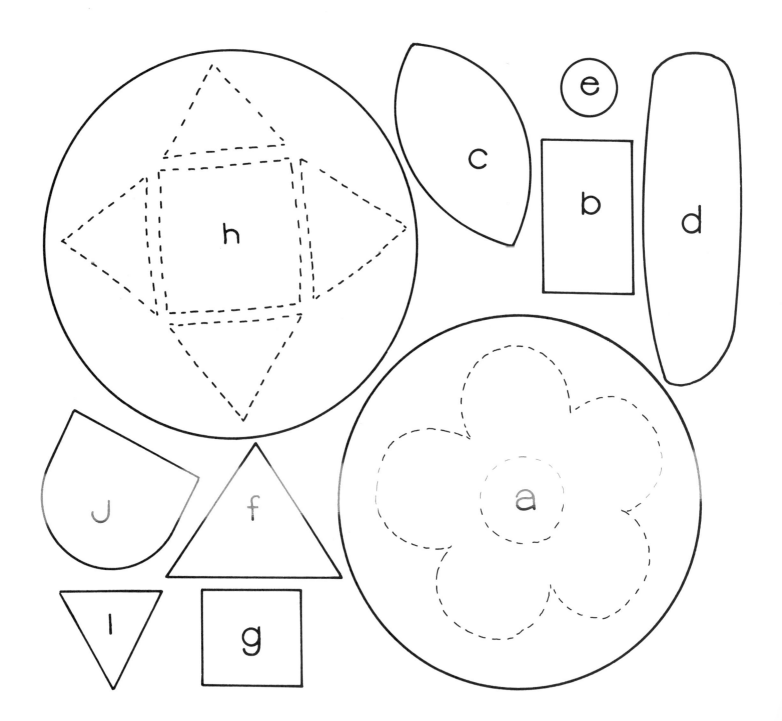

Woven Wall Hanging

When you get a hole in your socks, your mother darns it. That is, she weaves a patch with interlacing stitches. What she does is similar to what a weaver does when he is making cloth. In the old days, cloth was made on a loom. Today it is made by machine. Instead of weaving thread to make this wall hanging you will be removing them. The hanging you make will look attractive almost anywhere you put it.

Things You Need

piece of burlap fabric
ribbon, yarn, or colored string
curtain rod
needle and thread

Let's Begin

1. Fold over a little of the top edge of a piece of burlap and sew it down with a needle and thread. This is the hem into which you will later insert a curtain rod,

Fig. a. Use a running stitch (see Ball-Fringe Apron, p. 143, for instructions on how to do it).

2. "Weave" the hanging by carefully pulling out threads from the burlap fabric. Start by pulling about ten threads from the bottom and the sides (horizontal and vertical threads) of the burlap (see arrows, Fig. b). The vertical threads will pull out only as far as the hem on the top because of the stitches you made to sew the hem. Cut the vertical threads away when they reach these stitches.

3. On the right side, pull away threads at different places so that you have solid spaces and open spaces, Fig. c.

4. Pinch several threads together in the open places, and tie them with ribbons, yarn, or colored string. Tie as many as you wish, Fig. d.

5. Slip a curtain rod through the top hem and adjust it to the size of the wall hanging.

**6. Hang on a wall or door.

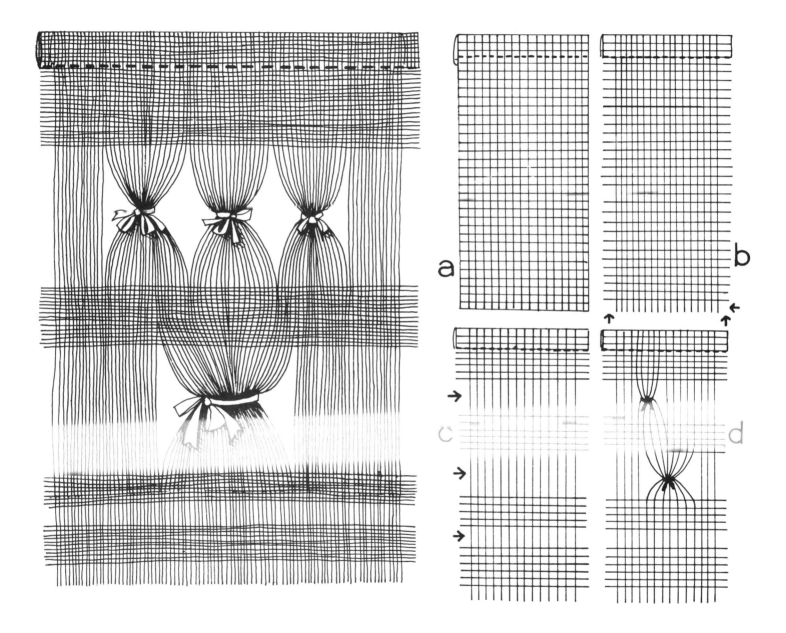

a

b

c

d

Dutch Folk-Art Dish

The United States is like the whole world in one continent. People from all over the globe came to find a home in America. They brought their customs and way of life with them. Different groups of people settled in different parts of the country.

Today, most of the customs of the first settlers have disappeared. In one of the eastern states, however, life goes on just as it did a hundred years ago. The Amish people of the Pennsylvania Dutch country still dress and live as they did when they first arrived in America. These people are famous for their decorative art, which can be seen on the sides of barns, buildings, and in the crafts they make. You are going to make a dish with Pennsylvania Dutch designs on it. It will look lovely hanging on a wall in the kitchen.

Things You Need

white plastic plate
tracing paper
pencil
scissors
poster paints
watercolor paintbrush
kitchen cleanser
clear nail polish

Let's Begin

1. If you don't have a white plastic plate, paint a colored plate with white poster paint. Add kitchen cleanser to the paint if it does not stick to the plate.
2. Trace the heart, leaf, and feather shapes from the book onto a sheet of tracing paper. Notice that there are two sizes for each shape, one drawn inside the other. Trace the size which fits your plate best.
3. Cut out the heart, feather, and leaf shapes from the tracing page.
4. Using these as patterns, trace the heart on the top and bottom of the plate with a pencil, then on the left and right.
5. After the hearts are drawn, add a stem under each heart and a circle in the middle of the plate, Fig. a.
6. Trace two leaves next to each stem, Fig. b.
7. Trace the feather under each stem, Fig. b.
8. Add to the design by drawing a pair of eyes between each heart. An eye is drawn as a circle with a rainbow shape over it, Fig. c.
9. Paint the designs with bright colors.
10. To preserve your plate, brush over the painted designs with some of Mom's clear nail polish. Be sure that the paint has dried completely first.

Swiss-Cheese Candle

Before electricity was invented, candles were very important. They provided light for nighttime living. Pioneer people worked, ate, and read by candlelight. Today, candles are used mostly for decoration. You know that Mom puts them on your birthday cake, and there are probably other candles around the house which look pretty, but are not used for light. What you need is a fun candle you can make for yourself. Since you are going to make a Swiss-cheese candle, be sure that no one puts it in the refrigerator!

Things You Need

paraffin or canning wax
tall candle
play clay
milk carton
ice cubes
2 cooking pots, one larger than the other
hammer
dishcloth
butter
coffee cup
scissors

Let's Begin

1. Cut off the top of a milk container that has been washed and dried, Figs. a and b.
2. Grease the insides of the milk carton with the butter.
3. Put a piece of play clay on the bottom of the milk carton.
4. Push a candle about as tall as the carton straight into the play clay, Fig. c.
5. Place the cup in the large pot and fill the pot with water a little higher than the cup.
6. Put paraffin or canning wax into the smaller pot.
7. Place the pot which has wax in it on the cup, Fig. d.
**8. Put the bottom pot (containing the cup and smaller pot) on the stove burner. Turn on the flame, and allow the water to boil until the wax is melted. If the water begins to spill, lower the heat.
**9. When the wax has melted, empty a tray of ice cubes into a dishcloth or towel, Fig. e. Hammer the ice into smaller pieces. Do not overhammer.
10. Fill the milk container with the ice bits, Fig. f.
**11. Carefully pour the melted wax into the milk carton all the way to the top, Fig. g.
12. Let the candle harden for a half an hour. Put the carton in the sink, and peel it away, Fig. h. (There will be some water from the melted ice.) You have just unmolded your Swiss-cheese candle.

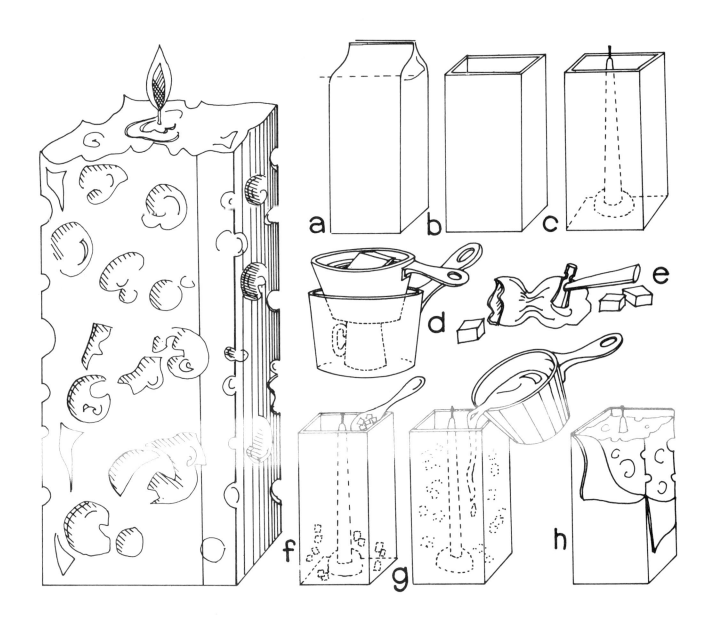

Patchwork Pillow

During the pioneer days, women saved all the scraps of material they could. Nothing was thrown away. Even the smallest piece of fabric could be used as a patch, or in a patchwork item. Patchwork objects are very pretty because of the combinations of different scraps which go into them. If you like to sew, then you will enjoy making this lovely patchwork pillow. It will make a lovely gift for Grandma. She might put it next to a patchwork quilt that her mother gave her.

Things You Need

scrap pieces of fabric
needle and thread
clothes iron
scissors
cotton stuffing

Let's Begin

1. Start by cutting about five equal length strips of different kinds of fabric. The fabrics can be of different thicknesses.
2. Place two strips together, making sure that their designs face one another, Fig. a.
3. Sew the two strips together, a little below the top edge, using the running stitch, Fig. b. (To do the stitch, see Ball-Fringe Apron, page 143.)
4. Sew the last stitch several times over itself before you cut the thread.
5. Sew all the other strips onto the first two, Fig. c.
**6. Use a medium-hot iron to flatten down all seams, Figs. d and e.
7. The front of the pillow will be the patchwork side. Make the back of the pillow by first placing the patchwork on a larger piece of fabric.
8. Cut out the back the same size as the front.
9. Place the front and the back together, Fig. f.
10. Sew the two pieces together with a running stitch near the edges, Fig. g.
11. Leave a little of one side unsewn.
12. Stuff the pillow with cotton stuffing.
13. Finish sewing the seam closed, Fig. h.
14. Go over the last stitch several times before you cut the thread.

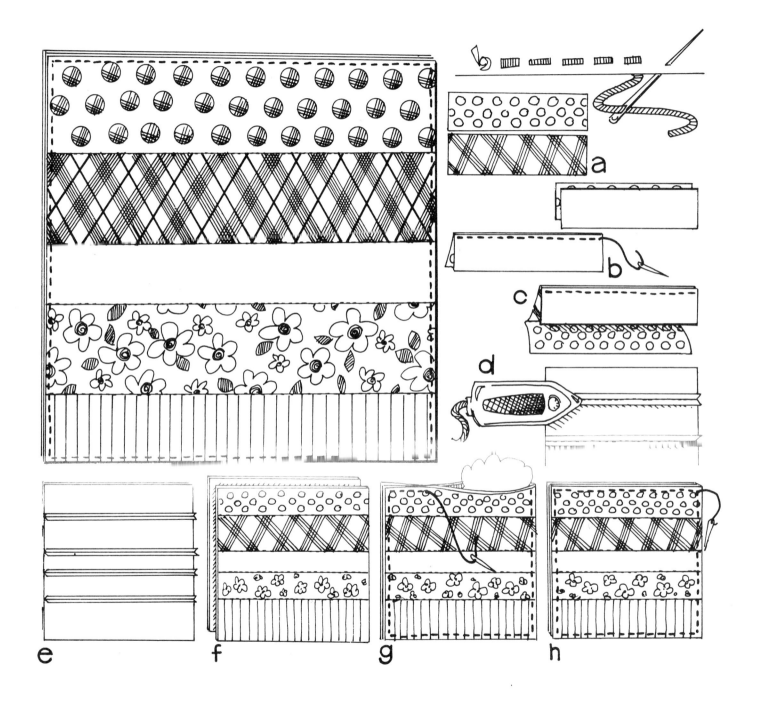

a

b

c

d

e   f   g   h

Quilted Tissue Bag

Do you have a box of facial tissue in your home? It is time to throw it away—the box, that is. What you need is a tissue bag. The bag is so pretty because it is quilted. When you quilt, the designs appear to be raised against the background. This tissue bag is nice because you can hang it or lay it almost anywhere in your home.

Things You Need

safety pins
felt
cotton stuffing
scissors
needle with a large eye
1 sheet of tracing paper
pencil
embroidery thread

Let's Begin

1. Cut three pieces of felt of exactly the same size. Make them as big as you want the bag to be. A good size is indicated by the large bag in the illustration.
2. Trace the tulip and bow design from the book onto a sheet of tracing paper.
3. Pin this tracing onto one of the felt pieces with safety pins, Fig. a.
4. Spread some cotton stuffing in the center of another piece of felt.
5. Put the piece of felt with the pinned tracing on it over the piece of felt with the cotton stuffing. (The stuffing is sandwiched between the two felt pieces, Fig. b.)
**6. Thread a needle with a large eye using embroidery thread.
7. Sew a running stitch (to do it, see Ball-Fringe Apron, page 143) through the tracing as well as through the felt and cotton stuffing, following the outlines of the tulips, stems, and bow.
8. When you have finished sewing along all of the outlines, pull the tissue away.
9. Sew a small hem on the top of the quilted pieces of felt as well as the third piece of felt, Fig. c.
10. Hold the front and back of the bag together with all hems on the inside.
11. Sew the pieces together with a running stitch around the sides and the bottom, Fig. d.
12. Sew the last stitch several times before you cut the thread.

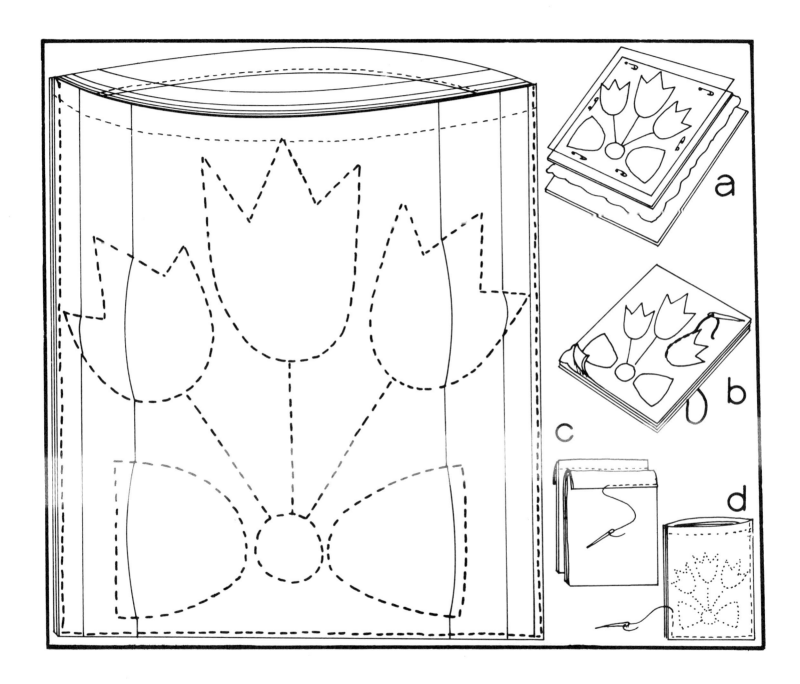

a

b

c

d

Play-Clay Pins

If you want to give a present to someone very special, a decorative pin is the ideal gift. These pretty pins will look wonderful on Grandma, and just as pretty on your Mom. Pin making is fun because it is like making cookies. You have to follow a recipe very carefully. Ask Mom for her help if you have a problem making the pins—she knows all about mixing and measuring.

Things You Need

2 cups cornstarch
4 cups baking soda
measuring cup
bowl
water
pot
poster paints
pencil
1 sheet of tracing paper
cardboard
rolling pin or soup can
spatula
wire rack or cookie sheet
pin backings (available at sewing counters)
liquid white glue
spoon and knife
watercolor brush
scissors
dishcloth
waxed paper

Let's Begin

1. Borrow some baking soda and cornstarch from Mom's kitchen.
2. Measure two cups of cornstarch and four cups of baking soda into a pot. Mix together with a spoon.
3. Add two and one-half cups of cold water to the mixture.
4. Place the pot over medium heat on the stove.
5. Stir everything together for about four minutes until the mixture has thickened to the consistency of mashed potatoes. Turn off the heat, and take the pot off the stove.
6. Cover the pot with a damp dishcloth.
7. When the dough has cooled, pick up half, and knead on a sheet of waxed paper for five minutes. That is, keep folding and pressing the dough with the thick part, or heel, of your hands.
8. Roll the dough between two sheets of waxed paper, not too thick or too thin (about one-quarter inch). Use a rolling pin or soup can.

(continued on page 167)

9. Trace the pin shapes (a–e) from the book onto a sheet of tracing paper. Cut out the shapes and trace them onto cardboard. Cut out the cardboard shapes.
10. Place the cardboard patterns on the dough and cut around the edges with a knife.
11. Remove the shapes with a spatula and place them on a wire rack or a cookie sheet.
12. Dry overnight. The thicker the cutouts, the longer they will take to dry.
13. Paint the designs on your pins with poster paints.
14. Glue a pin backing to the back of each pin with liquid white glue.

Playthings from other lands

Have you ever traveled very far? Maybe you journeyed to the beach or to the mountains. Or was it a trip to Grandma's house? You must travel long distances to find out what games boys and girls in other countries play, and also what toys they play with. Some children buy toys at a department store. Many children have to make their own. If you have a good imagination, you can create a toy from a piece of paper or a piece of wood. Handmade toys are just as exciting as a toy made by a machine. It doesn't really matter how the toy was made. The important thing is how much fun it gives the kids who are playing with it.

What is your favorite toy? It might be a pretty doll, a toy soldier, or a rubber ball.

Children in different parts of Africa play kickball with a ball made from straw. It is shaped like a soccer ball. In Japan, children make dolls, buildings, and animals out of folded paper. All it takes is a piece of paper folded in the right place, and presto, a great toy is born.

If you think that all of these foreign toys sound exciting, just wait until you tackle some of the projects in this chapter. They are all easy to make. If one wears out or breaks, you can easily construct another instead of running to the store. Usually you have to wait until your next allowance to buy another toy. When you know the secrets of good, homemade fun, a new toy is just minutes away.

Mexican Piñata

The children in Mexico love special holidays. They get a chance to break a papier-mâché animal called a piñata. The children swing sticks at the piñata, which is filled with little toys and candy. When it is broken, everyone scrambles for the goodies. Piñatas come in all sizes and shapes. Your piñata is shaped like a big bird.

Things You Need
1 large brown paper bag
1 package of crepe paper
1 sheet of tracing paper
pencil
scissors
stapler or safety pins
tape or paper paste
cord
wrapped candies and small toys
baseball bat
colored construction paper

Let's Begin
1. Cut two packages of crepe paper into strips, Fig. a.
2. Cut a fringe along the bottom edge of each rolled strip, Fig. b. Open up the rolls. You will have long fringe strips.
3. Fill a large brown paper bag with candy and small toys.
4. Gather the bag at the opening, and staple or pin with safety pins, Fig. c. Bag should remain a little open.
5. Poke a hole into the top of both sides of the bag with a sharp pencil, Fig. c.
6. Pass a length of cord through each hole and tie, Fig. c.
7. Tie both cords together, Fig. d.
8. Hang the bag by this loop onto a door handle. You will now transform the bag into a funny bird.
9. To make the bird, tape or paste the fringed strips to the bag starting at the bottom. Keep taping on strips as you move up the bag. Let the fringed strips overlap a little bit.
10. Make the head of the bird a yellow paper circle with white-paper-circle eyes. Staple the head to the top of the bag.
11. The bird's beak shape is shown in the illustration. Trace the beak shape on a sheet of tracing paper.
12. Cut out the tracing and use it to trace a beak on orange construction paper.
13. Cut out the beak and fold it along the dotted lines.
14. Paste the beak to the head.
15. Cut out funny wings and feet from colored construction paper and tape or paste them to the fringed bag.
**16. Hang the piñata in a doorway or on a tree branch.
17. Each person is blindfolded and spun around. He then tries to break open the piñata with the bat.

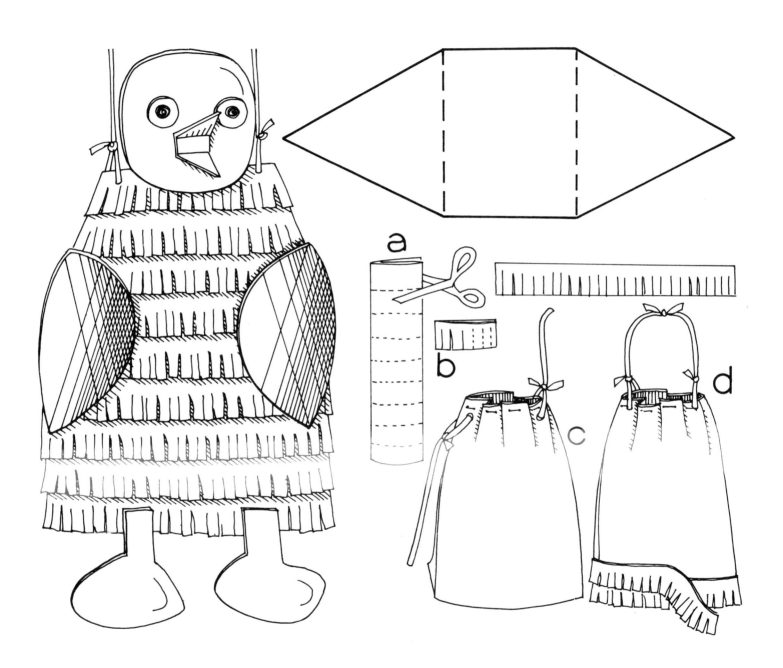

a

b

c

d

Ukrainian Pysanka Egg

It doesn't have to be Easter for you to enjoy dyeing eggs. The children of the Ukraine design some of the most spectacular dyed eggs. This craft looks very difficult but is well worth the effort it takes.

Things You Need

hard-boiled egg or blown egg (see below)
white crayon
egg or fabric dyes
small bowl

Let's Begin

**1. Use a hard-boiled egg or a blown egg. To blow out an egg, take a pin and twist it into the narrow end of an egg until it breaks through the shell, Fig. a.

**2. Remove the pin and make a hole in the other end. Make the hole on the wide end of the eggshell wider by chipping away a little bit of the shell with the pin.

3. Hold the egg over a small bowl and blow through the small hole in the narrow end of the shell. The insides of the egg will come out of the large hole in the egg.

4. Rinse the egg with cold water. Do not use soap.

5. The design is drawn on the egg with a white crayon. The design, as shown in the illustration, is drawn on both sides of the egg in the same way.

6. To copy the design, first draw two lines around the entire egg, from top to bottom and back to top, Fig. b.

7. Draw two lines going around the middle of the egg, Fig. c.

8. Draw a triangle in each "corner" of the egg on both sides, Fig. d.

9. Dip the egg in strong yellow dye solution.

10. Remove the egg and blot dry.

11. With the white crayon, fill in all the dark areas marked Number 1 in Fig. e.

12. Dip the egg in red dye solution.

13. Remove the egg and blot dry.

14. With the white crayon, fill in all the dark areas marked Number 2 in Fig. f.

15. Dip the egg in blue dye solution.

16. With white crayon, fill in all of the background, Number 3, in Fig. g.

**17. Hold the egg over the flame of a candle until the wax melts.

18. Wipe off the melted wax in a soft tissue.

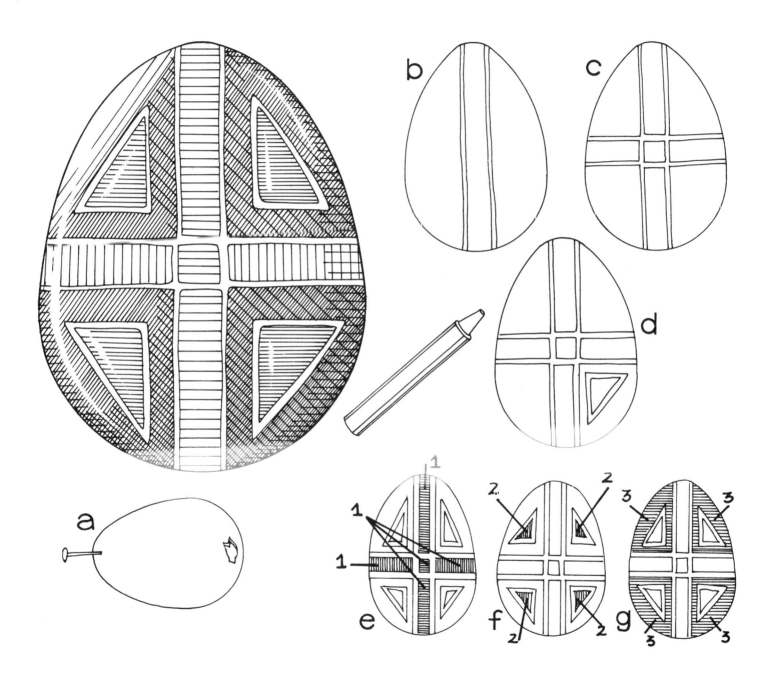

Japanese Origami Rocking Bird

The children of Japan enjoy making toys from paper. It is amazing what can be made from a simple sheet of paper. There is a name for this craft. It is called origami. The origami project shown on the opposite page is one of the most popular. The rocking bird can sit on your dresser or can be hung from the ceiling. If you make enough, you can have a flock of beautiful birds flying high above your room.

Things You Need

1 sheet of colored construction paper
crayons or colored felt-tipped markers
scissors
pencil

Let's Begin

1. Cut a piece of construction paper in a square (all sides equal).
2. Place the paper on the table so that the shape looks like a diamond, Fig. a.
3. Draw a small x and z in the corners that are on the left and right, Fig. a.
4. Fold corner x over to corner z making a sharp crease down the middle, Fig. b.
5. Bring corner x back to its original place, Fig. c.
6. Bring corner z to the fold in the center of the square and crease the corner down, Fig. d.
7. Bring corner x to the fold in the center of the square and crease the corner down, Fig. e.
8. Draw a small letter o on the new corners that are on the left and right.
9. Fold the paper in the middle so that both corners (letter o) meet, Fig. f.
10. Tilt the folded paper so corner o is on the bottom, Fig. g.
11. The tip of the paper shape (corner y in Fig. g) is then pushed down into the fold, Fig. h.
12. Use crayons or colored felt-tipped markers to draw eyes, wings, feathers, and feet on the bird.
13. Spread the bird apart slightly, and stand it on the two bottom points.
14. If you push on its tail, the bird will rock.

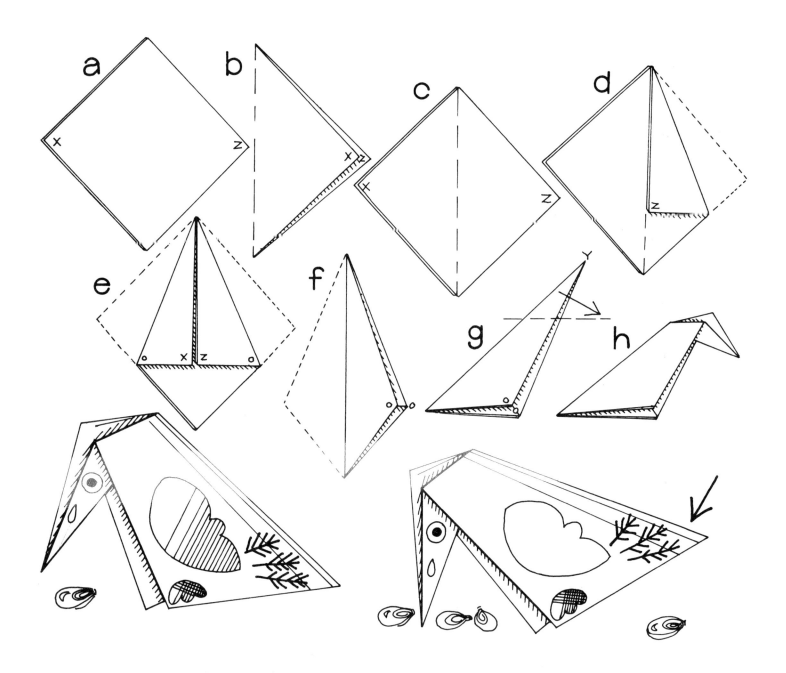

African Drum

The drum is one of the most interesting—and most primitive—of all musical instruments. In Africa it beats the rhythms of dances and songs, announces ceremonies and times of war.

The African drum you will make is modeled on an ancient instrument. It is a very pretty object and can be hung on a wall as well as "played."

Things You Need

oatmeal box
brown felt
yarn
poster paints
paintbrush
paper punch or a sharp pencil
scissors

Let's Begin

1. Paint an oatmeal box and its cover with a dark color.
2. Cut out two felt circles that are larger than the top of the box.
3. Punch an equal number of holes around the edge of the felt circles with a paper punch or with a sharp pencil, Fig. a.
4. Place a felt circle on the bottom and top of the box, Fig. b.
5. Tie one end of a long piece of yarn into one hole on the bottom circle of felt and knot it.
6. Bring the yarn up to a hole on the top felt circle, and push the yarn through.
7. Move the yarn down through another hole in the bottom circle and then up through a hole in the top circle.
8. Continue this process until you have gone completely around the box, filling all the holes of the felt circles with the yarn lacing.
9. If you need more yarn to finish the drum, tie an extra piece to the yarn already used.
10. Glue feathers to the top side of the drum.

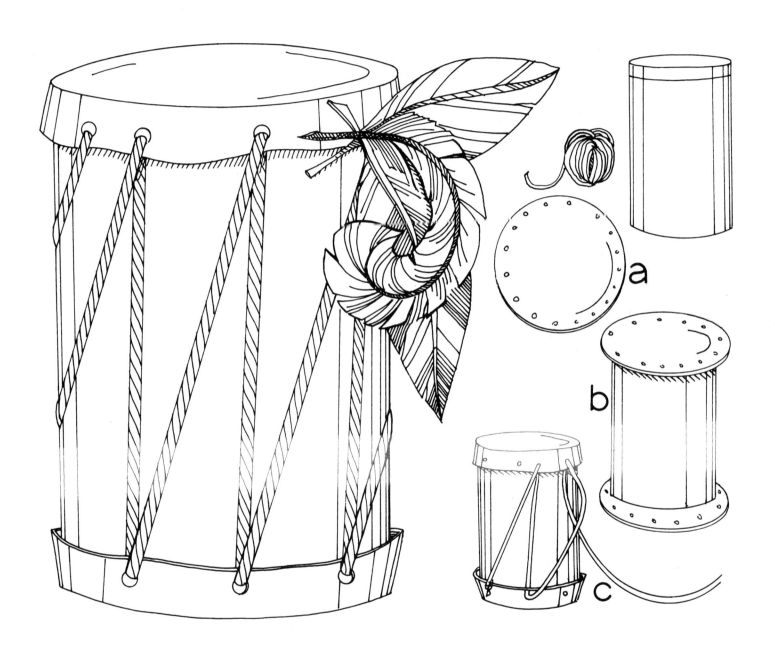

a

b

c

Polish Kaleidoscope Collage

Did you ever look into a kaleidoscope? A kaleidoscope is a small tube that contains small bits of colored glass and a reflecting mirror. When you look into the kaleidoscope and turn it, you see wonderful changing designs. Just as with snowflakes, you will never see two designs that look the same. If you like looking through a kaleidoscope, then you will enjoy this collage from Poland. It is just as beautiful and as colorful as any kaleidoscope design you will ever see.

Things You Need

colored construction paper
1 sheet of tracing paper
pencil
scissors
paper paste

Let's Begin

1. Trace all of the shapes from the book onto a sheet of tracing paper.
2. Cut out each shape. Trace two shapes each of d, e, f, g, and h, onto different-colored pieces of construction paper. Cut out shapes.
3. Trace remaining shapes onto a piece of construction paper that has first been folded. Place the dotted-line side of the shapes against the fold. Cut out two of each shape. When paper is opened, each shape is doubled to its complete form.
4. Draw a straight line across the center of a sheet of white construction paper.
5. Paste the flowers and leaves along the center line. Follow the drawing that shows where all the shapes should go.
6. Draw two stems going from the flowers to the center line.

Italian "Piggy in the Pen"

Here's a game that will test your skill. If you have lived on a farm you know how difficult it is to round up the pigs and get them in their pen. The pig in this toy is a ping-pong ball, and you have to get it into the box. Why not have a contest with your friends? See who will be the champion "Piggy in the Pen" player in your neighborhood. You'd better start practicing the minute you make it.

Things You Need

oatmeal box
cardboard tube from a roll of paper towels
scissors
length of yarn
ping-pong ball
liquid white glue
poster paints
paintbrush

Let's Begin

1. Trace around the end of the tube on the center bottom of an oatmeal box, Fig. a.
2. Poke a hole in the center of the drawn circle with a sharp pencil.
**3. Use this pencil hole to cut out the circle you drew on the bottom of the oatmeal box. Cut the circle a little smaller than the drawn circle.
4. Push one end of a paper-towel tube into the cutout circle.
5. For extra strength, spread glue around the place where the box and tube meet.
6. When the glue has dried, paint the box with poster paints and add designs if you wish.
**7. Twist a sharp pencil completely through the tube at a place a little below the bottom of the box, Fig. b.
**8. Twist a sharp pencil completely through a ping-pong ball, Fig. c.
9. Tie a length of cord or yarn through the holes in the tube and knot.
10. Tie the other end through the holes in the ping-pong ball and knot, Fig. d.
11. The idea of the game is to swing the ball up and try to catch it in the box. Hold the box by the tube and make an upward sweeping motion.

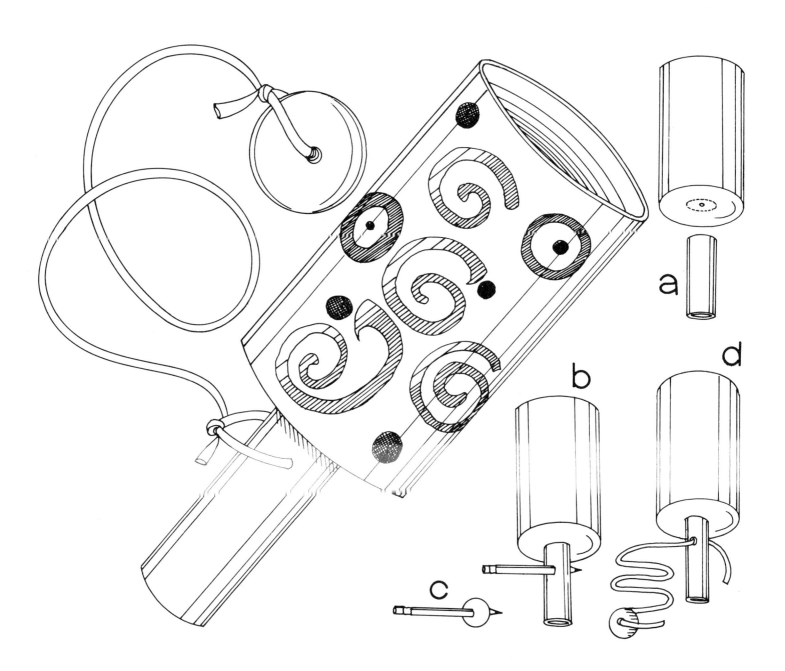

a

b

c

d

English Tops

Tops are fun to play with. All they need is a twist of the fingers to make them go. Make yourself a large collection of these English tops. Only one design is shown in the illustration, but with your imagination you can create some really way-out patterns. When you spin the tops, they will make you and your friends dizzy.

Things You Need

1 sheet of tracing paper
1 short (used) pencil
crayons or colored felt-tipped markers
cardboard
colored construction paper

Let's Begin

1. Trace the circle shape from the book onto a sheet of tracing paper.
2. Cut out the tracing and use it to trace several circles on a piece of cardboard or construction paper.
3. Cut out the circles from the cardboard or construction paper.
4. Copy the design from the illustration, drawing it onto the circle with crayons or felt-tipped markers.
5. Push a small pencil with a sharp point through the center of the circle.
6. Spin the pencil, and let the top spin. See the designs it makes on paper.

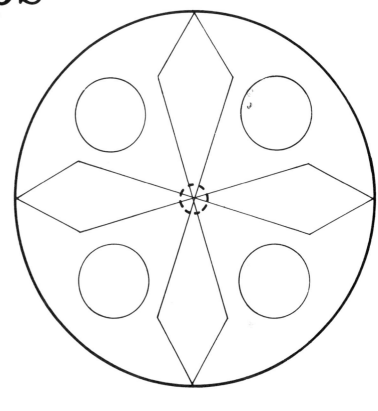

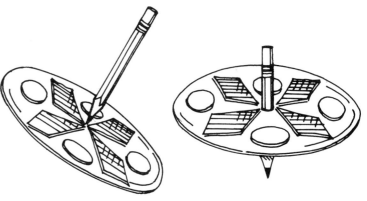

Learning is what you like

Everybody around tells you that going to school is important, but sometimes it really seems dull. Other times, you find yourself liking school a lot. When it *is* fun, it's usually because you're talking or doing or thinking about things that really interest you. Whether it's dinosaurs or the planets or numbers or drawing—learning seems to be a matter of following your interest as far as it will take you.

Or discovering an interest you didn't know you had.

This chapter should help you make some of those discoveries. In it you will learn things you never knew about, or re-learn things you forgot you knew. The toys included in this chapter *are* educational, but, more important, they're fun. And fun just may be the best teacher you've ever had.

Playing the Alphabet

All languages have an alphabet. The alphabet is a picture list of sounds in the language. Some alphabets have more symbols, or pictures, than others. The Oriental people have pictures that represent whole words as well as sounds. The English language has twenty-six letters. It starts with the letter a, and ends with the letter z. Do you know the rest of the letters? It is one of the first things you learned. Now it is time to learn how to make new words.

Things You Need

crayons or colored felt-tipped markers
colored construction paper
scissors

Let's Begin

1. Cut twenty-six squares out of colored construction paper.
2. Draw a capital **A** on one side, and a small **a** on the other side of one of the squares.
3. Do the same with all of the letters in the alphabet on the remaining squares of construction paper.
4. Make words with the letters. Make words that cross on a common letter, like the words in a crossword puzzle. Invent word games using the letters as a deck of cards . . .

ABCDEFGHIJKLMNOPQRS
TUVWXYZ

abcdefghijklmnopqrstuv
wxyz

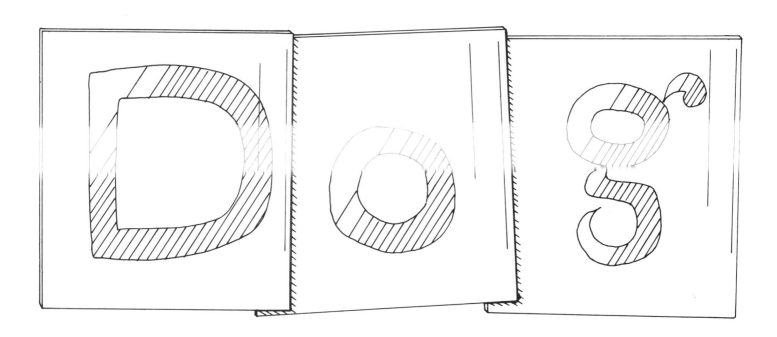

Learn to Count

"Countdown. 10, 9, 8, 7, 6, 5, 4, 3, 2, 1, blast-off!"

You hear these words whenever a rocket is being launched. This is a way of measuring time—of telling people how many seconds remain before the rocket leaves the ground. Numbers are symbols (pictures with a meaning) of quantities of things: 2 apples, 1 boy, 10 toys. Numbers are also written out: two apples, one boy, ten toys.

Numbers are useful because they tell us about how many things of anything there are. They are also used to help us determine the relations between quantities of things as in addition or subtraction. In other words, they are what we use to do mathematics.

Numbers are used everywhere. Everyone in the world knows and uses numbers. Now it's your turn to try . . .

Things You Need

paper

tracing paper
paper paste
pencil
scissors
crayons or colored felt-tipped markers

Let's Begin

1. Trace the circle with all its lines and numbers from the book onto a sheet of tracing paper.
2. Cut out the circle from the tracing paper.
3. Paste the tracing on a sheet of drawing paper.
4. Cut out the circle from the drawing paper.
5. Cut out the different numbers by cutting along the straight lines that cross through the circle, Fig. a.
6. Mix up the pie wedges, and try to put the circle back together as it was originally, Fig. b. The "secret" is to line up the short lines drawn along the edges of each wedge. If you match the short lines together, the numbers will go from 1 to 10.

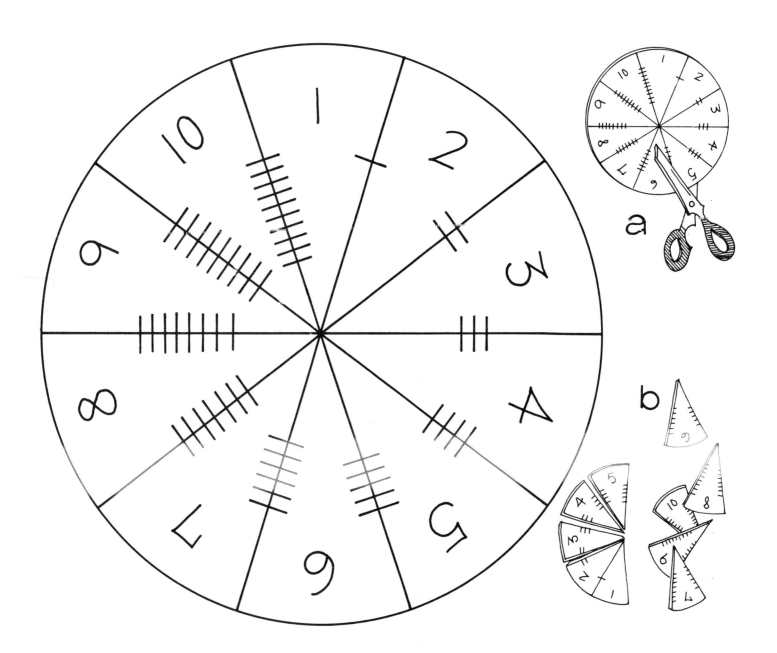

Learn Different Shapes

Probably one of the first toys your Mom gave you was a set of blocks. They were fun because you could stack one on top of another, and make all kinds of shapes. When you were finished playing with them, they could be knocked down and new shapes constructed. Every object has a shape. Certain shapes have special names. A wheel is a completely round shape—a circle. A block is square. If you put two blocks together, you will get a rectangle. Did you ever see a picture of a pyramid? It is shaped like a triangle. Now you can see how well you know the kinds of shapes. Start by looking in magazines and newspapers for circles, squares, and triangles.

Things You Need

1 large sheet of drawing paper
colored construction paper
1 sheet of tracing paper
pencil
scissors
crayons or colored felt-tipped markers
paper paste

old magazines or newspapers

Let's Begin

1. Trace the circle (Shape a), the triangle (Shape b), and the square (Shape c), onto a sheet of tracing paper.
2. Cut out the shapes from the tracing paper.
3. Use these shapes to trace a circle, triangle, and square, each onto construction paper of a different color.
4. Paste the shapes onto a large rectangular sheet of drawing paper, lining them along the left-hand side of the paper (see illustration).
5. Draw lines separating the different shapes as shown in the illustration.
6. Look through old magazines and cut out things that look like, or in part contain, the same shape as the shapes on the paper. (For example, an ice-cream cone has a triangle-shaped cone.)
7. Paste the shapes that match the circle, triangle, and the square next to the appropriate shape.

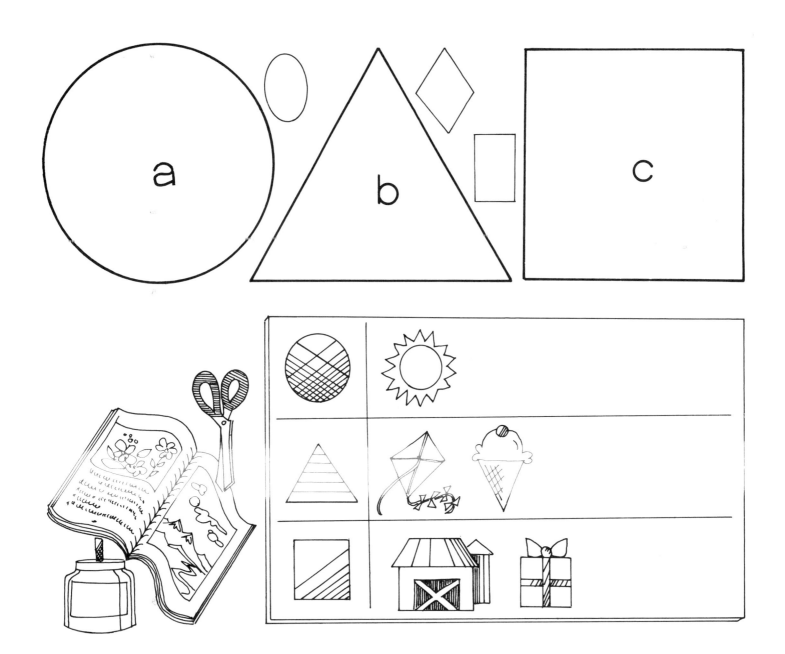

Clock-Face Time Teller

You hear the word "time" probably too many times during the day. "It's time to get up," says Mom. "It's time to correct your homework," says your teacher. "It's time to go to bed," says Dad. If you don't know how to tell time, it is *time* to learn. All you need is the Clock-Face Time Teller and a little instruction from Mom or Dad.

Things You Need

colored construction paper
piece of cardboard
1 sheet of tracing paper
crayons or colored felt-tipped markers
brass paper fastener
paper plate
pencil
scissors

Let's Begin

1. Trace around the edge of a large paper plate on a sheet of colored construction paper.
2. Cut out the circle.
3. Paste the circle on a sheet of cardboard. Cut out the circle from the cardboard.
4. Punch a hole in the center of the cardboard with a sharp pencil.
5. To place the numbers on the clock, first draw the 12 on the top and the 6 on the bottom of the circle.
6. Draw the 3 on the right and the 9 on the left of the circle, Fig. a.
7. Draw the other numbers between the numbers you have already drawn on the circle.
8. Trace the hands of the clock from the book onto a sheet of tracing paper. Draw the entire arrow for the big hand. Draw the arrow up to the dotted line for the little hand.
9. Draw a small hole on each hand where indicated.
10. Cut out the tracings and use them to trace the arrows onto colored construction paper.
11. Cut out the hands and punch a small hole on the bottom of each with a sharp pencil.
12. Push a paper fastener first through the hole in the little hand and then through the hole in the big hand, Fig. b.
13. Push the paper fastener with both hands through the hole in the center of the clock.
14. Spread the two ends of the paper fastener apart on the back of the clock.
15. Move the hands to tell time just like a real clock.

a

b

Learn about Money

Now you can have all the play money you always wanted. The purpose of this money is to help you understand the units of money. The dollar is the basic unit. You probably don't see too many of them in your pocket. But you do see a lot of coins. Pennies, nickels, dimes, and quarters are nice to have. You can buy bars of candy or toys with them. Do you know how many pennies in a nickel or in a dollar? If you are curious, get started on this project right away.

Things You Need

colored construction paper
1 sheet of tracing paper
pencil
scissors
crayons or colored felt-tipped markers

Let's Begin

1. Trace all of the circles from the book onto a sheet of tracing paper.
2. Cut out the circles from the tracing paper and use them to trace lots of different circles on colored construction paper. That is, many of each size.
3. Cut out the traced circles.
4. There are 100 pennies in a dollar.
   The large circle, Shape a, is a half-dollar. It represents 50 pennies.
   Shape b is a quarter. It represents 25 pennies.
   Shape c is a nickel. It represents 5 pennies.
   Shape d is a penny. There are—how many pennies in a dollar?
   Shape e is a dime. Even though it is smaller than a penny, it represents 10 pennies.
5. Mix and match the circles until you have one dollar. Here is one example: one dollar equals one half-dollar (50¢), plus one quarter (25¢), plus one dime (10¢), plus two nickels (5¢ each), plus five pennies (1¢ each).

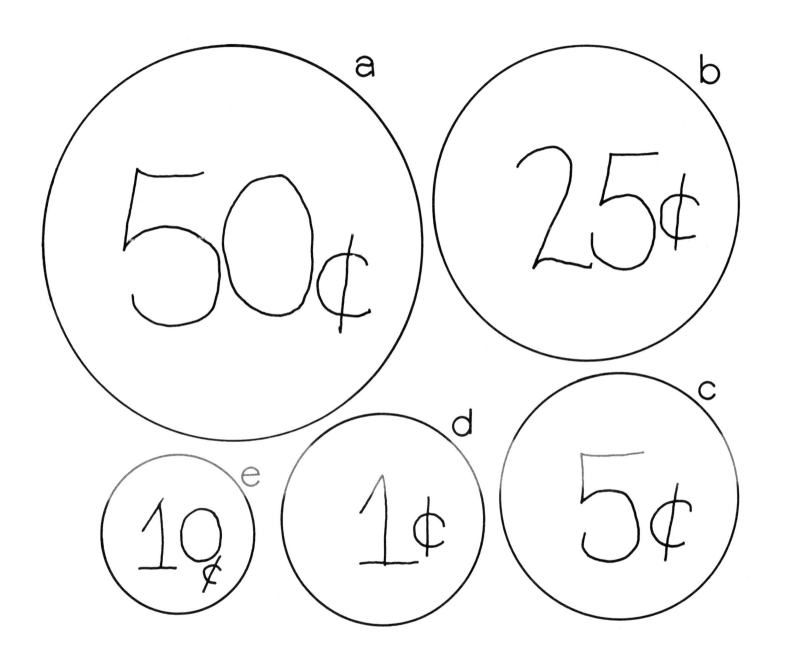

Centipede Measure-Maker

Do you know what an inch, a foot, and a yard are? They are measurements of length. Something can be an inch long, a foot long, or a yard long. When Mom measures you to see how tall you are, she uses feet and inches. When she wants to see how much you have grown from one year to another, she uses inches. You can grow one or two inches in a year. When she buys fabric, she buys it by the yard. These words are very important, and you should know something about them.

The centipede you will make will help you remember how many inches are in a foot, and how many feet are in a yard. It even shows you how long an inch is. Mom might even want to use it when she is making a new dress.

Things You Need

colored construction paper
1 sheet of tracing paper
pencil
scissors
crayons or colored felt-tipped markers

Let's Begin

1. Trace the three circle shapes, a, b, and c,
onto a sheet of tracing paper.
2. Cut out the traced circles and trace them onto colored construction paper.
3. Trace one Shape a on red construction paper, and draw a silly face on it.
4. Trace thirty-two Shape b circles on red construction paper. Draw a line down the middle of each circle with a crayon or colored felt-tipped marker.
5. Trace three Shape c circles on blue construction paper. Draw a star on each circle (see illustration).
6. Cut out all circles.
7. The centipede will be a yard long. A yard is made up of thirty-six inches, which is the number of circles you cut out including the head. A yard can also be broken down into three feet. Each foot is twelve inches long. To make your centipede, first put down his head, the red circle, which represents the first inch.
8. To make a foot, add eleven more inches or circles.
9. Each foot ends on the twelfth inch. Mark the twelfth inch with a blue circle. When all of the circles are in place you will have a centipede that is one yard, or three feet, or thirty-six inches long.

Tasty tummy ticklers

Eating is fun, but have you ever tried to cook? Watching Mom or Dad in the kitchen putting together something delicious is a fascinating experience indeed. Take a home-made cake. First there's the slippery beautiful eggs, which you've no doubt learned how to break yourself. Then a little sugar, some good butter, flour, flavoring, stirring. (People use electric mixers nowadays, but really, you should stir a batter at least once in a while by hand. You feel what it's like to put a cake together with muscle.) Now the careful baking until the layers have risen high and are tender and golden. What about chocolate icing? What about it! Is there anything better than scraping the icing bowl with your finger and popping a delicious lick of chocolate in your mouth? The finished cake is a sweet beauty. You wonder at the pleasure of making something and then being able to eat it. It seems almost too good to be true.

Now you can get into that mixing bowl with more than a finger's worth. You will be making many things to eat that will not only taste good but be unusual-looking (like the Happy Ice-Cream Clown). If you have helped Mom in the kitchen, now is her time to help you. Together you will create tasty tummy ticklers for you and your whole family to enjoy.

Happy Ice-Cream Clown

You've seen the clowns at the circus with their baggy pants and funny faces. But have you ever seen one made of ice cream? Now's your chance to make a refreshing ice-cream clown that you and your friends will love. You'll have a circus of fun in your own house making and eating this delicious snack.

Things You Need

ice cream, any flavor you like
ice-cream scoop
ice-cream cones
regular and miniature marshmallows
small candies for the eyes
gel icing in a tube
paper dishes
spoons

Let's Begin

1. Make the clown's hat from an ice-cream cone to which you've attached three small marshmallows with a dab of gel icing from a tube.
2. Place a scoop of ice cream on a paper plate, Fig. a.
3. Make the clown's collar from a row of marshmallows arranged around the bottom of the scoop, Fig. b.
4. Make the face using small round candies for the eyes, a miniature marshmallow for the nose, and gel icing from a tube for the smile, Fig. c.
5. Put the cone hat on the clown's head and eat with a spoon. Or put the clown in the freezer and enjoy later on.

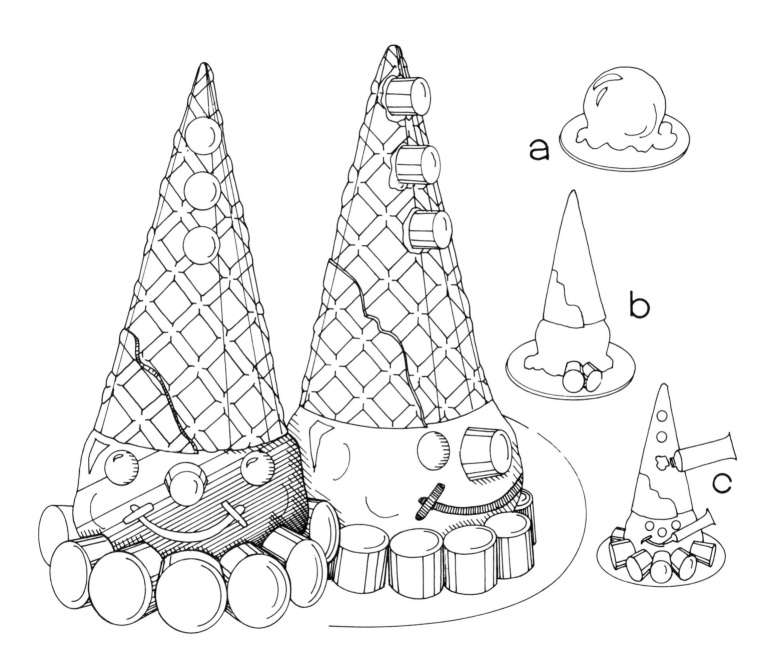

a

b

c

Marshmallow Boy and Dog

Owning a dog is a lot of fun. It is like having another brother or sister. Dogs love being with you and you love being with them. Now you can "create" the love of a boy and his dog in your kitchen. Or, at least, you can make a delicious marshmallow treat in the shape of the two companions.

Things You Need

regular and miniature marshmallows
toothpicks
colored construction paper
gel icing in a tube
tape

Let's Begin

THE BOY
1. Make the boy's body from three regular marshmallows put together with toothpicks.
2. Make an arm from two miniature marshmallows on a toothpick. Make two arms and push them into the middle of the body.
3. Make a leg from three miniature marshmallows on a toothpick. Make two legs and push them into the underside of the bottom marshmallow.
4. Make the cone hat by rolling a paper half-circle into a cone shape and taping it; put it on top of the head.
5. Draw a face on the boy with gel icing from a tube.

THE DOG
1. Make the dog's body from two regular marshmallows put together with toothpicks.
2. Make the head from another regular marshmallow put on the body with toothpicks. The head should be attached a little higher than the body.
3. Make a leg from two miniature marshmallows on a toothpick. Make four legs and push them into the body, two to the underside of each marshmallow.
4. Make the nose, tail, and two ears from miniature marshmallows by attaching them to the face with toothpick halves.
5. Draw on gel-icing eyes.

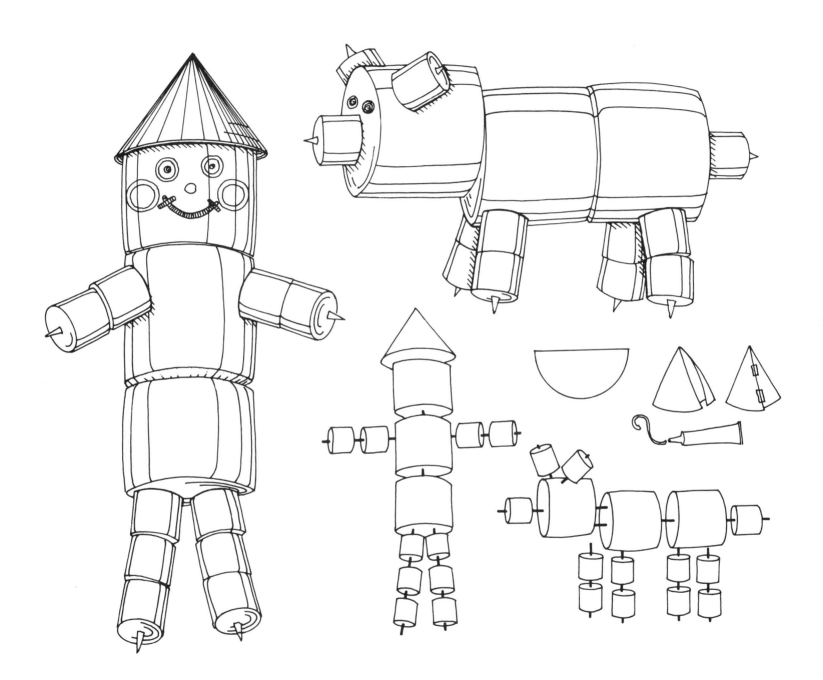

Decorate a Cupcake

Cupcakes are little cakes that can be eaten all by yourself. If you have a big appetite, a cupcake can be in your tummy in a few minutes. A large cake has to be cut into slices and shared by everyone because it is too big to be gobbled up by one person. Not the cupcake, which is like your own private treat. (Although it is always best to make baked goods from scratch, we will use mixes here to get you started fast.)

Things You Need

box of cupcake mix
cupcake pans
flutted paper muffin or cupcake cups
regular and miniature marshmallows, cookies
   and candies (see below for specific kinds)
frosting or gel icing in a tube
box of white frosting mix
box of chocolate frosting mix
food coloring

Let's Begin

1. Following the instructions on the box of cupcake mix, make the cupcake batter.
2. Place a paper muffin cup into each cupcake shape in your cupcake pan.
3. Spoon the batter into the cups filling them half full, Fig. a.

**4. Bake following package directions.
5. Decorate the cooled cupcakes following the ideas below, Fig. b.

HAPPY FACES
1. Frost a cupcake with pink, yellow, or chocolate frosting. Tint white frosting with food coloring to get pink or yellow.
2. Make the eyes from small round candy, the nose from a miniature marshmallow, the cheeks from large flat candies, and the mouth from a licorice string.

NAME CUPCAKES
1. Frost a cupcake with chocolate frosting.
2. Draw on a name with white icing from a tube.

SPRING DAISY
1. Frost a cupcake with white or colored frosting.
2. Make the petals from large flat round candies and the core from a small round candy.
3. Add a spearmint leaf and a licorice-string stem.

FUNNY ANIMALS
1. Frost a cupcake in any funny color.
2. Make animal ears from two cookies.
3. Make the nose from a large marshmallow or gumdrop, the eyes from round candy, and the mouth from tube frosting.

Funny-Shape Cake Bake

Now is the time for all good (or only so-so good) kids to bake a cake. Or many cakes— the recipe below allows you to assemble and decorate your layers in a variety of interesting, funny ways. Although you will use a mix, you should be very, very proud of the results. Why, some of the cakes will look so good, you may not want to cut into them!

Things You Need

box of cake mix, your favorite flavor
2 round or square baking pans
knife
packaged frosting mix
frosting or gel icing in a tube
candies (licorice stick for Sail Boat and
  marshmallow for Mr. Rabbit)
food coloring

Let's Begin

**1. Following the instructions on the box, make the cake batter.
**2. Bake the cake mix in either two square or two round baking pans.
  3. Assemble and decorate your cake when it has cooled following any of the ideas below.

THE BASEBALL
1. Put two round layers together with white frosting between them, then frost the entire cake.
2. Draw stitch designs on the cake with blue icing from a tube.

THE WRAPPED BOX
1. Put two square layers together with chocolate frosting between them, then frost the entire cake.
2. Draw a ribbon with red frosting from a tube and make a name tag with white frosting.

SMILING SUN
**1. Cut out wedges along the outer edge of one round cake layer with a knife, Fig. a.
  2. Place the second round layer on a large platter.
  3. Stick all of the wedges you cut from the first layer onto the outer edge of the second layer with a dab of frosting.
  4. Frost the top of this layer with orange frosting, Fig. b.
  5. Put the first layer (the one with the wedges cut out) on top of the layer on the plate.
  6. Frost the top of this layer with yellow frosting.

202

(continued on page 204)

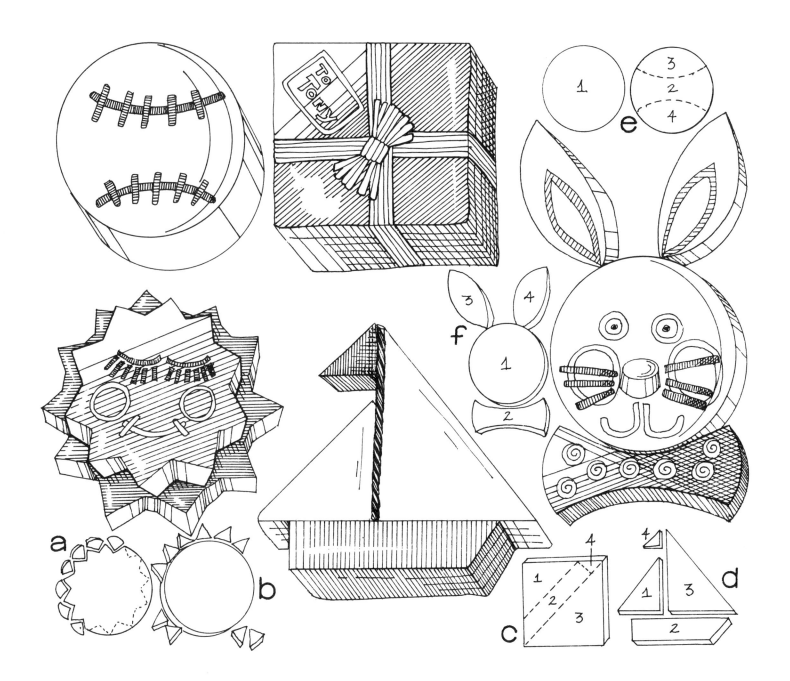

7. Decorate the cake with tube frosting.

SAIL BOAT
1. Put two square layers together with white frosting between them.
**2. Cut the stacked layers as shown in Fig. c.
3. Arrange the cake pieces to form a boat as shown in Fig. d. Leave space between pieces.
4. Frost the sails white, the boat and flag red (tint white frosting with red food coloring).
5. Put a licorice-stick mast between the sails and touching the flag. Push pieces together.

MR. RABBIT
**1. Cut one round layer as shown in Fig. e.
2. Arrange these pieces around the second uncut layer as shown in Fig. f.
3. Frost the face and ears with white frosting.
4. Frost the bow tie with yellow frosting (tint white frosting with yellow food coloring).
5. Use tube frosting to draw the face, and a marshmallow for the nose.

Fairy-Tale Castle

It would be wonderful to see some of the fabulous things you read about in fairy tales. Things like castles with their moats and turrets and towers, their battlements and flags and damsels in distress. Do you like castles? If you do, why not make your own? It will look—and be—good enough to eat.

Things You Need

shoe box
oatmeal or salt box
aluminum foil
ice-cream cones
assorted cookies
candies
marshmallows
frosting in a tube
colored construction paper
liquid white glue
toothpicks

Let's Begin

1. Cover a shoe box and the oatmeal or salt box with aluminum foil, Fig. a.
2. Glue the round oatmeal or salt box to the end of the shoe box, Fig. b.
3. Let the glue dry.
4. Stick the cookies to the foil-covered boxes with a little dab of frosting from a tube, Fig. c.
5. Add candies and marshmallows the same way you did with the cookies.
6. Top the castle with different-shaped ice-cream cones.
7. Make flags from triangles of colored construction paper and glue them to toothpicks.
8. Push the toothpicks into the tops of the ice-cream cones.
9. Add any other eatable decorations you please—use your imagination!

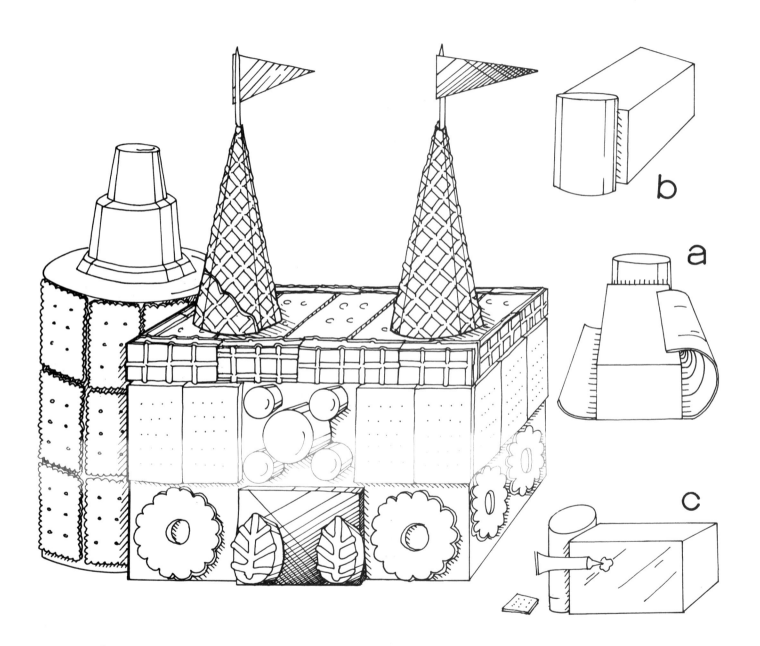

b

a

c

Everyone Loves Sugar Cookies

There are so many cookies for sale that it is difficult to have just one favorite. You probably like Mom's cookies the best. If you like homemade cookies, then you should make a batch of your own. Your cookies will be so delicious it is going to be difficult keeping Mom and Dad out of your cookie jar.

Food Things You Need

4 cups sifted flour
2½ teaspoons baking powder
½ teaspoon salt
⅔ cup soft butter
1½ cups granulated sugar
2 eggs
1 teaspoon vanilla extract
4 teaspoons milk
gel icing or frosting in a tube

Baking Things You Need

2 large bowls
waxed paper
cookie sheet
cookie rack
rolling pin
spatula

Other Things You Need

tracing paper
pencil
cardboard
paper
scissors

Let's Begin

1. Mix the flour, baking powder, and salt in a large bowl.
**2. Cream the butter and sugar together in another large bowl until the mixture is light and fluffy. Beat in the eggs and blend well. Add the milk and vanilla extract. Stir the mixture until it seems nice and light.
3. Slowly add the dry ingredients to the butter mixture, stirring everything until well blended.
4. Place the dough in the refrigerator.
5. Make cookie patterns by tracing the gingerbread boy, bird, and fish shapes from the book onto a sheet of tracing paper.
6. Trace the girl and boy cookie shapes. Follow the dotted lines for the girl shape.

207

(continued on page 209)

7. Cut out the tracings and, using them as patterns, trace shapes onto a sheet of cardboard.
8. Cut out the cardboard shapes.
**9. When the dough is firm enough to handle, turn on the oven to 400 degrees.
10. Sprinkle a sheet of waxed paper with a little flour. Put part of the dough on the paper. Keep the rest of the dough in the refrigerator.
11. Flatten the dough and put another piece of waxed paper over it. Roll the dough between the two sheets of waxed paper with a rolling pin, Fig. a.
12. Place a cardboard cookie pattern on top of the dough.
13. Cut the dough around the cookie shape, Fig. b.
14. Lift the cookie with a spatula, and put it on a buttered cookie sheet, Fig. c.
**15. Using whichever patterns you want, cut out cookies. Place several on a cookie sheet, and bake for ten minutes, or until they look brown.
**16. Remove the cookie with a spatula, and let them cool on a plate or a cookie rack.
17. Decorate the cold cookies with gel icings or frostings from a tube, Fig. d.

Let's have a party

Every year has many special days which are set aside for honoring people and events. There are the big holidays that everyone celebrates—things like Christmas and New Year's—and the special occasions observed and enjoyed by your friends and family only. Whatever the occasion, why not have a party (with Mom's permission, of course)? Whether its your birthday or George Washington's, it's great to get together with people you like to have fun.

Of course, you can go to the store to get "fancy" party fixings—or you can make them yourself. Read on and learn how to make all your own party decorations and favors—things like hats, noisemakers, and confetti balloons—as well as exciting games to play (have some small prizes or pennies on hand for the winners). This chapter will show you how to create your own invitations—in fact, how to get all the fun together and going. Take out your calendar and circle the day you want your party to happen. Then start to make things. And by all means—have a good time!

Special Invitations

If you're going to give a party you will want to invite all of your friends. How are you going to let them know what day and what time the party will be? Send a handmade invitation. This special invitation has three messages inside it. The outside announces your party. When your friends open it, the date and the time come into view. One look at your invitation and everyone will wish your party were tomorrow.

Things You Need

colored construction paper
1 sheet of tracing paper
pencil
scissors
crayons or colored felt-tipped markers

Let's Begin

1. Trace the cake shape from the book onto a sheet of tracing paper.
2. Cut a long strip of colored construction paper as high as the traced cake.
3. Cut out the tracing and use it to draw a cake on one side of the strip of paper, Fig. a.
4. Fold the paper on the left dotted edge of the cake drawing, Fig. b.
5. Fold the paper back along itself from the right dotted edge, Fig. c. Trim any excess paper away.
6. Cut around the cake except at the sides where there is a dotted line, Fig. d.
7. Use crayons or colored felt-tipped markers to decorate the front of the invitation as if it were a fancy cake.
8. Inside the card, write the place of the party, the day, and the time it will begin and end.

at toms House

On March 13

3:30 to 5:30

Come to a party

a

b

c

d

Surprise Favors

Parties—and especially birthday parties—frequently bring presents to you, the party-giver or guest of honor. A nice way to return the compliment is to provide favors for your guests. These Surprise Favors contain candy and may also be used as place cards at the table.

Things You Need

cardboard tubes from bathroom-tissue rolls
colored tissue paper
tape
scissors
wrapped hard candy
ribbon
colored construction paper
paper punch
crayons or colored felt-tipped markers

Let's Begin

1. Collect cardboard tubes from bathroom-tissue rolls long before the day of your party.

2. Fill each tube with wrapped candy.
3. Place the filled roll on a large sheet of colored tissue paper (also try colored cellophane or gift wrap), Fig. a.
4. Roll the paper around the tube and tape it together, Fig. b.
5. Tie the excess tissue onto one end of the favor with a length of ribbon or yarn. Keep one end of the ribbon long.
6. Cut a small name tag from colored construction paper.
7. Write the name of the person on the tag with crayons or colored felt-tipped markers.
8. Punch a hole on one end of the name tag.
9. Tie the long end of the ribbon into the punched hole in the tag, Fig. c.
10. Tie the other end of the favor with a shorter piece of ribbon.
11. Cut slits into the side paper frills to make a feathery fringe, Fig. d.

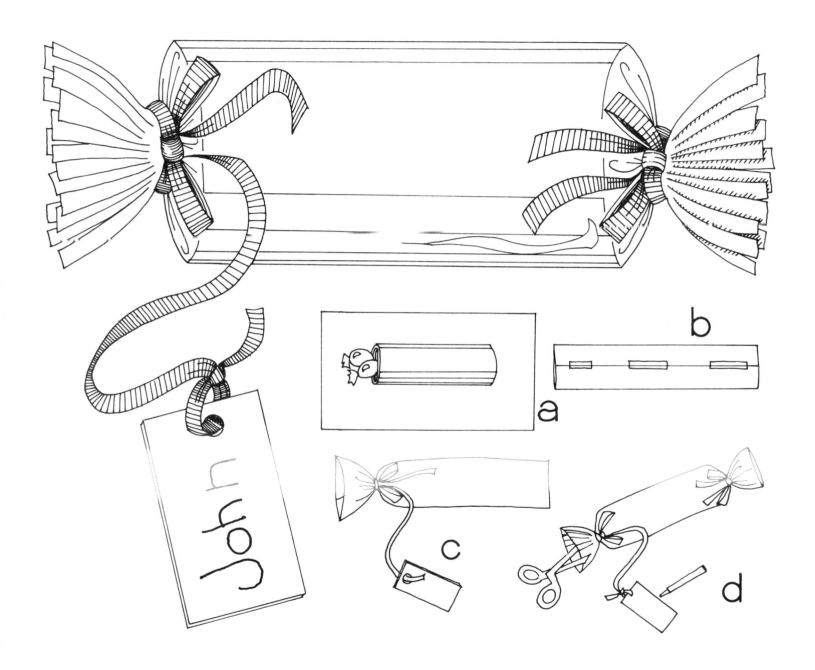

a

b

c

d

John

Paper Captain's Hat

Your party won't be complete unless your guests have hats to wear on their heads. You can go to the store and buy the pointed paper hats, but why not be different this year? Since you are going to make everything for your party, you should make the hats as well. All you need is a package of construction paper and you will be in business. Make the hats in all colors. Don't worry about the sizes. The bigger they are, the more fun your guests will have with them on their heads. If you really want to show your friends how creative you are, decorate your captain's hats with feathers or marshmallows, or draw designs on them.

Things You Need

large sheets of colored construction paper or
   large sheets of drawing paper
stapler

Let's Begin

1. Fold a large sheet of paper in half along the short side or width, Fig. a.
2. Keep the folded part on top and draw a line down the center of the paper, Fig. a.
3. Fold the two top corners, marked in the illustration with a letter x, over to the middle line on the paper, Figs. b and c.
4. Fold one of the bottom ends of the paper, marked with a letter z, over the two folded corners, Fig. d.
5. Turn the paper over, and do the same with the other bottom end, Figs. e and f.
6. Staple both ends of the hat (see illustration).
7. Decorate the hats with paper feathers or designs drawn with crayon or colored felt-tipped markers.

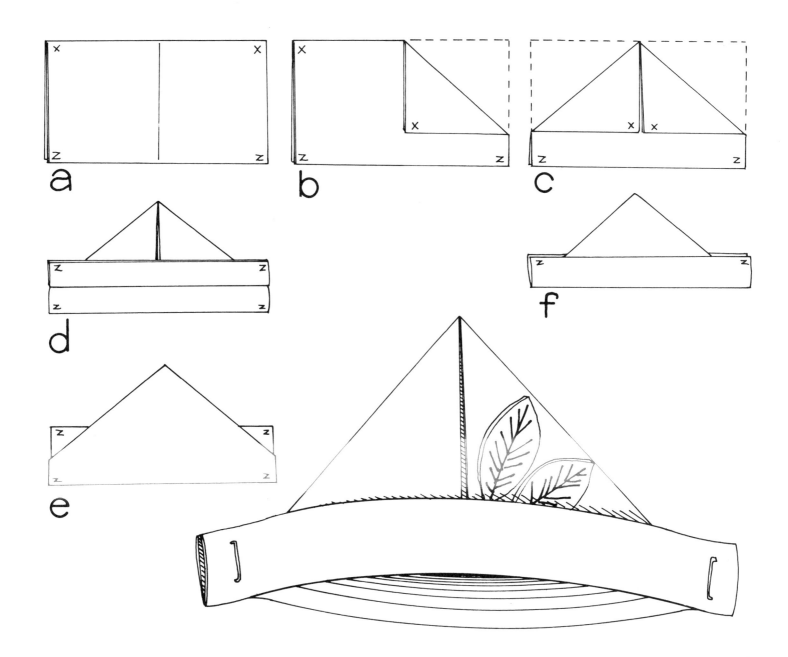

a

b

c

d

e

f

Four Fun-Filled Games

One of the fun parts of any party is playing games. Some of your favorite party games are pin the tail on the donkey and bobbing for apples. Now you will have four more fun-filled games to play. (With so much to do, you may not have any time to eat your cake and goodies.)

Things You Need

colored construction paper (including 1 large sheet)
tape
paper paste
crayons or colored felt-tipped markers
paper cups
rubber ball
soup cans
marshmallows
thread
string
drinking glass

Let's Begin

PIN THE NOSE ON THE CLOWN
1. Make the clown face from a large circle of light-colored construction paper. Make his hat from a triangle of blue paper. His collar can be any shape and any color.
2. Paste the face, hat, and collar onto a large sheet of white paper (see illustration).
3. Draw hair and eyes.
4. Make several noses by tracing around the edge of a drinking glass on red construction paper. Cut out the circles.
5. Hang the clown face on the wall.
6. Blindfold each guest and give him a nose that has a piece of tape attached to it.
7. Spin the person around, and see if he can pin the nose in the middle of the clown's face.

PAPER-CUP BOWLING
1. Place ten cups on the floor as shown by the triangle of circles in the illustration.
2. The aim of the game is to roll a rubber ball and try to knock down all of the cups.
3. Add up the scores. The person with the most points in five rolls wins a prize.

PENNY TOSS
**1. Remove the labels from tin cans by soaking them in warm water.
2. Write the numbers 1 to 5 on each can with an indelible felt-tipped marker.
3. Put the cans together on the floor.
4. Guests toss pennies onto the cans. If one lands in the can you win the number of pennies written on the can.

KISSING MARSHMALLOWS
**1. Thread a marshmallow onto a long length of cotton thread.
2. Hang it from a doorway.
3. A girl and a boy try to bite the hanging marshmallow at the same time.

Snapping Pop Guns

Noisemakers, horns, and rattlers are old friends at parties. To the familiar kinds you will want to add these Snapping Pop Guns. They are very easy to make. All you need is a stack of typewriter paper and a pencil. Make a boxful of these paper guns. You might want to use them after a party when you play with your friends.

Things You Need

1 sheet of typewriter paper or 1 sheet of newspaper
pencil

Let's Begin

1. The larger the paper the louder the pop. The paper should be longer than it is wide. Fold the paper in half along the long side.
2. Open the paper again.
3. Draw a small letter x on all four corners.
4. Fold all corners to the folded line marked with a letter z, Fig. a.
5. When all corners are in the middle, fold the paper in half, Fig. b. Folded corners should be inside. The folded line marked with the letter z is now on top.
6. Fold the paper in half again so that both corners marked with the letter z are together, Fig. c.
7. Fold the top edge of the corner z which faces you down so that it lies against the paper, Fig. d.
8. Turn the paper around and do the same with the other corner z, Fig. e.
9. To make the gun pop, first hold the two points marked letter z in your hand with the folded inside part facing away from you.
10. Snap your wrist hard. The folded inside part will pop out making a noise.
11. To pop the gun again, push the folded inside part back into the gun.

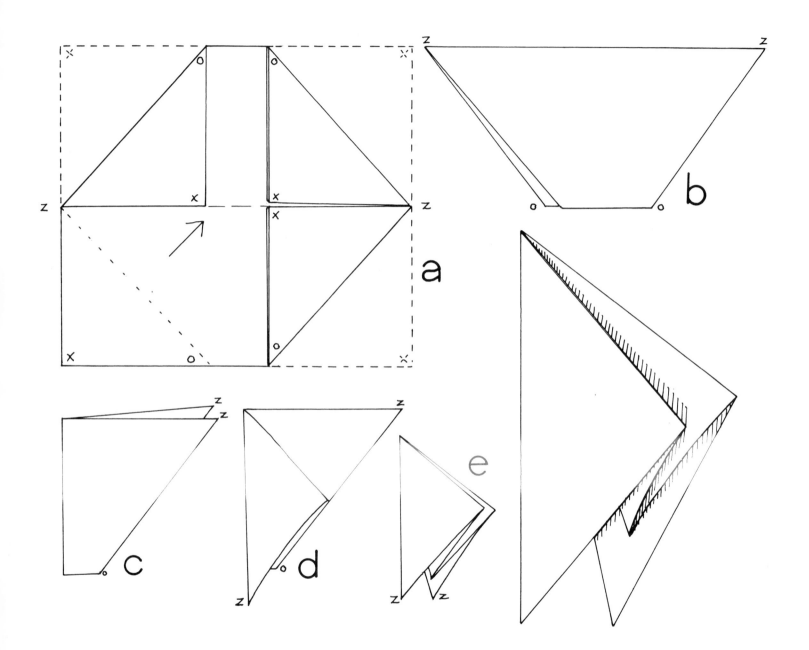

Confetti Balloons

One of the most important things you will be responsible for in getting ready for your party is decorating the house. Signs, streamers, and, of course, balloons should be scattered all around the house. When it's time to blow up the balloons, don't just fill them with hot air. Put a little something extra inside them. Have Mom buy some confetti. Before you blow up the balloons, put a little confetti in each. If you hang the balloons from the ceiling and you break them, it will rain confetti on your friends. (Remember to help Mom clean up all the spilled confetti after the party is over.)

Things You Need

colored felt-tipped markers
balloons
confetti
ribbon

Let's Begin

1. Put a little confetti in some of the balloons before you blow them up.
**2. Blow up the balloons and tie the end in a knot.
3. Use colored felt markers to draw designs on the balloons.
4. Tie a length of ribbon on the end of each balloon and hang them up.

Holidays are fun

Life would be less fun if you didn't celebrate holidays. You would probably do the same things day after day, and school would be an extra month or two longer! Holidays are fun because, among other things, you learn all about history. Most holidays commemorate important historical events, or the birthdays of famous people. When you are in school, the week before a holiday is usually spent learning all about the special day. Although this is enjoyable, the best part of any holiday is not being in school but out of it. Holidays mean time off from your everyday "job."

To get you in the holiday spirit, eight projects have been designed for you. Whatever type of holiday you like, there will be at least one project having to do with it which you will enjoy making. After you finish making the first holiday project you will want to make all of them. This is good because you should be ready for as many holidays as you can.

A Very Special Valentine

It is said that Cupid delivers messages of love. If you have never seen Cupid—or don't know where to find him—don't worry (he is a very busy person on Valentine's Day). Why not send your own messages? You will make these very special valentines and send them to all your favorite people. They will love your love notes—and love the fact that you made them yourself.

Things You Need

1 sheet of tracing paper
pencil
scissors
paper paste
red, white, and black construction paper
crayons or colored felt-tipped markers

Let's Begin

1. Trace the inside and outside heart shapes separately from the book onto a sheet of tracing paper. Also trace the arrow.
2. Cut out the hearts and arrow tracings.
3. Trace the heart with the scalloped edge onto white construction paper.
4. Trace the plain heart onto red construction paper.
5. Trace the arrow onto black construction paper.
6. Cut out the hearts and the arrow.
7. Paste the red heart in the center of the white heart.
8. Cut two slits through both hearts like the ones shown on the smaller heart.
9. Slip the arrow through the two slits.
10. Write your message on the heart with crayons or colored felt-tipped markers.

Washington's Birthday Cherry Tree

George Washington is called the father of his country. He was America's first President. If you don't know what he did when he was President, you do know what he did when he was small. He chopped down his father's cherry tree. Not being a bad little boy, he told his father what he had done. He could not tell a lie. His father was proud of him for telling the truth. Now, don't you go outside and chop down a tree. Make one for your bedroom instead.

Things You Need

1 sheet of tracing paper
pencil
scissors
green and red construction paper
paper paste

Let's Begin

1. Trace the tree from the book onto a sheet of tracing paper.

2. Cut out the tracing.
3. Use the cutout to trace two trees on green construction paper.
4. Draw a slit on each tree. One tree has a slit going from the top to the middle of the tree. The other tree has a slit going from the bottom to the middle of the tree.
5. Cut out the trees and the slits.
6. Trace the leaf shape from the book onto tracing paper. Cut it out and, using it as a pattern, trace onto green construction paper. Do the same with the cherry shape, but trace it onto red construction paper. Make several of each shape.
7. Cut out the leaves and cherries and paste them to the sides of both trees. Be sure that the leaves and cherries are pasted away from the center slit.
8. Fit the slit on the bottom of one tree into the top slit of the other tree.
9. Push the two trees together so that the top and the bottom of the trees line up.
10. Stand the tree up.

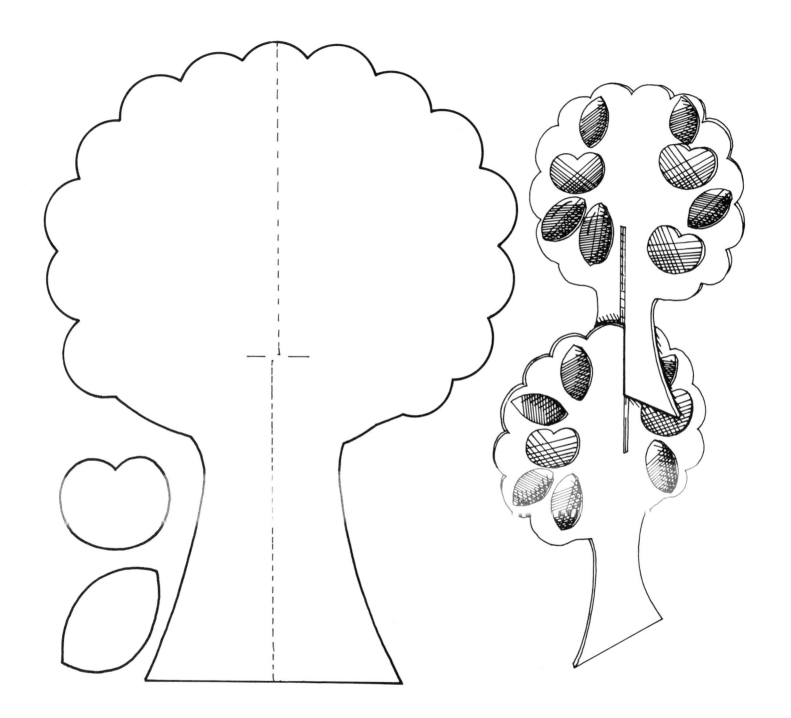

Tulips and Daffodils

Easter time is the flower season. This holiday arrives sometime during the spring when the flowers are starting to bloom. For a spring decoration, Easter-Egg Tulips and Daffodils will look as fresh as a bouquet of garden flowers.

Things You Need

blown eggs
indelible felt-tipped markers
drinking straws
green construction paper
liquid white glue
1 small clay or plastic flower pot
1 sheet of tracing paper
scissors
play clay
Easter grass
ribbon
pencil
pin or needle

Let's Begin

PRELIMINARIES

The tulips and daffodils are made from blown eggs. You will need at least two blown eggs for this project. To blow out an egg, see instructions in Ukrainian Pysanka Egg, page 200. Be sure to rinse the blown eggs; do not use soap.

TULIPS

**1. Make the hole on the wide end of a blown egg large enough to let a drinking straw fit through it. Push straw into egg.

2. Glue the straw to the eggshell. Let dry.
3. Hold the egg by the straw as you draw tulip petals on the shell with different colored felt-tipped markers.
4. Put a chunk of play clay into the bottom of a small flower pot.
5. Push the straws into the play clay.
6. Trace the tulip's leaf, Shape a, from the book onto a sheet of tracing paper.
7. Cut out the tracing and use it to trace leaves on green construction paper.
8. Cut out leaves and glue to the straws.
9. Fill the pot with Easter grass.
10. Tie a ribbon around the pot. Make a bow.

DAFFODILS
**1. Make a hole on the narrow end of a blown egg large enough to let a drinking straw fit through. Push straw into egg. Glue straw to egg and let dry.
2. Draw daffodil designs on eggshell with yellow and orange markers.
3. Trace the daffodil's petals, Shape b, from the book onto a sheet of tracing paper.
4. Cut out the tracing and use it as a pattern for cutting out petals on yellow construction paper. Punch a hole in the center of each petal.
5. Curl each petal upward.
6. Slip the petal on the straw and give it to the bottom of the egg.
7. Construct the pot of flowers the same way you did with the tulips.

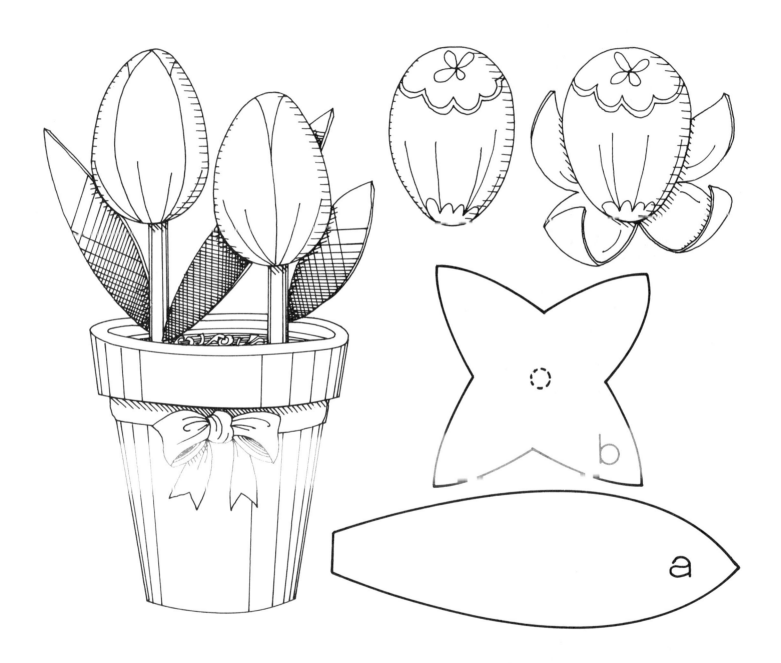

Fourth-of-July Hanging Flags

The Fourth of July is one of the most important holidays for the people of the United States of America. It was on July 4, 1776, that the Declaration of Independence was signed in Philadelphia. The United States became a free country. People were so very happy. Church bells rang and fireworks brightened the evening sky. The Liberty Bell was rung so hard that it cracked.

Today July 4th is celebrated with firework shows and programs about the meaning of the day. The most important thing to do is to show the Red, White, and Blue. In front of homes in your neighborhood, the American flag waves proudly. Why not bring some of the spirit of the celebration into your home with decorative hanging flags? They can be strung across a wall or hung, as patriotically as you like, in your window.

Things You Need

1 sheet of tracing paper
pencil
scissors
colored construction paper
tape
string
paper paste

Let's Begin

1. Trace the flag and the star separately from the book onto a sheet of tracing paper.
2. Cut out the tracings.
3. Use these cutouts to trace red, white, and blue flags and stars on construction paper.
4. Cut out the flags and stars.
5. Paste a star to each flag.
6. Fold the top of each flag along the dotted line (see illustration).
7. Place the folded top over a piece of string, Fig. a.
8. Tape the fold to the back of the flag, Fig. b.
9. Tape several flags onto the string, Fig. c.
10. Tape the string with the flags on a wall or across a window.

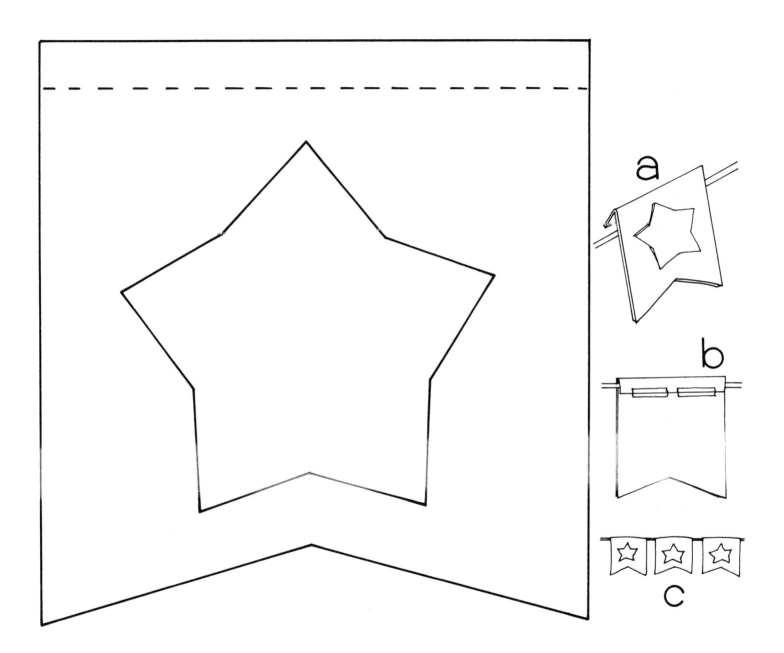

Carve a Halloween Pumpkin

Halloween is the day when witches, ghouls, goblins, and ghosts come out of hiding. It is fun dressing up in a costume and going trick-or-treating. If you are lucky, you can end up with a shopping bag of food, candy, and pennies. It is also fun to carve a big Halloween pumpkin. There is a song you should sing when you are carving the jack-o'-lantern:

First you get a pumpkin big, round, and fat.
Then you cut the top off, that makes the hat.
Then you cut the nose, the mouth and two eyes.
Making for the children a Halloween surprise.

Things You Need

1 pumpkin
knife and spoon
pie pan
birthday candles

Let's Begin

**1. First cut the top of the pumpkin, Fig. a. The top part is his hat.
 2. Use a spoon to scoop out all of the pulp and seeds. Save the seeds and put them in a pie pan, Fig. b.
**3. Use a knife to cut out the eyes, nose, and the mouth, Fig. c. Copy any of the shapes you see in the pumpkin illustrations.
 4. Poke a hole into the inside bottom of the pumpkin with a pencil.
 5. Put a birthday candle in the hole and light it. Put the "hat" on, Fig. d.
 6. Wash the pumpkin seeds you have saved with water. Sprinkle salt on the seeds and let them dry in the sun. In two weeks they will be delicious to eat.

Thanksgiving Placemats

A long time ago, the Pilgrims settled on the East Coast of America where they founded the Plymouth Colony. America was a strange country to them. Indians and wild animals lived in the forests and fields. Since the Pilgrims were the strangers in this new land, they had to learn how to live with the people and the creatures of America. Life was very hard at first, but the Pilgrims managed to endure. To celebrate this, and to express their thanks, they held one of the most famous dinners in history. It was the first Thanksgiving, and the colonists and Indians observed it together. Together they voiced their gratitude for all the things they had.

Today, Thanksgiving is the family holiday. If you don't have a turkey dinner in your own home, then you probably visit your aunts, uncles, or grandparents for dinner. The fun part of the day is watching the turkey being carved and eating all of the delicious food on the table. Now you can contribute to the Thanksgiving celebration by making turkey placemats for the table. Ask Mom how many people are visiting your home. Include yourself and your parents, too. Get started several weeks before Thanksgiving so your placemats will be ready when the guests arrive.

Things You Need

colored construction paper
1 sheet of tracing paper
crayons or colored felt-tipped markers
paper paste
scissors
pencil

Let's Begin

1. Cut out a circle larger than a dinner plate from orange construction paper.
2. Use the edge of a plate to draw a crescent shape on the paper circle, Fig. a. Use crayons or colored felt-tipped markers.
3. Draw a feather design on the crescent (see illustration).
4. Trace the turkey's-head shape and the small circle from the book onto a sheet of tracing paper.
5. Cut out the tracings.
6. Trace the head cutout onto brown construction paper and the circle onto red construction paper.
7. Cut out both shapes.
8. Paste the paper circle to the head (see illustration).
9. Paste the head to the body.
10. Put the dinner plates at your Thanksgiving dinner on the body part of your turkey placemats.

a

Chanukah Menorah

Chanukah is the Jewish Festival of Lights. It lasts eight days. During this holiday one candle is lit every day. Each day children receive gifts from their parents, and play games for pennies. The candles are placed in a menorah that is displayed in the house or by a window. You can celebrate Chanukah this year, and make your own menorah. It will be a lot of fun counting the days of this happy holiday.

Things You Need

colored construction paper
paper paste
drinking straws
scissors
pencil

Let's Begin

1. Fold a sheet of colored construction paper in four parts. Three parts should be exactly the same size and the fourth should be very small, Fig. a.
2. Fold the sheet into a triangle shape with the small fourth side tucked inside.
3. Paste the small side to the inside of the triangle.
4. Draw a menorah shape on construction paper big enough to fit on one side of the triangle. The menorah should have nine arms. (The ninth arm is for the candle used for lighting the other candles.)
5. Cut out the menorah and paste it to one side of the paper triangle.
6. Cut a small hole on the top fold of the triangle over each arm of the menorah.
7. Paste red paper flames to the top of nine drinking straws, Fig. b.
8. Place a straw candle into the middle hole.
9. Every night of the eight days of Chanukah add a straw candle to the menorah.

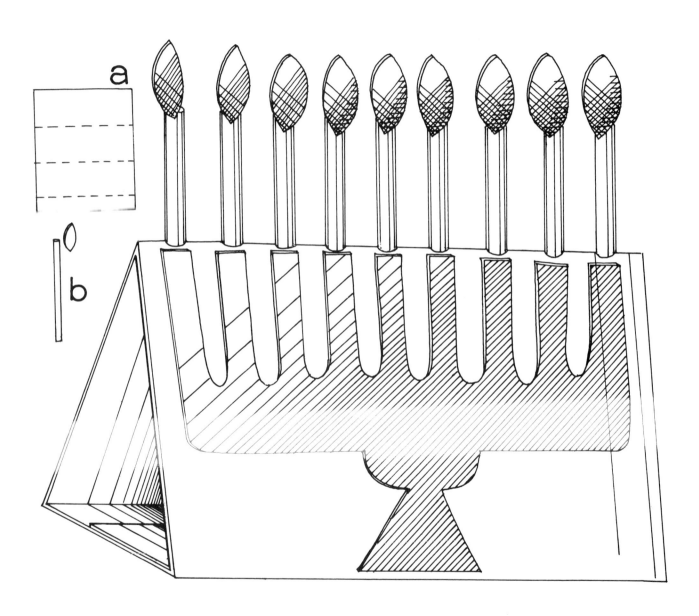

a

b

New Year's Eve Paper Hats

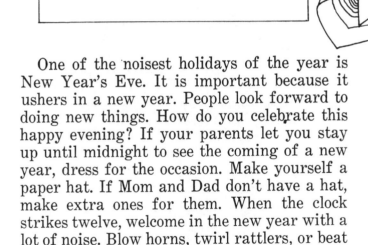

One of the noisest holidays of the year is New Year's Eve. It is important because it ushers in a new year. People look forward to doing new things. How do you celebrate this happy evening? If your parents let you stay up until midnight to see the coming of a new year, dress for the occasion. Make yourself a paper hat. If Mom and Dad don't have a hat, make extra ones for them. When the clock strikes twelve, welcome in the new year with a lot of noise. Blow horns, twirl rattlers, or beat a cooking pot with a large spoon.

Things You Need

colored construction paper
scissors
tape
stapler
ribbon

Let's Begin

1. Roll a sheet of colored construction paper to form a cone.
2. Tape the cone closed, Fig. a.
3. With scissors, trim the bottom edge of the cone to form an even circle, Fig. a.
4. Make a tassel for the top of the hat by cutting slits in a sheet of paper, Fig. b.
5. Roll the cut paper around itself to make a tassel and tape it in place on the top of the hat.
**6. Staple two pieces of ribbon onto both sides of the hat, Fig. c.

Santa is coming to town

When Thanksgiving Day is over, Christmas is just around the corner. People start counting the days before the arrival of jolly old Saint Nick. They want to be sure they buy Christmas presents for everyone they love. The streets are decorated with colorful lights, red candles, and ringing bells. Stores decorate their windows and the latest toys are put on display. People somehow look a little different. They are smiling more because this is the merriest of all holidays. It is the spirit of Christmas that brings laughter and happiness to the world.

During the weeks before Christmas you probably look at the newest toys, games, and sports equipment. You want to be sure that Mom and Dad know exactly what you would like to have this year. If you are lucky enough, Santa may be visiting your neighborhood department store. He will want to know what everyone wants for Christmas. With a jolly "Ho, ho, ho," he will leave for the North Pole and get ready for the long sleigh ride on Christmas Eve. Mom and Dad may ask you what presents you want, but it's nice to believe that Santa delivers them to the house on December 25th.

Whatever you get, it is the Christmas spirit of love that makes the day really special. Everyone in your family is so happy during this holiday season. Everyone is busy preparing for the holiday, making food and decorating the house. This year you can make many pretty decorations for every corner of your home. There can never be enough Christmas decorations. Every room should ring out with holiday cheer. Make this the best Christmas you have ever had.

Santa Centerpiece

"Ho, ho, ho!" says Old Saint Nick. What person does not know these words? They are very popular at Christmas time. If there is no Santa Claus in your home, it is time to bring the jolly fat man into your dining room. Every time your family sits down for dinner, Santa Claus and the spirit of Christmas will be with you.

Things You Need

milk carton
colored construction paper
scissors
paper paste
cotton balls
liquid white glue
plastic or real poinsettias
kitchen cleanser

Let's Begin

1. Cut the top off a washed milk carton at the point where the rounded spout begins, Fig. a.

2. Cover the carton with a piece of pink construction paper and tape it together. Or paint the carton with pink poster paint that has kitchen cleanser added to it.
3. Paste a red paper strip around the top of the carton, Fig. b.
4. Glue cotton balls to the bottom half of the carton, Fig. b.
5. Trace the moustache and eyebrow shapes from the book onto a sheet of tracing paper.
6. Cut out the tracings.
7. Use the cutouts to trace two moustache shapes and two eyebrows on white paper.
8. Cut out the moustache and eyebrows.
9. Also cut out two black circle eyes, a red circle nose, two pink circle cheeks, and a red mouth, all from construction paper.
10. Paste the eyes, nose, cheeks, and mouth to the carton, Fig. c.
11. Paste on the eyebrows and the moustache last.
12. Put plastic poinsettias into the carton. Or you can use real flowers, first adding a little bit of water to the carton.

a

b

c

We Three Kings

It was the Three Kings who brought the gifts to the Christ Child during the first Christmas. Since that time the job of delivering gifts has been given to Santa Claus and his helpers all across the world. But you can still have the Three Kings visit your home on Christmas. Get out your scissors and paste to make sure of their prompt arrival.

Things You Need

colored construction paper
scissors
paper paste
tape
crayons or colored felt-tipped markers

Let's Begin

1. Roll a sheet of colored construction paper into a tube, Fig. a.
2. Tape the tube together, Fig. b.
3. Cut out two squares on opposite sides of the bottom of the tube, Fig. c. These cutouts form the legs. One of them should face you.
4. Make the face from a strip of pink, yellow, or brown construction paper pasted to the top of the tube.
5. Make the beards from strips of paper that have slits cut along their bottom edges.
6. Paste the beards under the strip of paper that forms the face, Fig. d.
7. Decorate the kings with cut paper shapes, and use crayons or colored felt-tipped markers for added designs.

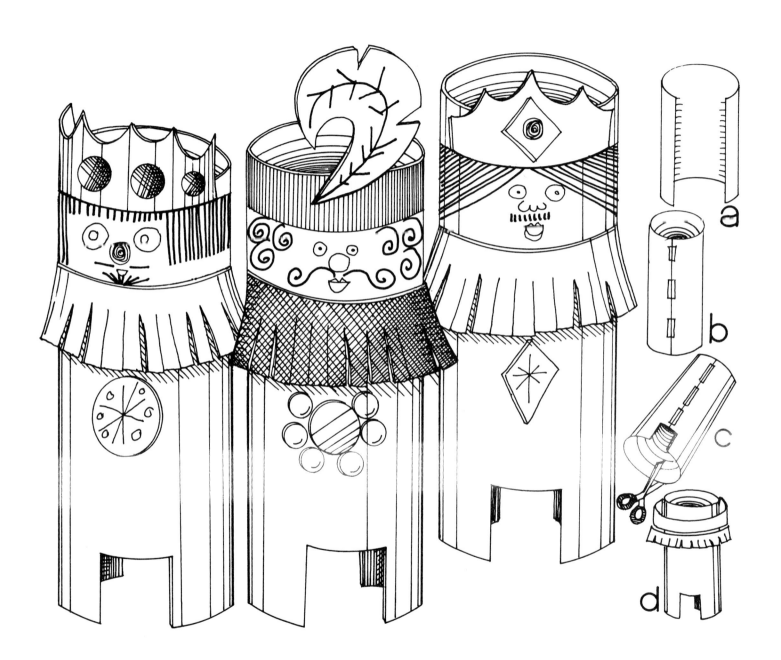

a

b

c

d

Tassel Table Tree

Nothing can take the place of a large Christmas tree standing tall in the living room. All of your family's favorite ornaments dangle from the branches. Although the tassel tree is not as tall and beautiful as a real Christmas tree, it will look pretty anywhere you want to put it. You might want a tassel tree in your room for the holidays.

Things You Need

1 large sheet of drawing paper
package of green crepe paper
scissors
paper paste
tape
yellow paper or gold stick-on stars
cardboard tube from a roll of paper towels

Let's Begin

1. Cut the drawing paper in a half-circle. It should be two times longer than it is wide, Fig. a.
2. Roll the half-circle into a cone, Fig. b.
3. Tape the cone together.
4. If the bottom of the cone does not form an even circle, trim it with your scissors.
5. Cut a package of green crepe paper into strips, Fig. c.
6. Cut slits in each strip halfway up, Fig. d.
7. Open the strips.
8. Paste a fringed strip to the cone at the bottom edge, Fig. e.
9. Keep gluing strips onto the cone, overlapping rows. Cover the entire cone.
10. Paste yellow construction paper stars or gold stick-on stars to the tree.
11. Stand the tree on a table. If it is small enough, stand the tree on a paper-towel tube, Fig. e.

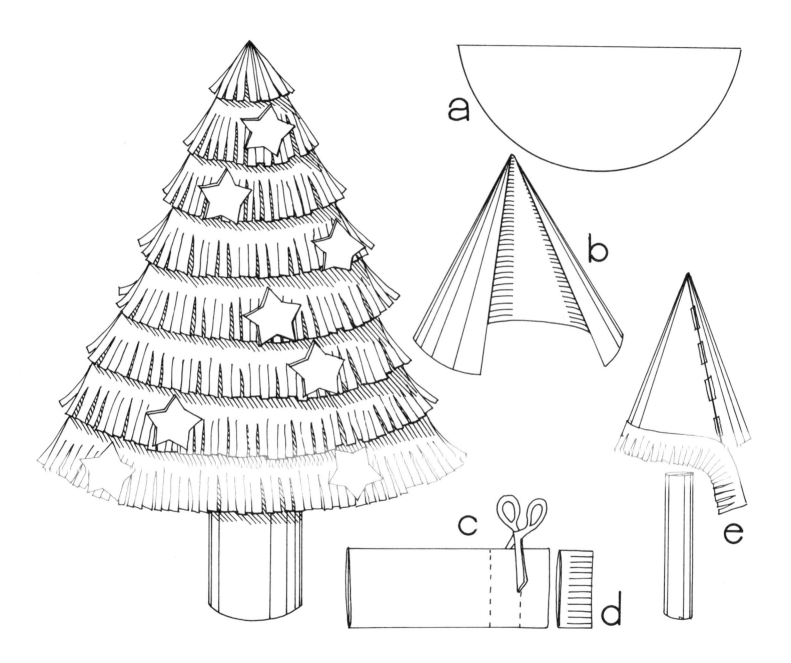

a

b

c

d

e

Mr. Snow the Snowman

Wintertime means snow and building snowmen and snowwomen. After you make one, you often want to bring it indoors with you. The problem is that it will melt in a few hours. Here is one snowman that won't turn to a watery puddle. Mr. Snow the Snowman will stay as crisp as new fallen snow all during the holiday season. Find him a place in your home this Christmas.

Things You Need

oatmeal or salt box
3-inch foam ball
4 one-inch foam balls
colored construction paper
1 sheet of tracing paper
white poster paint
drinking straw
liquid white glue
small length of scrap fabric
knife
scissors

Let's Begin

1. Trace the hat and broom shapes from the book onto a sheet of tracing paper.
2. Cut out the tracings.
3. Use the cutouts to trace a hat on black construction paper and the broom on yellow construction paper.
4. Cut out the hat and broom.
5. To make Mr. Snow, first paint a salt or oatmeal box with white poster paint, or wrap in white paper and tape.
**6. Cut a little slice from each foam ball with a knife, Fig. a. The flat side of the foam balls is the side that will be glued to the box.
7. Glue the large ball to the top of the box for a head.
8. Glue two of the small balls to the box near the top for the arms.
9. Cut two more slices from the remaining small balls opposite the first slices. The bottom slices help Mr. Snow to stand.
10. Glue the balls to the bottom of the box on opposite sides.
11. Glue the head of the broom to a drinking straw.
12. Glue the drinking straw to one of Mr. Snow's hands.
13. Make Mr. Snow's eyes, nose, mouth, and buttons from construction-paper circles and glue them on.
14. Tie a piece of scrap fabric around Mr. Snow's neck.

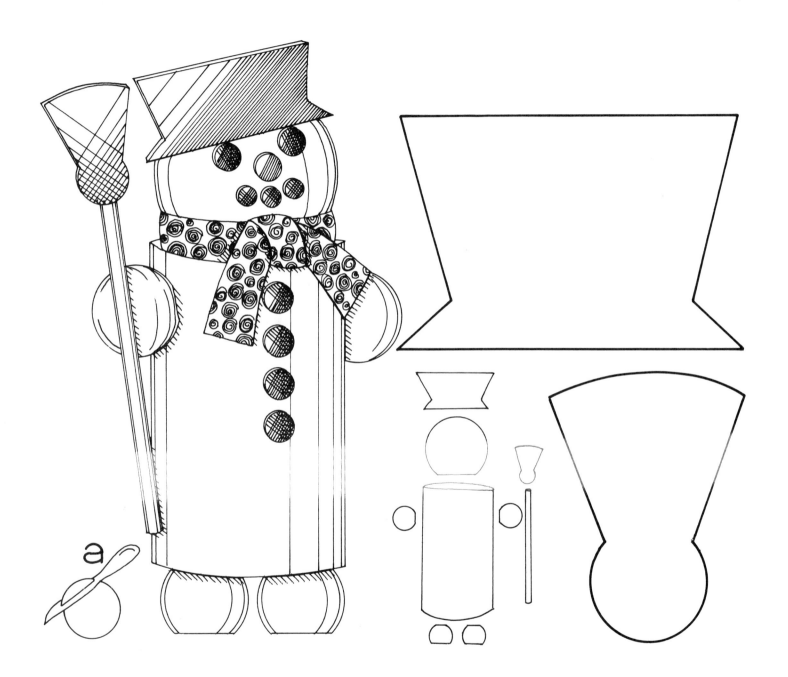

a

Holly Wreath

During the Christmas season your entire home is dressed in holiday attire. One of the first things your friends and relatives see when they come to your home is the wreath on your door. Wreaths come in all sizes and shapes. They can be made from almost anything. The most popular wreath is made from branches of pine with a big red ribbon tied to the bottom in a bow. If your door already has a wreath, then why not make one for the door to your room? It will provide a Christmas welcome for your friends when they come to visit you.

Things You Need

green and red construction paper
1 sheet of tracing paper
pencil
scissors
1 large sheet of cardboard or drawing paper
large plate
paper paste

Let's Begin

1. Trace around the rim of a large plate onto a large sheet of cardboard or drawing paper.
2. Using a smaller plate, trace a smaller circle shape in the center of the large one, Fig. a.
3. Cut out the outer circle first, then the inside circle, Fig. b.
4. Trace the leaf shape from the book onto a sheet of tracing paper.
5. Cut out the tracing.
6. Use the cutout to trace many leaves on green construction paper.
7. Cut out the leaves.
8. Cut out circles from red construction paper. (You can trace around a quarter for perfect circles.)
9. Paste the first leaf on the cardboard circle, Fig. c.
10. Paste the second leaf a little away from the first, overlapping it slightly, Fig. d.
11. Cover the wreath with leaves pasted slightly on top of each other.
12. Paste the red circles on the leaves for holly berries.
13. Use string to hang in a window or on a door.

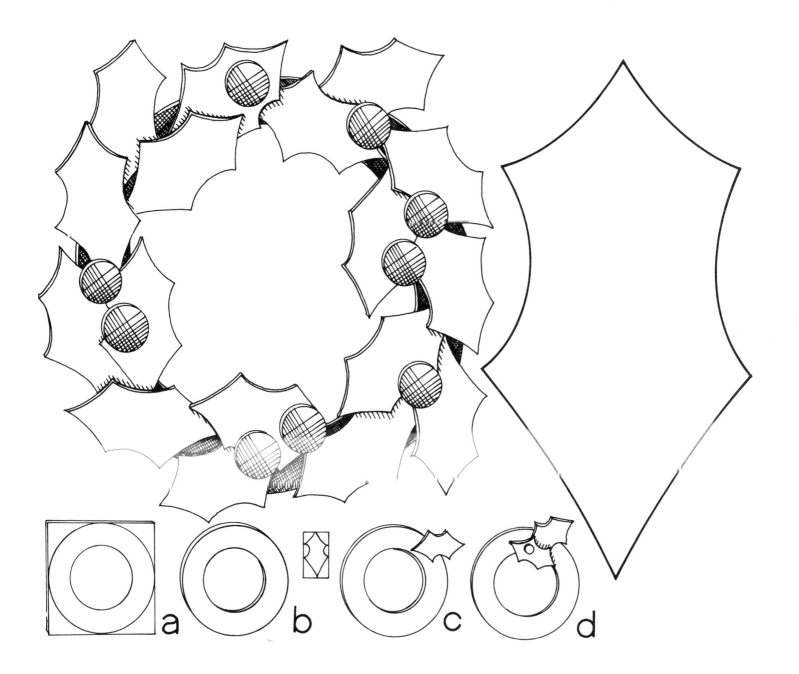

a

b

c

d

Tree Ornaments

Here are some more ornaments you can make for your Christmas tree. The last set of ornaments were made from paper. Now you are going to use other materials found around your home. Paper chains, bells, silver tassels, and candy cups will add the finishing touch to your already pretty tree. Be sure to find special places for these constructed ornaments.

Things You Need

aluminum foil
scissors
stapler
paper cone cups
pipe cleaners
kitchen cleanser
small Christmas balls
wrapped hard candy
colored construction paper
poster paints
paper paste

Let's Begin

SILVER TASSELS
1. Cut slits in a sheet of aluminum foil, Fig. a.
2. Roll the foil around itself in a tight circle, Fig. b.
3. Staple the foil together at the top.

4. Glue or staple a piece of paper or ribbon to the top of the tassel for hanging (see illustration).

BELLS
1. Paint paper cone cups with poster paints. If the paint won't stick to the cups, add a bit of cleanser to it.
2. Attach one end of a pipe cleaner to the wire loop of a small Christmas ball.
3. Push the other end through the top of the cone.
4. Twist the pipe cleaner into a small loop.
5. Tie a piece of string through the top loop.

CANDY CUPS
1. Paint paper cups with poster paints.
2. Staple a paper strip to both sides of the cup for a handle.
3. Fill with wrapped candy, and hang on a branch.

PAPER CHAINS
1. Cut construction-paper strips as long and as wide as the three links in the illustration.
2. Bend one strip into a circle and paste the ends together, Figs. c and d.
3. Put a second strip of paper into the circle and bend this strip into a circle, Figs. e, f, g. Paste the ends of this loop together.
4. Continue forming and pasting loops until you make a long chain.

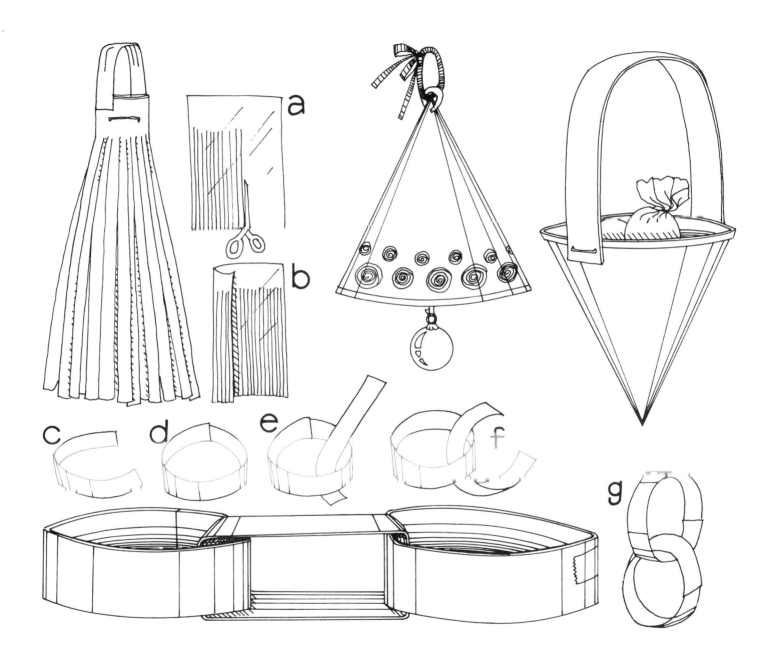

a

b

c   d   e   f

g

Paper Snowflakes

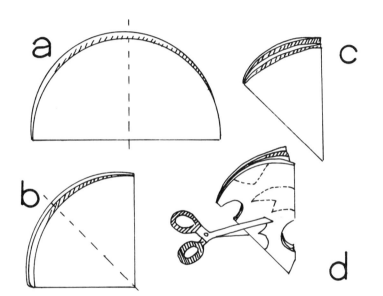

This year make your home look really wintery. Hang snowflakes in every room and in every window. When Old Saint Nick stops at your home, he will feel as if he is back at the North Pole. You might want to leave a few cookies or a piece of pie for this weary traveler.

Things You Need

typewriter or white drawing paper
scissors

Let's Begin

1. Cut white paper circles.
2. Fold the circles in half, Fig. a.
3. Fold the circles in half again, Fig. b.
4. Fold the circles in half again, Fig. c.
5. Cut out different shapes along the sides and the top of the folded circles, Fig. d.
6. Open the circles. You will never make two snowflakes exactly alike.

Puppets are almost people

Many of your best play friends are puppets. They are the closest thing to real people because they look and act as if they were alive. You can move their hands, legs, feet, mouths, and heads. By changing your voice, you can make them sound like different characters. They provide hours of fun for yourself and for your friends when they come to your home.

There was one famous puppet that became a real person. His name was Pinocchio. A woodcarver called Gepetto created him because he was lonely. Pinocchio was made from wood, but the day after he was created he began to talk. Gepetto was surprised but very happy. At last he had a talking friend. But Pinocchio was too curious about the world. He often ran away from Gepetto and would not come back for days. He even starred in a puppet show. Everyone was amazed to see a puppet without strings.

Pinocchio set out in search of new things. He met all kinds of people. He got in trouble several times. Finally he found himself in a really terrible situation. He became friends with a hooky player named Lamp Wick. They went to the Lands of Fun and Games when they should have been in school. It turned out not to be fun at all. Pinocchio finally escaped

but, in doing so, he landed in the ocean. He was swallowed by Monstro the Whale. Inside the whale's stomach he found Gepetto, who had been swallowed while searching for his little wooden puppet. They both managed to escape and ride to the shore on a tuna fish. Pinocchio saved Gepetto.

Gepetto and Pinocchio were finally together. They went home after their long search for each other. The next morning, when Pinocchio opened his eyes, he noticed something different. He was no longer a puppet. He was a real little boy. His good deed had made his wish to be real come true. Pinocchio and Gepetto lived happily for many years.

If you like the story of Pinocchio and enjoy playing with puppets, you are in for a treat. In this chapter you will make a puppet theater, scenery, puppets, tickets, and programs. A happy play, *Santina and the Whispering Willow*, is included. There is even a snack bar to sell tasty things to eat during the intermission. It is going to take many days, even weeks, before you finish all of the necessary things for a puppet show. But when you do, you will be the director of the best puppet theater in your neighborhood.

A Play—Santina and the Whispering Willow

Characters

NARRATOR
SANTINA
KING ANTHONY
PRINCE OF SIAM
PRINCE OF IRAN
PRINCE NOEL OF FRANCE
LITTLE BOY

ACT I

Scene: *The palace garden. A weeping willow tree is at the left of the stage.*

Curtain is closed throughout first speech

NARRATOR (*Spoken from backstage*)

In olden times, in the kingdom of Serene,
Lived the princess, Santina,
The fairest to be seen—
The lovely daughter of the great King
  Anthony.

Santina had a peacock with snow-white
  down
And a red marble throne,
And a bright golden crown.
She had a different dress for each day of
  the year.

In the palace garden stood an old willow
  tree.
Much closer to Santina than anything
  could be.

Open curtain

(*Enter* SANTINA *from the right side of the stage*)

SANTINA (*Looking at the willow tree*)
Oh dear willow, I will never leave thee.

(*Enter* KING ANTHONY. *He speaks from behind* SANTINA)

KING ANTHONY (*Softly*)
Oh lovely Daughter by the willow tree,
Turn your pretty face and look at me.

SANTINA (*Turns and looks at her father. She is in a daze*)
Dearest Father, are you speaking to me?

KING ANTHONY
An order has been sent to princes of the
  land.
A contest will soon be held to win your lovely
  hand.
The winner will have my kingdom.

SANTINA (*Turns away from her father and*

253

stares at the willow tree)
I don't like these words you are saying.
By my willow tree I want to be staying.

KING ANTHONY (*In an angry voice*)
And the winner will have my kingdom.

SANTINA (*Runs to the willow tree and puts
          her arms around it*)

Soon I will have to select a bridegroom.
Oh, my wise old tree,
How lovely is your bloom.
Please spread your weeping branches and
     comfort me.

Curtain

ACT II

Scene: KING ANTHONY'S *chamber. The king is
sitting at the right of the stage.* PRINCESS
SANTINA *is sitting in the middle of the stage.*

Open Curtain

NARRATOR (*Spoken from backstage*)
It is one week later in the early morning
Came the young Prince of Siam
With his hands bearing
Precious jewels from the Orient land.

(THE PRINCE OF SIAM *enters from the left.
He moves to the center of the stage and bows
in front of* SANTINA. *He holds out his hands
full of jewels*)

PRINCE OF SIAM
Diamonds, rubies, and a silver pearl ring
Are all yours, my sweet princess.
Take these valuable gifts I bring.
Your love is what I desire.

SANTINA (*Looking at the* PRINCE)
Kind prince, your fine jewels do not
Impress me,
And you are much too tall,
So I reject thee.

PRINCE OF SIAM (*With his head facing the
                  floor*)
Since it is me you do not want, I will leave.

(PRINCE OF SIAM *exits from the right*)

NARRATOR (*Spoken from backstage*)
The second suitor, very tall and bright,
Was a prince from Iran,
A stately, handsome knight.

(THE PRINCE OF IRAN *enters from the left.
He moves to the center of the stage and bows
in front of* SANTINA)

254

PRINCE OF IRAN (*Holding his hands apart*)
    I bring no jewels, only what you see.
    My handsome face is my gift to thee.
    I am sure that I will please.

SANTINA (*Feeling sorry for the prince*)
    It is a fact that you are quite handsome,
    But twiddling your thumbs
    Will be very hard for you to overcome.
    Oh handsomest of knights, you just won't do.

(PRINCE OF IRAN *exits from the right*)

KING ANTHONY (*Moves to* SANTINA)
    Such silly things does my daughter reject.
    Why couldn't you try to be a little less
        select?

SANTINA
    Oh kindest father, you will never get an
        heir to your kingdom this way.

Curtain

ACT III

Scene: *Outside the palace gates. On a dirt road
that leads to Serene.*

Open Curtain

NARRATOR (*Spoken from backstage*)

In the passing of time the nineteenth prince
Could not persuade,
Nor could he convince
The loyal Santina that he might win her
    love.

Now on the highway that leads to Serene
Walks Prince Noel of France,
Firstborn of a queen.

PRINCE NOEL
    Little boy, why does Santina turn so many
        away?

LITTLE BOY
    It is true that I'm a boy of five,
    But I am sure the secret
    Is easy to derive.
    It is the willow in her garden she will
        not leave.

PRINCE NOEL (*Shaking the* LITTLE BOY's *hand*)
    Thank you, you have told me very much.
    I must be traveling so I may touch
    The hand of beautiful Santina.

LITTLE BOY
    Many handsome princes passed this way.
    All brought gifts and promises,
    But none did stay
    To rule the kingdom of Serene.
    (*Exit* LITTLE BOY *from the left*)

PRINCE NOEL (*To himself*)
The mystery now has become very clear.
What the little boy has told me
Has given me an idea.
To the palace I must travel very quickly.

Curtain

(INTERMISSION)

ACT IV

Scene: *The palace garden.* SANTINA *is by the weeping willow tree.*

Open Curtain

(*During the following speech* PRINCE NOEL *searches for the willow tree. When he finds the tree he hides behind it.*)

NARRATOR (*Spoken from backstage*)
In the garden Prince Noel searched
    throughout,
        until he found the willow
        with its branches all about.
He climbed the old tree to the highest
    branch.

He listened from his branch so high
        and from inside the palace walls
        he heard a sad cry.
Santina rejected the twentieth prince.

(SANTINA *walks onstage and to the willow tree*)

SANTINA (*Very happy*)
Number twenty has heard my answer.
He pretended to be a prince
But he was only a dancer.
Dear willow, I am still as free as you.

PRINCE NOEL (*From behind the tree*)
Santina my dear, I am so fond of you.
You have such deep love
And remained so true.
Your kindness is music to my heart.

SANTINA (*Very surprised. Looks up at the tree*)
You startle me, but could this really be
That here I stand before you
Speaking words with my tree?
Then my love for you has been worthwhile.

PRINCE NOEL
Your love for me has been appreciated.
I am grateful for the young men
You have eliminated.
I am sleepy now, come back in the morning.

SANTINA
Oh speak no more, for I will go.
In the morning when I awake,
I will know
That the morning sun will lead me to you.

(*Exit* SANTINA *from the right*)

PRINCE NOEL (*Jumps down from the tree to
        the stage*)
It worked! She really thinks it has been
The tree
Who has been talking to her,
But it was really me.
Oh willow, the first part of my plan is done.

Curtain

ACT V

Scene: *It is the following day. The sun is shining brightly* (*pin a paper sun to the back curtain*). SANTINA *is by the willow tree in the
palace garden.*

Open Curtain

NARRATOR (*Spoken from backstage*)
In the morning of the very next day
The willow and Santina
Had many things to say.
He whispered softly to her of faraway
    places.

SANTINA (*Looking at the tree*)
The rays of the sun have brought me to your
Branches.
The night went by so fast
That there weren't any chances
To say how much I love you.

PRINCE NOEL (*From behind the tree*)
I remember a land with dragons all around.

SANTINA (*Very excited*)
Hurry, tell me more interesting things.

PRINCE NOEL
Please don't interrupt with the sound your
    tired voice is making.

SANTINA
I have lived behind these palace walls,
But over it I cannot see,
And you are so very tall.
Your stories of dragons, jesters, and snow-
    white doves must be true.

PRINCE NOEL
I love you, my princess, but I am sad of
Heart.
Oh lovely Santina,
We will have to part.
I'm dying of old age and to heaven I must go.

SANTINA (*Sniffling*)
Speak not these words, my faithful
    whispering tree.
You are the prince of my choosing.
Can't you see that I love thee?
If you must go, then I will follow you.

(PRINCE NOEL *jumps from behind the tree
in front of* SANTINA)

257

NARRATOR (*Spoken from backstage*)
At first Santina was as angry as can be,
Knowing that this young stranger
Was the voice of her favorite tree.
Then she knew that it was the Prince she
    really loved.

SANTINA (*Looking at* PRINCE NOEL)
So it was a prince who spoke of beautiful
Places,
Not my dearest willow tree,
Whom no prince replaces.
The willow tree will always be with me.

PRINCE NOEL (*Taking her hand*)
It is you I want to live with forever,
And with your willow tree.
You and I will never,
Never leave each other until the sun shines
No more.

(SANTINA *and* PRINCE NOEL *walk offstage*
while THE NARRATOR *speaks.*)

NARRATOR (*Spoken from backstage*)
And shortly after, Serene was to see
The loveliest of weddings
Beneath the willow tree.
They soon lived in a palace of their own.

It took twenty-nine men to move the willow
    tree.
And there it is standing
In its new home by the sea,
As another small Santina takes the willow
    to her heart.

And they did indeed live happily ever after.

Curtain

THE END

Puppet Theater

When your parents take you to the movies you go to a theater to see the show. If you have never seen a play at school or somewhere else, the actors perform on stage. If you want to put on a puppet show, then you will need your own theater or stage. This stage is very easy to make. All you need is a large cardboard carton and you can change your bedroom into a real performing theater.

Things You Need

large cardboard carton
knife or scissors
scrap fabric
string
needle and thread
poster paints
paintbrush
pencil
ruler

Let's Begin

**1. Cut away the top of the carton, Fig. a.
  2. Draw a stage opening on the front of the carton with a pencil. It should be shaped like a square with rounded corners on top, Fig. b.

**3. Cut out the stage opening, Fig. b.
  4. Measure with a ruler and note the distance from the top of the carton to the top of the stage opening.
  5. Draw a line around the other three sides of the box that is as far from the top as the distance you measured, Fig. c.
  6. Draw two x's at the front right- and left-hand edges of the box which are even with the top of the stage opening, Fig. c. Draw a line from the x points on both sides of the theater to opposite bottom corner, z.
**7. Cut away the triangular areas formed by the lines on both sides of the box, blackened area in Fig. c.
**8. Cut away the back of the carton up to the drawn line, blackened area in Fig. d. The remaining top part of the carton on the back and sides is called the curtain bar.
  9. Push out and forward the two triangle wings on the sides, Fig. d.
**10. Cut away the bottom of the carton, Fig. e.
  11. Place the theater on the back edge of a table with the wings facing front onto the table. Tape it to the table on the inside of the front and on the back wings, Figs. g and h.

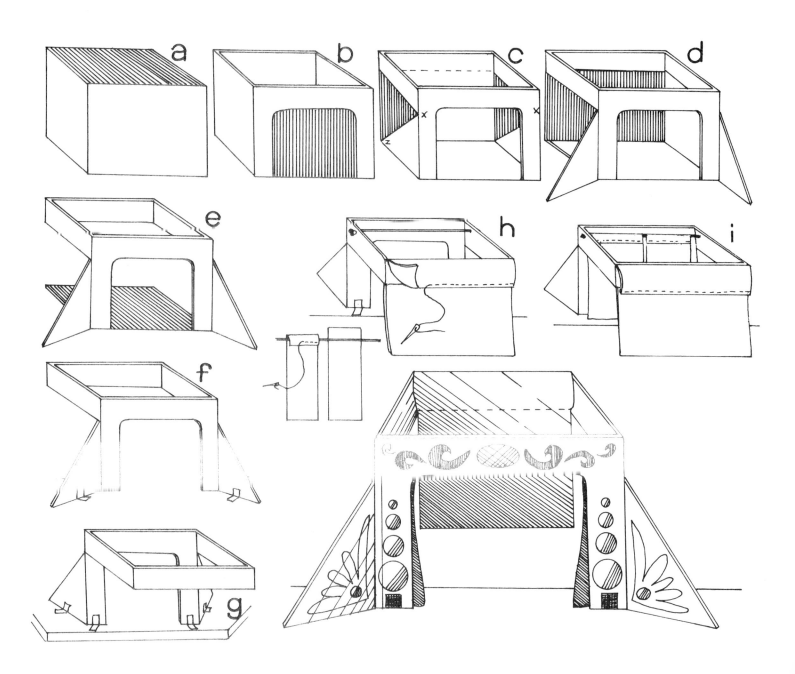

a b c d e f g h i

12. Cut a back curtain from the scrap fabric to fit the width of the back curtain bar. Add extra to the length of the curtain so that it can be wrapped around the curtain bar. Fold the curtain over the curtain bar and sew it as shown in Fig. h.
13. Make the front curtain from two pieces of fabric wide enough to cover the stage opening when "closed."
14. Punch a hole through each side of the theater a little bit back from the front. Run a cord through the holes and knot, Fig. h.
15. Fold the two front curtains over the cord and sew as shown, Figs. h and i.
16. Paint designs on the theater with poster paints. Work puppets from below back of table, sticking hands up through the open bottom of the theater.

Santina's Willow Tree

Weeping willow trees are very pretty because their branches seem to be kissing the ground. They look like huge green umbrellas, or giants with green hair. The willow is very important in this play. It is Santina's only love. She is very happy when she is in the palace garden by the willow tree. Although the tree can't talk, the prince in the tree talks as if he were the willow. Santina believes the tree is really talking. The willow tree is one of the important objects on your stage. Make it as pretty as you can.

Things You Need

cardboard tube from bathroom-tissue rolls
drinking straws
string
green construction paper
tracing paper
pencil
scissors
poster paints
paintbrush
colored felt-tipped markers
play clay

Let's Begin

1. Tie a handful of straws together close to the bottom, Fig. a.
2. Spread out the straws like a fan.
3. Paint the tube with brown poster paint.
4. Draw a bark design on the tube with a dark colored felt-tipped marker.
5. To put the tree together, push the straws into the top of the tube trunk. Wedge a piece of play clay into the bottom of the tube, Fig. b.
6. You can either cut out your own leaves or trace the leaf shape from the book. If you are going to trace the shape, first trace it onto tracing paper.
7. Cut out the tracing and use it as a pattern to trace many leaves onto green construction paper. Cut out leaves.
8. Glue the leaves to the straw branches.

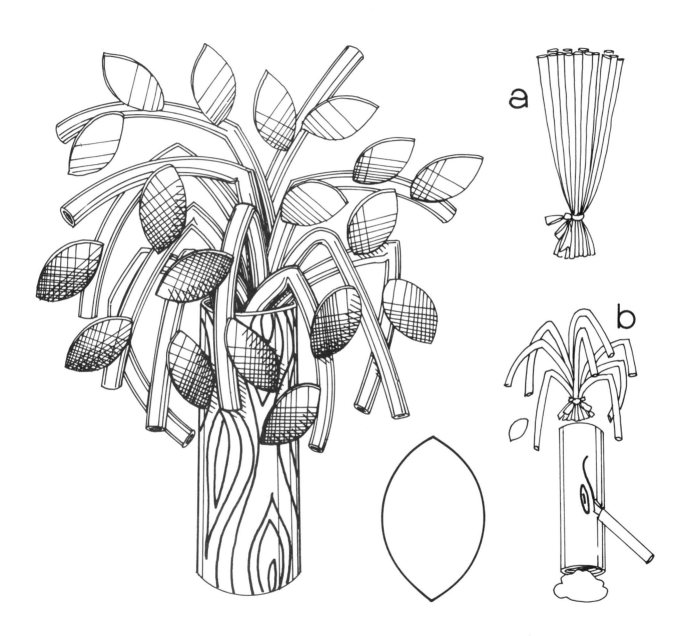

Ball-and-Pencil Puppets

Now that you have your stage and the weeping willow tree, it is time to make the principal characters. Santina, King Anthony, and Prince Noel of France are your three main characters. There are two other princes: the Prince of Siam and the Prince of Iran. When you make these two other princes, make sure their faces and clothing are different from those of the other characters. There is also a Little Boy who is very important in the story. Make a basic puppet shape and draw on a little boy's face. The puppets are made from pencils, ping-pong balls, and construction paper.

Things You Need

ping-pong balls or foam balls
pencils
colored construction paper
scrap fabric
needle and thread
colored yarn
liquid white glue
crayons or colored felt-tipped markers

Let's Begin

1. The puppet skirts should be cut wide enough to go around your hand with plenty of room to spare. They should be long enough to pass beyond your wrist. To make a skirt, first cut a sufficiently large piece of scrap fabric which is fairly rectangular.

2. Fold the fabric in half along the length, Fig. a.
**3. Thread a needle and knot the thread.
4. Sew the two sides of the fabric together a little in from the edges, Fig. a.
5. Sew the last stitch several times before you cut the thread.
6. Turn the skirt inside out.
**7. Thread the needle again.
8. This time sew a loose stitch around the top of the skirt a little down from the top edge, Fig. b. Do not cut the thread when finished.
9. To make the puppet, punch a sharp pencil into a ping-pong ball or a foam ball.
10. Add a dab of glue under the ball if it does not fit tightly on the pencil.
11. Push the pencil into the top of the skirt, Fig. c.
12. Pull the needle and thread tightly to trap the pencil, just under the ball.
13. Go over the last stitch several times before you cut the thread.
14. Glue on yarn hair and paper crowns, and draw faces with crayons or colored felt-tipped markers.
15. Add ribbon or yarn around the neck. Santina has beads around her neck.
16. NOTE: The Prince of Siam, the Prince of Iran and the Little Boy are made from the same puppet shapes as Prince Noel but only in different colors and with different faces.

Soap-Bottle Puppets

Your puppet show will be such a great success that you will have to perform it many, many times. What you will need for new performances is a new cast of actors. The same characters will be played by a different cast of puppets. You probably thought that empty plastic soap bottles should be thrown in the garbage. Save as many of these soap bottles as you can. They make wonderful hand puppets. With your finger in the bottle's spout, you can make a character do many things. Now you have a reason for helping Mom with the dishes. She will help you collect as many as you need.

Things You Need

small plastic soap bottles (the kind that
   dishwashing liquid comes in)
scrap fabric
needle and thread
ribbon and fringe
indelible felt-tipped markers

liquid white glue

Let's Begin

1. Make the puppet heads from plastic soap bottles with the opening turned upside down. Draw faces and hair on the bottles with indelible felt-tipped markers.
2. Glue yellow paper crowns on top of the face.
3. Make the skirt the same way as you did in the Ball-and-Pencil Puppets, page 310.
4. Pull the skirt around the indented part of the bottle. (See the dotted line in the King Anthony Puppet illustration.)
5. Cover the pulled stitches with bits of ribbon and fringe.
6. To work the puppets, put your finger into the opening of the bottle under the skirt.
7. NOTE: The Prince of Siam, the Prince of Iran, and the Little Boy are the same puppet shapes as Prince Noel but only in different colors and with different faces.

Paper-Bag Puppets

You probably thought that paper bags were used only for carrying groceries home from the supermarket, or for carrying your lunch to school. They make wonderful hand puppets, too. Your artistic creativity will be seen when these puppets are performing on stage. You can draw the entire face and body of paper-bag puppets. They are soft enough to bend and do all kinds of things, almost like the sock puppets. Mom will save all of her smaller grocery bags for you. Be sure to help her do the shopping, and carry some of the bags for her before you use them.

Things You Need

small brown paper bags

colored construction paper
crayons or colored felt-tipped markers
paper paste

Let's Begin

1. Draw King Anthony, Santina, Prince Noel, the Prince of Siam, the Prince of Iran, and the Little Boy, each on one side of a bag. (Only Santina, King Anthony, and Prince Noel are shown in the illustration.)
2. Paste crowns cut from yellow construction paper to the top of each bag puppet.
3. To work the puppets, put your hand inside the bags.

Programs and Invitations

Now that the scenery, theater, and puppets **are made, it is time to send out invitations for your performance. The invitation is a ticket that your guests have to present to you before the show begins. After they have handed you their ticket, give them a program that lists the characters and the person who is speaking for each character. Once all the tickets** have been collected, let the show begin. Dim the lights and open the curtain on the first performance of *Santina and the Whispering Willow.*

Things You Need

colored construction paper
scissors
crayons or colored felt-tipped markers

Let's Begin

1. **The program tells your guests all about the** play they are about to see. The names shown on the program in the book are only examples. You will write in the correct names of the people who will be speaking for the puppets. Copy the program information on sheets of colored construction paper.
2. Hand one to each guest as he arrives.
3. The invitations should be given to each invited guest a few days before the puppet show. Copy the invitation from the book as **many times as necessary on colored construction paper. Put in the appropriate date, time, and name.**
4. **Ask each guest to bring his invitation with him on the day of the puppet show.**
5. **Rip off the part of the invitation that says Admit 1 Person before letting the guest take his seat.**

Santina
and
the Whispering Willow

— o —

Voice of Santina - Mary

Voice of King Anthony
and Narrator — Greg

Voice of Prince Noel — Mark
boy and other princes

— o —

Play in 5 acts

Intermission after the
third act

— o —

Scenery, Puppets, Stage
Mary & Mark Smith

Refreshments - Mrs. Smith

Santina
and the Whispering Willow

o o o

Sat. - August 21, 19__
2:00 — 3:00

at Mary and Mark Smith's
Basement

- - - - - - - - -

ADMIT
1
PERSON

Snack Bar

Your puppet show has five acts. When you see a play at a theater there is an intermission after each act. This is so that the actors can have a little rest before the next act, and the audience can stretch and have something to eat or drink. Your intermission will come after the third act. Notice of the intermission will be written on the programs. Your guests will want a snack by the time the third act is over. Fill your snack bar with wrapped hard candy and a pitcher of fruit drink. Popcorn is also a good thing to have. Don't make the intermission too long. Your guests will be waiting to see what will happen to Santina and the willow.

Things You Need

large cardboard carton
scissors
tape
ruler
colored construction paper
paper paste
bowl of popcorn
candy
contact paper
paper cups
pitcher of juice or lemonade

Let's Begin

1. Tape the open end of a cardboard carton closed, Fig. a.
2. Turn the box upside down so that the taped end is on the bottom.
**3. Cut away one of the box's sides, Fig. a.
4. With a ruler, measure the depth of the inside of the box, Fig. c.
5. Measure the same depth on the cardboard side you removed, and draw a cutting line across the width.
**6. Cut away the extra cardboard from this side, Fig. b.
7. Fit this piece of cardboard into the box for a shelf.
8. Tape the shelf to the inside of the box.
9. Decorate the front of the box with a paper sign and arrows pointing to where the line should form.
10. Paste some paper decorations to the front of the box and write your Mom's name or your name on it. You might ask Mom for some contact paper to stick to the top of the snack bar. In case some juice is spilled, all you need is a wet sponge to wipe the top of the snack bar clean and dry. Put goodies on the shelf and you're in business!

a

b

c

Mrs. Smith's Snack Bar

Good-bye

Congratulations! You have come to the end of *Sticks & Stones & Ice Cream Cones*. It wasn't easy getting to this page. You spent many happy hours making these fun-filled crafts. There were probably many times when you thought you would never finish a project. If you tried your very best and completed the projects you liked the best, then you deserve an award. Consider yourself the proud recipient of the Certificate of Achievement you see in the book, and sign your name in the proper place. Remember, if you like to use your hands and make things, this book can be enjoyed over and over again.

Certificate of Achievement

AWARDED TO

_____

Phyllis Fiarotta

AUTHORIZED SIGNATURE

SNIPS & SNAILS & WALNUT WHALES

Nature Crafts for Children

Foreword to parents

This is a book of nature crafts for children. It shows how nature provides the artist or craftsman with raw materials as well as the sense of form, color, and harmony from which all beautiful or useful things are born. In making the projects found here, your children explore the relationship between natural things and the created object and come to know nature better while learning to use it in new and imaginative ways.

SNIPS & SNAILS & WALNUT WHALES belongs to the youth of today. It is written for children to understand. All specific measurements (inches and feet) are omitted, leaving the total creative process to the young artisan. Drawings accompany each craft project, and in some cases step-by-step illustrations are included. No guesswork is needed.

Some crafts will appeal to your children, others less so. Don't force them, just for creativity's sake, to make something they won't use. Let them decide which projects interest them most. They will automatically select the things most appropriate to their age group. Your children know themselves very well and what it is they most enjoy making.

The adult plays an important part in the construction process. Read through this book before you hand it over to your children. Look at all the craft items and see how the instructions are written. **You will notice the symbol ** in front of a direction. This means that potentially dangerous household equipment is called for, or that the execution of the step so marked may be too difficult for a child.** It is advisable for you to supervise this activity. Keep in mind your children's physical abilities and limitations. If you feel they cannot perform a particular task, you will have to do it for them. Allow youngsters to feel, however, that they are the ones creating the objects, even though it is you who have just bored a hole in a piece of cardboard or cut a length of string.

Every craft item in this book is presented in three parts: the drawing, the instructions, and a list of craft materials. Children should be encouraged to read through the instructions several times before they begin, and to study the drawings carefully. You will provide them with the necessary craft supplies and help them gather natural materials. Craft supplies can be bought in a stationery or art supply store, or at the stationery counter of department stores. Other items will be found in your kitchen or in the family tool box. Shop around in the woods, by the seashore, or in your backyard for twigs, rocks, sand, and any of the other natural craft supplies required. Every trip away from home can be a productive nature supply gathering involving the entire family. Don't forget to save all leftover items for future craft projects.

You and your children live in a time of renewed awareness of natural things and of the need for their conservation. We have learned the importance of the word "recycle" as it concerns the wise use of "waste" materials.

The craft boom has done its part to show us how our material resources may be reused constructively. This book should help take you and your children further in this direction, encouraging work which will create a real sense of accomplishment in its completion and display. With a little patience and devotion, all of the crafts in this book will become the natural wonders of your children's world.

Just for you

Starting at this moment, try to be aware of every natural object in front, above, and under you. Let the breeze part your hair and go grab a handful of autumn leaves. Gather stones, sand, shells, pine cones—any of nature's fascinating creations. Now you can use these earthly wonders to create beautiful things for you, your family, and friends. This book will open the gates to Mother Nature's wonderful kingdom.

There are many interesting crafts to make using natural craft materials like sand, snow, and flowers. Create a bouquet of dried flowers for the dining room table, a sand-casted plaster sunburst for your room, or a pine cone bird feeder for your feathered friends.

Look through the book and decide which craft item you would like to make first. It is very important that you read all directions not just once, but several times before you begin. If there is something you don't understand, have someone explain it to you. It is important that you study the drawings as well. You will be better able to understand the directions if you see how a craft is put together.

Your mom and dad will be very helpful to you. They will buy and help you find all the materials you will need for the projects you choose. If you have difficulty cutting, threading, sewing, or doing anything, ask for a helping hand. Once you learn the proper way to handle tools and materials, the construction of the items will be easier.

By now you should be as eager as a beaver to get started. Find a project you want to construct, and head for the hills in search of the natural things you'll need. Nature will provide enough craft materials for everyone (though you should never take more at one time than you actually require). Once you get going on the craftwork, you'll probably find it difficult to stop. That's the great thing about this book—reading it is like floating down a winding river with new treasures appearing at every turn of the shore.

Nature's gifts and where to find them

Nature's gifts can be found in the backyard, saved from trips to the beach or gathered on hikes and family picnics. It is a good idea to collect the gifts as you find them and to store them in a special place until you need them for a craft project. Try to keep your craft shelf well-stocked. If you need to supplement your craft supplies, many of the natural materials can be purchased from florists or in craft and hobby stores.

FLOWERS

• **Flowers** grow in fields or gardens, almost everywhere in nature. People who live in warm climates will have field flowers for a longer period of time than those living in cooler places. A florist can supply you with flowers anytime of the year, of course.

LEAVES

• **Leaves** grow on tree branches, bushes, vegetables, and flower stems. Tree leaves are best for the craft projects in this book. Fern and many evergreen branches, also needed for some of the projects, may be purchased from your local florist during any season.

TWIGS

• **Twigs** are small shoots or branches from trees or certain shrubs. Try not to remove twigs from living trees, but wait until they can be gathered from fallen branches. Certain "twigs" can be found along the seashore. These twigs are actually smooth wooden branches called driftwood—wood that is drifted or floated by the sea.

PINE CONES

• **Pine cones** are the seed carriers of pine trees. Other trees grow cones—like the larch and the spruce. The next time you pass a pine, spruce, or larch, look under the tree for fallen cones.

SEEDS, BEANS, AND NUTS

• **Seeds, beans, and nuts** are usually found in your kitchen—it's the first place to look. Fruits like oranges and melons contain seeds; some cooking spices are seeds, like unground mustard. Wild birdseed or parakeet seed can be bought at the five-and-ten-cent store, or at your local grocery. Dried beans and shelled nuts are also available at the food store. If you are more adventurous and live in the country, gather nuts in the woods. You can find acorns, black walnuts, and hickory nuts during the fall.

EGGS

• **Eggs** come from many kinds of birds, but we will use only chicken eggs for craft projects. These are sold in grocery stores, as you must know, by the carton.

STONES

• **Stones** can be found in all shapes, sizes, and colors almost everywhere you look in the outdoor world. Smooth white stones, sometimes called for in the projects, can be found at the seashore.

SHELLS

• **Shells** are best found by the seashore. Clams, oysters, and other shellfish can be bought at the fish market or in large supermarkets; enjoy eating them and then save the shells. Restaurants that specialize in fish dinners will also have a good supply of shells which should be available for the asking. Florists and hobby stores sell packages of pretty shells and there are the newer shell shops which carry all kinds of shells exclusively.

SAND

• **Sand** is found at the seashore or the desert. It can be bought at the hardware store or the florist.

FRUIT AND VEGETABLES

• **Fruits and vegetables** are usually found at the supermarket or grocery store. Some varieties are available only at special times of the year, while you can get others all year long. There may be a tree in your garden that produces fruit, or a plant that bears vegetables.

Other things you'll need

PAPER

- **White drawing paper** is important in craft projects as well as for drawing. Drawing paper is heavy, smooth paper that comes in pads or packages.

- **Colored construction paper** is heavy paper that comes in many wonderful colors. The sheets are sold in packages, and many paper sizes are available. Try to pick the correct size for the craft you will be making. Save all large scraps in a box or bag. You never know when you might need a little bit of color.

- **Tracing paper** is a light, transparent paper. When it is placed on a drawing, you can see the drawing through it. Tracing paper comes in pads.

- **Typewriter paper** is a white paper that is lighter than white drawing paper but heavier than tracing paper. You can see a drawing under it. It comes in packaged sheets.

- **Cardboard** is very heavy paper. You can find it backing shirts which come from the laundry or in packages of new clothes. Other boxes found around the house—like shoe and hat boxes—are made of it. Cardboard may also be bought in art supply stores. **Oaktag** is a kind of cardboard which you will probably have to buy; it comes in large sheets and is available at stationery and art supply stores. Save all pieces of cardboard you find in your home.

GLUES AND PASTES

- **Liquid white glue** comes in plastic bottles with pointed caps. This glue makes a strong bond when it dries and is used, therefore, for hard-to-glue crafts.

- **Paper paste** is a white, thick adhesive. It comes usually in a jar, and has a plastic spreader. Paper paste is best for sticking paper to paper.

COLORINGS

• **Poster paints** are paints that can be removed from your hands with water. They come in many colors and are sold in jars.

• **Watercolor paints** are little tablets of hard color that must be daubed with a wet brush to use. The paints come in a tin which has at least six colors in it.

• **Crayons** are colored wax sticks that are used for drawing.

• **Colored felt-tipped markers** are tubes or "pencils" of enclosed watercolor with a felt coloring tip. You draw with markers as you would with crayons.

FABRIC

• **Felt** is a strong, heavy fabric that comes in many colors. It is sold in small squares. It can be glued to a surface with liquid white glue.

• **Scrap fabric** is odds and ends of cloth that your mom saves from her sewing projects. You can also cut up old clothes for scrap fabric.

MOULDING MATERIALS

• **Plaster of paris** is a white powdery substance which, when united with water, hardens as it drys. It is available at hardware stores.

• **Paraffin** is a waxy material sold usually in blocks at supermarkets, hardware, and five-and-ten-cent stores. It is melted, and used for home canning or candle making.

• **Play clay** is any non-hardening modeling clay which comes in colors and is available at hobby, art supply, and five-and-ten-cent stores.

The flowers that bloom in the spring, tra la

Spring is perhaps the most magical of all the seasons. Nature performs one of her really miraculous tricks. Right before your very eyes, flowers and leaves seem to pop out everywhere. Just as the magician pulls a rabbit out of his hat, so spring changes the gray of winter into a starburst of color. You see and smell new life almost everywhere you go—feel new yourself.

Spring is just one part of nature's year-long mystery. After spring there's summer, during which all growing things flourish. Come autumn, flowers and leaves begin to die, but with their own subtle or brilliant colors going that make the world maybe even more beautiful than before. In the winter nature rests and the earth regains its strength. Then it's time for spring again, and those wonderful flowers that bloom, tra la.

If you like spring—to see, touch, and smell flowers—then this chapter is for you. With it, you'll capture spring's colors and be able to display their beauty all year long. Many of the projects here require flowers that have been dried—the book will tell you how—so you might want to start a dried flower collection now. Begin by gathering either garden or wild flowers (better ask Mom or Dad first if you intend to raid the garden), dry and save them for future craft use. After you have made some or all of the projects in this chapter you should know flowers better than ever. It's an acquaintanceship that's really nice to have.

Daisy Chains

As far back as two thousand years ago, people decorated their heads with flowers and leaves. You won't see many people walking around your neighborhood with flowers in their hair these days. In some countries, however, people still use flowers to decorate the top parts of their bodies.

The daisy chain is a craft you should do in the early summer; the daisy is in bloom at this time. If you live in an area where daisies don't grow, any flower with a long stem will do. The daisy is a wild flower, and can frequently be seen growing along the sides of country roads. Pick only enough daisies to use for this project. You wouldn't want to leave the countryside bare of flowers.

Things You Need

scissors
freshly picked daisies
butter knife
paper clip

Let's Begin

1. Cut daisies leaving a stem that is about as long as your hand.
**2. Starting a little way from the bottom, cut a small slit through all the stems, Fig. a. Make sure not to cut all the way through the bottom of the stem.
3. Pass the stem of one daisy through the slit of another, Fig. b. Pull the second stem all the way through the first.
4. Take a third daisy and pass it through the slit of the second daisy, Fig. c.
5. Continue by passing a new stem through the slit of the last attached daisy until you have a chain of daisies.
6. When you have made a chain as long as you want, attach the last stem to the stem of the first daisy with a paper clip. Try making a chain from other kinds of flowers, or mixing kinds in a single chain.

Sachet Bags

If you smell a pretty fragrance in a closet or drawer, it might mean that there is a sachet bag somewhere present. You can buy sachet bags—little cloth pouches filled with fragrant herbs and flowers—in stores, but it is much more fun to make one. Your room, bureau drawers, or closet will smell sweeter after you have finished this project.

Things You Need

flowers
scissors
shoe box or gift box with a lid
see-through fabric or netting
needle and thread
dime-store cologne
ribbon

Let's Begin

1. Collect roses or other flowers that smell sweet.
2. Cut away the stems and leaves with scissors.
3. Place the flowers in a shoe box or a gift box and cover.
4. Place the box in a dark, dry place like a closet or an attic.
5. Allow the flowers to dry for ten days.
6. Cut two rectangular shapes out of the fabric which are exactly the same size—the length of each shape should be longer than its width.
**7. Thread a needle with sewing thread, and knot the ends of the thread together.
8. Place the two fabric shapes together.
**9. Using a running stitch, sew down one of the long sides a little in from the edge. To make a running stitch, first push the needle through both pieces of fabric near the top of one side and pull the thread until it is stopped by the knot. Now push the needle back through both pieces of fabric a little way from the knot. Continue to pass the needle back and forth through the fabric making small, equally spaced stitches, Fig. a.
10. Now sew along the bottom leaving some extra fabric between your sewing and the bottom edge, Fig. b. Complete the bag by sewing up the other side. The last stitch should be sewn several times. Cut away the extra thread.
11. Cut slits into the extra fabric on the bottom of the bag to make a fringe, Fig. c. Be sure not to cut into the sewn stitches.
12. Sprinkle a little of the cologne on the completely dried flowers.
13. Fill the bag half-full of the dried flowers.
14. Tie the top of the bag with a ribbon and make a bow.

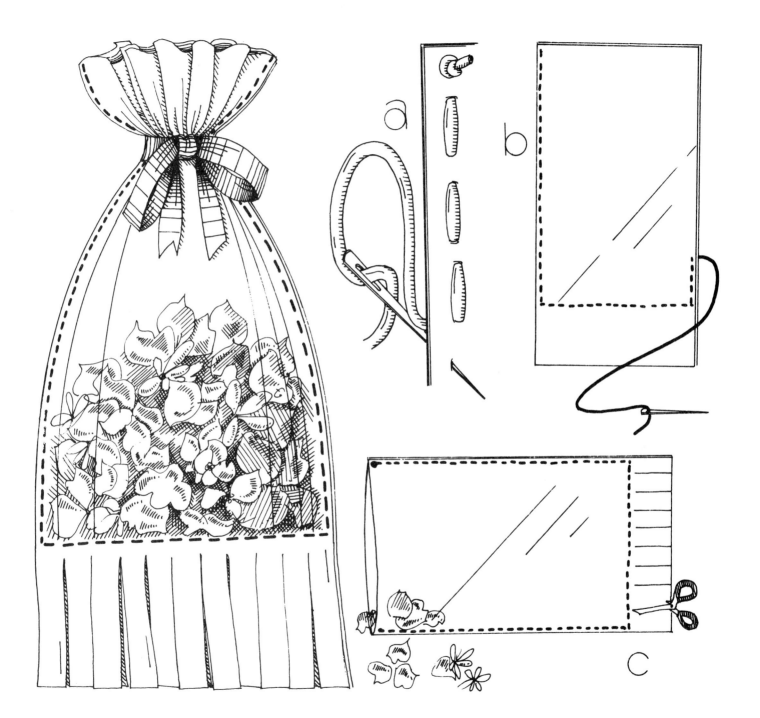

a

b

c

Flower Paperweights

A paperweight can be used by every member of your family. Dad can use one for his desk. Mom can use one in the kitchen to keep her bills in one place. Your sister or brother can use one for keeping homework papers together. You will have to read Sand-Dried Flowers, page 438, to make the dried flowers you will need for this project. You will need quite a few if you are going into the paperweight business—something you may find yourself doing after people get a look at one of these floral beauties.

Things You Need

glass ashtray or small jar with a lid
colored construction paper
pencil
scissors
liquid white glue
sand-dried flowers, see page 438
waxed paper

Let's Begin

1. Turn the ashtray upside down and place it on a sheet of colored construction paper.
2. Trace around the edge with a pencil, Fig. a.
3. Cut out the tracing with scissors, Fig. b.
4. Glue one or several of the sand-dried flowers on the cutout tracing.
5. Let the glue dry completely on the paper.
6. Place the paper with the flower on top of a piece of waxed paper, which will protect your working surface.
7. Squeeze liquid white glue along the edges of the construction paper cutout, Fig. c.
8. Fit the upside down ashtray onto the wet glue, matching the shape of the ashtray to that of the paper as exactly as you can.
9. Allow the paperweight to dry completely before you handle it.
10. Or, if you are using a jar with a lid, proceed as follows: Glue the flower to the inside of the jar lid. When the flower has dried in place, carefully screw the jar onto the lid, see illustration.

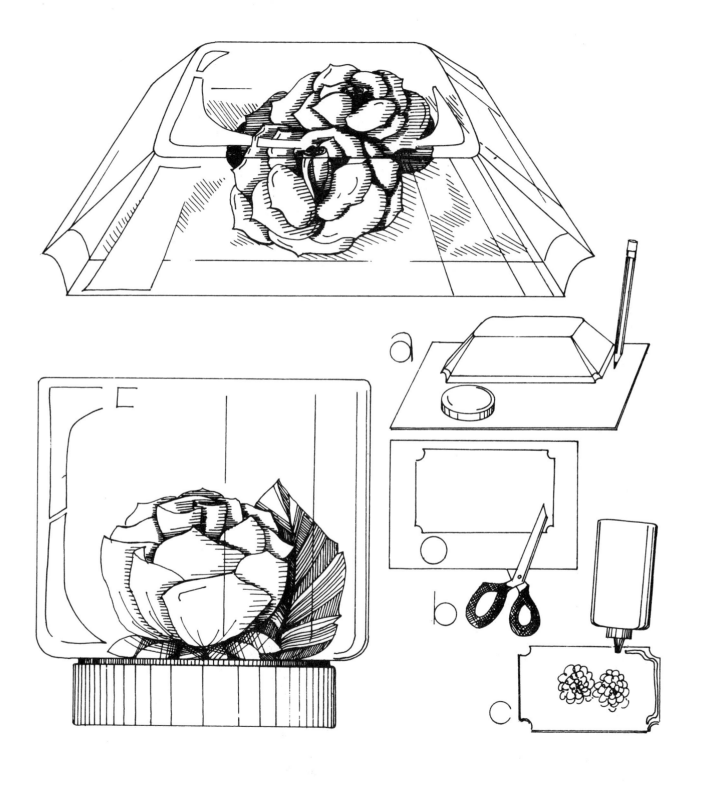

Still Life Paintings

Still life paintings show things that are inanimate—things which don't move—such as a bowl of fruit. You won't be painting in this project, but you *will* create a painting using dried flowers. Dried flowers retain some of their original color and make a beautiful picture when placed on a piece of colored construction paper.

Things You Need

scissors
cardboard, preferably oaktag
colored construction paper
paper paste
liquid white glue
sand-dried flowers, see page 438
colored felt-tipped marker or crayon

Let's Begin

1. Cut a piece of cardboard any size you wish.

2. Cut a piece of colored construction paper smaller than the cardboard. The paper should be cut so that when it is placed in the center of the cardboard, an equal amount of cardboard border shows on all four sides.
3. Center the paper on the cardboard and paste down.
4. Cut out a vase shape from colored construction paper.
5. Paste the vase near the bottom of the colored paper background, see illustration.
6. Glue a bouquet of dried flowers over the vase shape using large dots of the liquid white glue to fasten the flowers. Be careful that the flowers do not crumble as you work.
7. Cut a paper sign to fit on the cardboard border. Using the felt-tipped marker or a crayon, write your name and where you picked the flowers on the sign.
8. Paste the sign onto the cardboard border.
9. Glue a paper or a ribbon bow on the vase.

Flowers picked
and dried by
ANDREW KENE

Floral Note Paper

One of the nicest presents you can receive is a box of pretty stationery. Writing letters on special paper is somehow more enjoyable, makes you feel like you're sending more of yourself with every message. If you don't have a box of personal stationery why not design your own? Gather flowers, preferably of the daisy type rather than the rose. Flat flowers can be pressed more easily than bulky flowers. You might want to make extra sheets for gifts or even for display.

Things You Need

freshly picked flowers, leaves or ferns
white drawing paper
heavy books
envelopes
scissors
liquid white glue
paper cup
paintbrush
tweezers
colored construction paper
waxed paper

Let's Begin

1. Place "flat" flowers like daisies, leaves or ferns between two sheets of drawing paper.
2. Place the paper with the flowers between the pages of a heavy book, Fig. a.
3. Place more books on top of the first, Fig. b.
4. Let the flowers dry in the book for ten days.
5. After ten days, remove the paper and flowers.
6. To make a piece of note paper, fold white drawing paper in half. Trim the paper to fit the size of the envelope you will use. Do not cut away the folded edge.
7. Pour a little liquid white glue into a paper cup.
8. Using the paintbrush, paint the back of the pressed flowers with the glue.
9. Remove the flowers from the paper with tweezers, and glue them onto the top fold side of the paper, Fig. c. For fancier note paper, glue a strip of colored construction paper down the folded side. Glue the flowers onto this border.
10. Place a sheet of waxed paper over the note paper and put both in a book to dry overnight.
11. Write a note to a friend when the flower note paper has completely dried.

Dear Fred,
   I want you
to know that
I made this card
m...
fo...
Ih...

Grandma,
Last week
mom took
us, to pick
buttercups.
We picked
them and
put them
in a heavy
book. Mom →

a

b

c

Flower Découpage

Découpage is a way of decorating an object with pictures, cutouts or, in this case, flowers. The decoration is protected and made to look beautiful by coatings of a clear, hard finish. With a plate, dried flowers, and liquid white glue, you will make a beautiful découpaged craft that will look great in any room of your house. After you see how pretty your first project looks, you will be découpaging everything in sight.

Things You Need

book-dried flowers, leaves or ferns, see page 32
white paper or plastic plate
crayons
liquid white glue
paper cup
paintbrush
tweezers
plastic wrap or aluminum foil
stick-on picture hanger

Let's Begin

1. Start by making book-dried flowers, see page 292.
2. Decorate the inside rim of the plate with a crayon design.
3. Pour liquid white glue into a paper cup.
4. Paint the bottom of the inside of the plate with a coating of the glue, Fig. a.
5. Using the tweezers, carefully pick up the dried flowers and leaves from the paper. Arrange them on the glued surface.
6. Paint over the flowers with a light coating of glue, Fig. b.
7. Allow the glue to dry completely. While the plate is drying, cover the glue in the cup with plastic wrap or foil.
8. Give the entire plate a second coating of glue after the first coating has dried.
9. When dry, stick a picture hanger on the back of the plate to hang.

Pussy Willow Paintings

You know it's spring when you see pussy willows around. You probably think that they are meant for putting in vases only, but a beautiful form of painting can be done with the buds of pussy willow branches. In some areas of this country you can go out into the woods in the spring and find pussy willow. In most cases, however, you will have to buy branches of pussy willow from the florist.

Things You Need

white drawing paper
pencil
colored felt-tipped markers or crayons
pussy willow buds
liquid white glue
paper cup
paintbrush

Let's Begin

1. Draw a very simple design on a piece of drawing paper with a pencil, see the illustration for an example.
2. Color the drawing with felt-tipped markers or crayons. You can also make a drawing with pieces of colored construction paper cut into various shapes and pasted to the drawing paper.
3. Remove pussy willow buds from their branches.
4. Pour liquid white glue into a paper cup.
5. Paint an area on your picture with white glue.
6. Place pussy willow buds on the glued area.
7. Continue gluing pussy willow buds, wherever you want them on your picture.
8. Allow the pussy willow buds to dry.
9. The pussy willow buds can be tinted using colored felt-tipped markers.

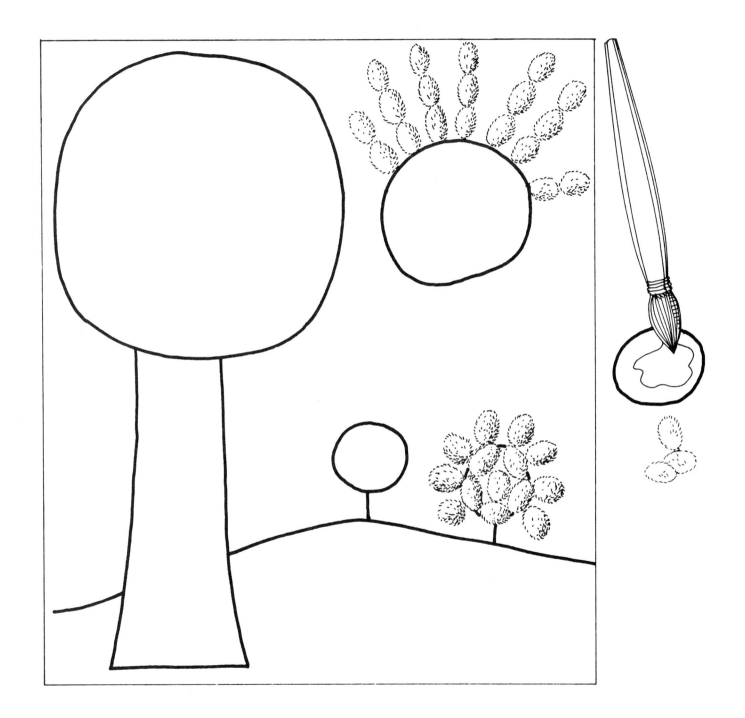

Stained Glass Collages

One of the most beautiful of all the art forms is stained glass. Churches all over the world are famous for their stained glass windows, and many old homes have small stained glass windows above their doors or elsewhere around the house. If you like stained glass windows, here is a craft that will give you something of the experience of making them yourself.

You won't be working with real glass, however. Flowers will form the basis of your picture. Waxed paper will seal the flowers down to produce the stained glass effect. You can hang several of these collages on your window or frame them for your bedroom wall.

Things You Need

white drawing paper

newspaper
waxed paper
book-dried flowers, see page 292
crayons
pencil or crayon sharpener
glitter (available at hobby or art supply stores)
iron

Let's Begin

1. Place a sheet of drawing paper on top of a piece of newspaper.
2. Place a sheet of waxed paper on top of the drawing paper. Arrange book-dried flowers, see page 292, on the waxed paper.
3. Remove the protective paper covering from old crayons and sharpen them over the flowers. Let the shavings fall evenly over the flowers.
4. Scatter glitter over the flowers and shavings.
5. Place a second sheet of waxed paper over the flowers and the decorations.
**6. Seal the two sheets together with an iron set at a low temperature.
7. "Hang" the collage in a bright window with tape.

Green is a leaf's special color

It's difficult to imagine the earth without nature's green—all the living green things which make it beautiful (and actually produce, through a process called photosynthesis, the oxygen we need to live). A tree growing out of the city pavement is a lovely green sight. The hills of the country are beautiful for, among other things, the many shades of green that extend from the valley to the top of the highest peaks. Nature has given the earth a soothing color to look at every day of the year, even in the cold of winter, when pine trees add their green color to snowy days.

Although green is for looking at, it is also for making wonderful crafts. The green we are concerned with here is that of the leaf, which provides us with many interesting project ideas. If you study a leaf very closely you will see a highway of veins. For the person who likes to paint or draw in lines, a leaf rubbing of this network is just what the doctor ordered. Leaves can be used to decorate things, and this chapter will show you how to stencil and print with them. You'll even be able to make a leaf "fossil" or leaf impression cast in plaster.

When you are gathering leaves, look for unusual shapes, different sizes, and different colors. Don't pick more leaves than you need—trees look funny if too many leaves are missing from them. You might start looking out the window for leaves right now, and when you go out bring a paper bag for collecting leaves with you. Invite your friends to join you on your leaf safari.

Leaf Printing

When you hear the word "printing," what comes to mind? Most likely it is putting words on a piece of paper by means of type. There are many kinds of printing using many different things to make impressions: sponges, carved wood, and carved potatoes. This project uses leaves to make prints. You will be amazed to discover how many different leaf printings you can make.

Things You Need

liquid white glue
tree leaves
cardboard
poster paint or an ink pad
paintbrush
white drawing paper

Let's Begin

1. Squeeze liquid white glue around the edges of the top side of a leaf, Fig. a. The top side of the leaf is the smoother of the sides—the one without raised veins or stem.
2. Glue the leaf onto a piece of cardboard, Fig. b.
3. Allow the leaf to dry on the cardboard.
4. "Ink" the leaf by painting a thin coating of poster paint on it, Fig. c., or by pressing the leaf surface onto an ink pad.
5. Make a leaf printing by pressing the "inked" side of the leaf onto a sheet of drawing paper. Press heavily on the cardboard.
6. Carefully lift the cardboard, Fig. d. Repeat the process as many times as you want for various design effects. Make other printers with differently shaped leaves.

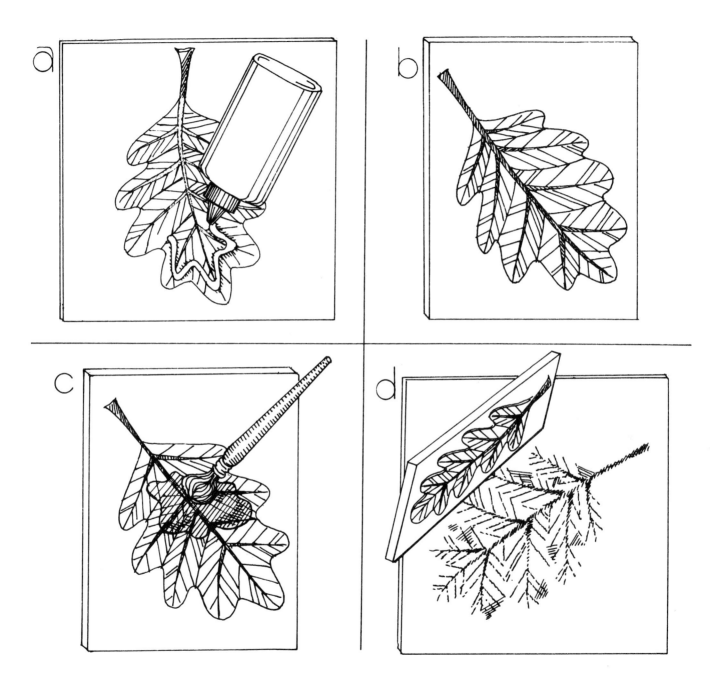

Leaf Stenciling

When was the last time you had to stencil something? It might have been a lettered heading for a homework assignment for school. The letters of the alphabet are stamped out of heavy cardboard in this kind of stencil and all you do is trace around the outline of the cutout letter with a pencil or pen. You can use leaves as stencils too. Gather all kinds of leaves, and you can make as many stencils as you want. You can stencil book covers, homework reports, or anything that needs nature's touch.

Things You Need

newspaper
paintbrush
poster paints
paper plate
sponge
tree leaves
white drawing paper
straight pins
old toothbrush
ice-cream stick

Let's Begin

SPONGE STENCILING
1. Spread newspaper over your working area to protect it.
2. Using a paintbrush, brush a little poster paint into the paper plate.
3. Wet a sponge, then squeeze all of the water out of it.
4. Place a leaf on a sheet of drawing paper.
5. Dip one end of the sponge into the paint. Dab the sponge up and down to get an even coating of paint on the sponge's surface.
6. Holding the leaf in place with your fingers, dab the painted side of the sponge over the leaf's edges and onto the paper, Fig. a.
7. Lift the leaf carefully to reveal the stenciled design.

SPATTER STENCILING
**1. Pin a leaf onto a piece of drawing paper with straight pins.
2. Pour a little poster paint into the plate.
3. Dip an old toothbrush into the paint. Shake off excess paint.
4. Holding the toothbrush over the leaf, rub the ice-cream stick across the bristles of the brush. The paint will spatter over the leaf and paper, Fig. b. Cover the paper around the leaf with spattering.
5. When the paint is dry, remove the pins and lift the leaf. Try spattering different colors of paint on top of one another for interesting effects.

a

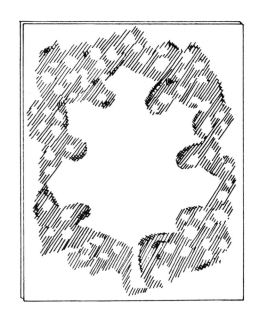

b

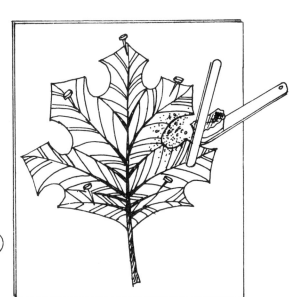

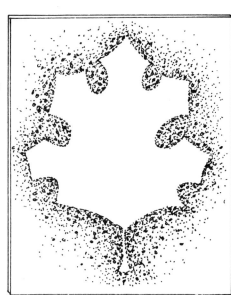

Leaf Rubbings

Making rubbings of different things can be a lot of fun. If you put a coin behind a piece of paper and rub a pencil over the paper where it covers the coin, an image of the coin will appear. What happens is that the raised surfaces of the coin "catch" the pencil strokes while lower surfaces do not. You may have done rubbings like this with other objects, but have you ever tried it with leaves? If you haven't, then you are in for some fun.

Things You Need

liquid white glue
tree leaves
typewriter paper or other lightweight paper
crayons

Let's Begin

1. Squeeze liquid white glue around the edges of the top side of several leaves, Fig. a. The top side of the leaf is the smoother of the sides—the one without raised veins or stem.
2. Glue the leaves onto a sheet of the paper, Fig. b. The raised sides of the leaves should face you.
3. Allow the leaves to dry.
4. Place another sheet of paper over the leaves, Fig. c.
5. Remove the protective paper covering from an old crayon.
6. Rub over the surface of the top paper with the side of the crayon, Fig. d. The veins and shape of the leaf under your rubbing will appear. Try using different colors of crayon for the different leaves, or for different parts of a single leaf.

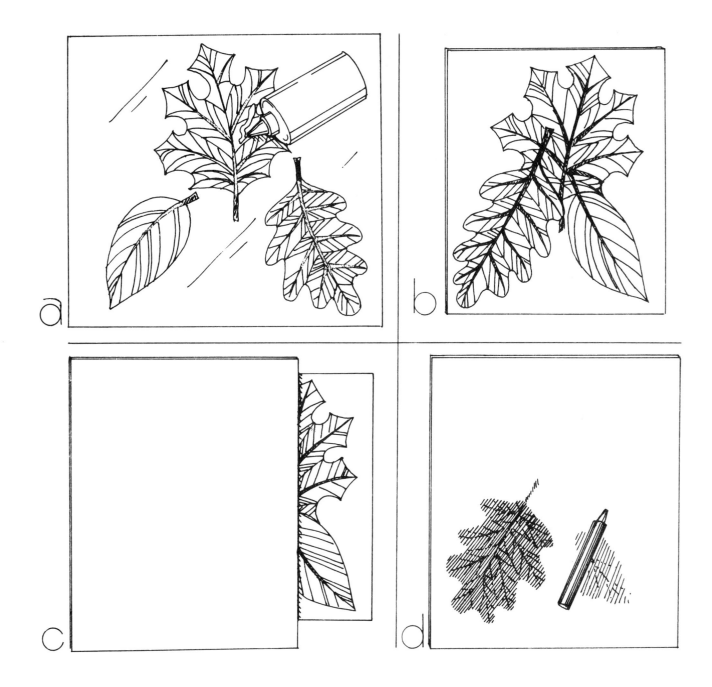

Leaf Casting

Millions of years ago, dinosaurs roamed the earth. When they were thirsty, they went to the rivers and streams for a drink of water. Little did they know they would leave something behind them that is still around today: their footprints in the mud. Over the years the mud hardened, and we can still see the size and shape of the dinosaurs' feet today. These hardened impressions are called fossils, and you can make something like them using leaves. All you need is plaster of paris, a little water, and a few minutes for drying. You won't have to wait millions of years for "fossils" of your own making.

Things You Need

disposable pie tin
large tin can
tree leaves
plaster of paris
spoon
paper clip
poster paint or watercolor paints (optional)

Let's Begin

1. Fill the pie tin with water, then pour the water into the can. Fill the pie tin again, this time half full, and add the water to the can.

2. Wet the top or smooth side of the leaf and stick it to the bottom of the disposable pie tin, Fig. a. The underneath or veined side of the leaf should face you.
3. Stirring all the while, add enough plaster of paris to the water in the can to make a mixture resembling loose whipped cream. Work as quickly as you can, and blend thoroughly.
4. Spoon some of the plaster of paris mixture onto the center of the leaf and spread it over the leaf until the leaf is covered, Fig. b.
5. Fill the pie tin with the remaining plaster of paris, Fig. c.
6. Set a paper clip into the plaster near the edge of the filled tin so that half of the clip remains in the plaster and half over the edge of the tin. The looped end of the clip will be used to hang the finished project.
7. In a half hour, remove the plaster carefully from the pie tin. The plaster is dry when it feels cool to the touch.
8. For an all-white casting, peel the leaf away now, Fig. d.
9. For a colored casting, paint the plaster before you peel away the leaf. When you remove the leaf, the leaf's impression will be white against a colored background.
10. Hang the casting by the paper-clip loop.

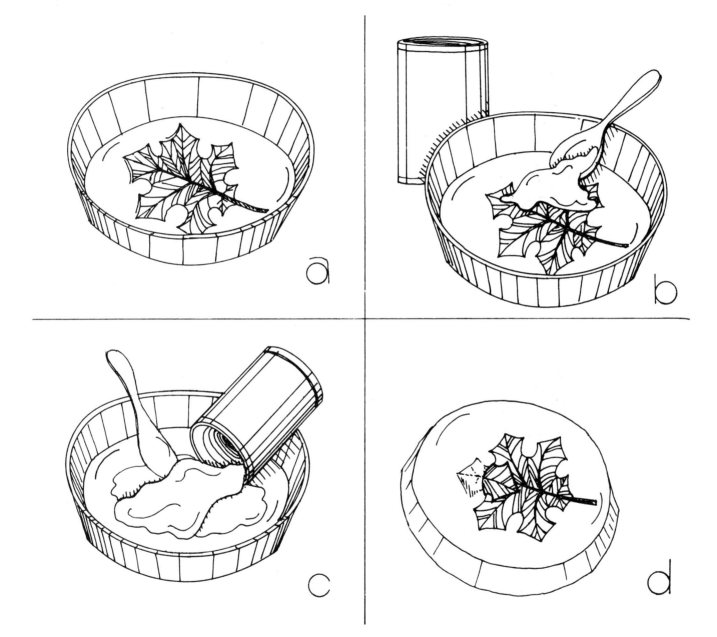

a

b

c

d

Fern in a Candle

Before Thomas Edison perfected the electric light bulb, and before the era of gaslight, people used candles as a source of light. People worked, ate, and read by flickering candles. Today, candles are found on top of birthday cakes, in churches, and as decorations in your home; you may even have one in your room. If you don't, here is a project that combines two of nature's products: wax and ferns.

Things You Need

scissors
pint or milk carton
butter
play clay (any non-hardening clay)
candle
2 saucepans, one larger than the other
small tin can
paraffin (canning wax)
fern

Let's Begin

1. Cut off the top part of a pint carton or half a milk carton, Fig. a.
2. Wash and dry the carton and butter the inside.
3. Place a ball of clay in the center of the bottom of the carton.
4. Choose a candle about as high as the cut carton.

5. Push the candle in the ball of clay at the bottom of the carton. The candle should stand up straight, Fig. b.
6. Fill the larger saucepan half full of water, and place on the stove.
7. Put the tin can in the center of the saucepan.
8. Add paraffin to the smaller saucepan.
9. Put the smaller saucepan into the larger. It should rest on the can in the water, Fig. c.
**10. Put the saucepan arrangement on a top burner of your stove. Turn on the stove carefully to a medium heat. The wax in the upper pot will melt slowly as the water begins to heat. Never take your eyes away from the melting wax.
11. When the wax has just melted, turn off the heat.
12. Put a fern into the carton. Trim the top if it comes above the edge of the carton.
**13. Carefully pour the melted wax into the carton, and up to the candlewick, Fig. d. Be sure the fern stands up straight.
**14. If you have not melted enough paraffin to fill the carton, allow the wax to harden in the carton before you melt and then add more wax.
15. When the wax has hardened completely, peel away the carton to unmold your candle, Fig. e.

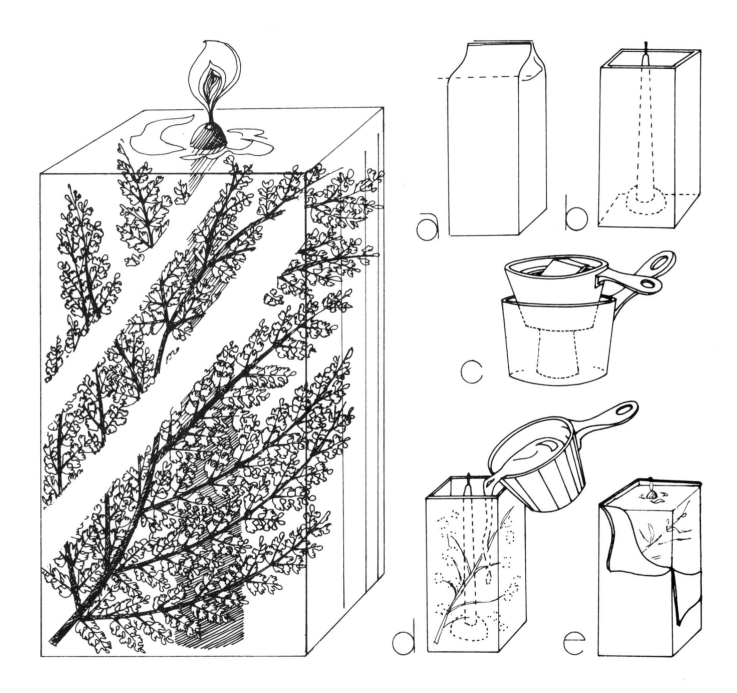

a

b

c

d

e

Wax Leaf Ropes

In ancient times, men frequently wore a bit of nature around their heads. If you look at pictures of famous men of the Roman Empire, you will see many of them wearing wreaths of golden leaves. This meant they had special power in the country. Leaf wreaths are also worn today as signs of peace and love. Necklaces, too, can be made like wreaths and spray-painted many different colors. You can make a leaf rope that can be worn about your head as a wreath, or used as a necklace.

Things You Need

paraffin (canning wax)
2 saucepans, one larger than the other
small tin can
newspaper
small tree or bush leaves
waxed paper
needle and thread
small tube macaroni

Let's Begin

**1. Melt wax as explained in *Fern Candle,* page 308.
**2. Remove the pot with the melted wax and place it on the newspaper.
**3. Holding a leaf by its stem, dip it completely into the melted wax. Repeat with all the leaves.
4. Place the waxed leaves on a sheet of waxed paper.
**5. Thread a needle with sewing thread.
6. When the leaves have hardened to the touch but are still warm, "thread" them. To do this, pass the threaded needle through the front of the leaf near the top and back through to the front near the bottom, see illustration.
7. Thread a tube macaroni between each leaf. Continue the alternate stringing of leaves and macaroni until you have a rope.
8. Tie the ends of the thread together when the rope is as long as you want it.

Placemats
and Coasters

Now is your chance to use nature to decorate your dinner table. You can design a set of placemats and coasters you will be proud to sit down to. Find the prettiest leaves you can. Gather all sizes and shapes. This craft would make a great gift for your relatives when you go visiting.

Things You Need

scissors
heavy white drawing paper or colored construction paper
liquid white glue
large tree leaves
waxed paper
heavy books
paintbrush
varnish or liquid plastic finish, available in hardware or art supply stores.

Let's Begin

PLACEMATS
1. Cut heavy paper into rectangles that are large enough to hold a plate and tableware.
2. Squeeze liquid white glue around the en-tire underneath or veined sides of the leaves, Fig. a.
3. Glue the leaves onto the paper in arrangements that please you, see illustration for an example.
4. Place a piece of waxed paper over the glued leaves.
5. Stack the books over the waxed paper.
6. When the leaves have dried, carefully peel away the waxed paper.
**7. Brush a coating of varnish or plastic finish on to the placemats covering the leaves thoroughly.
**8. When the first coating has dried, give the mats a second coating.
**9. When the second coating has dried, give the mats a third and final coating.

COASTERS
1. Cut heavy paper into square pieces somewhat larger than individual leaves.
2. Using liquid white glue, glue the leaves onto the paper, Fig. b. Be sure to glue them veined side down.
3. When the leaves are dry, cut them from the paper following their outlines, Fig. c.
4. Follow the same directions to finish the coasters as you did the placemats.

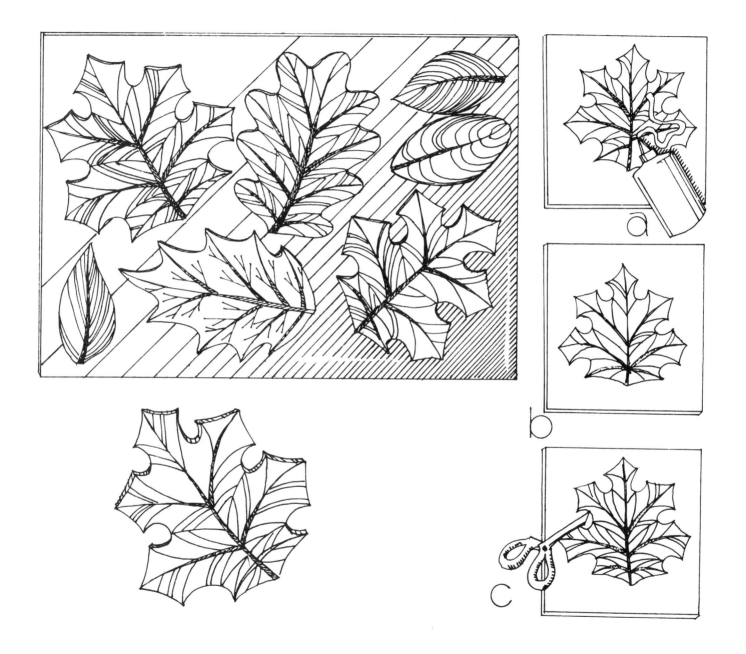

a

b

c

Glycerin Leaves

If you want to preserve a beautiful branch of leaves, this craft is for you. Glycerin—a colorless, odorless syrup that is very sweet—will do the trick. It comes from fats and oils, and is one of the by-products of soapmaking. After being treated with the glycerin, the leaves you collect become stiff, and won't disintegrate or fade. Depending upon the season and where you live, you may use green leaves or leaves that have just turned colors.

Things You Need

small branch with leaves, either green or just
  turning colors
newspaper
hammer
large jar
glycerin (available at drugstores)
scissors
colored construction paper
tall fruit drink can
colored felt-tipped markers or crayons
tape

Let's Begin

1. Place the branch on several layers of newspaper.
**2. With the hammer, tap the end of the stem until it is slightly crushed and feels soft, Fig. a.
3. In the jar, mix one part glycerin to two parts water.
4. Place the pounded end of the branch into the glycerin mixture. Leave the branch in the glycerin for two weeks, by which time the leaves should be preserved. They will have gotten thicker to the touch, and their color will have changed slightly.
5. Cut a piece of colored construction paper as high as the fruit drink can and long enough to wrap all the way around it.
6. Draw a design along the top length of the paper with colored felt-tipped markers or crayons, see illustration.
7. Tape the paper around the can, Fig. b.
8. Display the leaves in the can.

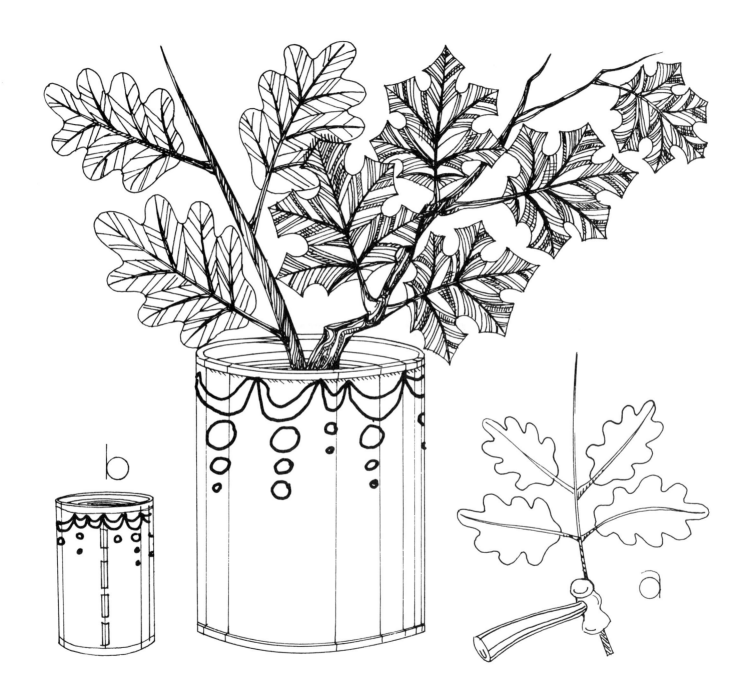

b

a

Lucky Clover Bookmark

"I'm looking over a four-leaf clover" is a line from a song composed many years ago. Four-leaf clovers are supposed to bring good luck and the song celebrates the discovery of one. Have you ever found a four-leaf clover? If you look long and hard, you may be able to locate some. In fact, you might well find clovers with five, six, seven, eight, even eleven leaves. Although most clover has only three leaves, clover with more than three leaves are often unearthed.

Although it would be nice to use a four-leaf clover for this craft, the more common three-leaf variety will do very well indeed. The bookmark you make with one will be lucky in that it will help prevent you from losing your place when you stop your reading.

Things You Need

clover, preferably four-leaf, but any kind will
  do
typewriter paper
heavy book
colored construction paper
liquid white glue
paper cup
paintbrush

Let's Begin

1. Put the clover between two sheets of typewriter paper. Press between the pages of a heavy book.
2. In a few days, check to see if the clover has dried. When it has, take it from between the pressing paper.
3. Cut a strip of colored construction paper a little longer than the book for which you are making the bookmark.
4. Pour a little white glue into a paper cup.
5. Paint the back of the clover with a thin coating of glue.
6. Carefully pick up the glued clover and place it on one end of the paper strip, see illustration. When the clover dries, your bookmark is ready for use.

Twigs are presents from a tree

Some of the most exciting crafts you can make come from things that grow right in your own back yard. They come from those huge growing things called trees. If you live in a big city, you may not see too many trees. You may have to travel to the country, or to a park to be really close to one. You really shouldn't have to look too far, however. Almost every part of the world has some trees growing on it. The only exceptions are the desert and the icy polar areas.

Making things from trees has always been important—not only to man, but to animals as well. Many animals use trees for building their homes. Birds make nests from small twigs. Beavers cut down trees to build dams across streams. Even chimpanzees use twigs as a tool to get termites out of termite holes.

The chimp puts a twig in the termite hole, and the termites cling to it. When the twig is taken out of the hole, the chimp has a tasty snack. It is interesting to think that people have copied the habits of animals and are today still building homes from wood cut from trees.

Unlike the chimp, we will use twigs for some good craftwork. Whenever you are near a tree and see some dead branches lying beneath it, collect them for the wood projects in this chapter. Remove the twigs, and stack them according to size. You will need very skinny twigs as well as fat ones. A twig hunt can be a lot of fun, but always remember not to take branches that are alive and have green leaves on them. There are plenty of "twig presents" under the trees to make the crafts which follow.

Charm Mobile

Do you know what a mobile is? It is a collection of objects that hang from another object, much bigger in size. This construction doesn't sound too exciting in itself. What is needed to make it more interesting is a light gust of wind. When wind passes through the hanging objects, they sway gracefully in all directions. They move, or become mobile.

You can gather a collection of your favorite things to make a mobile, or begin by using the objects suggested below. In either case, you will have a lot of fun making and watching this "action" toy.

Things You Need

scissors
colored construction paper
paper punch
colored felt-tipped markers or crayons
macaroni, sequins, stick-on paper stars, glitter
liquid white glue
string or yarn
small branch without leaves

Let's Begin

1. Cut different shapes from colored construction paper such as circles, stars, hearts, and triangles.
2. Punch a hole near the top of each paper shape with a paper punch.
3. Decorate the shapes with designs using crayons or colored felt-tipped markers, stick-on paper stars, or by adding macaroni and sequins with liquid white glue.
4. Tie one end of a length of string or yarn through the hole of each decorated shape.
5. Tie the other end of the string or yarn to an arm of the branch.
6. Tie a long length of yarn or string to both ends of the branch for hanging, see illustration.
7. Hang the mobile in your room in an open place so the charms may move freely.

Gumdrop Tree

Some of the strangest-looking things grow on trees. If you read some of your favorite stories, you learn that lollipops, ice cream cones, and even money can be found hanging in the forest. Nature is filled with surprises, but of a different kind than you sometimes read about. What you will find in the woods is a handful of acorns, a tasty apple, or a spindly pine cone. Only you can make a lollipop tree, or maybe a gumdrop tree. If you read on, you will soon have one growing in your own room.

Things You Need

ice-cream stick or spoon
plaster of paris
paper cup
small can
small branch without leaves
scissors
colored construction paper
tape
gumdrops or other candy
cellophane or plastic wrap
string or cord

Let's Begin

1. Using an ice-cream stick or a small spoon, mix water and plaster of paris in a paper cup until it has the consistency of heavy cream. Add water carefully at first to the plaster, mixing all the while; you don't want to add too much water too quickly.
2. Pour the plaster mixture into the can. Fill it halfway.
3. Wait a few minutes, and then push the end of the branch into the plaster in the can.
4. If the branch does not stand by itself in the plaster, hold it until the plaster sets enough for it to do so.
5. Cut a piece of colored construction paper as high as the can and long enough to wrap around it.
6. Wrap the paper around the can and tape it in place.
7. Stand a gumdrop on a piece of cellophane or plastic wrap that has been cut about three times larger than the gumdrop, Fig. a.
8. Bring the ends of the wrap over the top of the gumdrop, Fig. b.
9. Tie the wrap closed with a piece of string or cord, Fig. c.
10. After the plaster has hardened, tie the gumdrops to the branches of the tree.

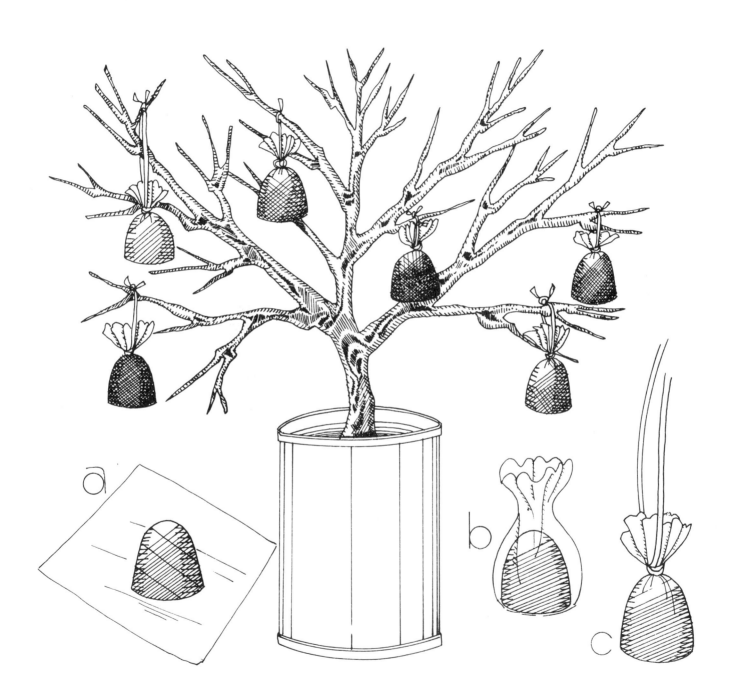

a

b

c

Tomahawk

When you think of the American Indian, many things may come to mind. He was one of the greatest woodsmen living in any country at any time in history. He made all of his own clothing, built his home, hunted his food, and made all of the tools he needed to live. One of the tools that was and still is today very important to him is the tomahawk. It was used as a weapon in wartime, and during peacetime it had a hundred-and-one uses. If you enjoy thinking about the American Indian and his way of life, then you may well want a tomahawk of your own.

Things You Need

thick twig
rectangular sponge
thick cord
scissors

Let's Begin

1. Find a thick twig that feels right in your hand for a tomahawk handle, see illustration.
2. Lay a rectangular sponge over the twig near one end.
3. Slip a thick cord under the twig at the bottom of the sponge, Fig. a.
4. Cross the ends of the cord over the sponge, Fig. b.
5. Bring the ends of the cord back under the end of the twig, Fig. c.
6. Pull the ends tightly on the underside of the twig and knot.
7. Cut away the excess ends of the cord.

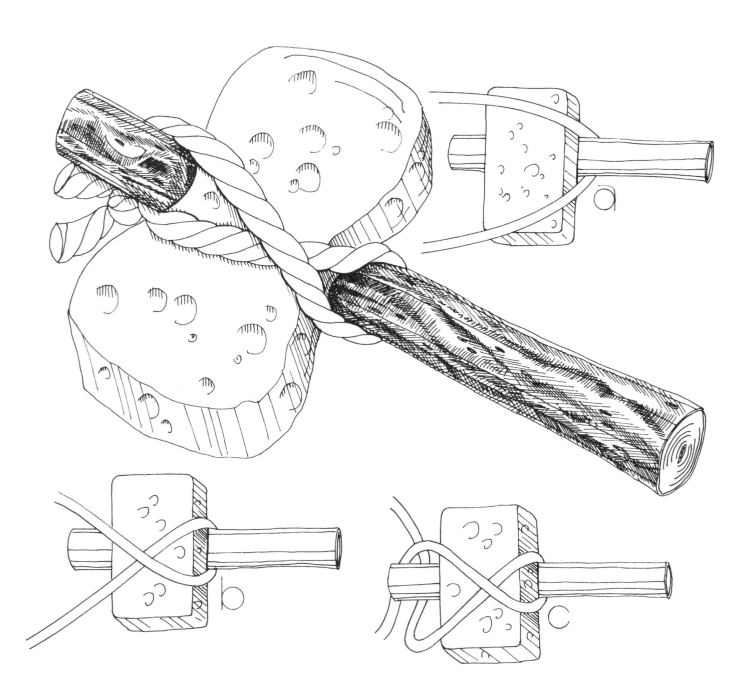

Eye of God

The Eye of God is an interesting craft that comes from Mexico. It is made with two twigs and different colored yarn. Two twigs are crossed and yarn is tied around them. If you use several colors, it will look like a big eye. This is how it got its name.

Things You Need

2 thickish twigs, one longer than the other
liquid white glue
colored yarn
macaroni or beads with large holes

Let's Begin

1. Make a cross with the twigs. That is, cross the smaller twig over the larger near the top of the larger.
2. Using liquid white glue, glue the two twigs together.
3. When the glue has dried, tie the end of a length of colored yarn around the point where the twigs cross on the back side of the cross, Fig. a.
4. Bring the yarn over arm 1 of the cross, down and then under it, Figs. b and c.
5. Bring the yarn behind arm 2. Bring the yarn over arm 2 of the cross, around and over, then behind it, Fig. d.
6. Bring the yarn down behind arm 3 of the cross, around and over, then behind it, Fig. e.
7. Bring the yarn behind arm 4 of the cross, around and over, then behind it, Fig. f.
8. You have now connected the four arms of the crossed twigs by wrapping the yarn around each arm in exactly the same way.
9. Repeat the procedure, doing four more yarn windings.
10. Continue to wrap the yarn around the cross, always moving outward along the arms. (You can use different colored yarns as you wind, or you can thread beads or tube macaroni onto the yarn).
11. Leave a little bit of wood visible at the top and on the sides of the arms. Let more wood show at the bottom.
12. Glue the end of the yarn to the back side of the Eye of God.

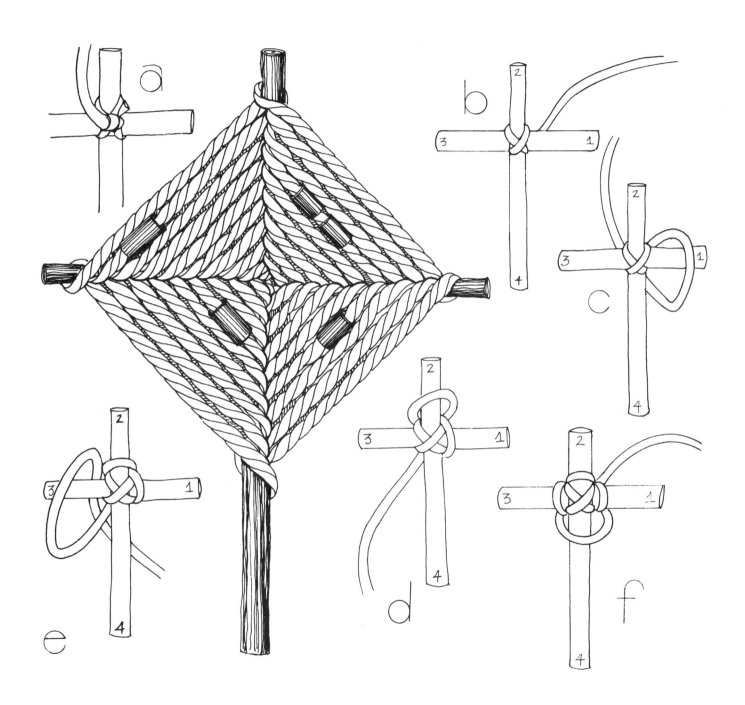

a

b

c

d

e

f

Picture Frame

If you would like to bring the adventure of the woods into your room, do it by framing some of your favorite outdoor pictures. If you don't have any, get some from magazines. Cut out pictures that interest you, and make your own frames. All you need is four twigs. No matter how big or how small your picture may be, you can make a frame to fit it.

Things You Need

4 twigs all the same size, or 2 of one size and 2 of another.
waxed paper
liquid white glue
thick cord
scissors
colored construction paper
ruler
pencil
tape

Let's Begin

1. Lay two of the same-sized twigs a distance apart on a sheet of waxed paper.
2. Lay the other two twigs across the first two.
3. Arrange the four twigs so that the ends of each stick out a little from the square, Fig. a.
4. Glue the twigs at the points where they cross, using the liquid white glue.
5. Let the frame dry overnight.
6. Tie an Indian knot around the twigs at each of the four corners of the frame. To make the Indian knot, first run the cord where two twigs meet from corner to opposite corner on what will be the underside of the frame, Fig. b.
7. The two ends of the cord will meet. Twist them around each other as if you were making an everyday knot on the front of the frame, Fig. c.
8. The two ends now go to the back of the frame, each end around one of the untied corners, Fig. d, back view.
9. Tie the ends together in a tight knot, Fig. e.
10. Cut a piece of colored construction paper to fit perfectly in the frame.
11. Use a ruler to draw a window in the center of the paper. There should be an equal amount of paper border on all sides of the window, Fig. f.
12. Cut out the window.
13. Tape a picture into the window. Make sure the picture is centered.
14. Glue the paper with the picture to the back of the frame.

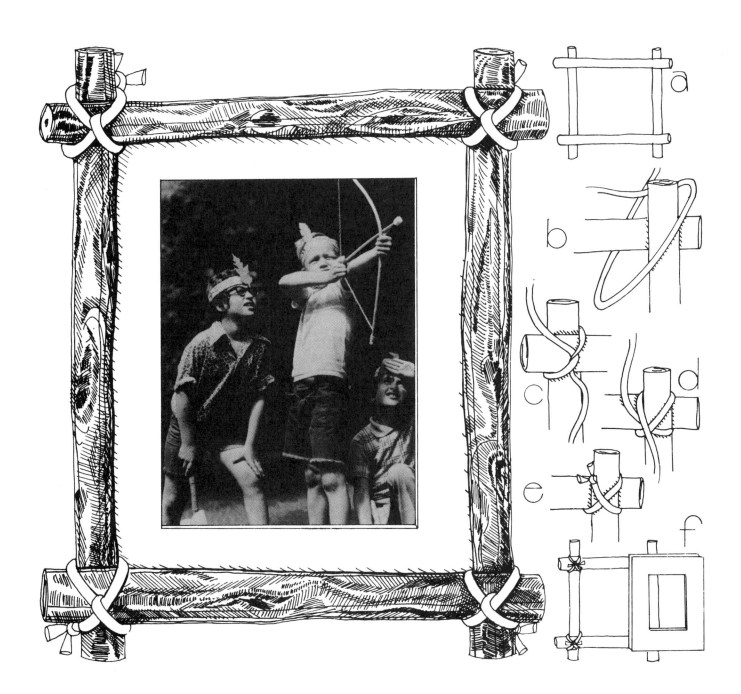

a

b

c

d

e

f

Tepee

The American Indian built a home that was comparatively simple to make. All he had to do was to chop down some tall young trees, cut off all branches, tie the narrow ends of the trees together, and stand the framework up. Around this he wrapped skins or bark from trees. In a matter of hours, he could construct a home for himself and his family.

You may not have room in your home for a large tepee, but you can learn the skills of the Indians by making a smaller version. If you make enough tepees, you can have a whole Indian nation.

Things You Need

scissors
small dish
pencil
cardboard
6 twigs
cord
liquid white glue
colored construction paper
colored felt-tipped markers or crayons
tape

Let's Begin

1. Cut a circle from the cardboard. Use the small dish to trace the circle.
**2. Cut out six small equally spaced holes around the outer edge, Fig. a.
**3. Saw the twigs so that they are equal in size (or maybe you can find six twigs of the same size).
4. Push one end of each of the twigs a little bit through the holes in the cardboard so that the little feet are the same length, Fig. b.
5. Gather all the twigs at the top and tie them together with a piece of cord, Fig. c. Add a dab of glue to the knot.
6. With crayons or colored felt-tipped markers, draw Indian designs on a long piece of colored construction paper that is as tall as the tepee frame and will fit around it. Tape pieces of construction paper together if you need a very long piece.
7. Wrap the paper around the tepee's frame, and tape the ends together, Fig. d.
8. Trim the bottom of the paper to the height of the inside cardboard circle, Fig. e.
9. Cut a triangular door out of the bottom edge of the paper cover.

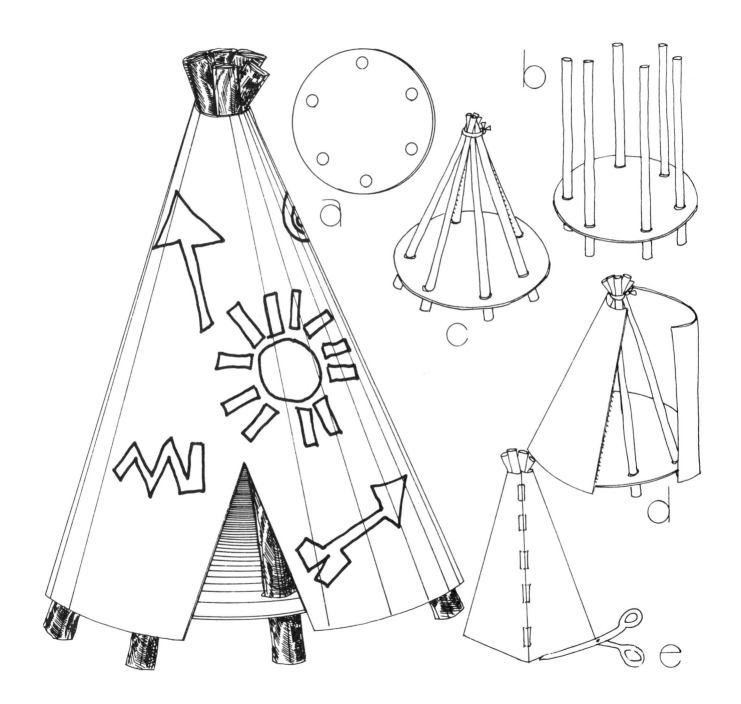

Log Cabin

When the first settlers came to America they built wooden homes. Not having the tools they needed with them, they devised a simple means of construction using logs to build their cabins. These structures had only one room with a fireplace. Everything was done in this one room. There are very few original log cabins still standing, but you can see something of what they looked like when you build one yourself. You can imagine how difficult it was to live in America many hundreds of years ago!

Things You Need

at least 14 twigs of the same thickness
saw
waxed paper
liquid white glue
colored construction paper
scissors
colored felt-tipped markers or crayons.

Let's Begin

**1. Saw all the twigs to the same length.
2. Place two twigs (group Number 1 in Fig. a) on a sheet of waxed paper a little away from each other, Fig. a.
3. Place two more twigs (Number 2) over the first two twigs. Arrange the twigs to look as they do in Fig. b.
4. Once the four twigs are in place, lift up one Number 2 twig and squeeze a dab of liquid white glue on the places where it touches the Number 1 twigs.
5. Glue the twig carefully in place on the Number 1 twigs.
6. Do the same with the other Number 2 twig, Fig. b.
7. Let the four twigs dry completely.
8. When dry, glue two more Number 1 twigs over the glued frame.
9. Follow with two more Number 2 twigs.
10. Keep building up twigs, letting each group of four dry before you add four more.
11. Make the roof out of a piece of colored construction paper folded in half. Cut the paper to fit neatly across the top of the cabin.
12. Draw a shingle design onto the roof with crayons or colored felt-tipped markers.
13. Cut a strip of colored construction paper to make a chimney.
14. Fold the strip in half and cut the ends of the strip into a point, Fig. c. Draw a brick design on it.
15. Cut two small slits in the roof, Fig. d.
16. Push the points of the chimney into the slits in the roof.
17. Glue the roof to the log cabin and your log cabin is finished.

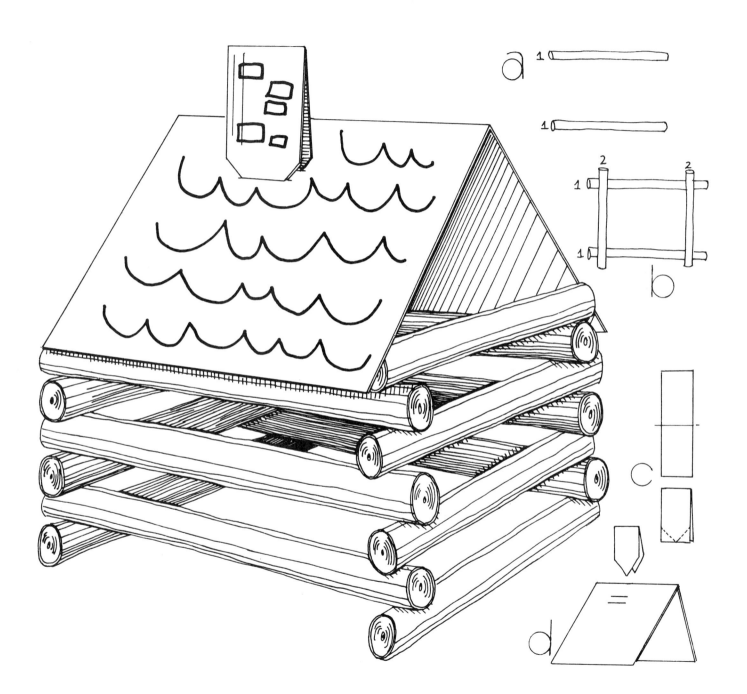

Bird Feeder

One important thing you and nature's feathered friends have in common, as you might well guess, is the need for food. You can help feed them by hanging one of these bird feeders outside your window, and putting birdseed in it.

Things You Need

cardboard or oaktag
scissors
pencil
ruler
liquid white glue
twigs
saw
waxed paper
cord

Let's Begin

1. Cut the cardboard into two triangles of equal size. Make the sides of the triangles longer than the bottom.
2. Using a pencil and ruler, draw a line down the three sides of each triangle a little way in from the edges, see dotted line in Fig. a.
3. Cut a slit from the points of the triangles to the points where the pencil lines cross. See the three heavy lines in Fig. a.
4. Cut out a triangular shape from the bottom center of each triangle, see shaded area in Fig. a.
5. Make folds along all the pencil lines.
6. Overlap the cut paper points on each corner and glue them down. This gives edges to the triangles, Fig. b.
**7. Saw all but three of the twigs to the same size. These three should be longer.
8. On a piece of waxed paper, lay out the right number of twigs to fit as a floor between the two bottom corners of each triangle. Use a long twig for the center twig of the floor, Fig. c.
9. Squeeze glue between all the twigs.
10. Squeeze glue on the bottom edge of each triangle.
11. Glue each triangle, with the folded sides facing in, across the twigs, Fig. d.
12. Let the glue dry overnight.
13. On a piece of waxed paper, lay out the twigs to fit one side of the feeder. Use a long twig on the top corner, Fig. e.
14. Squeeze liquid white glue between the twigs and on corresponding edges of each triangle. Glue triangles to the twigs, Fig. e. Let dry thoroughly.
15. Repeat the procedure of making a twig side and gluing it to the remaining triangle edges. Make sure that both long twigs are together at the top of the feeder.
16. Tie a length of cord around the two long top twigs for hanging the feeder.

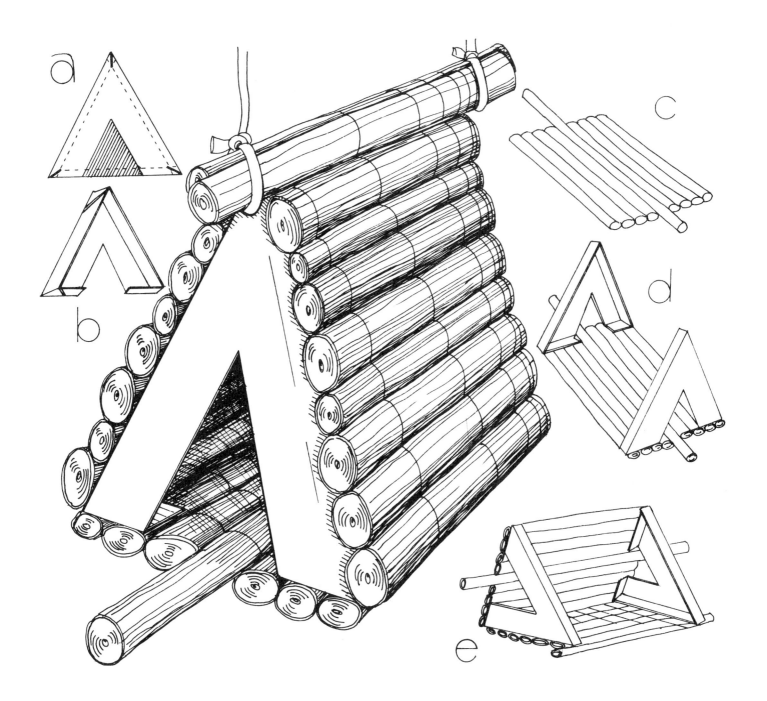

a

b

c

d

e

Fishing Pole and Bow and Arrow

When you think of the hunting tools of the Indians, you probably think first of bows and arrows. When the Indians went fishing they used a long pole with a hook attached to it. These were very useful food-gathering tools indeed. Today's bow and arrow and fishing pole really haven't changed all that much. Why not make some of your own? You will probably enjoy these even more than the kind you buy.

Things You Need

string
long, thin, straight twigs
short twigs
marshmallows
safety pin

Let's Begin

BOW AND ARROW
1. Tie string to both ends of a long, thin, straight twig. Pull it tightly so that the twig bends, see illustration. Don't make your bow too large to handle.
2. Make the arrows from shorter twigs with a marshmallow pushed on one end as an arrowhead.

FISHING POLE
1. Tie a string to one end of a long, thin twig.
2. Tie a safety pin (opened) to the end of the string. (Hope you catch a big one.)

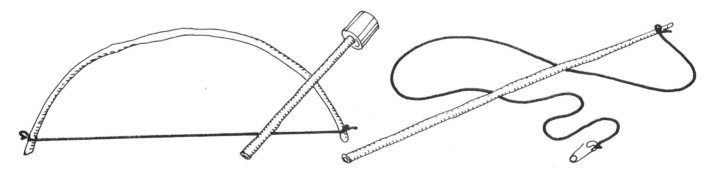

A pine cone is a nursery for seeds

A pine cone might be called a nursery for seeds. Seeds stay in this nursery until they are old enough to leave their rooms and fall to the ground to become a giant pine tree. Once this happens, the pine cone goes out of business and falls to the earth. Did you know that cones grow on other trees as well? Spruce, fir, and balsam grow cones. Unless you know the kind of tree you are looking at, you won't know what kind of cone you have.

Animals as well as people use the seeds of pine cones. Both squirrels and people eat the seeds. We call them Indian nuts, because the Indians used them for food. They are very tasty and can be used in cooking. You will not find seeds large enough to eat, so leave them to the squirrels.

The variety of Indian nuts that people eat comes from Europe. They grow in pine cones that are almost one foot long.

Pine cones are good to use in craft projects. Be sure to bring a large paper bag with you on your next journey into the forest, but never pick cones that are still on the trees. They are still alive and have not dropped their seeds. You may use any kind of cone for the crafts. If you can find a part of the forest where many cones have fallen, you should be able to gather enough for all the exciting projects in this chapter.

Wild Bird Feeder

If you live in the country you know that the wild birds are always looking for food. One way to feed them is with the kind of feeder that you put seeds into, and which birds come and perch on. There is another method of feeding these hungry critters. Believe it or not, a large pine cone, seeds, and a jar of peanut butter is all you need (you are not the only person who likes a good peanut butter dinner). Keep the jar of jelly in the house. If the wild birds ever taste peanut butter and jelly together, Mom will have to buy two jars of each—one for you and one for the birds!

Things You Need

cord
large pine cone
spoon
peanut butter
birdseed
waxed paper

Let's Begin

1. Tie the cord to the top petals of the pine cone.
2. Spoon peanut butter between the petals.
3. Place birdseed on the waxed paper.
4. Roll the peanut buttered pine cone in the birdseed.
5. Hang the feeder in a tree.

Feathered Friends

If you look at a pine tree, you will see birds flying in and out. Many birds nest in these trees because they offer good shelter and a nice place to live. You won't mistake pine cones for birds, unless they are decorated with paper wings and faces. You can make these pine cone birds if you follow the directions below. With a little imagination they will look like common birds you have seen in the forest. Collect long, round, and oval pine cones for this craft.

Things You Need

different shaped pine cones
pencil
scissors
colored construction paper
liquid white glue
crayons
string

Let's Begin

HANGING BIRD
1. Choose a long pine cone.
2. Cut two paper wings from colored construction paper and glue them to the sides of the pine cone, see illustration.
3. Cut a strip of paper twice as long as it is wide.
4. Fold the paper in half.
5. Cut out a circle from the folded paper, leav-ing part of the fold uncut, see illustration.
6. Cut a very small slit into the folded side of the circle.
7. Cut a small beak shape from construction paper and push it into the cut slit. Draw an eye on both sides of the beak.
8. Open the paper head slightly, and glue over the wide end of the pine cone.
9. Tie string to a top petal and hang.

TURKEY
1. Lay a round pine cone on its side.
2. Cut several paper feathers from construction paper, see illustration.
3. Draw vein designs on the feathers with crayons.
4. Glue the feathers into the top petals of the pine cone.
5. Cut a head and neck out of construction paper, see illustration. Draw an eye on the head and glue on a red paper circle under the eye for a wattle (the fleshy piece of skin turkeys have under their necks.
6. Glue the head to the bottom of the pine cone.

OWL
1. Stand an oval pine cone on its bottom end.
2. Cut round paper eyes and a beak out of construction paper.
3. Glue the eyes and beak to the top of the pine cone.

Pine Cone Elves

Santa Claus is lucky because he has a group of faithful helpers. These elves help make the toys and load the sled for that all-night sleigh ride. You may or may not believe in Santa's elves, but a collection of these cute creatures would be fun to have.

Things You Need

scissors
cardboard
liquid white glue
small beads or dried beans
small, round pine cones
acorns, large beads, small foam balls
colored felt-tipped markers
yarn
pipe cleaners
colored construction paper
tab from soft-drink can
cotton tufts
stick-on paper stars
toothpick

Let's Begin

1. Cut a circle from the cardboard.
2. Glue two small beads or dried beans to the center of the cardboard circle. These will be feet for the figures.
3. Let the beads or beans dry.
4. Press the top petals of a pine cone on a table to make a flat surface (you will glue the head to this surface).
5. Glue the bottom of the pine cone to the feet on the cardboard circle. Make sure the feet stick out just a little.
6. When the cone has dried on the circle, glue an acorn, large bead, or small foam ball onto the top of the cone for a head.
7. Draw on eyes with felt-tipped markers.
8. Wrap a pipe cleaner around the upper part of the cone for arms.

ANGEL ELF
1. Glue yarn to the head for hair.
2. Make a book out of a folded square of colored construction paper and glue to the hands.
3. Use the tab from a soft-drink can for a halo.

MUSICIAN ELF
1. Make hair out of a strip of colored construction paper cut into a fringe.
2. Make a cone hat out of a circular piece of colored construction paper which is slit to the center and wrapped around itself. Glue the hat to the head.
3. Fold a strip of paper back and forth for an accordion and glue it to the hands.

MAGIC GODMOTHER ELF
1. Glue cotton tufts to the head for hair. Add stick-on paper stars to the hair.
2. Top a toothpick with a stick-on paper star. Glue wand to the pipe cleaner arms.

Cone Flowers

In this chapter the scales of a pine cone are referred to as petals. If you study a pine cone very carefully it looks very much like a flower made of wood. Just like a flower, a pine cone has petals that are closed while it is growing. When the cones are fully grown, they open their petals and spread their seeds so that new plants can grow. Collect an assortment of pine cones and you can create a garland of pretty cone flowers.

Things You Need

pipe cleaners
medium-sized round pine cones
scissors
colored construction paper
drinking straws
liquid white glue

Let's Begin

1. Wrap a pipe cleaner around the last ring of petals at the bottom of a pine cone. Twist ends together leaving one end of the pipe cleaner longer than the other end, Fig. a.
2. Cut a circle from colored construction paper twice as large as the bottom of a pine cone.
3. Cut circular petal shapes around the edge of the circle and make a small hole in the middle, Fig. b.
4. Push the longer end of the pipe cleaner through the center of the paper petals, Fig. c.
5. Twist the end of the pipe cleaner tightly around the top of a drinking straw.
6. Add a dab of liquid white glue where the pipe cleaner is wrapped around the straw. Let dry overnight.
7. Cut out green construction paper leaves and glue to straw stems.

Candle Holder

Candles are becoming more popular each and every day. You may have a decorative or funny candle somewhere in your room or elsewhere in your home. There is a special fascination about candles. It is fun to watch the flame dance with its favorite partner, the soft breeze that makes it flicker in all directions. The flame moves to every whisper and vibration in the room. If you talk to it, it seems to be talking back to you.

If you enjoy candles, then you will need a safe candle holder. You can make one with pine cones and a tin can. It can be used in your room for your enjoyment, or placed on the dining room table during the holiday season. Enjoying candles can be fun, but you must be extra careful with them. Candles involve fire, and you know how dangerous that can be. When you light a candle, always be careful.

Things You Need

yarn
small, round pine cones
tin can with label removed (soak off with hot
    water)
red poster paint or paper
paintbrush
ribbon
play clay (or any non-hardening clay)
candle

Let's Begin

1. Tie two pieces of yarn together around the last ring of petals at the bottom of each pine cone, Fig. a. Be sure each side has a length of yarn hanging from it.
2. Tie two pine cones together by knotting one length of yarn of one pine cone to another length of yarn on a second pine cone, Fig. b.
3. Continue tying pine cones together to form a string of pine cones long enough to fit around the tin can.
4. Paint the tin can with red poster paint or cover with red paper.
5. Arrange the cones around the bottom of the can, see illustration.
6. Tie a ribbon around the can and into a bow.
7. Stick a large ball of play clay onto the bottom of the tin can.
8. Push a candle into the clay.

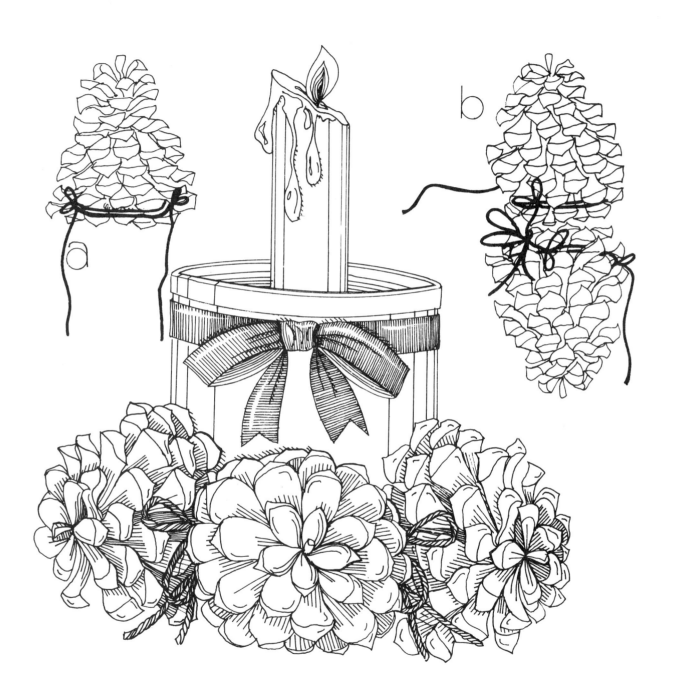

Door Wreath

When you are visiting friends and relatives at Christmas time, the first thing you notice is the wreath on the door. You can buy a pretty wreath at the store, but maybe this year you and your family can make one with pine cones. You may just have the most spectacular Christmas wreath in your neighborhood this holiday season.

Things You Need

pipe cleaners
small, round pine cones
pencil
large sheet of cardboard
compass or large plate and small plate
scissors
green poster paint
paintbrush
paper punch
red construction paper
string

Let's Begin

1. Wrap a pipe cleaner around the last ring of petals on the bottom of each pine cone and twist the ends together, leaving one end longer than the other, Fig. a.
2. Draw a large circle on the sheet of cardboard with a compass opened as wide as it will go or trace around a large plate.
3. Draw a smaller circle in the center of the larger circle with the compass or small plate.
**4. Cut out the larger circle from the cardboard.
**5. Cut out the smaller inner circle, Fig. b.
6. Paint the cardboard wreath shape with the green poster paint.
7. Punch a hole in the center of the rim, green side facing you, Fig. c.
8. Take one of the prepared pine cones and slip the end of the pipe cleaner through the punched hole.
9. Place a second pine cone next to the first cone on the circle. Mark, with a pencil, the center point where the second pine cone falls on the wreath.
10. Punch a hole through this pencil point.
11. Push the end of the pipe cleaner of the second cone through the second hole.
12. Twist the pipe cleaner ends of the first and second cone together on the underside of the wreath.
13. Continue marking points, punching holes, inserting pine cones, and twisting together pipe cleaner ends until the wreath is covered with cones.
14. Cut a bow from paper, Fig. d.
15. Punch two holes in the middle of the bow.
16. Put a pipe cleaner through the two holes.
17. Twist the pipe cleaner ends of the bow around a pine cone on the wreath.
18. Wrap the string around the top cone— and hang on a door.

Tall Tree

Pine cones grow on pine trees, but did you ever see a tree with just pine cones instead of branches? Of course you haven't. But you can make one very easily. Gather many small, round pine cones that are about the same size and shape. If you arrange them according to the directions, a beautiful pine cone tree will be the result. Place this tree in your bedroom, or maybe Mom can use it as a centerpiece for the dining room table.

Things You Need

large sheet of cardboard
compass or large plate
pencil
scissors
liquid white glue
small, round pine cones
white drawing paper
tape
ribbons

Let's Begin

1. Draw a large circle on the cardboard with a compass or trace around a large plate.
**2. Cut out the circle with the scissors.
3. Glue pine cones along the rim of the circle, Fig. a.
4. When the glue has dried, roll a piece of heavyweight paper into a cone that will fit into the ring of pine cones, Fig. b.
5. Tape the cone together.
6. Trim the bottom edge of the cone so that it will stand straight in the ring of pine cones.
7. Glue a second ring of pine cones on top of the first ring, placing each new cone between two previously attached cones. Glue cones to cones, pressing new cones closely against the paper cone.
8. Build rings of pine cones to the top of the paper cone. Each new ring should rest on the previously glued ring. The taller the paper cone, the taller your tree will be.
9. Tie lengths of ribbon into bows.
10. Glue ribbon bows onto the tree.

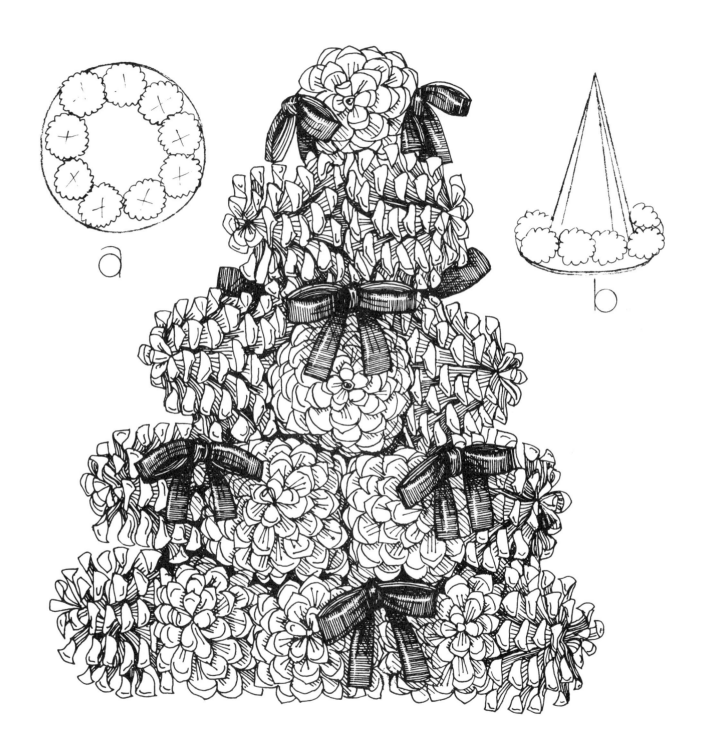

a

b

Small Christmas Tree

Christmas has its own special feeling. One of the things that creates that feeling is the annual shopping for the Christmas tree. You want one that is full so that it can be completely covered with decorations and lights.

It's too bad that Christmas can't be around all year long. The tree starts to turn yellow, and that is a sign that the holidays are over. You can keep a touch of Christmas all year long, however, by making a pine cone Christmas tree. Choose a large pine cone, and decorate it as you do a Christmas tree. Take it out whenever you get the Christmas feeling, even if it's during the hot summer months.

Things You Need

liquid white glue
paper cup
paintbrush
large well-formed pine cone
glitter or plastic snow
tiny glass balls or beads
scissors
yellow or gold stick-on paper stars

Let's Begin

1. Pour a little liquid white glue into a paper cup.
2. Paint the glue on all the petal tips of the pine cone.
3. Sprinkle glitter or plastic snow on all glued petals.
4. Shake off the excess glitter or snow.
5. Let the pine cone dry.
6. Glue tiny balls or beads wherever you wish on the pine cone. Some beads may be wedged between the petals.
7. Cut out shapes like stars and hearts from colored paper and glue them to the tree.
8. Attach a stick-on paper star to the top of the pine cone tree.

Beans, nuts, and seeds before they grow up

You learned from the last chapter that Indian nuts live and grow in pine cones. All seeds grow inside some kind of "home." Many of these homes are your favorite things to eat—fruits like watermelon. Beans and nuts are also seeds. The largest of all seeds is that tropical delight, the coconut. The shell of the coconut houses and protects the seed or meat within. Beans, seeds and nuts have one thing in common. If you plant them in the ground and give them proper care, they will grow into the living plants themselves. In this chapter, however, you will be making exciting crafts with seeds, not planting them.

There are many wonderful projects to make with seeds, things like bean bags, cantaloupe seed necklaces, and a fleet of walnut shell ships. As you look through this chapter, make a list of the different kinds of seeds you will need, and start collecting them. (Save watermelon seeds instead of spitting them into the garbage can or at your friends!) Let all seeds dry and place them in jars. You will enjoy making seed crafts, not to mention the fringe benefits derived from eating that great cold slice of melon or those delicious walnut meats!

Walnut Ships

One of the most adventurous journeys you could take would be on a sailing ship. Imagine being the captain of a three-masted clipper riding the waves to unknown places. Very few people are lucky enough to travel this way. If you've always wanted this type of life, start learning all about ships and how they are built. Or make your own fleet with walnut shells, toothpicks, and paper. Now you can be the captain of a sailboat, a three-masted clipper, and a pirate ship. All are seaworthy, and will give you hours of fun on the high seas of your bathtub.

Things You Need

play clay (any non-hardening clay)
walnut-shell halves
scissors
colored construction paper
liquid white glue
toothpicks
colored felt-tipped markers or crayons

Let's Begin

1. Press small balls of clay into walnut-shell halves. Continue by following the directions for one or more of the ships described below.

SAILBOAT
1. Cut a triangular sail from the colored construction paper. Don't make the sail larger than toothpick size.
2. Using liquid white glue, glue the sail to a toothpick. Leave enough toothpick at the bottom to push into the clay, see illustration.
3. Let the sail dry.

CLIPPER SHIP
1. Cut three squares from colored construction paper. Make one a little smaller than the other two.
2. Draw a design—like the cross in the illustration—on the smaller square with colored felt-tipped markers or crayons.
3. Push toothpicks through the tops and bottoms of each sail, see illustration. Leave enough toothpick mast at the bottom to push into the clay.
4. Cut an anchor from colored construction paper and glue it to the side of the shell.

PIRATE SHIP
1. Cut two rectangles from the colored construction paper, one larger than the other.
2. Decorate the larger rectangle with a pirate's skull and crossbones, see illustration.
3. Using liquid white glue, glue the sails, with the larger one on the bottom, to the toothpick, see illustration.
4. Let the sails dry. Push toothpick into the shell.

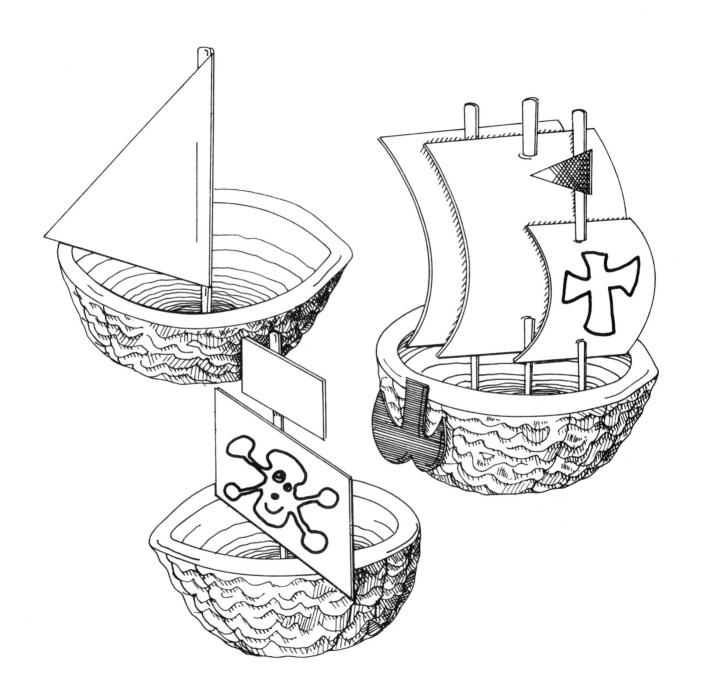

Walnut Animals

There are certain animal pets that you can have in your house. Others, you'll just have to make. Here is the opportunity to create a zoo of animals for your bedroom. After you have finished making the four creatures in this project, you can start designing many more on your own for your collection.

Things You Need

walnut-shell halves
colored construction paper
pencil
scissors
liquid white glue
poster paints or colored felt-tipped markers
paintbrush
pipe cleaners or cord

Let's Begin

1. Place the flat side of a walnut-shell half on a piece of colored construction paper.
2. Trace the outline of the shell with a pencil, Fig. a.
3. Cut out along the shell's outline.
4. Squirt liquid white glue onto the rim of the shell, Fig. b.
5. Place the paper cutout on the glue and make one or more of the animals described below.

WHALE
1. Color the shell gray or blue with poster paint or a colored felt-tipped marker.
2. Cut out a tail from blue construction paper, see illustration.
3. Using liquid white glue, glue the tail to the underside of the shell, see illustration.
4. Cut out two white construction paper eyes and a blue fringe of spouting water and glue them to the shell.

PLATYPUS
1. Color the shell brown with poster paint or a colored felt-tipped marker.
2. Cut out feet, tail and nose from orange construction paper, see illustration.
3. Using liquid white glue, glue the parts to the underside of the shell, see illustration.

TURTLE
1. Color the shell green with poster paint or a colored felt-tipped marker.
2. Cut out the head, feet and tail from green construction paper, see illustration.
3. Using liquid white glue, glue the parts to the underside of the shell, see illustration.

MOUSE
1. Color the shell gray or white with poster paint or colored felt-tipped markers.
2. Cut out ears from pink construction paper and whiskers and eyes from white.
3. Using liquid white glue, glue the parts to the shell, see illustration.
4. Glue a cord or pipe cleaner tail to the shell.

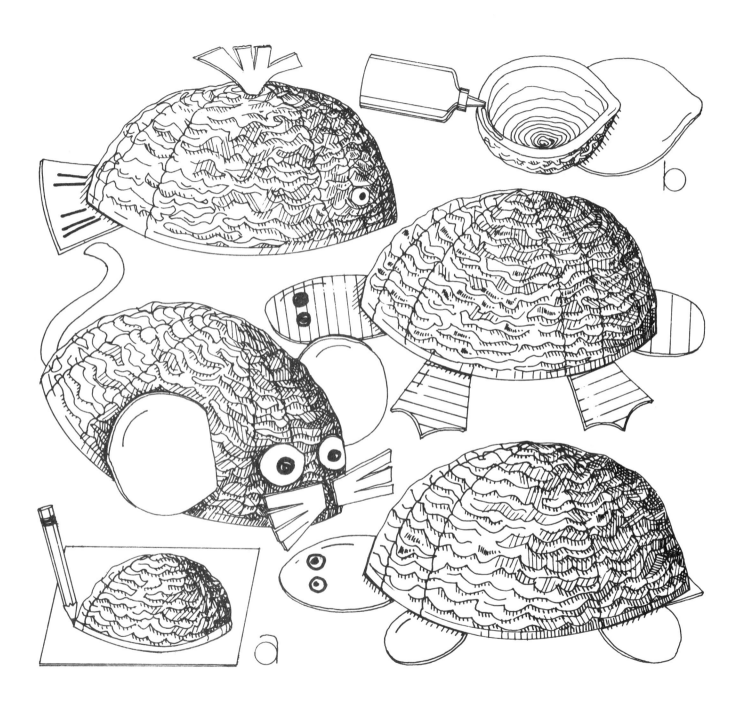

a

b

Walnut Photo Case

If you have any photographs or pictures you would like specially mounted, then you can make a pretty photo case out of walnut shells. Use pictures that are small. (If you don't have photographs, cut pictures from newspapers or magazines.) Once you have selected your favorite pictures, make one or several of these photo cases. They make wonderful gifts for any member of your family, especially those who live far away from you. You can never get tired of seeing the people and things you love so very dearly.

Things You Need

walnut-shell halves
photographs or pictures
pencil
scissors
liquid white glue
felt or fabric

Let's Begin

**1. Divide a walnut very carefully into two perfect halves. Mom or Dad can help by putting the pointed end of a knife into the seam of the back blunt end of the shell to twist it open.
2. Place the flat rim of the shell over the part of the photograph you want to show in your case.
3. Trace around the shell pressing the pencil deep into the photo, Fig. a.
4. Repeat with another photo or picture.
5. Cut out the photos or pictures along the pencil line.
6. Squeeze liquid white glue around the rim of the shells, Fig. b.
7. Place the backs of the cut photos onto the glued shells matching the shapes of photos to shells. Let them dry.
8. When the photos have dried, put the two shells together as they were before the walnut was opened.
9. Cut a small rectangle out of felt or fabric for a hinge.
10. Glue the fabric over both shell halves on one side, Fig. c.
11. Open the case when the fabric hinge has dried.

a

b

c

Acorn Grapes

Most people think that squirrels are the only animals that eat acorns. What you didn't know is that people eat acorns too. The Indians used acorns as snacks, to make a hot drink, and as flour for making bread. Although acorns are very bitter when eaten raw, they lose some of their bitterness when boiled for about two hours. Acorns from white oak trees are sweeter than other kinds. If you are not in the mood for a bowl of roasted acorns, then use these green shelled nuts in art projects, such as acorn grapes.

Things You Need

acorns
cellophane or plastic wrap
scissors
pipe cleaners
green construction paper
paper punch

Let's Begin

1. Place an acorn on a piece of cellophane or plastic wrap and cut the wrap into a square about three times larger than the acorn.
2. Put the acorn in the center of the wrap. The point of the acorn should be facing down with the "little cap" facing up, Fig. a.
3. Bring all of the corners of the wrap up and over the base of the acorn, Fig. b.
4. Twist the wrap ends tightly around the base of the acorn, Fig. c.
5. Twist a pipe cleaner around the twisted wrap leaving one end longer for a stem, Fig. d.
6. Make many acorn grapes in the same way.
7. To make a cluster of acorn grapes, start by twisting two pipe cleaner stems together, Fig. e.
8. Continue to twist together pipe cleaner stems with wrapped acorns.
9. Cut a paper leaf from green construction paper.
10. Punch a hole in the leaf and twist a pipe cleaner into the hole, Fig. f.
11. Tightly twist together the pipe cleaner leaf to the pipe cleaner stems of the grape cluster, see illustration.

Nut Tree

Autumn is the nut season. Trees that bear nuts are usually ready for harvest during this season. If you walk in the woods in autumn, you will see squirrels and other animals gathering hickory nuts, acorns, and an occasional black walnut. Most of the nuts you buy in the store grow in other parts of the world, however, and very few can be found in the woods near your home. In any case, only one type of nut grows on any tree. But the tree you are going to make contains all of your favorite nuts.

Things You Need

tape
colored construction paper
scissors
waxed paper
liquid white glue
mixed nuts and peanuts, all in their shells

Let's Begin

1. Tape two sheets of construction paper together, one on top of the other.
2. Roll the paper to form a cone, Fig. a.
3. Tape the cone together, Fig. b.
4. Trim the bottom edge of the cone so that the cone stands straight, Fig. c.
5. Place the cone on a sheet of waxed paper.
6. Glue walnuts, or the largest nuts you have, along the bottom of the cone. Squeeze a dab of glue to the side of the nuts and press them in a ring all around the bottom of the cone.
7. Let the nuts dry before you glue on the second ring of nuts.
8. Keep gluing on rings of nuts letting each ring dry before you add the next ring, see illustration.
9. When the tree is complete, carefully peel away the waxed paper.

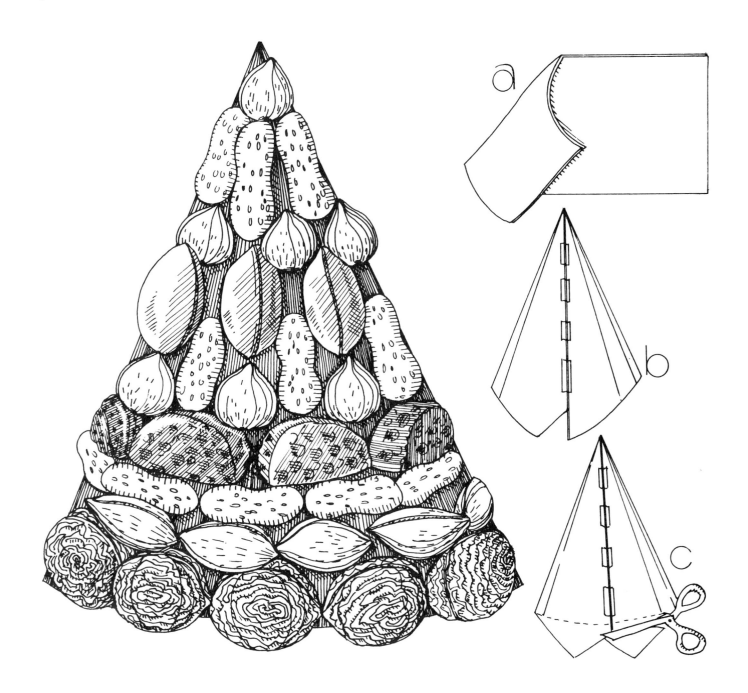

a

b

c

Bean Layering

Dried beans, the kind people use when they make homemade soup, come in many shapes and colors. You know how good they are to eat, but did you know that they can be used in a variety of craft projects? One of the prettiest is bean layering. Mom may store beans in old jars with different beans in each one. Usually you don't want to mix the beans together in a single jar, at least if you want to use them. But there is a beautiful way of mixing different beans to look at. The result is layers of different colors and sizes of beans neatly packed into a jar. It will make a pretty addition to the kitchen or to a special corner in your room.

Things You Need

large jar with a lid

spoon

dried lentils, kidney beans, black-eyed peas, split peas, or any other kind of dried beans

Let's Begin

1. If the jar has a label, place it in water and soak until the paper label slips off. In any case, wash the jar and lid, and dry carefully.
2. Spoon the first kind of bean into the jar to form the first layer, which can be as high as you wish.
3. Carefully spoon the second different layer of beans onto the first in the jar.
4. Spoon layers of different kinds of beans on top of each other until you reach the top of the jar.
5. Screw the lid on tightly.

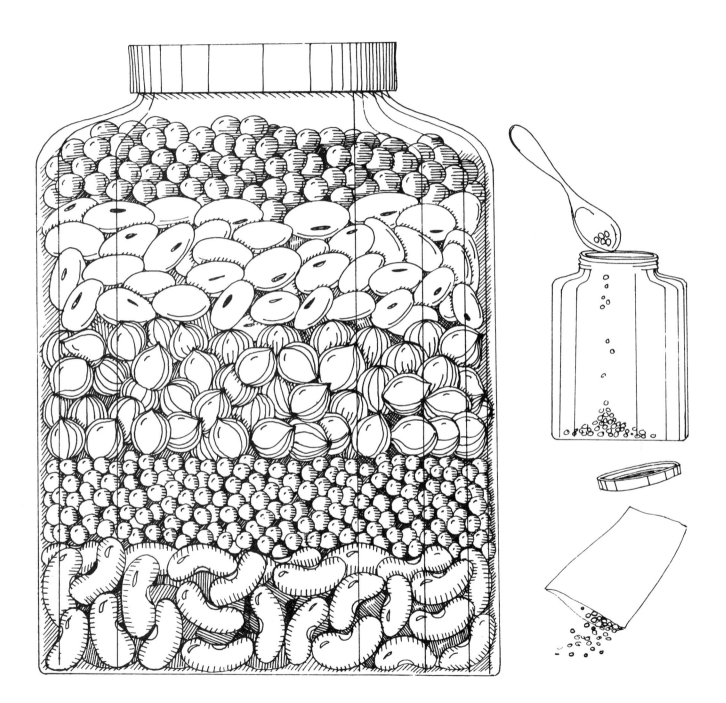

Hobnail Glasses

A hobnail is a short, thick-headed nail that was used at one time for shoeing horses. It is used today for attaching soles and heels to shoes and is a very strong nail to use. Hobnail glass got its name because it looks as if someone had driven hobnails into it. It's quite bumpy, but also very pretty at the same time. You can't make hobnail glass, but you can still see what it looks like. All it takes is some time and patience, some split peas, and a coating of white paint.

Things You Need

drinking glass or goblet
liquid white glue
paper cup or plate
paintbrush
dried split peas
white poster paint

Let's Begin

1. Wash the glass and dry it completely.
2. Pour a little white glue into a small paper cup or plate.
3. Decide on a design that you would like to create on the outside of the glass. It can be repetitive rows covering the entire glass, or just a simple design like a heart, see illustration.
4. Dip the end of a paintbrush handle into the liquid white glue. Dab the glue on the outside of the glass in the pattern you have decided upon.
5. Let the drops of glue dry just a few minutes, then put a split pea on each drop. Glue the flat side of the split pea to the glass.
6. Finish your design, and let the glued split peas dry overnight.
7. Paint the entire outside surface of the glass with white poster paint.
8. Use the glasses for holding a small bouquet of flowers.

364

Bean Bags

Probably one of the earliest games played by children was a toss game. A rock or some other object was used. Somewhere along the line a bean bag was invented. It is softer than a rock, and can be used in many different ways, such as a pincushion or a paperweight. The bean bag has always been used for games like hot potato (keep the bean bag in the air and not in your hands as you toss it around a circle of players). If you have never played with a bean bag, it's time you did. You and your friends can spend hours creating games and having fun with one another.

Things You Need

scissors
scrap felt
liquid white glue
lentils

Let's Begin

1. Cut two circles of the same size from scrap pieces of felt.
2. Decorate one or both circles with felt cut-outs in one of the designs shown in the illustrations: small circles and a smile make a Happy Face; two bars with shorter cross bars make a Baseball; a number 1 and a cent sign (¢) make a Penny; a circle with scallops makes a Flower. Or make up your own designs.
3. Squeeze liquid white glue along the edges of the design pieces. Glue the felt shapes onto the circles in their proper design.
4. Turn over the circle with the design facing down.
5. Squeeze liquid white glue around the edge of the circle with the design. Leave a little bit of the edge unglued for an opening.
6. Place the other circle over the glued circle.
7. Press the two circles together with your hands.
8. Let the circles dry overnight.
9. Spoon dried lentils into the opening of the glued circles. Fill half full.
10. Squeeze glue onto the open edges of the circles. Press together with your fingers.
11. When the newly glued edge of the circle has dried, use the bags in tossing and catching games.

Birdseed Squiggles

You can make a million-and-one different designs with Birdseed Squiggles. No two will ever be the same. You can use these crazy crafts to decorate your room. (Make sure your pet parakeet doesn't get hungry because you've taken all his seeds to make the squiggles!)

Things You Need

liquid white glue
waxed paper
birdseed
spoon
paper bag
string

Let's Begin

1. Remove the cap of a bottle of liquid white glue. Squeeze a squiggly design on a sheet of waxed paper, Fig. a. Be very careful when using the glue not to allow too much to come out of the bottle so that you get lumpy lines.
2. With a spoon, slowly sprinkle birdseed over the squiggly design, Fig. b. Be sure that the birdseed covers all of the glue.
3. Let the design dry overnight.
4. When dry, tilt the waxed paper into the paper bag to remove and save all of the extra seeds that did not dry on the glue.
5. Carefully peel away the waxed paper from the hardened seed squiggle.
6. Tie a length of string into a loop in the squiggle and knot it.
7. Hang the squiggle in a window or on a wall.

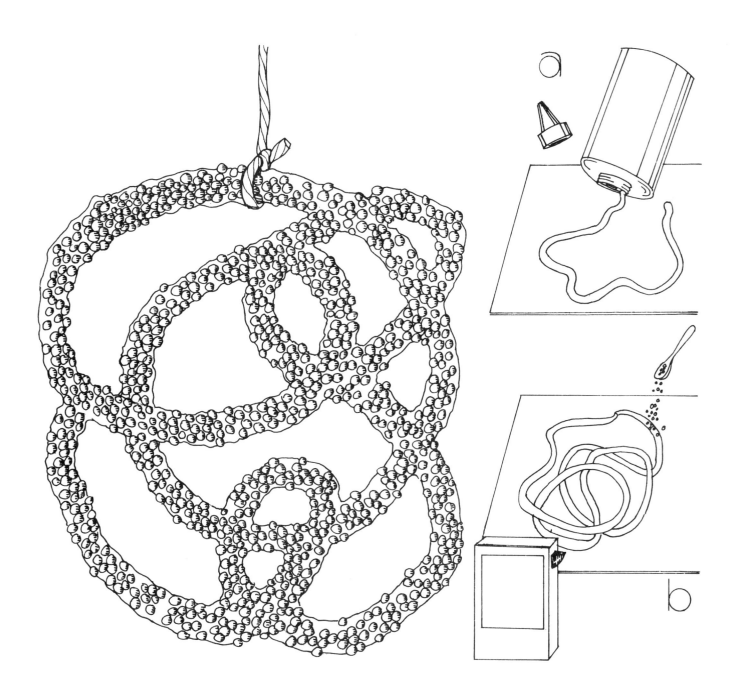

Seeded Pencil Holder Can

If you like to draw and write, you will need a place to keep your pencils and crayons. A tin can is an ideal pencil holder. It may not be pretty to look at with all of the writing on it, however. To make it more attractive, add a seeded cover to the outside of the can. You create the design in this interesting craft.

Things You Need

scissors
construction paper
coffee can
newspaper
liquid white glue
paper cup
paintbrush
melon, sunflower, bird, or spice seeds
tape

Let's Begin

1. Cut a piece of construction paper as tall as a coffee can and long enough to fit around the can with a little extra length.
2. Lay the construction paper on the newspaper.
3. Pour liquid white glue into a paper cup.
4. Paint a section of the construction paper with the glue, a little bit in from the end, Fig. a.
5. Sprinkle one kind of seed to the glued area.
6. Blow away any seeds that have not fallen onto the glue.
7. Paint another area with glue and sprinkle on another kind of seed.
8. Again, blow away any extra seeds.
9. Cover the paper with seeded areas. Do not add seeds to the ends of the paper. They will be taped together around the can.
10. Let the paper dry overnight.
11. Carefully roll the seeded paper around the can, Fig. b.
12. Overlap the ends that have no seeds glued to them. Tape or glue them together.
13. Brush glue on the part of the paper that has no seeds, Fig. c.
14. Sprinkle seeds on the glued surface.
15. When dry, paint these seeds with liquid white glue. Put pencils or whatever in the can.

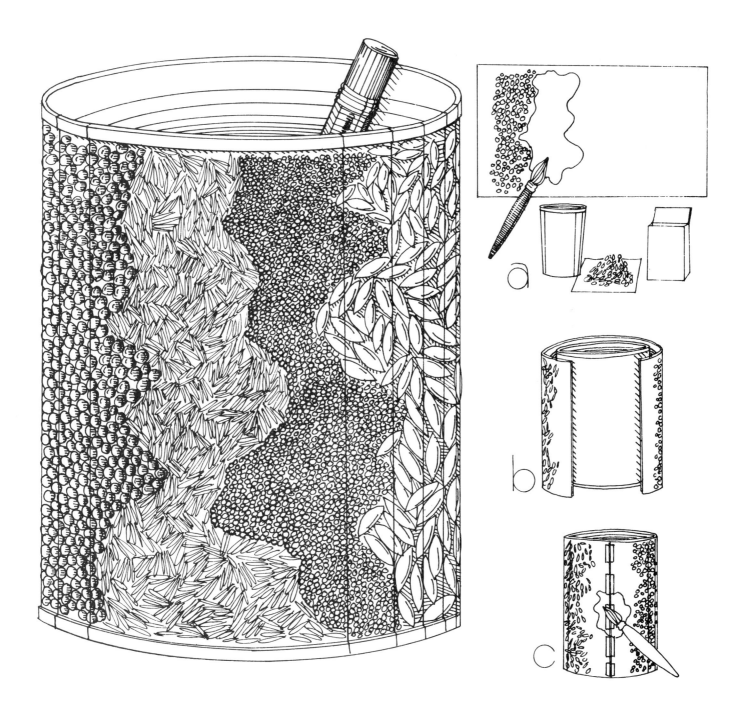

Melon Seed Necklace

Ever since people began to wear jewelry, natural things were strung and worn around the neck and wrists. Indians used shells for necklaces; some tribes in Africa use bones; and whale teeth and tusks are used by the Eskimos. Seeds were also used as beads. They were strung by themselves, or mixed with some of the items just mentioned. The necklace in this craft uses only seeds. Whatever melon your family enjoys, save and use the seeds from it. If your family enjoys all types of melon, you will have a large collection of neckware.

Things You Need

cantaloupe or honeydew melon seeds
box of dye or food coloring
small bowl
spoon
paper towel
needle and thread

Let's Begin

1. Wash the seeds.
2. Mix dye according to package directions in a small bowl, or use food coloring, and add the seeds.
3. Remove the seeds with a spoon from the coloring after a short time, and place them on a paper towel.
4. Let the seeds dry overnight.
**5. Thread a needle with sewing thread and knot the ends of the thread.
**6. Sew the seeds onto the thread, see illustration.
**7. Cut away the needle after you finish threading all of the seeds. Knot the ends of the thread together.

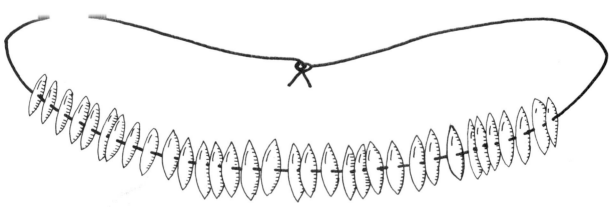

372

Which came first, the chicken or the egg?

Do you know which came first? Wait a minute. Chickens come from eggs, so the egg must have come first. But eggs come from chickens . . . It's all rather confusing if you stop to think about it. Better not spend too much time trying to solve this mystery. Nobody has yet been able to pick one or the other for first place. Might as well just be happy that there are chickens laying eggs so that you can look at them, eat them, and—you guessed it—make things from them.

This chapter shows you many crafts you can make with eggs, or more exactly, egg shells. All of the projects require whole empty eggs, half egg shells, or pieces of egg shell. Eggs are fun to work with because of their shape and because they can be painted, dyed, and colored with crayons. Since they have an inside, you can put things in them and use them in all ways to make fun toys and pretty decorations for your room. If a member of the family is celebrating a birthday, many lovely gifts can be made with egg shells.

It would be nice if you could get some of the wonderfully colored eggs the wild birds lay. It *is* possible for you to locate such priceless egg shells. The next time you are in the woods, look on the ground under trees for blue, green, brown or speckled pieces of egg. But don't worry, really, if you can't find any. You will have more than your share of fun with the plain old chicken eggs to be found in your local supermarket.

Blown Eggs

There are many projects in this chapter that require blown eggs—eggs that have had their contents removed without breaking the shells. You have to use blown eggs in these crafts because the egg—and the craft—will go bad if you leave the white and yolk inside the shell. Blow out eggs whenever they are to be used for cooking and save the shells for future craftwork.

Things You Need

straight pin
egg, at room temperature
bowl or dish

Let's Begin

**1. Twist a pin into the top or pointed end of an egg. Twist back and forth until you break through the shell, Fig. a.

**2. Keep twisting the pin into the egg until you break through the membrane that lies just under the shell.

3. Remove the pin.

**4. Make another hole by twisting the pin into the other end of the egg just as you did before, Fig. b.

5. Make this hole a little larger by carefully poking away some of the shell with the tip of the pin, Fig. c.

6. Remove the pin.

7. Hold the egg over a bowl or dish, with the large hole down.

8. Blow through the small hole. The egg will flow slowly through the larger hole, Fig. d.

9. Rinse the egg under cold running water. Do not wash with soap.

10. Store blown egg in a used egg carton. Do not use until thoroughly dry.

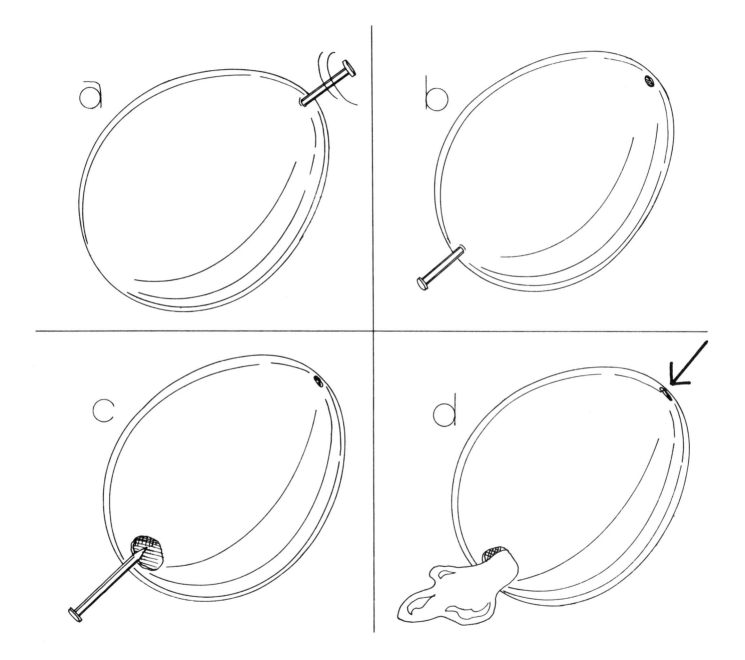

Batik Eggs

It's fun coloring eggs during the Easter season. One way to do this is to use dyes and a white crayon. This is a form of batik. Batik is a method of putting designs on fabric or a smooth surface by using dyes and wax. You put wax where you don't want any color—dyes can't penetrate it. Batiking is really very simple to do. With a little patience you will create a beautiful egg that any chicken would be proud to sit on.

Things You Need

blown (or hard-boiled) eggs, see page 374
white crayon
egg dye or food coloring
paper cups or glasses
spoon
paper towels
rubber cement

Let's Begin

CRAYON BATIK
1. Draw a free-hand squiggly design over a blown or hard-boiled egg with a white crayon, Fig. a.
2. Mix egg dye or food coloring in a paper cup or a glass that is three-quarters filled with water.
3. Dye the egg by dipping in the coloring solution. Because blown eggs are lighter than hard-boiled eggs, you may have to hold down a blown egg with a spoon.
4. Carefully lift the egg out of the dye with a spoon.
5. Place the egg on paper towels to dry.

RUBBER CEMENT EGGS
1. Dip the brush on the cap of a rubber cement bottle into the glue. Dribble squiggly designs onto a blown or hard-boiled eggs, Fig. b. Do not brush the rubber cement on the eggs as if you were gluing something.
2. Hold the egg a few minutes until the rubber cement dries.
3. Dye the egg just as you did for the Crayon Batik egg. Dry thoroughly.
4. Rub the rubber cement off the dried egg with your fingers.

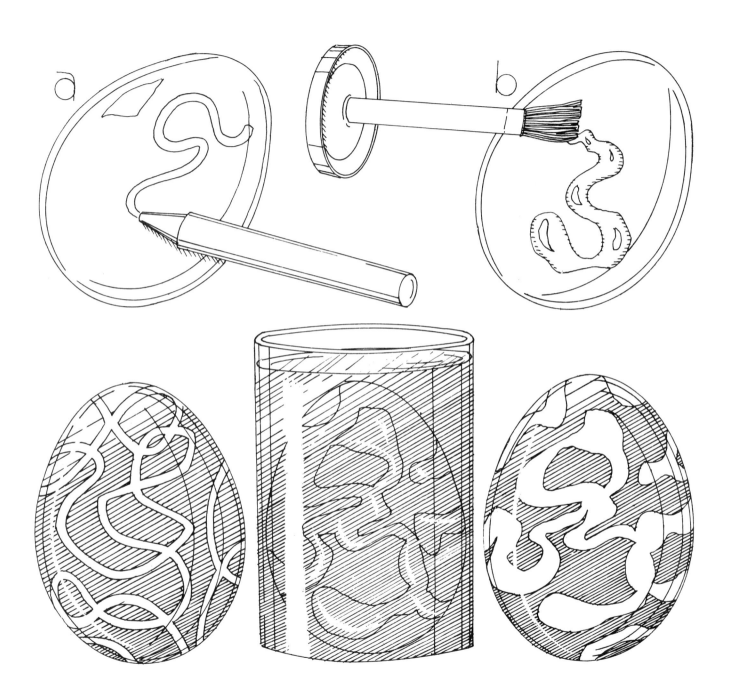

Patchwork Eggs

A craft your great-grandmother may have done was patchwork quilting. During olden times, women used every scrap of material they had saved and sewed them together. They used this patchwork sheet to make clothing, curtains, or bedspreads. You won't need a needle and thread for this patchwork project. A dab of glue and an egg will create an old-fashioned delight for you or as a gift.

Things You Need

scissors
colored tissue paper or scraps of fabric
liquid white glue
paper cup
paintbrush
blown (or hard-boiled) eggs, see page 374

Let's Begin

1. Cut colored tissue paper or scrap fabric into square or rectangular shapes. Each shape should be about the size of postage stamps.
2. Pour liquid white glue into a paper cup.
3. Paint an area of the egg with glue, Fig. a.
4. Place the first tissue or fabric cutout on the glued part of the egg, Fig. b.
5. Paint another section of the egg with glue.
6. Place the second tissue or fabric cutout overlapping the first on the egg. They can overlap as much as you like and in any direction, Fig. c.
7. Cover the entire surface of the egg in this manner with either tissue or fabric shapes. If some ends turn out not to be glued down on the egg, lift them up and add a bit of glue.
8. Smooth out all of the glued patches with your fingers before you set the egg aside to dry.

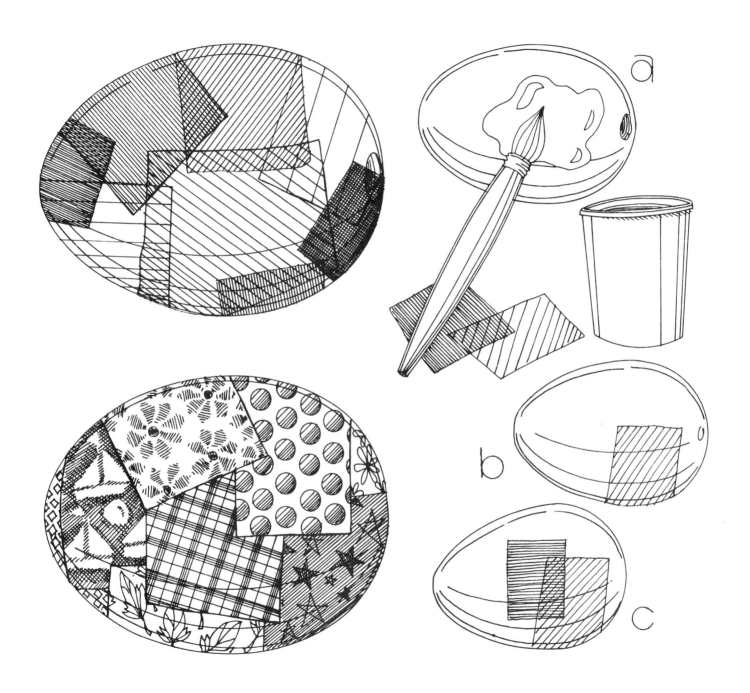

Egg Paperweights

If your homework papers get lost or fall under the table, then you need a paperweight to keep them in place. Mom or Dad may need one for their important papers. No matter who needs a paperweight, they are fun to make and decorate.

Things You Need

blown eggs, see page 374
straight pin
paper collar, see Egg Characters, page 382
spoon
plaster of paris
paper cup
waxed paper or small funnel
egg dyes or food coloring
liquid white glue
colored yarn or thick cord
scissors
sequins
gold or colored stick-on paper stars

Let's Begin

**1. Poke away at the larger hole of a blown egg with a straight pin until the hole is the size of a shirt button or could take the spout of a small funnel, Fig. a.

2. Make a paper collar for the egg to stand in. See Egg Characters, page 182, for directions.

3. Stand the egg in the collar with the large hole facing up.

4. Put several spoonfuls of plaster of paris in the papercup. Stirring all the while, add water until the mixture looks a little thicker than milk.

5. Place the spout of a real or paper funnel into the hole. To make a paper funnel, roll waxed paper into a cone and cut open the tip, Fig. b.

6. Pour or spoon the liquid plaster into the egg through the funnel, Fig. c. Remove the funnel, and fill the egg to the very top with the plaster of paris mixture.

7. Let the plaster that is in the egg dry overnight. If the plaster shrinks in the egg, add freshly mixed plaster the following day

8. Dye the egg if you desire.

9. Squeeze liquid white glue onto the egg in rings or in a checkerboard pattern, Fig. d.

10. Place pieces of yarn on top of the glue lines.

11. Trim the ends of the yarn with scissors.

12. Use liquid white glue to decorate the eggs with sequins or stick-on paper stars.

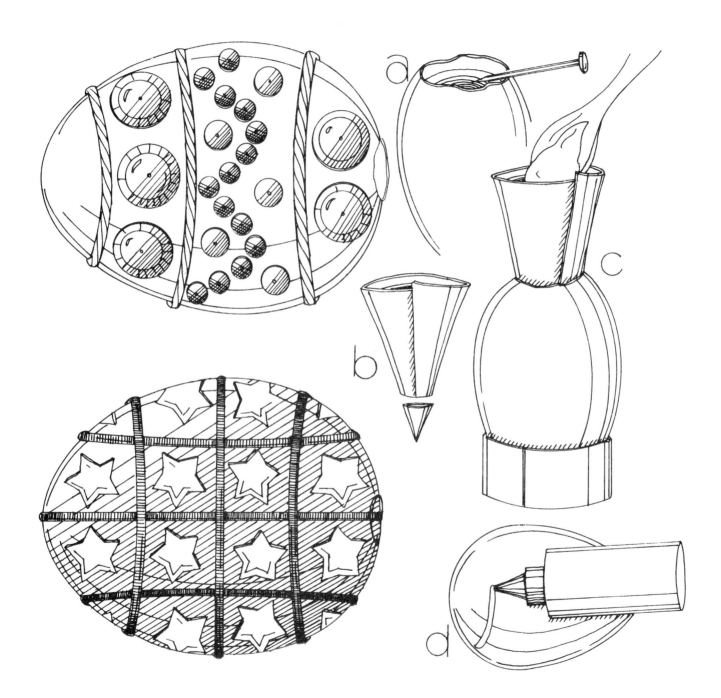

Egg Characters

Who are your favorite characters? You may have gone to the circus and loved the clown. What about that visitor from outer space you saw in a scary movie? Whoever or whatever they are, you can have your favorite characters with you whenever you want. All it takes is a carton full of blown eggs and a little imagination.

Things You Need

blown (or hard-boiled) eggs, see page 374
crayons
egg dye or food coloring
paper cups
spoon
paper towels
scissors
colored construction paper
liquid white glue
feather
yarn
beads or beans
pipe cleaner

Let's Begin

1. Draw a face on a blown egg with crayons.
2. Mix egg dye or food coloring as for Batik Eggs, page 376 , and dye the eggs.
3. Make paper collars, which will act as little stands to hold the eggs upright. To do so, cut a strip from colored construction paper, Fig. a. Roll the strip into a circle overlapping the ends until you have a collar that eggs will rest in snugly, Figs. b and c. Cut any excess off the strip ends. Using this strip as a guide, make as many collars as you will need. Draw designs on strips with crayons and glue the ends together.
4. Finish by decorating the eggs to make the characters below.

RABBIT: Glue pointed colored construction paper ears to the head.

LADY: Make a hat from a circle of colored construction paper with a smaller circle cut out of the middle of it, see illustration. Add a paper feather.

INDIAN: Glue colored construction paper feathers to a paper circle headband made like the egg collar.

MAN: Glue tied-yarn hair to the head.

MARTIAN: Glue beads or beans to a pipe cleaner. Twist around the head.

CLOWN: Make a hat from a small colored construction paper cone (roll a square of paper into a cone shape, tape the ends together) and add paper trimming to the bottom edge.

MONKEY: Glue round colored construction paper ears to egg, see illustration.

Egg Village

Now you can be the builder of your own village. All it takes is a half-a-dozen blown eggs, and you'll be just about ready to set up shop. You will need a few improvements, perhaps, before the permanent residents move into their new community.

Things You Need

6 blown eggs, see page 374
crayons
egg dye or food coloring
paper cups
spoon
paper towels
scissors
heavy cardboard
liquid white glue
colored construction paper
Easter grass (artificial toy grass, purchasable at the five-and-ten-cent store)
waxed paper
paintbrush
twigs
play clay (any non-hardening clay)
candy wafers and spearmint leaves

Let's Begin

1. Draw windows and doors on blown eggs with crayons, Fig. a. Mix egg dye or food coloring as you did for Batik Eggs, page 376, and dye the eggs.
2. Cut a square of heavy cardboard as large as you want the area of your village to be.
3. Squeeze big dabs of liquid white glue onto the heavy cardboard where you want the egg houses to go. Wait five minutes and then place the decorated eggs on the glue. Allow the glue to dry completely.
4. Fold rectangular pieces of colored construction paper in half for the roofs. Trim the folded paper to fit the eggs.
5. Draw a roof design on the roofs with a crayon, Fig. b.
6. Glue the roofs to the eggs with the liquid white glue.
7. Cut some Easter grass into little pieces like confetti and place on waxed paper.
8. Pour some liquid white glue in a paper cup.
9. Paint the tips of the twigs with glue.
10. Roll the glued twigs in the cut-up grass.
11. Stick balls of play clay to the cardboard near the eggs, and stand the twig trees in the clay.
12. Squeeze squiggles of glue over the cardboard.
13. Scatter Easter grass over the squiggles on the cardboard.
14. Add a candy wafer path and spearmint leaf bushes, see illustration.

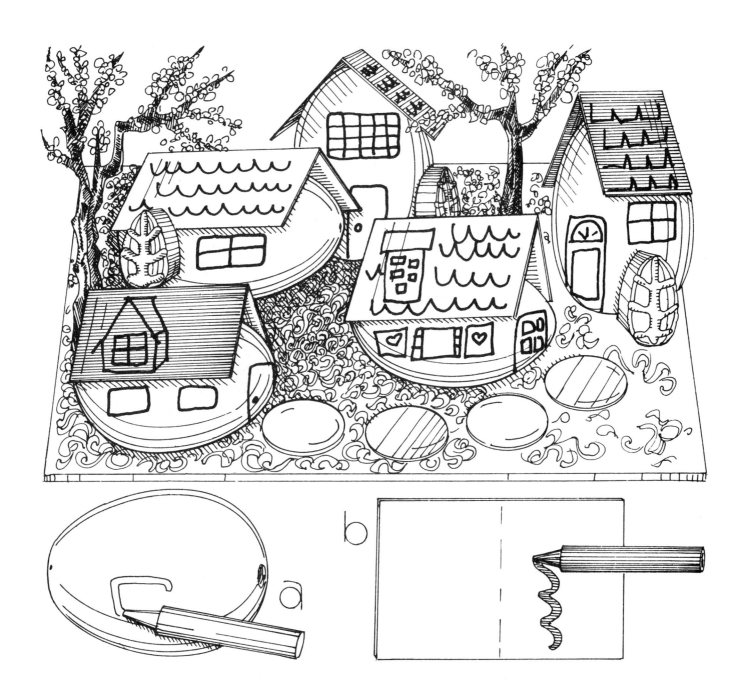

Pot of Tulips

You don't want to tiptoe through these tulips. They break too easily. As a matter of fact, they are as fragile as a carton of fresh farm eggs (they *are* eggs!). Save the cracked egg shell halves that are usually thrown away when eggs are cooked, wash carefully, and let dry. Now you can use these egg shell halves to make a pretty pot of flowers for the kitchen or your bedroom.

Things You Need

cracked egg shell halves
egg dye or food coloring
paper cups
spoon
paper towels
scissors
paper or plastic drinking straws
liquid white glue
colored construction paper
colored felt-tipped markers or crayons
play clay (any non-hardening clay)
small flower pot
Easter grass (artificial grass, purchasable at the five-and-ten-cent store)

Let's Begin

1. Choose the best-shaped egg shell halves you have saved.
2. Mix egg dye or food coloring as you did for Batik Eggs, page 376, and dye the egg shells.
**3. Stems will be made from straws. Cut slits into one end of each of the straws with scissors, Fig. a.
4. Push back the two cut ends of each straw. Flatten out the curve of the ends with your fingers, Fig. b. Paper straws work best.
5. Squeeze liquid white glue on the cut ends. Let the glue dry several minutes.
6. Press the glued ends of each straw to the bottom ends of dyed egg shell halves, Fig. c.
7. Let the straws dry completely on the shells.
8. Cut leaves from colored construction papers and draw veins on them with crayons or colored felt-tipped markers.
9. When the straws are dry, glue paper leaves onto them. Paper straws and some plastic straws can be colored green with a colored felt-tipped marker.
10. Push a big ball of play clay into the bottom of the flower pot.
11. Push the straws into the clay.
12. Cut a strip of colored construction paper. Cut slits into the paper. Don't cut completely through the paper, Fig. d.
13. Roll the fringed paper and glue, Fig. e.
14. Glue these tassels inside each tulip, see illustration.
15. Fill the pot with Easter grass.

a

b

c

d

e

Egg Shell Mosaic

Looking through a kaleidoscope is like seeing a continuous, always-changing mosaic. Mosaics are paintings made of bits of glass or tile. Glass and tile aren't the only things that you can use to make mosaics. The butterfly mosaic you are going to make is made with egg shells that have been broken into small pieces. Once all of the pieces have been dyed, a butterfly as real as life will bring springtime to your special room.

Things You Need

pencil
heavy paper or cardboard
liquid white glue
cord or colored yarn
scissors
egg dye or food coloring
paper cups
paper towels
spoon
cracked egg shells
waxed paper
rolling pin
paintbrush

Let's Begin

1. Draw a simple butterfly design for your mosaic on a piece of cardboard or heavy paper with a pencil, Fig. a.
2. Squeeze a line of liquid white glue on all the pencil lines of the drawing, Fib. b.
3. Lay cord or yarn along the glued lines, Fig. c. Cut away the extra yarn or cord with scissors.
4. Mix egg dye or food coloring as you did for Batik Eggs, page 376, and dye cracked egg shells.
5. Place the dyed egg shells between two sheets of waxed paper.
6. Crush the shells by rolling a rolling pin over the waxed paper.
7. Pour liquid white glue into a paper cup.
8. Brush an enclosed area of the design with a thick coating of liquid white glue, Fig. d.
9. Sprinkle the crushed egg shells onto the glued area, Fig. e.
10. Repeat gluing and sprinkling shells, filling in all areas of your design.
11. Let the shells dry overnight.
12. When the designs are dry, tip the paper to remove any shells that did not stick to the glue. Brush a coating of glue thinned with a little water over the entire surface of the shell design.

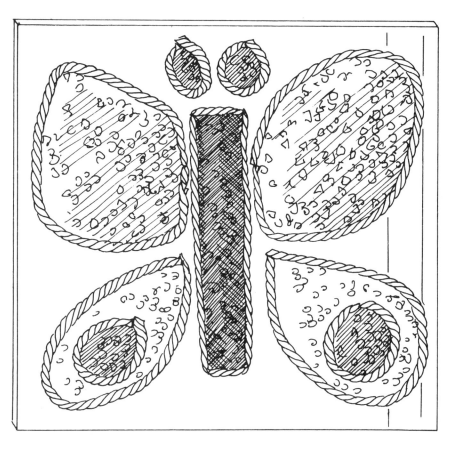
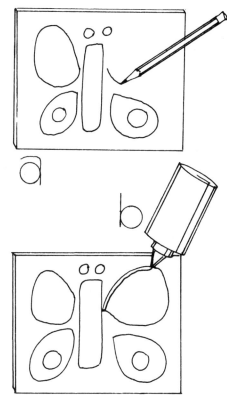
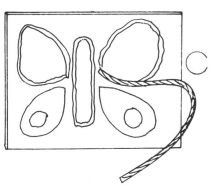

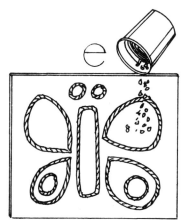

a

b

c

d

e

Egg Tree

Have you ever seen a tree with eggs hanging from it? The only way you will ever see one is to make one. You will need a small branch and some decorated blown eggs to complete this unusual tree.

Things You Need

small tin can
plaster of paris
paper cup
small branch
scissors
ribbon
liquid white glue
blown decorated eggs, given in this chapter

Let's Begin

1. Remove the label from the tin can by soaking it in warm water. Dry completely.
2. Put several spoonfuls of plaster of paris into a paper cup. Stirring all the while, add water until the mixture looks like heavy cream.
3. Pour the plaster of paris mixture into the tin can almost to the top.
4. Wait a few minutes and then stand the branch straight in the plaster.
5. Cut the ribbon into small pieces. Tie a knot in the center of each piece. Glue ribbon at the knots to the tops of the eggs.
6. When the glue is dry, tie the eggs to different limbs of the branch.
7. Tie a ribbon bow around the can.

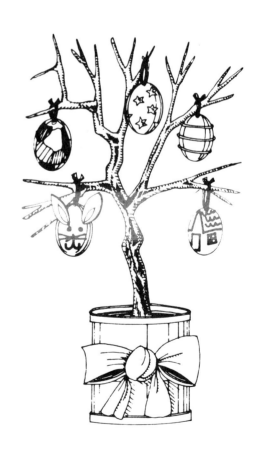

Stones can be found everywhere

Stones are among the most common objects found almost everywhere. By the sea, up a mountain, even in the city, you will see stones of all sizes, shapes, and colors. Some are opaque, and some you can see through. Stones, or rocks as we may sometimes call them, were formed in two ways. Some came from inside the center of the earth where it was very hot. Others were made by pressure for millions and millions of years. You might have a rock collection of your own own. If you do, you know how much fun it is collecting them.

Stones are used frequently in jewelry when they are of special value. Pendants, bracelets, and rings are made with stones of many kinds. Besides starting a stone collection, there are lots of other things you can do with them. As you read through this chapter, you will see how you can make stone people and animals, as well as games and stone sculptures. Even if you never liked stones before, after finishing some of the crafts, you may be hooked on a new hobby.

Now is the time to start collecting stones in all sizes, shapes, and colors, and to store them away for future projects. (Besides making crafts, stones can be used in fish tanks, in flower pots, or when playing with your favorite toys.) Make sure that you don't throw stones at anyone or at anything, though—they can hurt. Better use them to make one of the beautiful creations that follow.

Rock Collection

Do you collect rocks or stones? If you do, and they are here and there in your dresser drawers or a toy chest, why not display them neatly? Save as many egg cartons as you can for this project. They make good collection boxes because you can put one stone in each of the egg compartments. If you don't have a collection of pretty stones, start getting one together. Wherever you go with your friends or family, look around for interesting stones. Stone collecting can become a facinating hobby for you. There are many books that will help you identify all of the rocks you collect. Why not start collecting now?

Things You Need

scissors
colored construction paper
egg carton
liquid white glue
12 very special stones
colored felt-tipped markers or crayons

Let's Begin

1. Cut a piece of colored construction paper large enough to cover entirely the outside lid of an egg carton.
2. Using liquid white glue, glue the cut paper to the top of the lid. Make sure all of the edges are glued down neatly.
3. Wash and dry your special stones.
4. Glue one stone into each compartment of the egg carton.
5. Use a crayon or colored felt-tipped marker to write where the rocks were collected, and the type of rocks they are, on the carton.

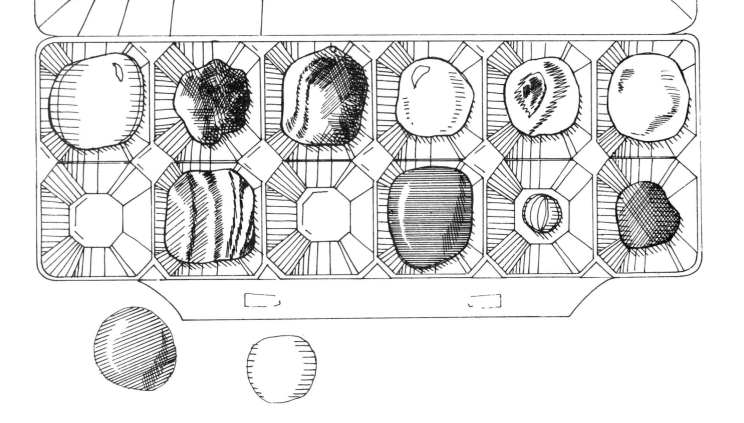

Indian Pebble Game

The Indians used natural things in their games. They played many games that involved rolling stones. Signs and symbols were painted or carved on the stones, and games of skill and luck were played with them. This game is fun to play anywhere, especially when the rain is pelting against your window. This is the time to gather all of the braves together for a day of skill and excitement.

Things You Need

15 smooth pebbles (small stones)
nailpolish
scissors
colored construction paper
coffee can
colored felt-tipped markers or crayons
tape

Let's Begin

1. Wash and dry the pebbles.

2. Paint an X on five of the stones with nailpolish.
3. Paint an O on five of the stones with nailpolish.
4. Paint a Z on five of the stones with nailpolish.
5. Let the nailpolish on all the stones dry.
6. Cut a piece of colored construction paper as high as the coffee can and long enough to wrap around it.
7. Draw Indian designs on the paper with crayons or colored felt-tipped markers, see illustration for some examples.
8. Wrap the paper around the can, and tape the paper ends together.
9. When the painted letters on the pebbles are dry, place them in the can.
10. To play the game, each player in turn puts his hand in the can and pulls out one pebble. When all of the pebbles are picked from the can, the one who has the most of one kind of letter wins the round. Repeat several times.

Basket of Fruit

Fruit arranged in a pretty way in a basket looks good enough to be eaten—and usually is. The stone fruit we will make in this craft would be hard to swallow, but makes a beautiful decoration nonetheless. It will be a lovely addition to any room in your home.

Things You Need

different sized stones (round and smooth)
poster paints
paintbrushes
liquid white glue
green construction paper
scissors
pipe cleaners

Let's Begin

1. Choose stones of appropriate shapes, as indicated below, and decorate to make fruit.

APPLE (A). Paint a medium-sized stone red with a pink highlight. Glue on a green construction paper leaf.
ORANGE (B). Paint a medium-sized stone orange with brown speckles, and add a brown star on top.

MELON (C). Paint a large stone green with light green squiggles going from one end of the stone to the other.
PLUM (D). Paint a small stone purple with a pink circle highlight.
STRAWBERRY (E). Paint a tiny stone red with black speckles. Glue on a green construction paper star-leaf.
PEACH (F). Paint a medium-sized stone pink with a yellow circle highlight. Glue on a green construction paper leaf.
BLACKBERRY (G). Paint tiny stones black with blue dots.
GRAPEFRUIT (H). Paint a medium-large stone yellow with brown speckles and add a brown star on top.
LEMON OR LIME (I). Paint a small oblong stone yellow or green with brown speckles and add a star on top.
PEAR (J). Paint a medium-sized oblong stone yellow or light-green with a white circle highlight. Glue on a green paper leaf.
GRAPES (K). Glue small stones together with liquid white glue. When dry, paint them purple or light-green. Glue on a large green construction paper leaf. Glue two twisted pipe cleaners to the cluster for vines.

People and Pets

Creatures made of stone? It sounds like they might come from outer space. Not really. They come from your neighborhood—at least the stones you make them from do. Look carefully for the stones of the right size, and this happy family of stone creatures can be all yours. With paint and dabs of glue, their stone faces will come to life.

Things You Need

large, medium, and small flattish stones
waxed paper
liquid white glue
poster paints
paintbrushes
ice-cream stick

Let's Begin

BOY
1. Place two small flat stones on a sheet of waxed paper. These will be the boy's feet.
2. Squeeze a large dab of liquid white glue on the top of the stones.
3. Let the glue dry for five minutes, and place a medium-sized stone body on top of the feet.
4. Let all the stones dry.
5. When dry, squeeze a dab of glue on top of the body, wait five minutes, and add a smaller stone for the head.
6. When the stones have dried, paint the fig-

ure to resemble a boy, using poster paints, see illustration.

MOTHER
1. Place a large stone on a sheet of waxed paper.
2. Using liquid white glue, glue two medium-sized stones on top of each other, and then glue both onto the top of the large stone, see illustration.
3. Glue a small stone for the hair bun onto the very top of the figure.
4. Let all the stones dry.
5. Break an ice-cream stick in half, and glue the halves onto the figure for the arms.
6. Using poster paints, paint the figure to resemble a mother, see illustration.

DOG
1. Place four small flat stones on a sheet of waxed paper. These will be the dog's feet.
2. Using liquid white glue, glue a medium-sized stone body to the four feet.
3. Glue a small stone head onto one side of the body stone, see illustration.
4. Glue another small stone onto the other side of the body stone for a tail.
5. Glue tiny pebbles to the head for the ears, see illustration.
6. Let all the stones dry.
7. Paint the figure to resemble a dog, see illustration.

Stone Sculptures

Have you ever poured wet sand on top of itself to make strange, icicle-like forms? If you have, then you know what interesting sculptures you can create. Stone sculptures look almost like sand sculptures. They are wide at the bottom and thin at the top. Create a dozen or so of these sculpture groups and make an outer space scene, or just place individual sculpture groups anywhere you like about your room.

Things You Need

disposable aluminum pie tin
flat, smooth beach pebbles (small stones) of different sizes
liquid white glue

Let's Begin

1. Turn the pie tin upside down. Make indentations in the bottom of the tin with the largest stones wherever you want to build a sculpture.

2. Squeeze liquid white glue into the indentations in the pie tin.
3. Place the largest pebbles onto the glued indentations.
4. Let the pebbles dry completely. Then squeeze a dab of glue onto the top of each pebble and allow to dry for about five minutes before carefully adding a layer of smaller pebbles. Let the new layer of pebbles dry completely.
5. Squeeze a dab of glue onto the top of the new layer of pebbles and let dry for five minutes before adding more pebbles. Be sure each layer of pebbles is completely dry before adding more glue and pebble layers. You will be building sculptures from large to increasingly smaller pebbles.
6. When this set of glued pebbles has dried, add another set just as you did with the last.
7. Continue building sculptures in this way. Make some sculptures taller than others. Be sure to let the glue dry for five minutes on one layer before adding another.

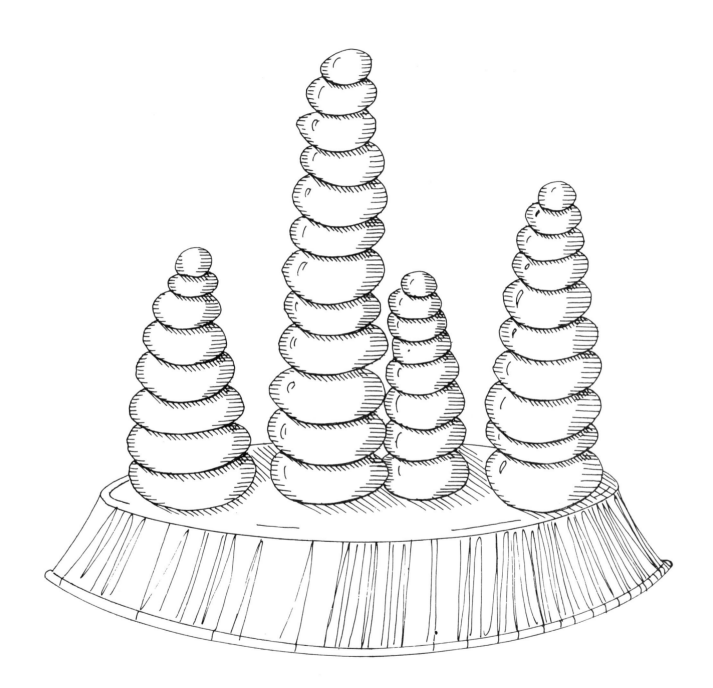

Rock Pendant

Rocks can be found in many different colors. This project asks that you look for the most beautiful rock you can find. Don't just choose any stone. Look for one that is shiny, colorful, or in some way interesting or unusual. If you have a back yard, there is probably a wonderful rock just waiting to be wrapped with yarn and worn as a pendant around your neck.

Things You Need

beautiful rock
colored yarn
scissors
liquid white glue
paper cup
waxed paper
paintbrush

Let's Begin

1. Wash and dry your rock.
2. Place the rock in the center of a length of yarn and wrap the rock by twisting the two ends of yarn in every direction around it, Fig. a.
3. Tie the two ends of the yarn tightly at the top of the rock with a double knot, Fig. a.
4. Make a loop in the yarn by tying the two ends of the yarn into a second double knot a little up from the first knot, Fig. b.
5. Trim the ends of the yarn with scissors.
6. Pour a little liquid white glue into a paper cup.
7. Place the wrapped rock on a sheet of waxed paper.
8. Paint the entire rock and yarn with a thin coating of liquid white glue, Fig. c. Use your paintbrush for this. Be sure the loop at the top remains open.
9. Let the glue dry.
10. When dry, slip a piece of yarn through the yarn loop.
11. Knot the two ends of the yarn to make a necklace that will fit over your head.

Mosaic in Plaster

The use of stones to create pretty mosaic designs is not a new art form. Stones were used to make mosaic floors many thousands of years ago. They were set in cement, and beautiful designs were created. Many ancient palaces have mosaic floors, walls, and ceilings, and all were done in bits of cut stone. Your mosaic will add an old-world tradition to your new-world bedroom.

Things You Need

bottom of a small gift box
sheet of aluminum foil
cord
coffee can
plaster of paris
long stirring stick
food coloring
plastic spoon
small smooth stones
scissors

Let's Begin

1. Line the inside of the bottom half of a gift box with a sheet of aluminum foil. Be sure to press the foil into the corners.
2. If you plan to hang your mosaic, punch two holes on the underside of the box near the top. Insert a piece of cord, and tie the ends loosely inside the box, Fig. a.
3. Fill the coffee can about half-full with plaster of paris.
4. Stirring all the while, add water until the mixture looks like heavy cream. Add a little bit of food coloring if you wish the background of the mosaic to be colored.
5. Pour the plaster into the foil-lined box bottom, Fig. b.
6. Quickly spread and smooth the plaster evenly in the box bottom with the plastic spoon.
7. Push pebbles halfway into the plaster, creating a design, Fig. c. Work fast, because the plaster will dry quickly.
8. The plaster will be completely dry in an hour.
9. If you wish to take the mosaic out of the box, trim away any extra foil with scissors.

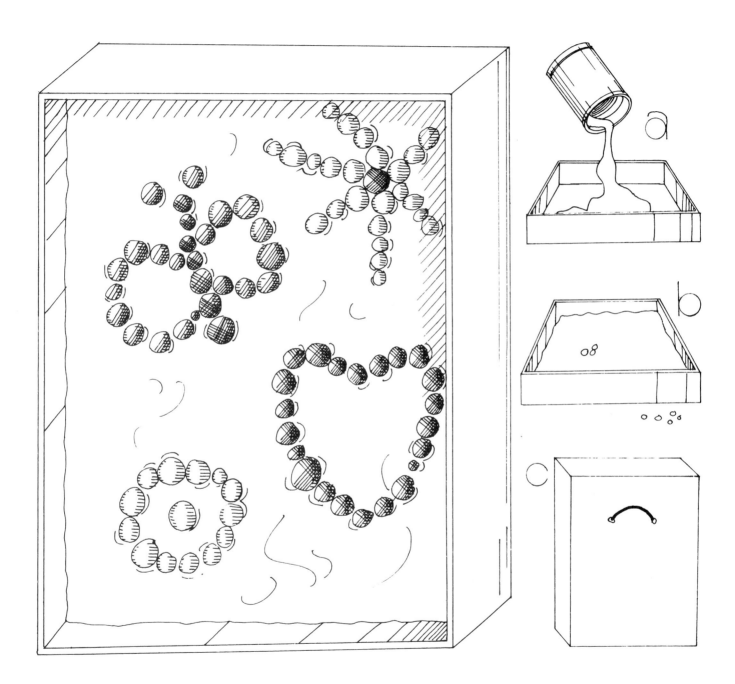

a

b

c

Stone Paperweights

Stones are very heavy and so can make excellent paperweights. For this project, look for stones with interesting shapes and fascinating colors. (You might even find many-colored stones or ones with stripes going all around them.) Paperweights make wonderful presents for any member of your family.

Things You Need

large smooth stones
poster paints
paintbrush
waxed paper
liquid white glue
paper cup

Let's Begin

1. Wash and dry a large smooth stone.
2. Using poster paint, paint the entire stone a color of your choice. If the stone is particularly beautiful in itself, you may wish to omit this step and skip to step 4.
3. Let the paint dry.
4. Paint a design on the stone that you like, or for the snail, paint a spiral line, see illustration for examples. Let the design dry.
5. Place the stone on a piece of waxed paper.
6. Pour liquid white glue into a paper cup, and carefully brush a coating of glue on the stone. Don't scrub on the glue or you may smudge your design.
7. Let the glue dry on the stone.

8. To make the snail's head, cut out a long-rounded shape and glue it to the bottom of the stone. Draw eyes on it.

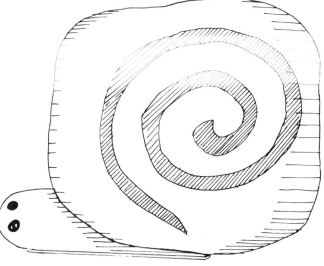

A shell was once a home

A sea shell that you collect at the shore was once a home, the living protective part of the soft creature within it. The shell grows with its "occupant." When that occupant dies, the shell does too (its the creature's outside skeleton, and like a human skeleton, it remains after the body is gone). The sea washes the empty shell to the shore. There you pick it up and probably wonder about what kind of strange and beautiful thing it is.

There are basically two shell types: the clam and the snail. If you are a practiced shell collector, you know that many varieties of these shells exist. The clam types are usually flat or dish-like, while the snail types are usually spiral or cone-shaped. Shellfish provide food for people and other animals, like seagulls. They even provide protective homes for some of the other creatures of the deep. The hermit crab will make an empty shell—a shell whose original occupant has died—his own home, while small fish will protect themselves under a clam shell to escape the hungry jaws of a larger fish. All shell inhabitants are among the earth's oldest living things.

It's wonderful to think about these things—to collect and look at sea shells—but did you know that shells can be used in wonderful craft projects? They can be used to decorate a comb, strung for a necklace, transformed into animals, and made into many more beautiful items. All it takes is some glue, string, paint, and a box of different type of shells. If you don't live near the ocean, don't worry. Hobby stores and other craft counters carry shells of all sizes and shapes. Mom and Dad will help you to locate the places where shells can be bought. It doesn't matter where you get your shells, really. As long as you have a few, a world of fun things to make is at your fingertips.

Shell Necklace and Pin

Shells can be used in many decorative crafts, but most craftsmen use these underwater treasures for jewelry. If you can get to the beach, collect a wide assortment of small shells. You can usually find them where the waves break on the shore. If you don't make it to the ocean, your local hobby store most probably carries bags of small, colored shells. Create an entire jewelry wardrobe with shells, a different design for every day of the week.

Things You Need

scissors
colored yarn or cord
liquid white glue
small shells
cardboard
heavy paper or fabric
safety pin
poster paints
paintbrush

Let's Begin

NECKLACE
1. Cut yarn into small pieces.
2. Tie a knot in the middle of each piece of yarn, Figs. a and b.
3. Squeeze a dab of liquid white glue into the opening or near the top of each sea shell.
4. Press the knots of the yarn pieces into the glue, Fig. c.
5. Let the yarn in the shells dry.
6. When dry, tie the shells onto a length of yarn at different intervals. The yarn should be long enough to make a necklace that will slip easily over your head when knotted.

PIN
1. Cut a round or oblong shape from the cardboard.
2. Cut a small paper or fabric hinge about the width of the closed safety pin and not much longer, Fig. d.
3. Slip the paper or fabric cutout through the closed safety pin, Fig. d. This will be the clasp.
4. Glue the back of the paper or fabric with the safety pin to the back of the cardboard near the top. Make sure you glue the part of the safety pin that doesn't open to the cardboard, not the other way around.
5. Paint the top side of the cardboard with poster paints.
6. Glue small sea shells in a pretty design to the painted side of the cardboard.

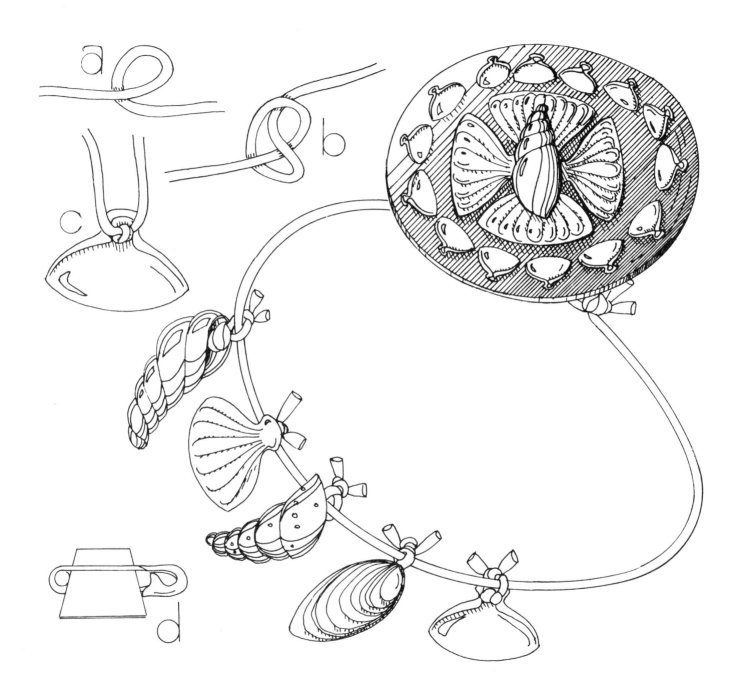

Slowpoke Turtle

It was the slowpoke turtle that managed to beat the speedy hare in that famous race you've undoubtedly heard about. Turtles can't move very fast, but when they have to go somewhere, usually nothing stops them. On your next trip to the beach, look for the makings of this slow-moving animal. You will need a large round shell, five small flat shells, and an oval-shaped shell. The best oval-shaped shell to use is a cowry shell, and you can purchase it at your local hobby or shell store if you can't find one. All of the shells you need can be bought in hobby stores.

Things You Need

liquid white glue
large, round shell
white drawing paper
scissors
four small flat shells
waxed paper
piece of broken shell
pipe cleaner
long, oval shell (cowry shell)
colored felt-tipped markers or crayons
paintbrush

Let's Begin

1. Squeeze liquid white glue around the bottom edge of the large, round shell, Fig a.

2. Place the glued side of the shell onto a piece of paper.
3. When the glue has dried, trim away the excess paper with scissors, Fig. b.
4. Squirt glue on the top of the four small flat shells.
5. Using the large, round shell as a guide, arrange the four shells on a sheet of waxed paper in "feet position," two on one side of the large, round shell, and two on the other side, Fig. c.
6. Place the large, round shell paper-side down over the four glued small shells.
7. Use the piece of broken shell for a tail. Put a dab of glue on top of it, and glue it under one end of the large shell.
8. Let the turtle dry.
9. Cut a pipe cleaner in half, and glue one of the pieces to the inside of the long, oval shell, Fig. d. Let it dry.
10. Gently push the other end of the pipe cleaner neck into the paper on the underside opposite the tail of the large, round shell.
11. Bend the shell head up, pushing all of the extra pipe cleaner into the paper, Fig. e.
12. Once the turtle's head is in place, glue the pipe cleaner to the paper.
13. When dry, draw eyes on the turtle's head using colored felt-tipped markers or crayons.

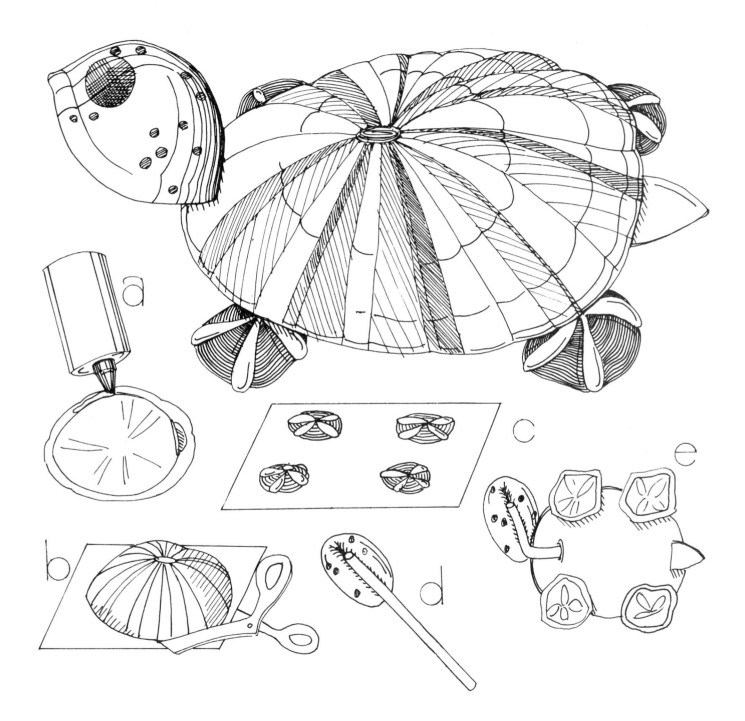

a

b

c

d

e

Butterfly Mobile

Butterflies appear to dance from one flower to another. This ballet is one of the main attractions of spring. If you enjoy watching a field of graceful butterflies, then a mobile of shell butterflies is what you need in your room.

Things You Need

pencil
tracing paper
scissors
cardboard
liquid white glue
flat shells of 2 different sizes or kinds (preferably mussel and scallop shells)
poster paints
paintbrush
pipe cleaners or drinking straws
beads
paper punch
yarn
plastic coffee can lid
paper clips

Let's Begin

1. Trace the butterfly body shape onto a sheet of tracing paper with a pencil.
2. Cut out the tracing.
3. Using the tracing as a pattern, trace the body shape onto a piece of cardboard.
4. Cut out the butterfly body from the cardboard.
5. Using liquid white glue, glue the bottom end of two large shells (mussel shells) to the top of the body shape at places marked by an X on the body shape in the book.
6. Glue two smaller shells (scallop shells) to the bottom of the body shape at places marked by an O on the body shape in the book.
7. Using poster paint, paint spots on the shells and eyes on the body.
8. Fold a pipe cleaner in half.
9. Glue a bead to each end of the pipe cleaner.
10. When the beads have dried, glue the folded point of the pipe cleaner to the back of the top of the butterfly body shape.
11. When the pipe cleaner has dried, punch a hole near the top of the butterfly's head with a paper punch.
12. Tie a piece of yarn through the hole, leaving one end long.
13. Make several more butterflies.
14. Punch well-spaced holes in the plastic coffee can lid with a paper punch, one hole for each butterfly you have made.
15. Push the yarn ends of each butterfly up through the holes in the lid.
16. Tie the ends of yarn to paper clips.
17. Punch two more holes opposite one another, near the edge of the lid.
18. Push two lengths of yarn down through the holes, and knot in place. Use these strands to hang your mobile.

Shell Flowers

On your next excursion to the seashore, gather a bagful of sea shells and save them for a pretty bouquet of shell flowers. Once you have made a lovely vase full of these "blossoms," your family and friends will enjoy looking at them just as they would the real thing.

Things You Need

small, flat shells (shells which look like flower petals)
liquid white glue
pipe cleaners

Let's Begin

1. Squeeze a large dab of liquid white glue onto the inside of the shells at their narrowest points.
2. Place one end of a pipe cleaner into the glue to form shell petals, Fig. a.
3. Let the glue dry completely.
4. Twist as many shell petals together as you want to form a flower, Fig. b. If you are lucky enough to have a long, cone-shaped shell, glue it onto a pipe cleaner and use it as a center petal for your flower.
5. Add a shell to the stem of a finished flower for a leaf, see illustration.
6. Make as many shell flowers as you like, and arrange them in an attractive vase or jar.

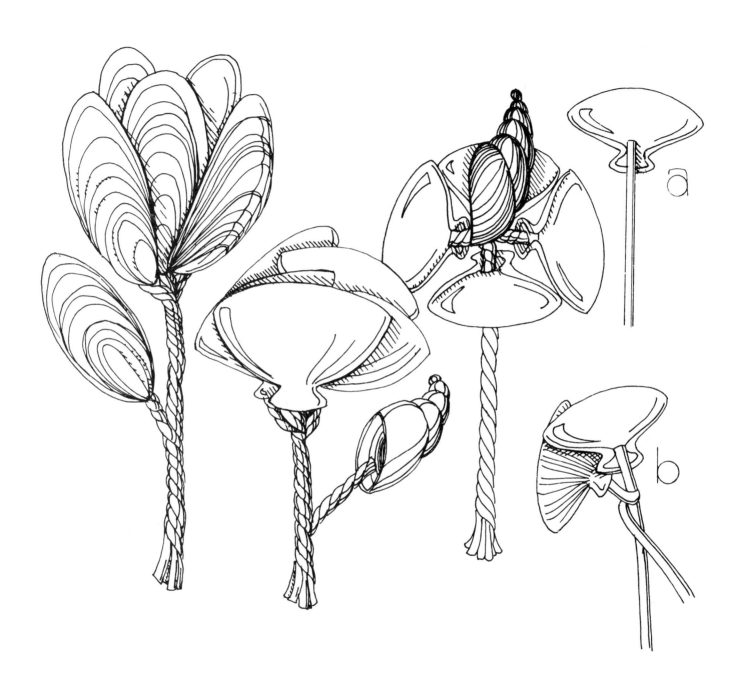

a

b

Picture Frame

Most picture frames you see in the stores are made of wood or metal. They are usually painted a solid color, or left unpainted. If you have pretty pictures you want framed and you don't want a plain-looking frame, use shells and cardboard to make as many frames as you need. Any picture will look great behind a shell-studded frame. All you need is a dab of glue, some paint, shells, and a piece of cardboard. You might want to surprise Mom and Dad with a beautifully framed picture of their favorite person, You.

Things You Need

scissors
heavy cardboard
pencil
ruler
poster paints
paintbrush
liquid white glue
different kinds of shells
tape

Let's Begin

1. Cut the cardboard to the size and shape you want your frame to be.
2. Draw a square or a rectangle in the center of the cardboard with a pencil and a ruler. There should be an equal border on all sides of the shape you draw.
**3. Cut out the inside shape with scissors.
4. Paint the frame with poster paint, and let it dry.
5. Using liquid white glue, glue shells on the dried cardboard frame in a pretty design.
6. Center your picture in the cutout area on the underside of the shell frame.
7. Tape the picture to the frame when it is in the right position.

Standing Planter

If you or any member of your family enjoys growing plants, then this craft is sure to please. To make it, you will need large sea clam shells. These are the ones people generally use for ashtrays or candy dishes. The sea clam shells are best found at the beach. Make many planters with them, and start yourself on a new hobby, growing flowers in your home. When your plants get too big for the shell, get a larger flower pot, or plant them in the garden. You may be the only horticulturist (a person who grows plants) on your block!

Things You Need
large sea clam shell
liquid white glue
three large beads or marbles
soil
seeds

Let's Begin

1. Turn the clam shell upside down.
2. Squeeze three large dabs of liquid white glue onto the shell as shown in the illustration.
3. Let the glue dry for five minutes on the shell.
4. Push the beads or marbles into the glue.
5. Let the glue dry overnight.
6. Turn the shell onto its bead legs.
7. Fill the shell with soil.
8. Plant a few seeds in the soil following all of the instructions given on the back of the seed package.
9. Water the seeds as the soil in the shell dries.

Collage Box

By now, you have probably collected quite a few seaside things for your craftwork. Why not display your salty treasures in a collage box? Collage boxes are very popular today. To make one, you begin by dividing a large box into smaller compartments. In each compartment you place one or more objects arranged in a pretty design. Shells are not the only things you can gather at the beach and use for your collage box. Pieces of coral, driftwood, sea glass, and shiny stones are other collectables that can be found near the surf. Collect a bagful of nature's wonders the next time you go to the beach (or, for that matter, anywhere you can). You may want more than one collage box for all of the treasures you bring home.

Things You Need

paintbrush
poster paints
bottom half of a flat gift box
ruler
pencil
construction paper
scissors
liquid white glue
sea shells, driftwood, sea glass, beach stones, coral or other natural things

Let's Begin

1. Paint the inside of the box with blue or green poster paint.
2. Make a center wall for the inside of the box from a strip of construction paper as long as the longest side of the box. Add a little more paper to the length on both ends of the strip to make fold-over tabs, Fig. a.
3. Fold back the paper tabs on both ends just enough so that the center wall fits perfectly in the box, Fig. b.
4. Squeeze liquid white glue onto the outside of each tab.
5. Place the wall in the center of the box, and press the tabs to the sides, Fig. c.
6. Make cross walls from strips of construction paper cut as long as the distance between the side of the box and the center wall. Add extra paper on each side of the strips for tabs.
7. Fold and glue the cross walls into the box just as you did with the center wall. You can glue as many cross walls as you wish into the box making compartments of whatever size you wish.
8. Glue your beach treasures into the small windows with liquid white glue.
9. You can hang your dried collage on the wall using string or a stick-on picture hanger.

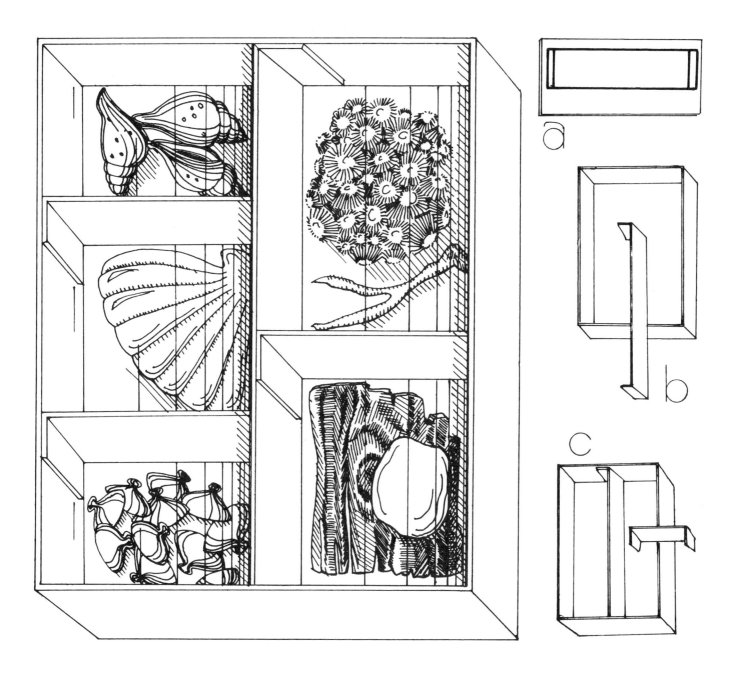

a

b

c

Shell Comb

No matter where you are, you carry a creature that is all mouth and no body. It's your hungry comb with more teeth than a baby shark. Hair is the only food that will satisfy its appetite. If your comb is rather dull-looking, then it's time to give it a face lift, and decorate it with tiny shells. Collect or buy small shells to decorate the top of your comb. You probably won't want to carry this comb with you all the time, since some of the shells might come off. If you have a comb, brush, and mirror, you can glue shells onto all three items and have a matching set.

Things You Need

comb
liquid white glue
small sea shells

Let's Begin

1. Start with a washed comb or buy an inexpensive one at the store.
2. Squeeze liquid white glue on the band above the teeth of the comb. Cover the entire top of the comb.
3. Let the glue dry for several minutes.
4. Place small shells on top of the glue. Some can face up and some down. Make your own design. Let it dry thoroughly before use.

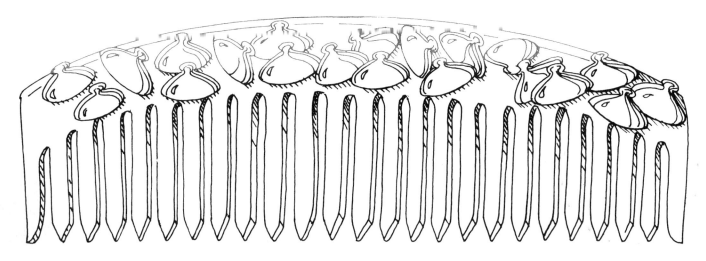

Sand is a blanket by the sea

Dipping your burning toes in the cool ocean is a real treat on a hot, sunny day at the beach. The sand can get very hot unless it is chilled by the rushing waves. Even when it is hot, sand has a soft, silky touch that feels good when you run your fingers or toes through it. Billions upon billions of tiny rocks, shells, and other natural things have been ground fine to create this soft, sandy blanket. It is nice to lie on, bury yourself in, or build a sand castle with. If you dig a hole deep enough in the sand, you will find the ocean at the bottom of it.

Sand has many craft uses. The projects in this chapter will prove to be very interesting. Did you know that you can make a plaster sunburst using sand as a mold or dry flowers in it? Well, you can. You can also dye sand and pour it in different colored layers into jars and glasses, creating beautiful patterns. If you've never constructed a sand castle at the beach, all of the directions for making one are given. It is true that the best place to find sand is by the ocean or in the desert. Don't worry, however, if you live inland or in the city. Sand is available in hardware and hobby stores where it is sold by the bag. Everyone, no matter where they live, can have the pleasure of creating projects with sand. By making the crafts that follow, the thrills of the beach can be yours all year long.

Super Sand Castle

Imagine crossing over a moat filled with hungry crocodiles and entering a castle as large as a football field. What excitement there must have been when kings, queens, counts, and princesses ruled the world. If you had lived hundreds of years ago and were lucky enough, you might have been a Knight of the Roundtable or a princess or a king.

There aren't too many castles to live in these days, but you can do the next best thing by building one when you go to the beach or neighborhood sandbox. Why not bring some play soldiers with you when you go to make this very special fortress?

Things You Need

scissors
colored construction paper
liquid white glue
toothpicks
shoe box
coffee can
funnels
small pail
soup can
sand

Let's Begin

1. Sometime before your trip to the beach or neighborhood sandbox, cut triangles from colored construction paper.
2. Using the liquid white glue, glue the triangles to the toothpicks for flags.
3. Take the flags, shoe box, coffee can, funnels, and soup can with you to the beach or sandbox.
4. Use the wet sand that is near the water if you are at the beach. (Take a gallon of water with you if you are going to build your castle in a sandbox)
5. Fill the shoe box with wet sand.
6. Turn the box upside down onto the flat sand.
7. Unmold the sand by carefully lifting up the box.
8. Fill the cans with wet sand.
9. Turn the cans upside down, the larger one at the side of the shoe-box-molded sand, and the other at the end of it, see illustration. Carefully, lift the cans.
10. Fill a small pail with wet sand and carefully turn it upside down on top of the shoe-box-molded sand. Lift the pail.
11. Fill a funnel with wet sand and carefully turn it upside down on the pail-molded sand. Do the same on the coffee-can molded sand.
12. Add the paper flags to the castle as shown in the illustration.
13. Make windows in the castle by poking holes carefully into the sand with your finger.

Sand-Casted Sun

The sun is very important to every living creature and plant, and without it the earth would be colder than your freezer (in fact, there would be no life on earth without the sun). If you have ever seen fanciful drawings of the sun, you will notice that sometimes it is shown smiling and sometimes not. This sand-casted sun has a happy face. Put it in your room, or give it to someone you like as a very pretty present.

Things You Need

large gift box
aluminum foil
sand
pie tin
plastic spoon
plaster of paris
coffee can
paper clip

Let's Begin

1. Line the bottom and the sides of a gift box with aluminum foil. Be careful to get the foil into the corners.
2. Scoop sand into the box.
3. Sprinkle water onto the sand so that it is wet enough to make a hole if you poke your finger into it.
4. Smooth the sand evenly in the box.
5. Press the bottom of a pie tin completely into the sand, Fig. a. Don't press beyond the rim.
6. Carefully lift the pie tin from the sand. You should have created an impression of the bottom and sides of the pie tin in the sand.
7. Make a face design on the bottom of the impression with your fingers, Fig. b.
8. Poke a design into the side of the impression with your fingers, Fig. b.
9. Stirring all the while, mix plaster of paris and water in the coffee can until it looks like loose whipped cream.
10. Quickly spoon the plaster into the impression in the sand, Fig. c.
11. Smooth the top of the plaster with the back of a plastic spoon.
12. Open a paper clip, Fig. d.
13. Push one end of the open clip into the plaster near the top of the sun, Fig. e.
14. The casting will dry very slowly because of the wet sand. In ten days, remove your casting and hang. (To speed up the drying, place the box of sand in the sun.)

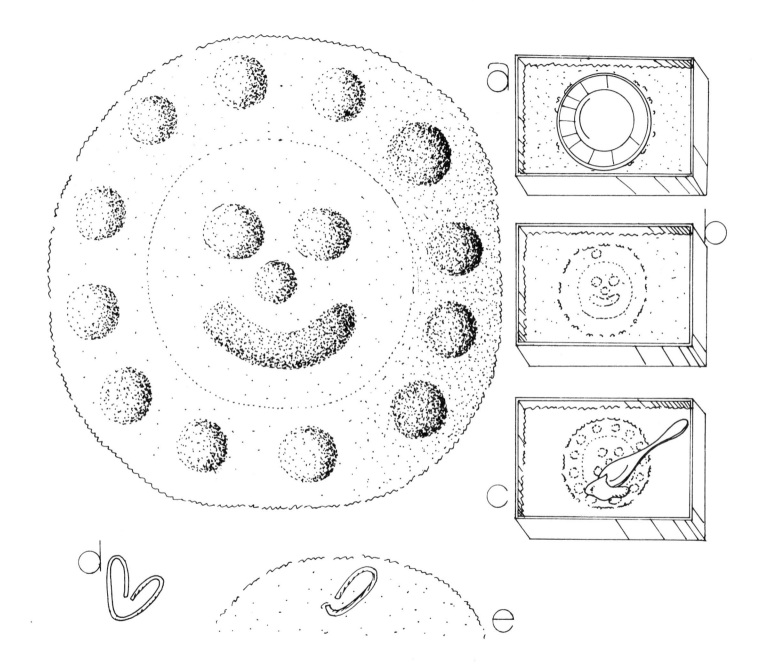

Fantasy Sculptures

Have you ever imagined that you were someone else living in a different time? If you have, then you have been in the world of fantasy. There are no real things in a fantasy (though the fantasy seems and is very real). Everything is designed in the halls of your imagination. You create the characters, the setting, and the story. These sculptures are fantastic because they come from your imagination and can be whatever you want them to be: animals, plants, or just strange things. Here is a craft that can be enjoyed anytime you feel like a little fantastic daydreaming.

Things You Need

plastic spoon
plaster of paris
coffee can
sand
waxed paper
poster paints
paintbrushes
sequins

Let's Begin

1. Stirring all the while, mix water and plaster of paris in a coffee can until it looks like cream.
2. Quickly stir enough sand into the plaster of paris to make the mixture look like thick whipped cream. Work fast, because the plaster dries quickly.
3. Pour some of the plaster mixture from the can onto a piece of waxed paper creating towering squiggles, Fig. a.
4. Spoon the remaining plaster out of the can in long creations, Fig. b.
5. Squeeze the tall squiggles to create unusual designs. Do this quickly before the plaster hardens.
6. When the sculptures have dried, paint and decorate them using poster paints and sequins, and remove from waxed paper.

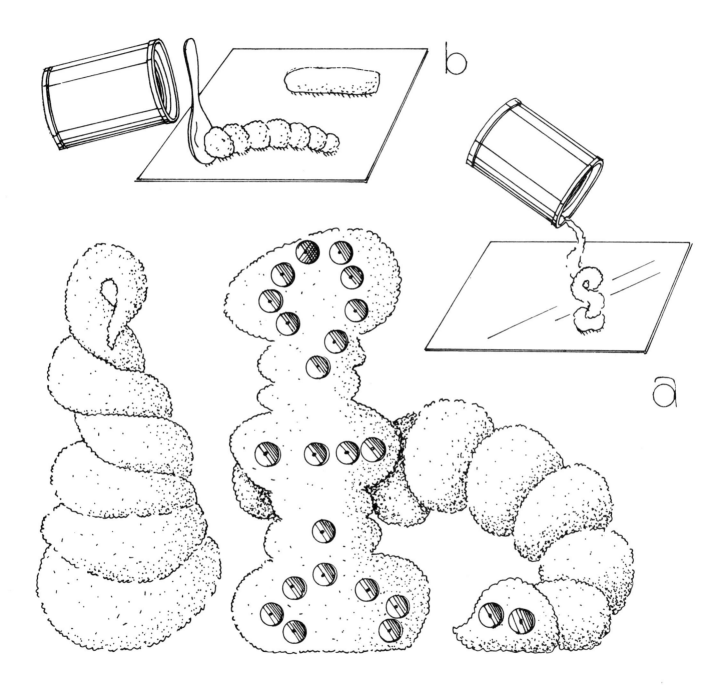

b

a

Apple Pin Cushion

"An apple a day keeps the doctor away," but if you bite into this one you may find yourself the not-so-happy recipient of a house call. You'll get a mouth full of sand! The Apple Pin Cushion is a gift Mom may have wanted for a long time. Pins and needles get lost very easily. When they are placed in this apple, the sand will hold them in place until it's time to sew the hole in your sock or that tear in your pants. If you like to sew, then you might want to make an Apple Pin Cushion for yourself.

Things You Need

scissors
scraps of red and green felt
needle and thread
plastic wrap
tablespoon
sand
rubber band

Let's Begin

1. Cut two circles from red felt, Fig a. They should be as large as the finished apple illustration.
2. Cut a leaf shape from green felt.
**3. Thread a needle.
4. Place the leaf between the two felt circles, Fig. b.
5. Start to sew the two circles together at the leaf shape with a small running stitch, see the directions given in Bean Bags, page 366.
6. Sew small, tight stitches halfway around the edge of the circle, Fig. c. Leave the threaded needle in place in the middle of your sewing.
7. Cut five large squares of plastic wrap.
8. Place the squares on top of each other.
9. Spoon three tablespoons of sand on top of the wrap stack, Fig. d.
10. Gather the ends of the plastic wrap around the sand, and twist rubber band tightly around the gathered wrap, Fig. e.
11. Trim the gathered wrap with scissors, Fig. f.
12. Place the bag of sand between the two red circles of felt, Fig. g.
13. Let gathered end of the wrap stick out from the circles near the green leaf. This will be the stem.
14. Finish sewing the circles together, Fig. h.
15. Sew the last stitch several times to form a knot before you cut away the thread.

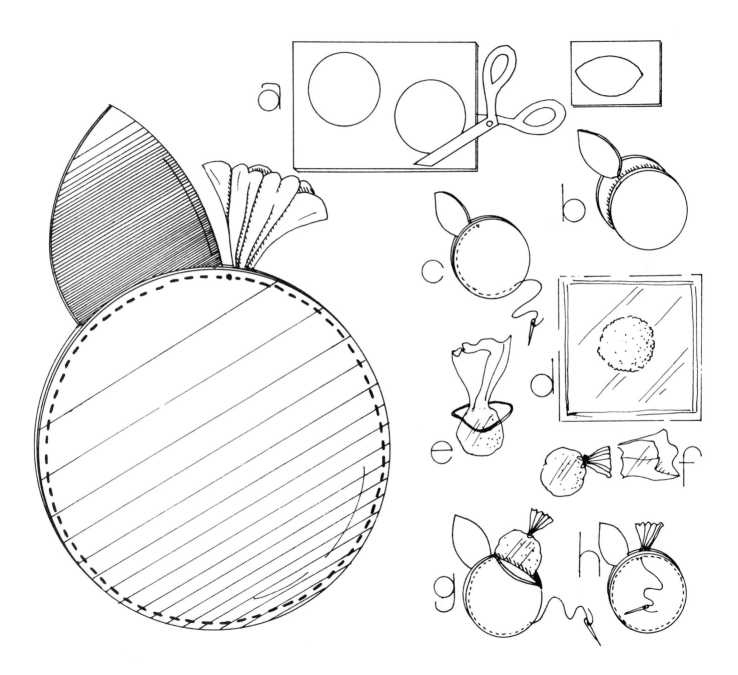

a

b

c

d

e

f

g

h

Bubble Bird Cage

Most of our flying feathered friends could not live in a bird cage. They must live and eat outdoors. There are several types of birds that can be kept in a cage: parrots, parakeets, and finches. You may already have a pet bird, but nothing like the caged creature you will make in this project. If you look at the illustration, you will wonder how it is made. The secret is using a balloon, but you will have to read further to unlock the mystery.

Things You Need

round balloon
string
colored yarn
liquid white glue
paper cup
waxed paper
paintbrush
sand
straight pin
tracing paper
pencil
scissors
yellow construction paper
paper punch

Let's Begin

1. Blow up a round balloon.
2. Knot the neck of the balloon, or tie it closed with a piece of string.
3. Tie a length of yarn to the neck of the balloon.
4. Wrap the yarn around the balloon in all directions, Fig. a.
5. After wrapping, tie the loose end of the yarn to the neck of the balloon.
6. Pour liquid white glue into a paper cup.
7. Place the yarn-wrapped balloon on a sheet of waxed paper.
8. Paint all of the yarn with liquid white glue.
9. Sprinkle sand evenly onto another sheet of waxed paper.
10. Roll the balloon over the sand to coat the yarn completely with sand, Fig. b.
11. Let the yarn dry thoroughly.
**12. Break the balloon with a straight pin.
13. Carefully peel away the broken balloon from the inside of the yarn.
14. Trace the bird shape from the book onto tracing paper. Cut out the tracing
15. Using the tracing as a pattern, draw the bird on a sheet of yellow construction paper.
16. Cut out the bird and draw an eye on it.
17. Punch a hole in the bird's head with a paper punch or with the point of the pencil.
18. Tie yarn through the hole on the bird.
19. Tie the bird in the cage, see illustration.
20. Tie yarn to the top of the cage for hanging.

a

b

Sand Pouring

Sand pouring may not sound very interesting to you, but when the sand is colored, you can make many beautiful objects with it. Collect several small jars with lids, and bring home a bag of sand the next time you are at the beach. Once the sand is dyed, start making different colored sand layers in the jars. You can use these sand-poured jars as paper weights or as decorations in your room.

Things You Need

paper cups
fine sand
powdered fabric dyes or food coloring
plastic spoons
paper towels
small jars with lids
paper clip

Let's Begin

1. Fill paper cups half-full with sand.
2. Add water to each cup to cover the sand completely.
3. Add different colors of powdered fabric dye or drops of food coloring to the water and sand. The more coloring you add, the deeper the color of the sand.
4. Stir the sand, water, and dye with a plastic spoon, Fig. a.
5. Let the sand sit in the dye and water for fifteen minutes.
6. Pinch the edge of the cup so you can pour out most of the water without spilling the sand. Pour out the water.
7. Spoon the sand from each cup onto separate sheets of paper toweling, Fig. b. Keep colors separate.
8. Spread out the sand and let it dry.
9. Spoon a layer of colored sand into a small jar which you have washed and dried well, Fig. c.
10. Carefully spoon different layers of colored sand on top of one another into the jar, Fig. d. The last layer should barely come to the neck of the jar.
11. Open a paper clip to form a straight piece of wire.
12. Holding the wire against the inside of the jar, push the wire down through all the layers of sand, Fig. e.
13. Pull the wire out of the jar and you will see how it pulls the different layers into each other.
14. Make these designs around the entire jar.
15. When the design is finished, spoon sand to the top of the jar and screw on the lid, Fig. f.

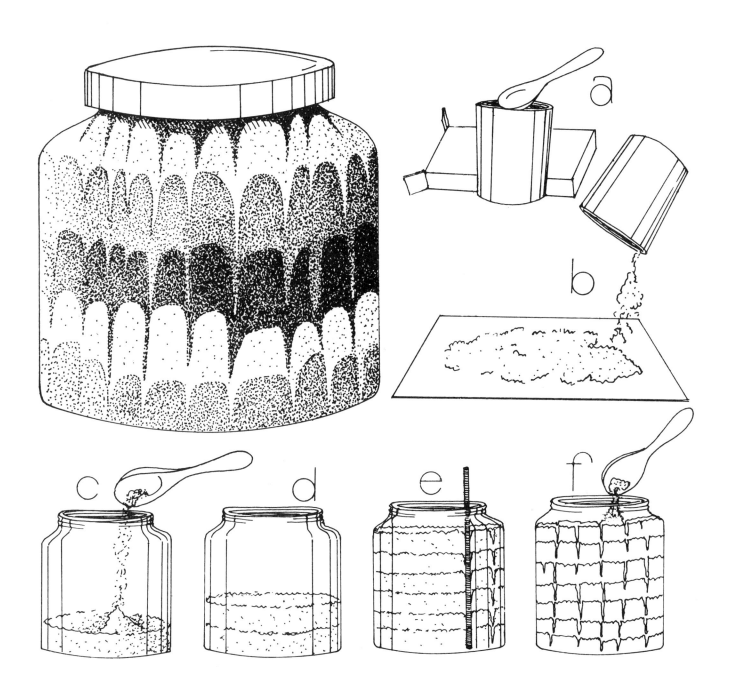

Sand Painting

Because sand can be dyed any color, it can be used to create beautiful paintings. As an artist uses paint on a canvas, you will use colored sand. The subject for this sand painting is a butterfly and an apple on a branch. Find pictures of these natural beauties, and decide what colors to dye your sand. Once you start working on this painting, you won't be able to put it down.

Things You Need

pencil
heavy white drawing paper
sand
paper cups
boxed dyes or food coloring
plastic spoons
paper towels
liquid white glue
paintbrush

Let's Begin

1. With a pencil draw the design shapes as you see them in the illustration on a sheet of heavy paper, Fig. a.
2. Dye and dry the sand as described in Sand Pouring, page 434.
3. Pour liquid white glue into a paper cup.
4. Using the paintbrush, fill in one of the design shapes with the glue, Fig. b.
5. Sprinkle one color of dyed and dried sand over the glued area, Fig. c.
6. Repeat gluing design shapes and sprinkling on different colored sand in different areas of your design.
7. Let the painting dry.
8. When the painting has dried, tip it over a paper towel to remove any excess sand that did not glue in place, Fig. d.

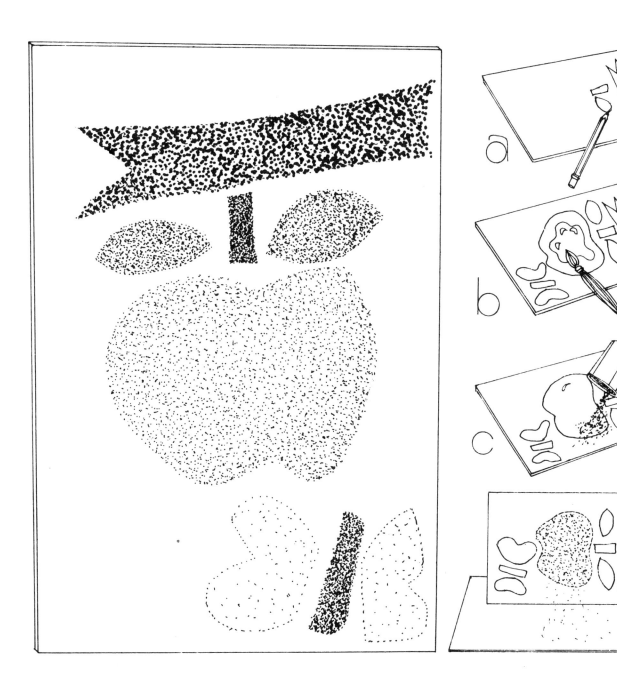

Sand Dried Flowers

There is always a need for a bouquet of lovely flowers. The bouquet you will make will consist of dried flowers—flowers with soft colors that last a long, long time. Gather flowers from the fields or from your garden, and start drying them immediately. Once you have dried enough flowers, start making bouquets and garlands for every room in your home.

Things You Need

cardboard box
sand
scissors
freshly picked flowers
drinking straws or florist sticks
beading wire (purchasable in five-and-ten-cent stores) or pipe cleaners
green construction paper
liquid white glue

Let's Begin

1. Fill the cardboard box half-full with sand.
2. Cut away most of the stem from each flower. The remaining stem should be as long as your middle finger, Fig. a.
3. Push the stem of each flower into the sand, Fig. b.
4. Sprinkle a thin layer of sand over the flowers making sure to cover them completely, Fig. c. If you have a thick flower with many petals, such as a rose, open the petals slightly, and fill in the spaces between the petals with sand.
5. Place the box in a dry place like a closet or an attic.
6. Let the flowers dry in the sand for two weeks.
7. When the flowers have dried, carefully tilt the box and pour out the top sand.
8. Carefully lift out the flowers.
9. Florists sell green wooden sticks that can be used as stems for your flowers. You can also use drinking straws. Carefully attach flowers to the stems with beading wire or pipe cleaners, Fig. d.
10. Cut out leaves from green construction paper.
11. Glue the leaves to the stems of the flowers.

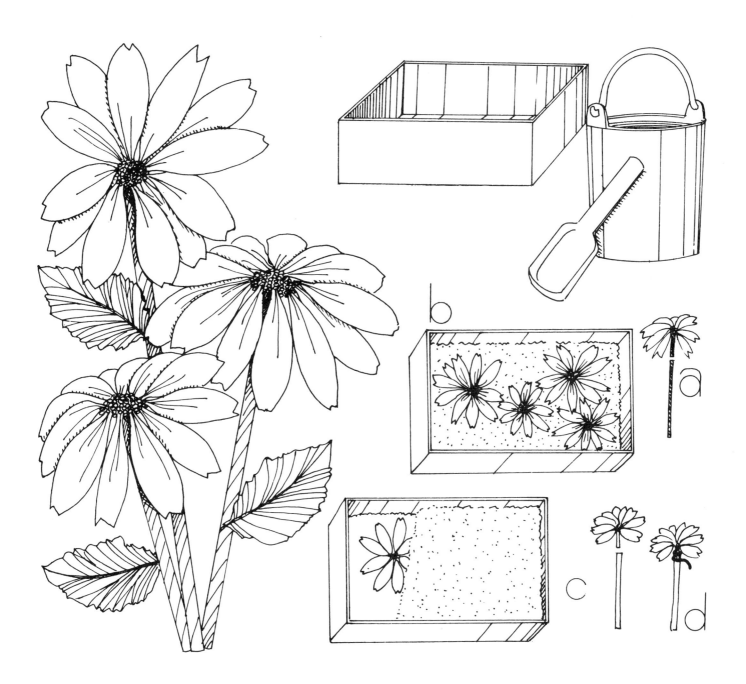

b

a

c

d

Cactus Terrarium

A terrarium is a closed container in which small plants or animals live in a controlled atmosphere. You won't be using small animals for this project, just cactus plants. Have Mom or Dad buy one or more cacti, then find a jar large enough to contain them. Add a rock or rocks to this glass-enclosed, desert. Add some water when you cannot see moisture beads on the inside of the glass jar. Your cactus terrarium will be a treasure that will seem to draw you into its miniature environment.

Things You Need

large jar with a lid
sand
small cactus plants
tiny rocks
hammer and nail

Let's Begin

1. Wash and remove the label from a large jar.
2. Add sand to the jar.
3. Plant small cactus plants in the sand.
4. Add some pretty rocks.
5. Sprinkle just enough water into the jar to wet the sand.
6. Screw on the lid.
**7. Make small holes in the lid with a hammer and nail.

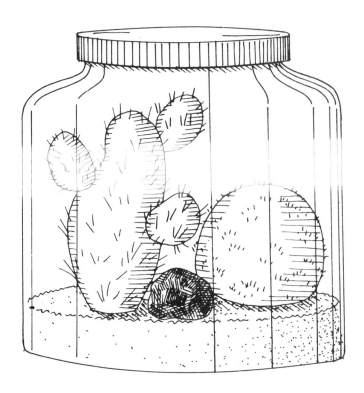

Fruit is a beautiful sweet

You know you like candy, but what about fruit? Both contain sugar—that's probably the big attraction. But though candy may come first when you want something sweet, there are times when nothing but fruit will do. Think of a cold crunchy apple or a sweet and sloppy slice of watermelon. We say that fruit is nature's candy, but it is so much more. Take a good look at a peach or a bunch of grapes sometime. You'll never see such a beautiful candy bar. Fruit's a beautiful sweet—to your eye and hand as well as your sweet tooth.

You are probably wondering why there is a chapter on fruit in a craft book. Many interesting things can be made with fruit. Most fruits required for the projects here can be obtained easily at the supermarket. If you enjoy outdoor adventure, however, you may want to hunt for fruit yourself. Blackberries, raspberries, and blueberries grow in most parts of the country during the summer. Don't look for berries in the forest, however. They grow where the trees end and the fields begin. They will be useful when you want to make berry ink.

Since fruit is available at the store all the time, have Mom or Dad buy only that amount you will need for the crafts you intend to make right away. Unless you use (or eat) the fruit immediately, it will spoil. And speaking of eating, try to refrain from ingesting your craft materials or your project will very much lack something. Although that orange would be delicious, you're going to be out a beautiful and fragrant pomander ball!

Caramel Apple Friends

You don't have to travel very far to enjoy a good caramel apple. All it takes is a bag of caramels, a bowl of apples, and some funny face-making assorted candies. Your Caramel Apple Friends will be amusing—not to mention—delicious companions.

Things You Need

two saucepans, one larger than the other
small tin can
1 package vanilla caramels
spoon
jelly apple sticks
4 to 6 apples
candies, sprinkles, coconut
waxed paper
cookie sheet

Let's Begin

1. Fill the larger saucepan half-full with water.
2. Place a small tin can upside down in the water.
3. Put the smaller pot on the can in the larger pot, Fig. a.
4. Add caramels to the smaller pot. (Do not use the chocolate fudge that are sometimes packed with the caramels.)
**5. Place the saucepan arrangement on top of the stove and turn the burner on to a medium heat. Stir the caramels with a spoon until they melt. You can also melt caramels in a single saucepan directly over a low heat. If you do, add a teaspoon of milk and stir constantly.
6. Push a jelly apple stick into the top of a washed and dried apple.
**7. Dip the apple into the melted caramel, coating it by swirling it in the melted caramel, Fig. b. Be sure that the entire apple is covered with caramel.
8. Hold the apple by the stick and make silly faces with candy trimmings. Work fast. The following are instructions for making the caramel apple faces:
Face A. Use chocolate sprinkles for hair, gumdrops for eyes and nose, and string licorice for the mouth.
Face B. Use chocolate chips for hair, chocolate-coated dots for eyes and nose, and an orange slice for the mouth.
Face C. Use coconut for hair, sourballs for the eyes, and red hots for the nose and mouth.
Face D. Use string licorice for hair, candy wafers for the eyes, and miniature marshmallows for the mouth.
9. Place the decorated apple upside down on a sheet of waxed paper placed on a cookie sheet, Fig. c.
10. Spoon remaining caramel onto waxed paper. Press the caramel flat, to make caramel candy drops.

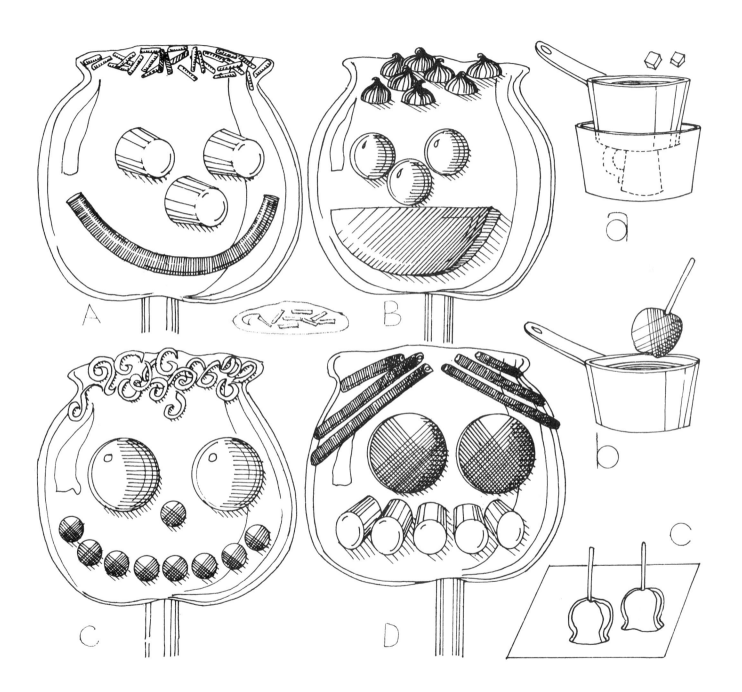

Apple-Head Puppets

Did you know that apples make wonderful puppets? You create the costumes for the puppets and decorate the apple heads to make funny faces. Choose apples that aren't too perfect for this project because you won't be able to eat them after the puppet show is finished.

Things You Need

apples
spoon
toothpicks
miniature marshmallows, gumdrops or grapes
cotton napkin or handkerchief
3 rubber bands

Let's Begin

1. Remove the stem from an apple.
**2. Scoop out a deep hole in the top of the apple with a spoon, Fig. a.
3. Break toothpicks in half.
4. To make faces, push the toothpick halves through miniature marshmallows, gumdrops, or grapes and then into the apple.
5. Place a cotton napkin or handkerchief over your hand as shown in Fig. b.
6. Wrap and twist a rubber band not too tightly around the three extended fingers as shown in Fig. c.
7. Push the hole in the apple head over the top (middle) finger. The two side fingers work as arms. Make as many puppets as you wish, but give each a unique candy face.

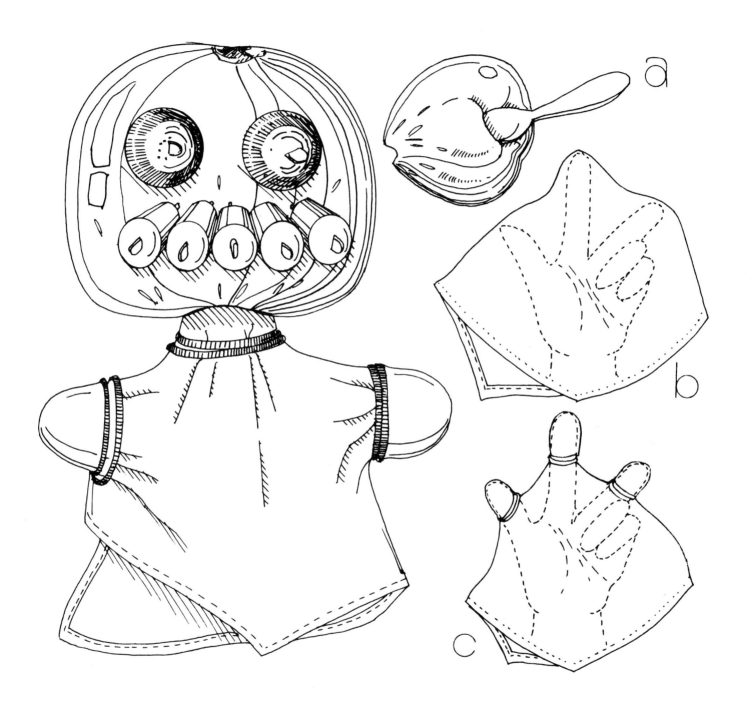

Fruit Printing

Have you ever cut a piece of round fruit in half? If you have, then you know that the exposed surface has a pretty design. Every fruit you cut in half reveals a different pattern. You can use cut fruit to make prints. Get yourself a stack of paper and a bowl of fruit, and experiment with different fruits and colors. Once you have mastered fruit printing, you can make beautiful prints for your room.

Things You Need

knife
apples, oranges, lemons
poster paints
paper plate
paintbrush
white drawing paper

Let's Begin

**1. Cut a piece of fruit in half, Fig. a.
2. Pour a little poster paint into a paper plate. Spread it evenly over the bottom of the plate with a paintbrush, Fig. b.
3. Press the cut side of the fruit into the paint.
4. Lift the fruit from the plate.
5. Press the painted fruit onto white drawing paper. Be careful not to move the fruit as you print, Fig. c.
6. Carefully lift the fruit to see the print.

a

b

c

Orange Pomander Ball

People have always placed sweet-smelling things in their drawers or closets to make them smell especially fresh. The most popular freshener is the sachet bag filled with dried lilac. Another old-fashioned closet sweetener is the orange pomander ball. Pioneer women used this spicy-smelling ball to remove unpleasant odors from the kitchen. You will want to have a pomander ball in your room as Mom or Dad will undoubtedly want one for their closet or dresser drawers.

Things You Need

whole cloves
orange
cinnamon
plastic bag
ribbon or netting
string

Let's Begin

1. Push the pointed stems of whole cloves into the skin of an orange, Fig. a. Cover the entire orange with cloves, see illustration.
2. Sprinkle cinnamon into a plastic bag.
3. Place the orange in the bag, Fig. b.
4. Hold the top of the bag as you shake the orange in the cinnamon.
5. Remove the orange from the bag.
6. Tie a length of ribbon around the orange and knot it, Fig. c.
7. Tie a second ribbon criss-crossing the first ribbon at the bottom, and knot at the top.
8. Tie a length of string around the knotted ribbons.
10. Hang the ball in a special place. The orange will eventually shrink in size and become hard, but should not lose its scent.

a

b

c

Pear People

Pears are fruit with a shape that may remind you of a person sitting on the floor. Now all you need to add is a face, arms and legs. With everything in place, your pear person will entertain you and your family enormously.

Things You Need

fresh pears
toothpicks
grapes
knife
maraschino cherries

Let's Begin

1. Stand a pear upright on its wide bottom.
2. Make two arms and two legs by pushing two grapes onto each pick, see illustration.
3. Push the toothpicks into the pear for the arms and legs.
**4. Cut a maraschino cherry in half with a knife.
5. Break a toothpick in half.
6. Push each half toothpick through each half of the cut maraschino cherry.
7. Insert the maraschino cherry halves into the pear for eyes. You may make many pear people for a funny bowl of fruit.

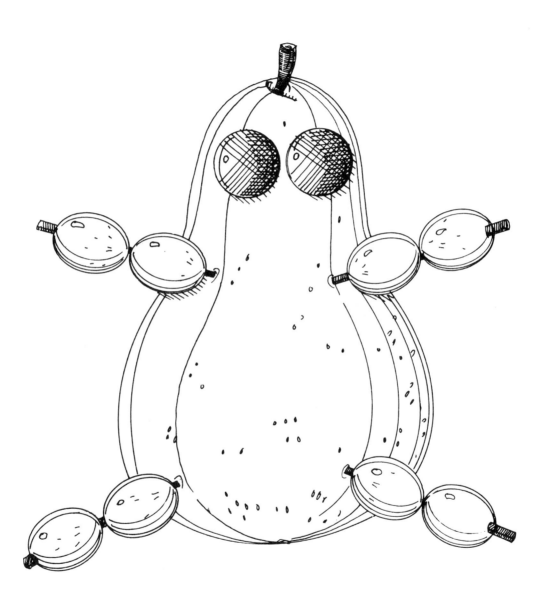

Canned Fruit Animals

If you like what's inside a closed can of fruit, then you'll love what you can do with the contents once the can is open. You can make all of your favorite animals from canned fruit. And you get to eat them for a fabulous dessert.

Things You Need

spoon and spatula
canned pineapple slices, peach halves, apricots, and pears
paper towels
small paper plates
cake decorating gel in a tube

Let's Begin

1. Spoon out the canned fruit onto paper towels. Blot the fruit until it is dry.
2. Use a spatula to lift the fruit onto a small paper plate.
3. Make the animals as described below:

LION: Place a peach half on top of a pineapple slice. Use cake decorating gel to draw a lion face on the peach half.

MONKEY: Use a pear half and add apricot halves for ears. Draw a monkey face on the pear with cake decorating gel.

RABBIT: Use a peach half for the face. The ears are made from peach slices. Draw on a face and ear design with cake decorating gel.

BEAR: Use a peach half for the face and add apricot halves for the ears. Draw on a face with cake decorating gel.

For serving, animals can also be placed on a slice of pound cake or a dish of jello.

Berry Ink

When you write a letter to a friend or to your grandparents, you probably use a ball-point pen. Before the ball-point pen was invented, people used a fountain pen that contained ink or a stick pen that had a point which was dipped in ink. It is very tiresome dipping a pen continuously into ink, but if you've never written in this way it could be fun. You will enjoy writing even more if you make your own ink. All you need is some ripe berries and something to crush them with. Believe it or not, this was one of the ways writing ink was first produced.

Things You Need

ripe cherries, blueberries, blackberries or
  strawberries
small jars with lids
spoon
paper towels
paper cups

Let's Begin

1. Remove stems and leaves from ripe berries and place them in a small jar.
2. Press the berries to a pulp with the back of a spoon, Fig. a.
3. When the berries are crushed, add a little water. The more water you add, the lighter the color of the finished ink will be, Fig. b.
4. Stir the mixture well, Fig. c.
5. Place a sheet of paper toweling over a paper cup. Push the paper towel down into the cup, Fig. d.
6. Slowly pour the berry mixture through the towel in the cup, Fig. e.
7. Let all of the liquid drain through the towel. Remove the towel and throw it away.
8. Pour the strained ink back into the jar and screw on the lid.
9. Use a straight or fountain pen to write with the berry ink.

a

b

c

d

e

Cranberry Necklace

Almost anything can be strung to make a necklace providing it is small enough. Cranberries are good to use because they are firm and have no pits. They are also quite round and look like large red beads. With the addition of construction paper charms, this necklace will look pretty around your neck. The kids at school as well as the teachers will be amazed at your creation.

Things You Need

needle and thread
scissors

colored construction paper
whole fresh cranberries

Let's Begin

**1. Thread a needle with a long length of thread.
 2. Cut small charm shapes from colored construction paper.
**3. String cranberries onto the thread using the needle. Alternate berries with paper charms, see illustration.
 4. Knot both ends of the string of cranberries to form a necklace.

456

Even you
can love vegetables

How many times have you heard that awful command, "Eat your vegetables, they're good for you!" Well, they are, but they can also be delicious. It may take a while to like vegetables, but once you do, you really do. A sweet and buttery ear of corn, tender peas served, perhaps, in a little cream, even spinach—properly prepared—these vegetables could make you forget the meat and dessert. No, you won't *have* to eat any vegetables to tackle this chapter (this is not a cookbook), but you may learn to love them if only by making wonderful crafts that use them.

Unless you have a vegetable garden, all the vegetables you will need will have to be freshly bought. If they have been in the house for days or weeks, they may be too old to use. One of the projects in this chapter calls for a potato as a printing press. If the potato you use is not firm, it will be hard to carve designs into it. In order to make a carrot necklace, you must have a hard carrot. If you don't, the individual carrot beads will droop on the string.

Look through the chapter and see what vegetables you will need for the crafts you want to make. Go shopping for them with Mom or Dad. After you complete your projects, you may want to sample some of the "raw materials" yourself. Even you can love vegetables—as mouth-watering craftwork or simply beautiful eating.

Carrot Necklace

Carrots are supposed to be good for your eyesight. They can also do wonders for your neck. Wonders for your neck? Yes, if you turn them into a pretty orange necklace. Carrots can be sliced and strung on a string to create a most unusual piece of neckware. Be very careful, however. Don't wear your necklace in the vicinity of a hungry rabbit!

Things You Need

large carrots
potato peeler
knife
string or dental floss
needle with a large eye
typewriter paper

Let's Begin

1. Scrape the outside of a carrot with the potato peeler, Fig. a.
**2. Cut the carrot into medium-sized slices, Fig. b.
**3. Thread the needle with enough string or dental floss to go over your head when the necklace is completed.
**4. Thread the carrot slices by pushing the needle through the center of each slice, one by one, Fig. c. Leave a little space between each slice as you thread.
5. Tie the ends of the string together to close the necklace.
6. Lay the necklace on a sheet of paper, Fig. d.
7. Place the paper in a dry place, such as a closet or in the attic so that the necklace can dry completely.
8. Your necklace should be ready to wear in ten days.

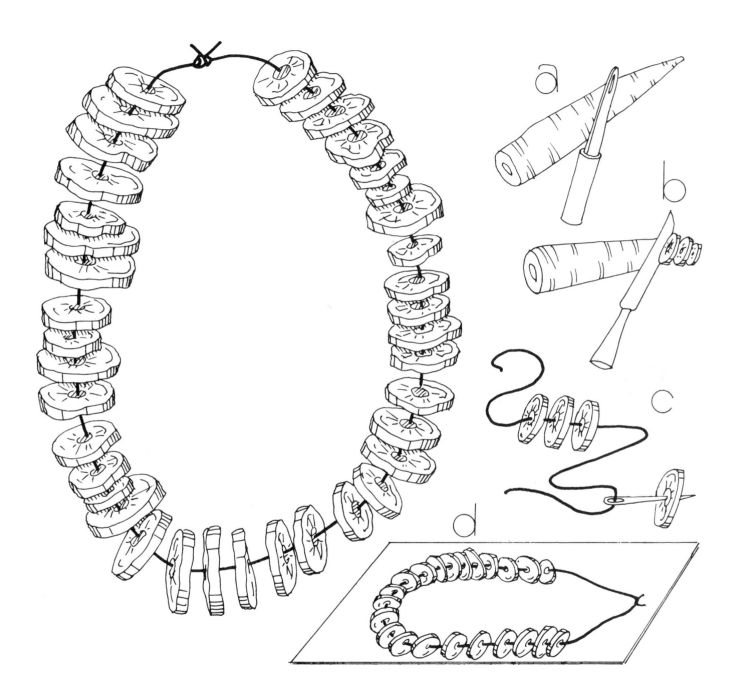

Colored Celery Tree

Have you ever wondered how a tree gets water from the soil? It's not too difficult to understand. Water first enters the roots that are in the ground. From the roots, the water travels up "tubes" in the tree all the way to the top of the branches. Every branch and leaf is nourished through these tubes. If there is no moisture in the ground, the tree will die.

If you want to see this process for yourself, this project will help you do it. You will need water, a stalk of celery, and two different colored food dyes. Do this project in the evening, or just before you go to bed. When you wake up in the morning you will see that your celery stalk has absorbed the dyed water and that the leaves have changed colors.

Things You Need

knife
celery stalk with leaves
2 drinking glasses
boxed dyes or food coloring (2 colors)
spoon

Let's Begin

**1. Trim away part of the bottom of the celery, Fig. a.

**2. Slice halfway through the center of the celery stalk with a knife, Fig. b.

3. Fill two glasses at least three-quarters full with water.

4. Add a different color of dye or food coloring to the water in each glass. Mix well with a spoon. Add enough dye to make a very strong or dark solution, Fig. c.

5. Place the two glasses next to each other. Slip one end of the cut celery stalk into one glass and the remaining end into the other glass, see illustration.

6. Let the celery remain in the dye overnight. In the morning, the different dyes will have traveled up the celery stalk and the leaves will have colored beautifully.

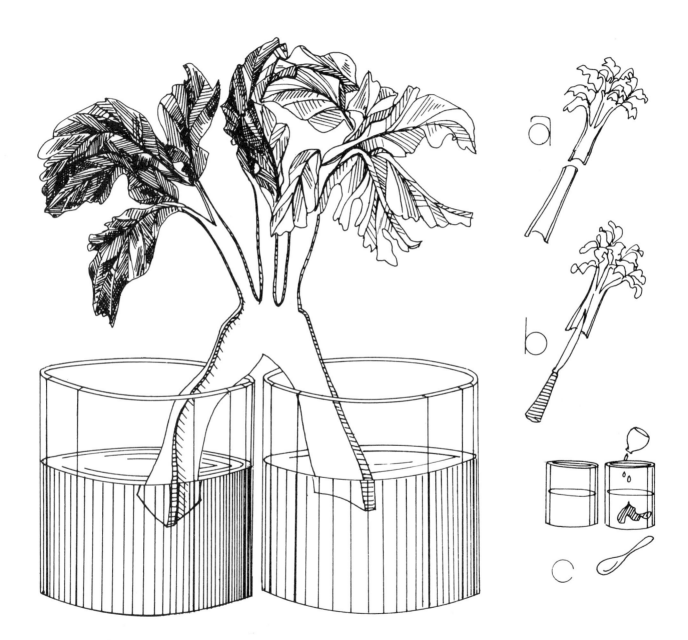

a

b

c

Painted Pumpkins and Gourds

A favorite Halloween craft is the decoration of pumpkins and gourds. Fall is actually the only time of the year you can do this because pumpkins and gourds are harvested then. Even if it is not the jack-o-lantern season, you can still think of unusual faces and designs to paint on a gourd or a pumpkin. Hold onto your ideas, and when the right season arrives, get ready to make this craft. Place the completed projects behind your front door or on your window sills to keep the Halloween spirit at your very own house during this spooky time of year.

Things You Need

pumpkins and gourds
mild soap
poster paint or model airplane enamels
kitchen cleanser
paintbrush

Let's Begin

1. Wash pumpkins and gourds with mild soap and water. Let them dry completely.
2. Mix a little kitchen cleanser to poster paints in small paper cuts. You can also use model airplane enamels.
3. Use oil-base paints to create a wonderful assortment of autumn friends, see illustration for examples.

Popcorn Painting

The Indians were probably the first to enjoy a tasty bowl of popcorn. They would dry the kernels and save them for popping during the winter and spring months. If it weren't for the Indians, you probably wouldn't be able to munch on a bag of buttered popcorn while watching a horror movie.

Popcorn can be dyed and used in many creative projects. Why not try your hand at a popcorn painting? You can make a lovely flower that will add a delicious touch to your room.

Things You Need

pencil
white drawing paper
popping corn
cooking oil
pot with lid
paper cups
food coloring
spoon
paper towels
liquid white glue

Let's Begin

1. Draw a simple design on a sheet of paper such as the one you see in the illustration.
**2. Have Mom or Dad pop some corn for you. Follow the instructions which come with the popping corn.
3. Fill cups with water and add different colored food coloring to each one.
4. Add a few popped corn kernels into each of the colors, Fig. a.
5. Stir the kernels once and quickly remove them from the cups with spoon. Place them on a paper towel to dry, Fig. b.
6. Let the colored popped corn dry completely.
7. Fill in an area of your design with liquid white glue. Place one of the colors of the dried popped corn on the glue.
8. Glue and fill in all of the areas of your design using a different colored corn for each area.
9. Let the popcorn painting dry overnight.

a

b

Artichoke Flowers

Have you ever eaten a flower? If you like to eat artichokes, then—guess what—you have eaten one of nature's edible flowering plants. Artichokes are the unopened flowers of a thistle-like plant. Thistle plants produce a purplish blossom and have many thorns. You might find them growing wild along the highways in the country.

Artichokes, like other vegetables, can be dried. Since they resemble flowers, the dried plants can be included in a bouquet of dried flowers, or placed in a vase by themselves. Artichokes are a seasonal vegetable, so you will have to check with the grocery store to see if they are being sold.

Things You Need

pencil
artichoke
cotton
poster paints
paintbrush

Let's Begin

**1. Push a sharpened pencil into the base of an artichoke, see illustration.
2. Stuff cotton between some of the leaves of the artichoke.
3. After a few days the artichoke will begin to dry slightly. Push more cotton between as many leaves as you can.
4. The artichoke leaves will be tightly arranged, but as the artichoke dries, insert more cotton, between the leaves. When the artichoke has been stuffed with as much cotton as possible, let it dry completely. The drying time will differ, depending on what part of the country you live.
5. When the artichoke has dried, remove all of the cotton that is between the leaves.
6. The artichoke flower can now be painted with poster paints. If you have spray paint in a can, use this, but let Mom or Dad help.

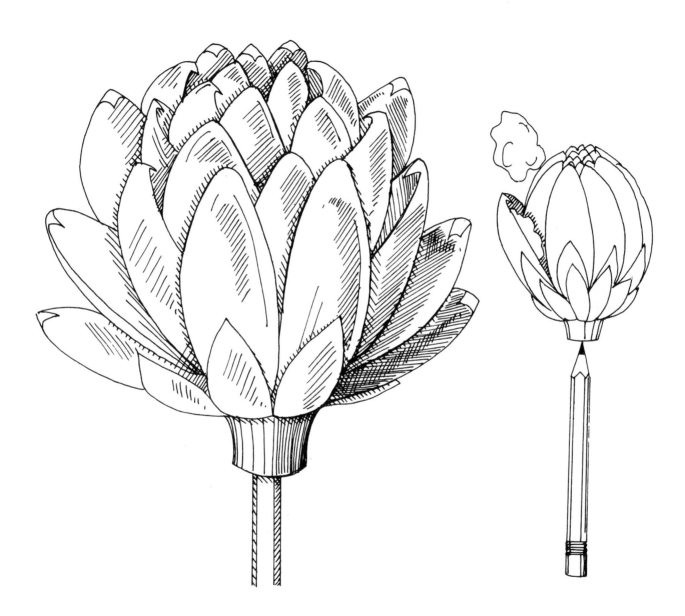

Potato Face

There is a vegetable that has more eyes than you do but can't see a thing. Do you know what it is? It's the brown-skinned potato. Of all the vegetables cooked in your home, the potato is probably the one you like the most. Shoestring, mashed, french-fried, scalloped—these are some of the many potato preparations you have probably tasted. All of them are delicious, each in its own special way.

Potatoes grow in every shape imaginable. Some are round, some are long, and some are twisted. No matter what the shape, you can design a hundred different faces for it. Use your imagination to make a clubhouse of potato-face pals.

Things You Need

tracing paper

pencil
scissors
colored construction paper
toothpicks
large potato

Let's Begin

1. Using a pencil, trace all of the features from the book onto a sheet of tracing paper.
2. Cut out the features from the tracing paper.
3. Place the tracing paper cutouts on colored construction paper and trace around them.
4. Cut out the features from the colored construction paper.
5. Break toothpicks in half.
6. Push a toothpick through a paper feature and then into the potato.
7. Create a different look by adding a hat, glasses, or a mustache.

Potato Printing

To make a potato print, you carve a design on the surface of a cut potato, paint it, and press the painted design onto a piece of paper. What you get is an impression with an interesting texture. Even the largest potato doesn't have a very wide surface once it is cut in half, so you will probably want to repeat a single design in interesting ways all over your paper. The design in the illustration is of a three-leaf clover. Your print could show a bouquet of clover or clover prints arranged in an interesting scattered design. Create your own potato printer design, print it on the things that belong to you. Potato printing is a lot of fun, especially on days when you have to stay indoors.

Things You Need

knife
potatoes
paper towels
water-color felt-tipped markers
potato peeler
poster paints
paper plate
paintbrush
paper

Let's Begin

**1. Cut a large potato in half, Fig. a
  2. Blot moisture from the potato's surface with a paper towel.
  3. Draw a simple design on the potato's surface with a colored felt-tipped marker, Fig. b.
**4. With a potato peeler or knife, scoop away the part of the potato that surrounds the drawn design, Fig. c. The design should be raised above the potato's surface.
  5. Pour a little poster paint onto a paper plate.
  6. Spread paint over the plate with a paintbrush.
  7. Either press the potato into the paint or brush the paint directly onto the design, Fig. d.
  8. Press the painted potato design onto a piece of paper.
  9. Lift the potato carefully to see your print, Fig. e.

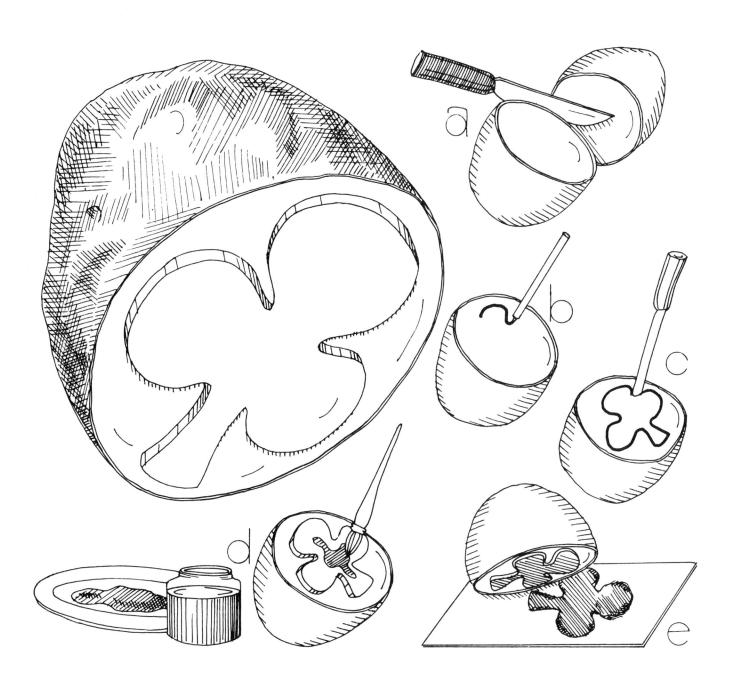

a

b

c

d

e

Sweet Potato Plant

When you plant a seed, you never get to see what is happening below the soil. It takes one to two weeks before the green shoot breaks through the surface of the dirt. Now you can watch the entire growing process by planting a sweet potato in a glass. You will see the roots grow first and then watch a beautiful, leafy plant sprout out of the potato top.

Things You Need

toothpicks
sweet potato
glass

Let's Begin

1. Push four or more toothpicks halfway into a sweet potato. They should be inserted in the bottom third of the potato, see illustration.
2. Place the potato in a glass with the toothpicks resting on the top rim.
3. Pour water into the glass. Make sure the end of the potato is in the water.
4. Place the glass on a window sill or any place where it will get a good deal of light. It will take a few weeks before you see roots growing out of the sides and bottom of the sweet potato. Keep the water level in the glass constant. Soon purplish sprouts will grow from the top of the potato.

5. You can leave the plant in the glass, or pot the sweet potato in soil, as you wish.

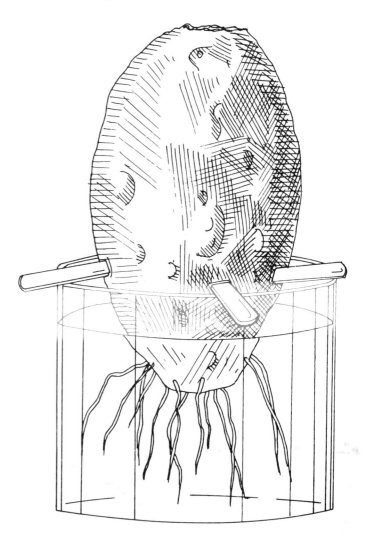

Nature is filled with wondrous things

Nature is all around you. Even if you live in a large city, nature in the form of birds, bugs, and buds live with you In the country it is easy to locate natural wonders. All you have to do is head for the nearest tree. It's not quite that simple in the city, but if you look carefully, you will surely find something "natural" to delight you. It might be a weed growing through the crack of the pavement outside your apartment It might be a sparrow nesting in a hole in a brick wall You might even see a spider web stretched across a corner of the ceiling in a little-used room.

Of course, natural things and their products are used by people every day no matter where they live. Did you know that things like sugar, salt, feathers, and bones are all part of nature? We have been using natural materials for craftwork, and this chapter should take us even further in this special enjoyment of them. We will use the rain to produce fascinating prints, a sponge's surface to make a lunar landscape, a wishbone for a good luck necklace. There are so many wonderful moments in this chapter, it's time to get started right away. Perhaps you'd like to begin with a craft that uses everyday sugar in a new way—to make a "mountain" of rock candy you will find delicious to eat.

Feathered Peace Pipe

The Indians smoked a peace pipe as a gesture of love and understanding with their fellow tribesmen and the settlers of the Old West. Perhaps you could use one after playing a particularly hard game, or whenever you think things might be better for a little calm and quiet.

Things You Need

small paper cup
red construction paper
pencil
scissors
liquid white glue
red glitter
drinking straw
feathers

Let's Begin

1. Turn a small paper cup upside down on a piece of red construction paper.
2. Trace around the rim of the cup with a pencil, Fig. a.
3. Cut out the traced red circle.
4. Stand the cup up on its base.
5. Push a pencil through the center of the cup on an upward angle, and out through the opposite side, Fig. b. See the dotted line in the illustration.
6. Using liquid white glue, glue the red circle onto the top of the cup. Fig. c.
7. Spread some glue over the top of the red circle.
8. Sprinkle red glitter over the glue, Fig. d.
9. Push the straw through the two holes in the cup. Let a little of the straw poke through the other end, see illustration.
10. Glue the straw in place.
11. Glue large feathers to the straw.

a

b

c

d

Salt Play Clay

You know how much fun it is to get a package of clay and mold strange creatures from it. Did you know that you can make a non-messy clay in your own kitchen? All of the ingredients you will need for it can be found in the cupboard. You will probably need Mom's or Dad's help with this project. For being so helpful, why not make them a play-clay pendant or medallion.

Things You Need

measuring cup
flour
salt
old saucepan
food coloring
spoon
waxed paper
rolling pin
cookie cutters
plastic drinking straws
scissors
liquid white glue
sequins
yarn
macaroni

Let's Begin

1. Measure one cup of water, one-half cup of flour, and one cup of salt in an old saucepan and mix. Add food coloring if you want to make a colored clay.

**2. Place the saucepan on the stove over a very low heat. Stir continuously.

**3. When the mixture is as thick as rubber, remove the saucepan from the stove.

4. Spoon part of the clay onto a floured sheet of waxed paper, Fig. a.

5. Roll out the clay with a rolling pin, Fig. b. If the clay is sticky, sprinkle with more flour.

6. Cut out designs from the clay with cookie cutters. Punch out a small hole near the top of each cutout with a straw.

7. Roll the scraps of clay into balls.

8. Push the balls of clay onto a plastic drinking straw leaving a little space between each ball, Fig. c.

9. Let the clay shapes and balls dry for a few days.

10. Cut and remove the straw from the balls, which will be used for beads.

11. Using liquid white glue, glue sequins to the cookie shapes.

12. Tie a cookie shape to the middle of a piece of yarn.

13. String the beads on the yarn and tie the ends together.

14. You can make a clay bowl by shaping rolled-out clay with your hands. Press macaroni into the sides before the clay hardens, see illustration.

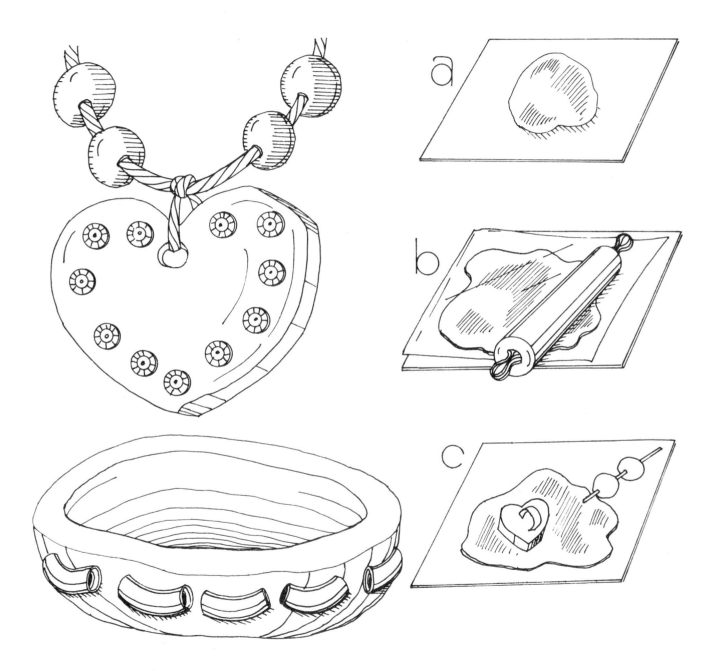

a

b

c

Wheat Sunburst

Wheat is one of the most important plants in your life. If you enjoy eating cereal for breakfast, check out the ingredients on the box. Somewhere between the sugar and the food coloring you should find the word "wheat." All products that contain flour started out as wheat. Some of your favorite food such as cake and cookies are made with wheat in the form of flour.

Wheat is a member of the grass family, and produces a crown of kernels. When wheat turns golden brown, it is time to harvest it. If you can find a field where wheat grows, pick a small bundle. If you can't, it can occasionally be bought at the florist's where it is sold to make dried plant arrangements. Your Wheat Sunburst will make a glorious decoration for your wall.

Things You Need

wheat
waxed paper
liquid white glue
colored yarn

Let's Begin

1. Place an uneven number of wheat stalks in a circle on a sheet of waxed paper, Fig. a. The wheat stalks should overlap one another in the center. They should also be exactly the same distance apart.
2. Squeeze a large dab of liquid white glue onto the overlapping ends of the wheat stalks.
3. When the glue has dried, carefully peel away the waxed paper.
4. Tie one end of a length of yarn to a stalk of wheat near the center of the sunburst, Fig. b.
5. Take the other end of the yarn and weave it in and out of the stalks as if you were weaving a basket.
6. You can tie a different colored yarn to the first as you weave along for a more colorful sunburst. Warm colors, such as yellow, orange, and red, are especially pretty.
7. After you have woven several circles of yarn, tie the end onto the stalk nearest to it. Hang the sunburst on a wall.

a

b

Corn Husk Doll

The Indians were the first to make the corn husk doll. Corn husks were dried, tied, and fashioned into squaws, chiefs, and braves. All additional features were made of corn husk. Faces were painted, and sticks were used to make arms and sometimes legs.

The corn husk doll you will make differs from the original Indian design. This doll is created with yarn, which when properly tied produces all of the parts of the body. Your creativity and imagination will transform these characterless shapes into your favorite storybook figures. Use other materials to create clothing, and glue on facial features.

Things You Need

12 corn husks
yarn, string or cord
scissors

Let's Begin

1. The next time you get fresh corn, save twelve husks or outside "leaves." Gather the husks, and tie them tightly together at one end with the yarn or string, Fig. a.
2. To make the head, tie the husks a little way down from the top knot, Fig. b.
3. Gather three of the husks, and tie them together halfway down for an arm. Gather and tie three more husks, at the opposite side of the doll to form another arm. Cut away most of the excess corn husk that is below the knots, Fig. c.
4. To make the body, tie the remaining corn husks halfway between the head and their ends, Fig. d.
5. Make the legs by taking three husks and tying them together a little up from their ends, Fig. e.
6. Make the other leg the same way.
7. Decorate with colored felt-tipped markers, construction paper, fabric, or any other craft supplies you may have.

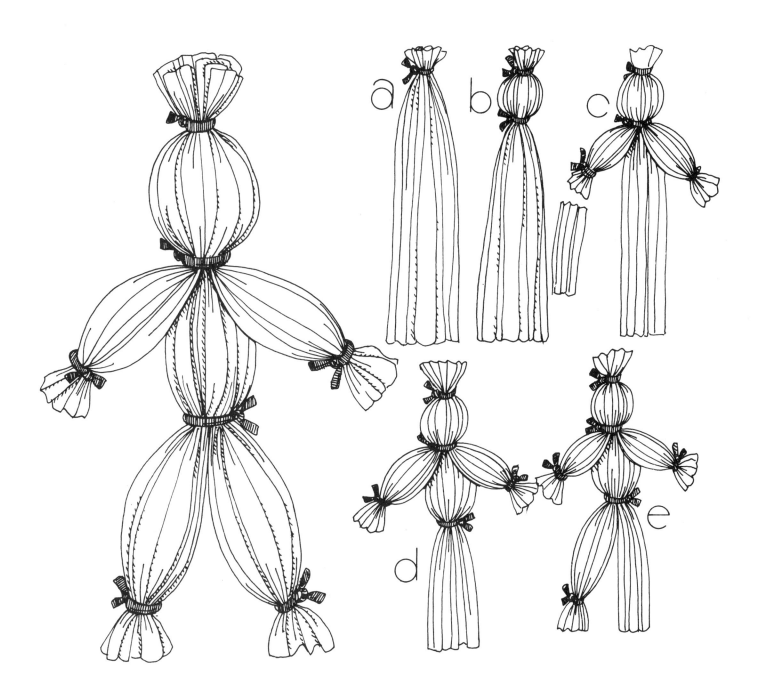

a

b

c

d

e

Sponge Printing

A sponge is a marine animal with a very soft skeleton. It lives in warm, salty water and pretty much stays put on the ocean's floor. Only underwater currents move a sponge from one place to another. People in Europe dive for sponges, and sell them strung on cords like popcorn on streets and in the stores.

People in your house probably use sponges for washing dishes and counters. In most cases these sponges aren't once alive creatures of the sea. Real sponges are very expensive. The sponges most people use are manufactured. These are flat rather than round, but have pores just like the living variety. Use only flat sponges for this printing project.

Things You Need

colored felt-tipped markers
flat sponges
scissors
poster paint
paper plate
paintbrush
white drawing paper

Let's Begin

1. Draw designs on a sponge with a colored felt-tipped marker, Fig. a.
**2. Cut out the designs with scissors.
3. Spread a little paint on a paper plate with a paintbrush.
4. Dip the cut sponge shape or a chunk of sponge into the paint on the plate, Fig. b.
5. Press the painted side of the sponge onto a sheet of white drawing paper.
6. Carefully lift the sponge from the paper to reveal your print.
7. Let the sponge print dry.

Sugar Rock Candy

Rock candy looks like precious crystal stones good enough to be strung as glass beads or set in a gold ring band. Only you get to eat these beautiful stones. Open your own sweet shop featuring rock candy hanging like grapes on a vine. By following some simple directions, you can make a little Rock Candy Mountain for your own enjoyment right in your own room.

Things You Need

measuring cup
small saucepan
granulated sugar
spoon
empty glass jar
heavy cord
pencil

Let's Begin

1. Put one cup of water into a small saucepan.
2. Pour two cups of granulated sugar into the water.
**3. Heat the water and sugar on the stove over a medium heat, Fig. a.
**4. Continue stirring until the sugar melts.
**5. Keep adding sugar and stirring until it melts.
**6. Stop adding sugar when you see that it will no longer dissolve in the water. That is, until you see sugar lying on the bottom of the saucepan.
**7. Remove the pot from the stove.
8. Let the liquid cool until it is just warm.
9. Pour the liquid into a clean glass jar.
10. Tie one end of a piece of heavy cord around the middle of a pencil.
11. Place the pencil over the top of the glass jar letting the cord fall into the liquid, Fig. b.
12. Crystals will begin to form in a few hours, Fig. c.
13. The next day, remove the cord from the jar.
**14. Pour the sugar liquid back into the saucepan, reheat and cool it just as you did before.
15. Pour the liquid back into the jar and reinsert the cord with the crystals into it. More crystals will form.
16. If you repeat this procedure every day, the crystal candy will grow bigger and bigger. When it has reached a size that pleases you, snip off any excess string and enjoy.

a

b

c

Crystal Garden

Natural crystals were formed when the earth cooled down millions of years ago. Now they can be grown in your own home. One of the main ingredients for this project is salt, which is itself a crystal. If you look at it under a microscope, salt crystals look like diamonds. You will find this project one of the more exciting natural crafts in this chapter because you can watch the crystals grow larger day by day.

Things You Need

6 charcoal briquets
disposable aluminum pie or pastry tin
measuring cup
salt
liquid bluing
ammonia
coffee can with lid or jar with lid
food coloring in 4 colors

Let's Begin

1. Place six charcoal briquets in the aluminum pie or cake tin, Fig. a.
2. Measure one-quarter cup of salt, bluing, and ammonia and pour all ingredients into a coffee can or jar. Mix them together.
3. Squeeze or sprinkle different food colors onto four of the briquets, one color for each briquet. Squeeze or sprinkle all four colors onto the fifth briquet. The remaining briquet is not to be colored.
4. Pour the salt mixture evenly over the briquets, Fig. b.
5. Place the tin in a warm place.
6. The crystals will start to grow in a very short time.
7. Mix the same solution of salt, bluing and ammonia in the can or jar and cap tightly.
8. Add some of the solution over the garden every two days to keep it growing.

Mushroom Prints

Mushrooms are one of nature's most interesting creations. They grow in damp, dark places and can pop up through the ground overnight. They have no roots, no leaves and no flower, but they can be found in bright fiery reds and oranges or in snow-white puffs. Some mushrooms are edible but many more are very poisonous. Don't ever eat a mushroom that you find in the woods. If you like to eat these tasty plants, Mom or Dad will buy them and make a tempting dinner with them.

Mushrooms grow in all shapes, sizes, and textures, each with a very interesting design under the cap or head. You can make a print of this beautiful design on books or as paintings in full color. If you don't live near the woods, have Mom or Dad buy several mushrooms at the food store. If you are lucky enough to have the forest in your back yard, choose an odd-shaped mushroom and start printing immediately.

Things You Need

liquid white glue
paper cup
paintbrush
shiny paper or oaktag
piece of corrugated cardboard
mushroom
straight pins
small bowl

Let's Begin

1. Pour a little of the liquid white glue into a paper cup and add just a drop or two of water. Mix with a paintbrush.
2. Place a piece of shiny paper or oaktag on a sheet of corrugated cardboard.
3. Break off the stem from the cap of the mushroom, Fig. a. You may want to remove some of the outer edge of the cap if it hides too much of the gills on the underside.
4. Paint a circle of glue on the center of the paper. The circle should be a little larger than the mushroom, Fig. b.
5. Press four straight pins into the outer rim of the mushroom.
6. Hold the mushroom over the glued area. Do not let the mushroom touch the glue.
7. Press the pins through the paper and into the corrugated cardboard, Fig. c.
8. Quickly place a bowl over the mushroom, Fig. d.
9. Remove the bowl twenty-four hours later.
10. Carefully lift the mushroom off the paper to see the print, Fig. e.

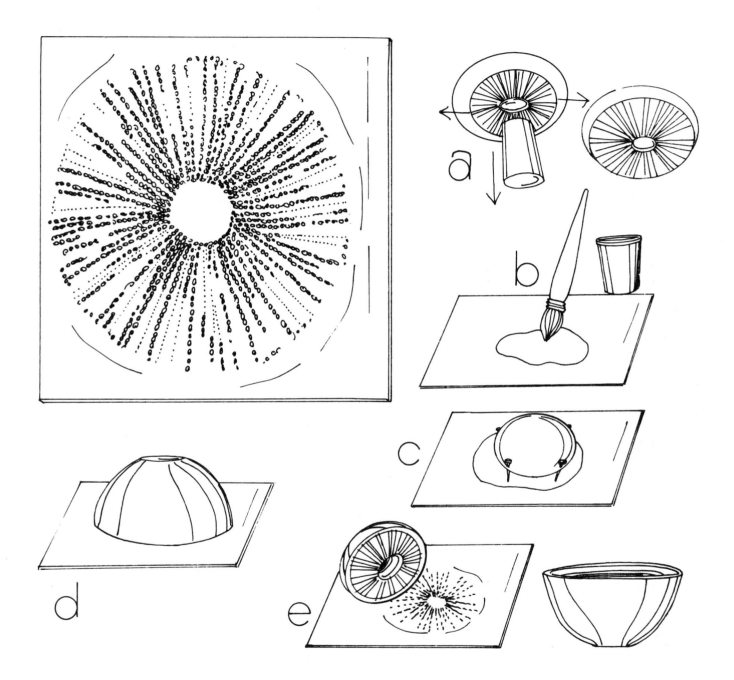

a

b

c

d

e

Web (Printing) Painting

The spider weaves his web to catch insects for a tasty dinner. The web has a sticky surface which holds a bug entangled in it. Try as it might, the trapped insect must wait for the hungry weaver to claim its catch. Only the spider can climb this circular ladder with a thousand rungs.

A spider web is very beautiful, but unless moisture or the rays of the sun strike it, you will probably pass it by. Sometimes you walk right into a web, and how uncomfortable it is having those silky strands dance about your face! Webs are so hard to see because they are so thin. On your next trip into the forest, bring a can of spray paint and a piece of paper with you. The following directions will enable you to print some of the most beautiful designs in nature's pattern book.

Things You Need

white drawing paper
paint in spray can
spider web

Let's Begin

1. Take a walk in the forest and bring white paper and a can of spray paint with you. Find a spider web. Webs are usually found between branches of bushes or between two growing things, such as weeds or garden flowers.

**2. Hold the can of spray paint at arm's length away from the web. Spray quickly with a back and forth motion, Fig. a. Be sure that the wind is blowing away from you when you spray paint so you won't breathe in any of it. Cover the web with a thin coating of paint. The paint will look like tiny beads on the fine strands.

3. Quickly place a piece of paper on the web. It is better if you curve the paper first in the center of the web and straighten it out very carefully along the sides, Fig. b.

4. Let the web dry on the paper. Your finished print will contain some of the web.

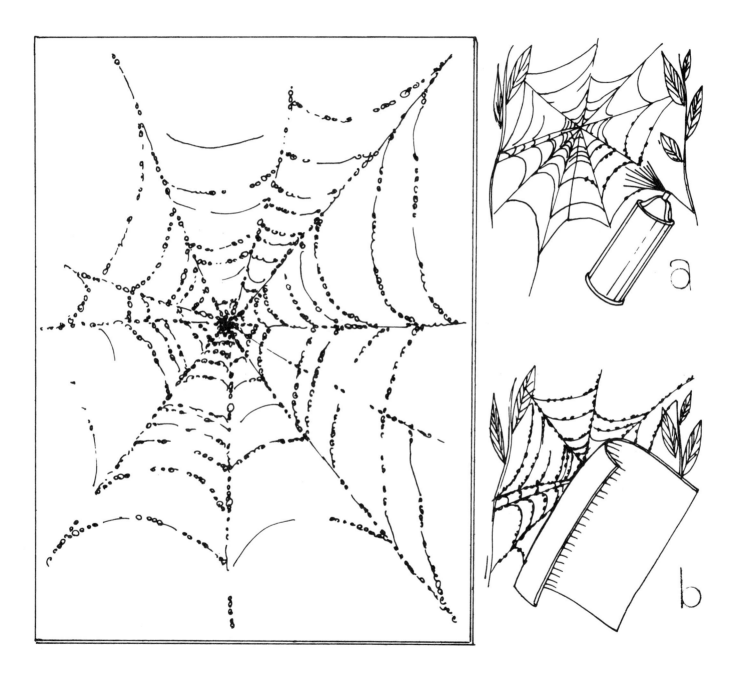

a

b

Rain-Spatter Painting

Here is a project that will make you wish for a rainy day. Are you surprised? Rain-Spatter Painting is so much fun you will do a rain dance every night until Nature rings out her cloudy sponge over your home. All you do is spread paint on a sheet of paper and let the rain create the painting for you. This project can be done by the front door or—with Mom or Dad's supervision—by an open window. If you have to go outside, take your raincoat, umbrella, and boots so that you won't catch a cold. You don't want to spend any of those cloudless days inside in bed!

Things You Need

poster paints

paintbrush
white drawing paper
rain

Let's Begin

1. Paint different colored shapes on a sheet of white drawing paper, Fig. a.
2. When it rains, put the painting outside for just a moment, Fig. b. You might want to wear a raincoat so your arm won't get wet.
3. Take the painting inside. Hold the paper flat so that the drops on the paint won't run.
4. Place the paper on a flat surface, such as a table or the floor.
5. Let the rain dry and see the different patterns it has created.

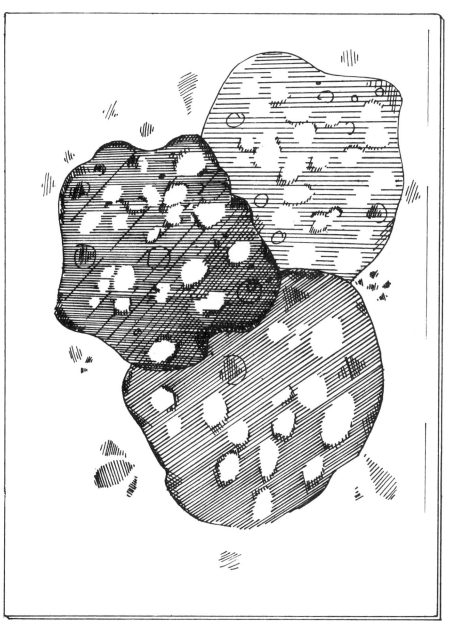

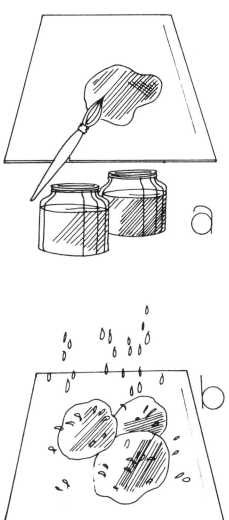

a

b

Two Happy Snowmen

Winter is the season when raindrops fall to earth as fluffy snowflakes. If you are lucky enough to live in a part of the country where snow occasionally covers the ground, then you know how much fun it is to make a snowman. It takes a wet snow to form a really good snowman because it packs very easily. Why not make a really creative snowfriend by adding to it things you have in your home? Make construction paper facial features, wrap an old belt around the snowman's waist, top his head with a cap. No matter how big or small your snowman may be, dress him up in a "Sunday-go-to-meeting" costume. He will be the talk of your neighborhood.

Things You Need

fresh-fallen, wet snow
3 twigs, 2 short and 1 long
charcoal briquets
scissors
colored construction paper
crayons
large belt
paper cups
carrot

Let's Begin

1. Before the snow starts to fall, save three twigs and charcoal briquets and put them in a safe place.
2. Cut a round head and mittens from colored construction paper, see illustration.
3. Draw a face on the head with crayons.
4. Push the two small twigs through the mittens and the long twig through the head.
5. After the snow stops falling, roll a snowball with your hands.
6. Roll the snowball in the fallen snow pushing it into the snow. Continue to roll it until it is large enough for a little snowman.
7. Stick the head and arms into the ball. Add a belt around the middle of the ball, see illustration.
8. To make the large snowman, roll two snowballs, the bottom ball larger than the top ball.
**9. Lift the smaller ball onto the top of the larger ball.
10. Press two paper cups into the head for eyes, a carrot for the nose, briquets for the mouth and buttons, see illustration.
11. Add a hat and scarf.

Wishbone Pendant

What is your favorite part of the chicken? The wishbone, of course! What's it going to be this time: a new toy, a snowy day, or a new pair of pants? No matter what you want, don't break that wishbone! Save it for this craft project. You can make a lucky wishbone necklace. Wear it around your neck, and if you ever need a quick wish, it will be with you at all times.

Things You Need

dried wishbone
cord or yarn

Let's Begin

1. Let a wishbone from a chicken or turkey dry completely.
2. Tie a length of colored yarn or cord at its center around the neck of the wishbone.
3. Tie the ends of the yarn into a knot to make a necklace that will fit over your head.
4. You can paint the wishbone with poster paint or with Mom's nailpolish.

The smooth, shiny, slippery stone

In this chapter you will make masks and scenery for an actual three-act play, The *Smooth, Shiny, Slippery Stone,* which is included. You will direct the play and impersonate the characters in it. Imagine having a real show in your own home! Invite your friends over so that they can see the performance. Their applause will tell you how very well you've done.

The play has a message for you. It tells all about how the animals under the Oak Tree try to get rid of something left behind by people after a happy picnic. Luckily, the problem is solved when one of the people—the Little Boy—comes back for it. Had he not returned, the waste object would have remained for a long time, perhaps forever. The idea is, people should try to leave the outdoors clean of litter. Keeping nature free from picnic or other disposables is a way of showing our happiness with our surroundings. If you happen to come across a piece of paper or a tin can in the woods or at the beach, pick it up and toss it into the nearest garbage can. You may not hear a "Thank you!" from a tree, a rock, or a stream, but you can be sure you have done the right thing.

Now that you know the message and what you can do to keep the outdoors clean, it's time to get on with the show! Your performance should help you and your friends learn about nature and how people and nature can live together. It should also be a lot of fun.

Oak Tree and Smooth, Shiny, Slippery Stone

Although the Oak Tree cannot move by itself, the wind can bend and dip its branches. This happens in the Third Act, and makes all the creatures in the forest aware that the Little Boy is approaching.

Things You Need

newspaper
tape
scissors
large fruit juice can
plaster of paris
spoon
green and brown construction paper
paper paste
aluminum foil

Let's Begin

OAK TREE
1. Lay a sheet of newspaper flat on a table or on the floor.
2. Loosely roll the paper at one end to the center crease of the newspaper, Fig. a.
3. Lay a second sheet of paper over the unrolled part of the first sheet of newspaper, Fig. b.
4. Continue rolling newspaper to the center crease of the second sheet of paper.
5. Keep adding new sheets of paper to the center creases, rolling five to ten sheets of newspaper together.
6. Tape the roll together.
**7. Cut four deep slits into one end of the roll of newspaper , Fig. c.
8. Put your finger into the roll, and pull out the center sheet of paper to form a floppy, fringed pole-like tree, Fig. d.
9. Make three fringed poles.
10. Fill a can half-full with plaster of paris. Mix the plaster with water in the can until it looks like heavy whipped cream.
11. Push the three poles into the plaster mixture in the can. Be careful that the can does not tip over.
12. Cut leaves from green paper and paste them to the fringe branches.
13. Cut a piece of brown construction paper as high as the can and long enough to wrap around it. Tape it around the can.

SMOOTH, SHINY, SLIPPERY STONE
1. Make the shiny stone from aluminum foil rolled into a large smooth ball.

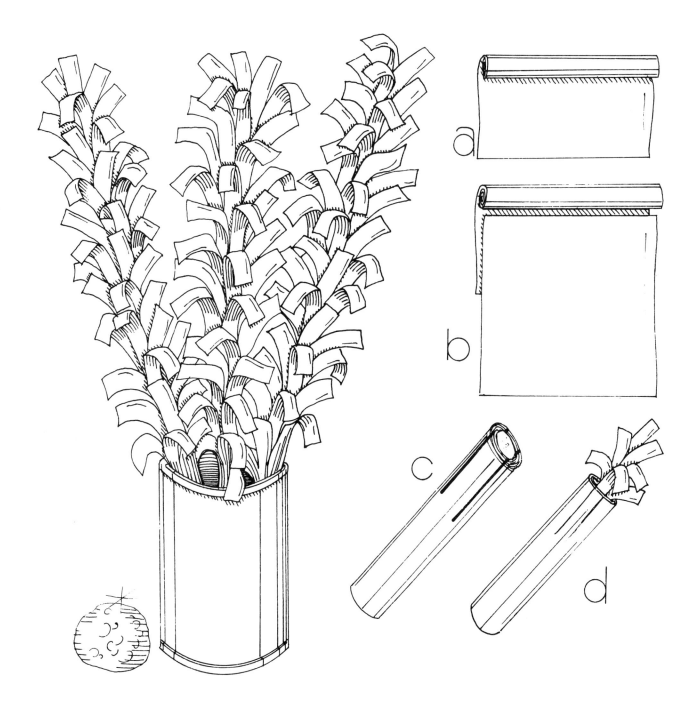

a

b

c

d

Owl and Molly Mole

In the play, it is Molly Mole who finds herself in trouble. With the aid of her friends, she is freed from the shiny stone that has fallen on top of her home. Owl is the wisest of all creatures, and solves the riddle of the shiny stone.

Things You Need

large brown paper bags
colored felt-tipped markers or crayons
scissors
colored construction paper
paper paste
crepe paper
tape

Let's Begin

OWL
1. Put a bag over your head and feel for your eyes through it. With a crayon, lightly make an X where each eye lies behind the bag. Remove the bag.
2. Cut two large circles for eyes from yellow construction paper.
3. Using colored felt-tipped markers or crayons, draw black circles in the centers of the yellow-paper eyes with short lines around them, see illustration.
4. Using paper paste, paste the eyes on the bag over the Xs you have drawn.
5. Cut a beak and top feathers from colored construction paper, and paste them onto the bag, see illustration.
6. Make the body feathers from long strips of colored paper or crepe paper. Cut slits along one side of the paper, half-way up.
7. Tape or paste each fringe strip to the bag starting at the bottom. Overlap the strips upward to the beak.
8. Cut out two circles through the eyes so that you can see out once you slip the mask over your head.

MOLLY MOLE
1. Mark eyes with an X just as you did for Owl.
2. Roll colored construction paper into a cone and staple or tape it together.
3. Trim the bottom edge of the cone so that it can stand straight.
4. Color the tip of the cone beak using colored felt-tipped markers or crayons.
5. Tape the cone to the bag near the closed end.
6. Cut out two eyes, two ears, a paper bow, and lips from colored construction paper, see illustration. Draw black circles on the center of the eyes.
7. Paste the eyes onto the bag over the Xs you have drawn; paste the other places, see illustration.
8. Cut out two circles through the eyes so you can see out once you slip the mask over your head.

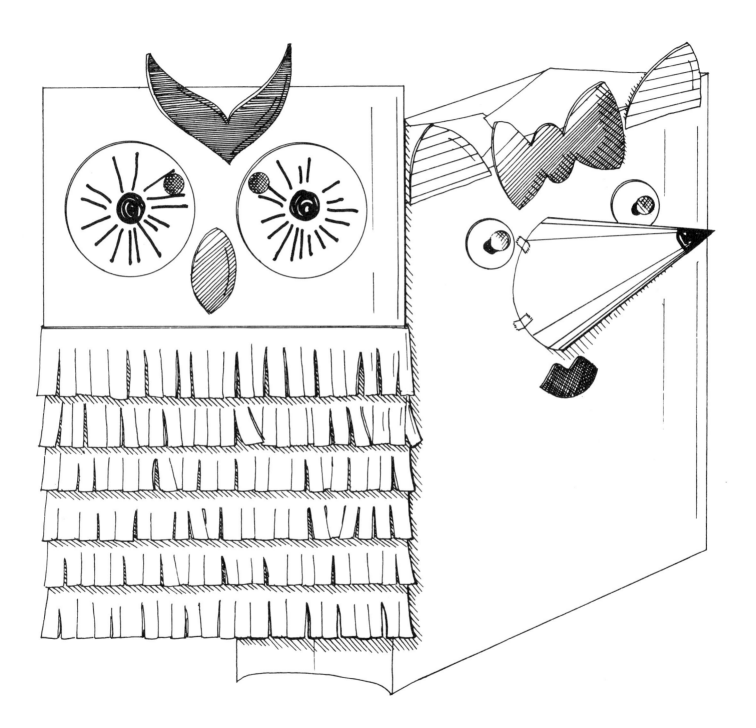

Squirrel and Mr. Turtle

Squirrel is the character who alerts the creatures of the forest to Molly Mole's problem. He is a busy character, always looking for nuts to store away for the winter. Mr. Turtle is the one who drags the shiny stone from Molly's home. (Actually, he would rather spend the day in the pond eating insects and fish.)

Things You Need

large brown paper bag
colored felt-tipped markers or crayons
scissors
colored construction paper
paper paste
drinking straws
tape
cardboard
stapler
yarn or string
oaktag
ribbon

Let's Begin

SQUIRREL

1. Put the bag over your head and feel for your eyes through it. With a crayon, lightly mark an X where each eye lies behind the bag. Remove the bag.
2. Cut out two ears, two eyes, two eyebrows, and a nose from colored construction paper, see illustration.
3. Using paper paste, paste the eyes on the bag over the Xs you have drawn; paste the other shapes on the bag in the proper places.
4. Draw a mouth under the nose with colored felt-tipped markers or crayons.
5. Cut deep slits into one end of both straws.
6. Tape on straw whiskers on both sides of the nose.
7. Cut a bar-like length of cardboard for the tail.

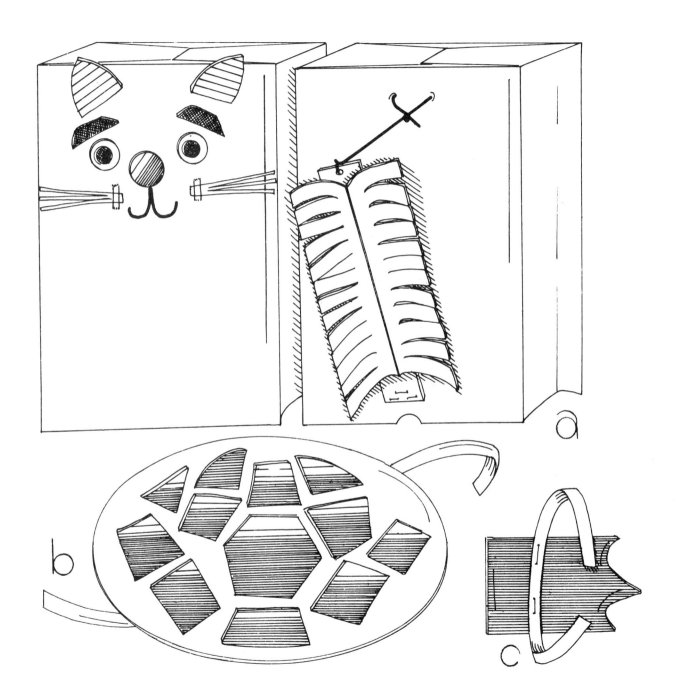

a

b

c

8. Cut two strips of colored construction paper as long as the cardboard.
9. Cut slits along one side of each piece of construction paper.
10. Paste the strips to the cardboard with the uncut edges meeting at the center, Fig. a.
11. Staple the tail to the bottom of the back of the bag, Fig. a.
**12. Using a paper punch or a sharp pencil, punch a hole in the cardboard and two holes in the bag near the top of the back and to one side. Tie a string through the hole in the top of the tail and tie it into the two holes in the bag with a big knot so that the tail swings outward, Fig. a.
13. Cut out two circles through the eyes so you can see out once you slip the mask over your head.

MR. TURTLE
1. Cut out a large oval from a sheet of oaktag. If you can, make the oval from green oaktag.
2. Cut out a six-sided shape from green construction paper and paste it to the center of the oval, Fig. b.
3. Cut out more green paper shapes and paste them around the center shape.
4. Staple a ribbon long enough to go around your waist to the underside of the oval shell, Fig. b.
5. Cut hands and feet like the ones in Fig. c. Use green construction paper.
6. Staple ribbons to the underside of the feet and hands, Fig. c.
7. Tie the shell around your waist, and the hands and feet around your wrists and ankles. To portray the turtle, walk on your hands and feet.

The Smooth, Shiny, Slippery Stone

*A play about the forest and the
animals who live there*
by Noel Fiarotta

Characters

OWL
MOLLY MOLE
SQUIRREL
MR. TURTLE
LITTLE BOY
OAK TREE

ACT I

SCENE I

Scene: *Morning in the forest. The squirrel's
home in the* OAK TREE.

Open Curtain

SQUIRREL *(Yawning, stretching, and covering
his eyes with his paws)*
It must be morning! I wish the birds
wouldn't chirp so loudly. They wake me up
every morning. *(Opening his eyes)* Who
turned the lights on! Who?

OWL *(Perched above* SQUIRREL'*s home)*
Who! Who! Who!

SQUIRREL *(Looking from the hole of his home.
He sees the* OWL)
That's all you ever say.

OWL
I have been awake all night and now I want
to get a good day's sleep. Don't make so
much noise. I'm sleepy!

SQUIRREL
Why don't you sleep at night like I do?

OWL
I sleep better in the day because I see better
at night. It's the only time I can find food
to eat.

SQUIRREL
If you are hungry why don't you join me for

breakfast? I have plenty of food stored away. More than enough for next winter.

OWL
Thank you very much, but I would be poor company. I would be asleep before I could get the first acorn to my mouth. *(Yawning)* I'm so very sleepy.

SQUIRREL
Some dark and rainy morning you must eat breakfast with me.

OWL *(Closing his eyes. Mumbling in a sleepy tone)*
Dark . . . rainy . . . morning. Okay. Good day!

SQUIRREL
Good Nighhh . . . t! I mean good day to you. *(Hopping back into his home)* It's so hard getting to know him. He sleeps all day. I think I will eat breakfast under the tree. Maybe someone will join me. *(Looking all around his home)* Now, where did I hide those hickory nuts?

Curtain

SCENE II

Scene: *Under the* OAK TREE.

Open Curtain

SQUIRREL
This looks like a good place to eat breakfast. I guess I will have to eat all by myself. *(Looking around)* There is nobody in sight.

MOLLY MOLE *(From under the ground. In a muffled voice)*
Help! Help! Help! I can't get out!

SQUIRREL
Did I hear someone crying for help? It sounds like it is coming from the mole's home. *(Looking for the* MOLE's *home)* Is that you, Molly Mole?

MOLLY MOLE *(In a muffled voice)*
Yes! Something is covering the entrance to

my home. Help me. I don't know if it is a stone or branch.

SQUIRREL (*Looking at the stone and scratching his head*)
I have never seen a stone like this before. It is so shiny. You push and I will pull and maybe we can move it.

MOLLY MOLE (*In a muffled voice*)
I'm pushing as hard as I can.

SQUIRREL
I'm pulling as hard as I can. It is just too heavy for us. Maybe Mr. Turtle can help us. He is walking this way. (*Waving his paw*) Oh Mr. Turtle, can you help us?

MR. TURTLE (*Looking all around*)
Us? I only see one of you. I mean I only see you, Squirrel. Who else might you be talking about?

SQUIRREL
Molly Mole is trapped in her home with a shiny stone rolled over it. We were wondering if you could help us remove it.

MR. TURTLE (*Looking at the stone*)
With my strength it will be removed faster than a rolling acorn. Tie a vine around the shiny stone and I will pull it away with my teeth.

(*With the vine in Mr. Turtle's mouth, the shiny stone is removed*)

MOLLY MOLE (*Climbing out of her home in the ground*)
Oh thank you very much, Mr. Turtle and Squirrel. I thought I would never get out.

MR. TURTLE
I am glad I could help.

SQUIRREL
You are lucky Mr. Turtle was walking this way.

(MR. TURTLE, SQUIRREL, *and* MOLLY MOLE *examine the shiny stone*)

SQUIRREL (*Scratching his head*)
What is it? I have never seen a stone so shiny.

MR. TURTLE *(Touching it)*
It doesn't feel very hard. It is rather smooth.

MOLLY MOLE *(Also touching the stone)*
It's slippery. It must be a smooth, shiny, slippery stone. But how did it get here?

SQUIRREL
Who placed it here? Who? *(Pause)* Who?

OWL *(Flying down from his branch in the* OAK TREE*)*
Did I hear someone say, "Who?" *(Angrily)* All this noise is keeping me awake. What seems to be the matter?

MR. TURTLE
We are trying to find out who placed this—correct me if I'm wrong Molly Mole—smooth, shiny, slippery stone over her home. *(Looking suspiciously at* OWL*)* Did you roll this stone over Molly's home?

OWL
I did not. I saw everything that happened last night from my branch in the Oak Tree. Nothing strange happened last night. It must have been rolled during the day. Maybe one of you did it.

MR. TURTLE
It could not have been me. I stayed in the pond all day eating insects and fish.

SQUIRREL
I was busy collecting acorns and pine nuts several trees from here. I have to collect extra because sometimes I hide them and forget where they are when winter covers the ground and trees with snow.

MOLLY MOLE
I slept all day long yesterday. Besides, it was my home that was covered by the stone.

SQUIRREL *(Puzzled)*
How can we find out who placed the smooth, shiny, slippery stone over Molly Mole's home?

OWL
By the end of the day we will have the answer. My wisdom will solve this mystery. But first, I must get some sleep. We will meet by the smooth, shiny, slippery stone when the sun moves to the other side of the sky.

*(*MR. TURTLE *goes back to the pond,* MOLLY MOLE *returns to her home in the ground,* SQUIRREL *scampers to his tree home, and the* OWL *goes to sleep on his branch)*

Curtain

ACT II

SCENE I

Scene: *Afternoon in the forest. An important meeting under the Oak Tree.* MOLLY, SQUIRREL, *and* MR. TURTLE *are waiting for* OWL.

Open Curtain

MR. TURTLE
Where is Owl? He is the one who called for a

meeting. Did you see him in the tree, Squirrel?

SQUIRREL
I didn't notice. I was in such a hurry to be on time. He is probably still sleeping.

OWL (*Flying to the ground from his branch*)
I am as awake as a fully bloomed daisy on a sunny day. I needed a few more seconds to gather my thoughts.

SQUIRREL
How can you think when you are sleeping?

MR. TURTLE
When I sleep, my head is like the forest at midnight.

OWL
Enough of this chatter. The meeting shall begin. (MR. TURTLE, MOLLY MOLE, *and* SQUIRREL *sit together in front of* OWL(We will start at the beginning. Molly Mole, you will speak first. Tell me everything you remember.

MOLLY MOLE
Yesterday I was gathering food in the early morning sunshine. When I had eaten enough, I crawled back into my home and fell asleep. When I awoke this morning, everything was dark.

OWL
When did you fall asleep?

MOLLY MOLE
Very early in the morning. I don't see too well, but it was shortly after the sun peeked over the trees.

OWL
Did you hear any strange noises during the day?

MOLLY MOLE
I don't hear very well since I spend so much time in the ground. The world was as quiet as a mushroom growing on a damp log. This is all I remember.

OWL
You have helped greatly. We will have the answer when the toads sing their evening lullaby. What do you remember, Mr. Turtle?

MR. TURTLE
I spent all day in the pond eating insects and

509

fish. When the sun was shining directly over me, I heard strange loud sounds.

OWL
What kinds of sounds?

MR. TURTLE
The sounds of people talking, yelling, and laughing. I didn't see any people by the pond. It was as noisy as a cornfield of magpies. This is all I remember.

OWL
You have said many helpful words. We will now have the answer before the birds settle down to an evening's rest. And now, Squirrel, it is your task to tell me the missing facts. Think very carefully.

SQUIRREL
I was collecting acorns and pine nuts several trees from here. When I returned in the evening, before the sun set, I saw footprints on a path near the oak tree—big ones, middle-sized ones, and small ones. It looked like a very busy deer path. This is all I remember.

OWL
I am now certain we will have the answer while the sun is in the late afternoon sky. We will have lunch and return when we are full.

(MR. TURTLE, MOLLY MOLE, SQUIRREL, *and* OWL *return to their homes*)

Curtain

SCENE II

Scene: *One hour later under the* OAK TREE.

Open Curtain

OWL
Now that we have eaten, I have some bad news to tell you.

MOLLY MOLE
You didn't find who placed the smooth, shiny, slippery stone over my home.

OWL
More serious than that!

SQUIRREL
Don't keep us waiting. What is it?

MR. TURTLE
Yes, please don't make us wait another minute longer.

OWL *(Very sad)*
While we were busy doing our work, many people sat under this tree. The footprints you saw, and the noise you heard were made by people having a picnic. You were fast asleep, Molly Mole, that is why you didn't hear anything.

SQUIRREL
Then a people must own it and placed it over Molly's home.

OWL
That is correct.

MOLLY MOLE *(Puzzled)*

Then what is the big problem?

OWL
The smooth, shiny, slippery stone doesn't belong in the forest. It should have been taken away with the people who had the picnic.

MR. TURTLE
And now we must get rid of it by ourselves.

MOLLY MOLE
I'm too small to move the stone!

SQUIRREL
So am I!

MR. TURTLE
I could only move it several inches before I get tired.

OWL
With all of my wisdom I can't fly with it in my claws.

ALL
What are we going to do?

OAK TREE *(In a mighty voice)*
I was the only one who saw what happened. It was fun seeing the people having a good time in the forest. It is not fair to us if we

have to live with the things people leave behind.

MR. TURTLE
You are right! It isn't fair.

MOLLY MOLE
Especially when it is dropped on your home . . .

SQUIRREL
. . . and we can't get rid of it.

OWL
Can you help us, Oak Tree?

OAK TREE
No, only the wind can bend my branches. I can only provide food, home, and safety for you, the animals of the forest. This is why I'm here.

OWL
Let us go back to our homes and try to solve our new problem. If anyone can come up with a solution, wake me up.

(MR. TURTLE, MOLLY MOLE, SQUIRREL, and OWL return to their homes)

Curtain

ACT III

Scene: *It is late afternoon.* MR. TURTLE, SQUIRREL, MOLLY MOLE, *and* OWL *are asleep in their homes.*

Curtain

(*A strong gust of wind causes the* OAK TREE's *branches to shake wildly*)

OAK TREE
Wake up! Wake up! There is a stranger walking towards us.

(SQUIRREL *pops his head out of the tree,* MOLLY MOLE *pops her head out of the ground,* MR. TURTLE *pops his head out of the lake, and* OWL *opens his eyes*)

OWL (*Very mad*)
Can't an owl get a good day's sleep! What is going on in this forest? It must be you,

512

Squirrel. You have already disturbed my sleep twice today.

SQUIRREL
I was also sleeping, so it could not have been me.

OWL *(Calls from the tree)*
Molly Mole and Mr. Turtle, did you disturb my sleep? It is important that I find the answer to the problem.

MOLLY MOLE
Not me, Owl.

MR. TURTLE
Not me, Owl.

OWL
Then who? Oh my dear, did I just say, "Who?"

SQUIRREL
We must get his attention.

After some whooing and chattering the LITTLE BOY *looks up)*

LITTLE BOY
Hello, little squirrel and owl. I wish I knew what you were saying. Don't be so angry. It is a lovely day.

SQUIRREL *(To Owl)*
He wants to talk to us.

OWL
We have to turn his attention to the shiny stone.

SQUIRREL
We will have to show him why we are so angry.

*(*SQUIRREL *and* OWL *stand in front of the shiny stone)*

LITTLE BOY
What's this? Oh, it is the aluminum foil I rolled into a ball and used for a catch ball. You are mad because I forgot to take it with me.

*(*MOLLY *and* MR. TURTLE *join* SQUIRREL *and* OWL*)*

LITTLE BOY
You too came to complain to me about the

aluminum foil ball I left behind. I came back here today because I wasn't sure I cleaned the picnic area. Don't worry, I will take it away from here. I must be extra careful and look high and low for all things that don't belong in the forest. I know I should keep the forest as clean as when I arrived here. Good-bye, friends of the forest.

OAK TREE *(In a mighty voice)*
A stranger walks in the forest. Be very careful. It was the wind and my branches that woke you from your sound sleep.

MOLLY MOLE *(Frightened)*
A stranger! Where?

OAK TREE
Coming closer.

(As the little boy enters the scene, OWL, MOLLY, MR. TURTLE, *and* SQUIRREL *hide in their homes)*

LITTLE BOY
This looks like the place where we had the picnic. *(Looking around)* I think we took all of the paper and food with us.

SQUIRREL *(Pokes his head out of his home. chattering)*
Chatter, chatter, chatter. *(To Owl above him)* So he's the one who placed the smooth, shiny, slippery stone over Molly's home.

OWL
I was correct when I told you I would have the answer today.

SQUIRREL
If it belongs to the little boy he must see it. It might be something special.

OWL
He must take it with him. I am sure the little boy can find a home for this shiniest of stones.

(The LITTLE BOY *leaves the forest with the shiny stone)*

OWL *(Happily)*
I guess that solves both problems. We know who placed the shiny stone on Molly's home . . .

SQUIRREL

   . . . and the stone is no longer in the forest.

MR. TURTLE

   I am very glad the Little Boy took it with him. It would take me many years to drag it out of the forest.

MOLLY MOLE

   If all people would take with them all the things they brought with them into the forest, it would be a cleaner place.

MR. TURTLE

   And a beautiful place to visit.

SQUIRREL

   And a clean home for us.

MR. TURTLE

   Now that the mystery is solved, I'm going back to the pond and snap at a few sunfish.

MOLLY MOLE

   A little house cleaning wouldn't hurt. Much sand fell into my home today.

(MR. TURTLE *and* MOLLY MOLE *wave good-bye to* SQUIRREL *and* OWL. *They go to their homes*)

SQUIRREL

   It never hurts to gather a few extra acorns for a rainy day. What are your plans for today, Owl?

OWL

   I should be on my branch fast asleep. Night-time will be here very soon. I'll be wide awake. It is all your fault, Squirrel!

SQUIRREL

   Since you didn't sleep well today, sleep long and hard tonight. When the birds sing their morning song, you can join me for breakfast.

OWL

   Breakfast? That sounds like a good idea. If I can keep my eyes closed and fall asleep, it will be my pleasure to join you in the morning. Did I say good morning? Good day, Squirrel!

SQUIRREL

   Good day, Owl. Sleep well, and I will see you at breakfast.

(OWL *flies to his branch and* SQUIRREL *hops off into the forest to search for acorns and pine nuts. The forest is quiet and clean once more*)

Curtain

THE END

Good-Bye

Isn't nature fascinating! If you have reached this page, then you have roamed through a kingdom more spectacular than any built by man. You have stood on top of the tiniest grain of sand or in the shadow of a mountain. Things grew before you and a rock-candy crystal became a tasty treat. Nature's discards were changed into beautiful crafts. You should be very proud of yourself. For your achievements and dedicated service to nature, you have the right to wear this "I CREATE WITH NATURE" medal.

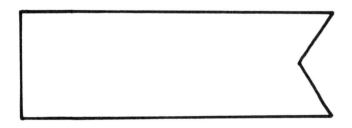

Things You Need

scissors
colored construction paper
pencil
tracing paper
paper paste or tape
colored felt-tipped markers or crayons

Let's Begin

1. Cut a circle from colored paper about the size as the medal in the illustration.
2. Trace the ribbon shape from the book onto tracing paper, then cut out the tracing.
3. Use the tracing to draw two ribbon shapes on blue construction paper.
4. Using paper paste or tape, attach the ribbons behind the paper medal.
5. Write the official message on the medal with crayons or colored felt-tipped markers.